The New Left and Labor in the 1960s

The New Left and Labor in the 1960s

Peter B. Levy

University of Illinois Press   URBANA AND CHICAGO

© 1994 by the Board of Trustees of the University of Illinois
Manufactured in the United States of America
1 2 3 4 5 C P 5 4 3 2 1

This book is printed on acid-free paper.

Library of Congress Cataloging-in-Publication Data

Levy, Peter B.
    the new left and labor in the 1960s / Peter B. Levy.
       p.   cm.—(The Working class in American history)
    includes bibliographical references and index.
    ISBN 0-252-02074-X (alk. paper).—ISBN 0-252-06367-8 (pbk.) :
alk. paper)
    1. New Left—United States 2. Trade-unions—United States—
Political activity 3. Working class—United States—Political
activity I. Title. II. Series.
HN90.R3L495   1994
303.48'4—dc20   93-30844
                                                CIP

To Jessica Ann and Brian Edward Levy

Contents

Abbreviations   xi

Acknowledgments   xv

Introduction   1

1 We Shall Overcome: Labor and
the Emergence of the New Left   7

2 Coalition Politics or Nonviolent Revolution   26

3 Vietnam   46

4 Black Power   64

5 The Counterculture   84

6 Debating the Labor Question   108

7 Organizing the Unorganized   128

8 Solidarity on the Labor Front   147

9 Testing the Political Waters   167

Conclusion   187

Appendix: Theory, Methodology,
and Historiography   197

Notes   203

Bibliography   257

Index   277

Illustrations follow page 102.

Abbreviations

ACFE	Applachian Committee for Full Employment
ACLU	American Civil Liberties Union
ADA	Americans for Democratic Action
AFL–CIO	American Federation of Labor-Congress of Industrial Organization
AFT	American Federation of Teachers
AFSCME	American Federation of State, County, and Municipal Employees
AJC	American Jewish Congress
ALA	Alliance for Labor Action
AWOC	Agricultural Workers Organizing Committee
CAPAC	Cleveland Area Peace Action Committee
CFM	Committee for the Miners
CLUW	Coalition of Labor Union Women
CNVA	Committee for Nonviolent Action
CP	Communist Party
COFO	Council of Federated Organizations
COME	Committee on the Move for Equality
COPE	Committee of Political Education
CORE	Congress of Racial Equality
CUFAW	Citizens United for Adequate Welfare
CWA	Communication Workers of America
DRUM	Dodge Revolutionary Union Movement
ELRUM	Eldon Axle and Gear Revolutionary Union Movement
ERAP	Economic Research and Action Project
FEPC	Fair Employment Practices Commission
FSM	Free Speech Movement
FRUM	Ford Revolutionary Union Movement
FSU	Free Student Union
HFS	Highlander Folk School

IAM	International Association of Machinists
ICWU	International Chemical Workers Union
ILA	International Longshoremen's Association
ILGWU	International Ladies' Garment Workers' Union
ILWU	International Longshoremen's and Warehouseman's Union
IS	International Socialists
IUD	Industrial Union Department
IUE	International Union of Electrical Workers
JOIN	Jobs and Income Now
LCCR	Leadership Conference on Civil Rights
LERA	Labor for Equal Rights Now
LID	League for Industrial Democracy
LNS	Liberation News Service
MFDP	Mississippi Freedom Democratic Party
MFLU	Mississippi Freedom Labor Union
MFU	Maryland Freedom Union
MOBE	National Mobilization Committee to End the War in Viet Nam
NAACP	National Association for the Advancement of Colored People
NALC	Negro American Labor Council or Afro-American Labor Committee
NCUP	Newark Community Union Project
NER	Network of Economic Rights
NFWA	National Farm Workers of America
NMU	National Maritime Union
NO (SDS)	National Office (SDS)
NOW	National Organization of Women
NSA	National Student Association
OCAW	Oil, Chemical and Atomic Workers
PL	Progressive Labor
RA	Radical America
RAFT	Rank and File Team
RWDSU	Retail, Wholesale, Department Store Union
SANE	Committee for a SANE Nuclear Policy
SCEF	Southern Conference Educational Fund
SCLC	Southern Christian Leadership Conference
SDS	Students for a Democratic Society
SEIU	Service Employees International Union
SLAM	Southern Labor Action Movement
SLAP	Student Labor Action Project

SLID	Student League for Industrial Democracy
SNCC	Student Nonviolent Coordinating Committee
SPU	Student Peace Union
SSOC	Southern Student Organizing Committee
SWP	Socialist Workers' Party
TAA	Teaching Assistants Association
TWU	Transport Workers Union
UAW	United Automobile Workers
UE	United Electrical Workers
UFT	United Federation of Teachers
UFW	United Farm Workers
UFWOC	United Farm Workers Organizing Committee
UMW	United Mine Workers
UPWA	United Packinghouse Workers of America
WSA	Worker Student Alliance
YPSL	Young People's Socialist Alliance

Acknowledgments

In the ten plus years that I have worked on this book, I have received invaluable help and support from more people than I can recognize here. Needless to say, their comments and suggestions have immeasurably improved the final product, even if I have not always heeded them.

From the moment I knocked on his door, shortly after he returned to Columbia University, and asked him to direct my dissertation, Eric Foner supported my work and provided keen and incisive criticism and direction. No wonder that many others have rushed to take his classes, asked him to direct their dissertations, or to comment on their manuscripts. James P. Shenton, Ron Grele, John Garraty, and Eric Hirsch similarly read this work when it was in its dissertation stage and offered valuable suggestions that allowed me to improve upon my original work in a variety of ways. I must doubly thank Ron Grele for providing me with access to many interviews from his own research on the 1960s, which are now part of the esteemed Columbia University Oral History Collection. Although I never had a class with Ken Jackson, his collegiality on the basketball court and on other occasions helped sustain me during some of my more trying moments. William Leuchtenburg, Rosalind Rosenberg, and Robert McCaughey aided me during the early stages of research and, more important, as teachers helped sharpen my sense of the craft of history.

Many of my graduate school friends read or listened to me discuss parts of my work and deserve special commendation. Let me briefly thank Barbara Tischler, Myra Sletson, Mark Kaminsky, Avital Bloch, Richard Giardano, Cliff Hood, Bob Cvornyek, Mary Curtin, Mary Beth Brown, Gail Radford, and Cheryl Greenberg. In my years at Rutgers University and at the Center for Labor Studies in New York City, I also benefited from comments and encouragement I received from Tim Coogan, Colin Davis, Jan Lewis, Elliot Rosen, Warren Kimball, Dan Rosenberg, Harriet Kram, and Mike Musuraca. Mike Musurca and I have gone on the road a couple times with our research at labor history conferences and I must thank him for putting up with me in these endeavors. Since joining the faculty at York College I have been blessed with an incredibly supportive set of peers, from my chairpersons, Chin Suk and Phil Avillo, to my colleagues in the Department of History and Political Science. Let me also recognize my office mate, Hugh Sherman, and good friend Chip Miller for pushing me, in nice ways, to finish this book.

A number of historians, trade union officials and political activists (sometimes one-in-the-same) have commented on parts of this work at conferences or as readers of sections of the book, including Robert Cherny, Irving Bluestone, Larry May, Nelson Lichtenstein, Staughton Lynd, Jo Ann Argersinger, John Barnard, Sidney Fine, and the editors of *Peace and Change* and *Labor History.* All of their comments helped me tighten my arguments and forced me to push my thoughts and research in new directions.

Unfortunately, I have always been terrible at remembering names, so I have to thank anonymously all of the librarians and archivists who have aided me over the past ten plus years. To the librarians at the reference desks and the interlibrary loan and microfilm departments at Columbia University, the New York Public Library, Rutgers University-Newark Campus, Johns Hopkins University, and York College, thank you. To the archivists at the Walter P. Reuther Library, the State Historical Society of Wisconsin, and the Tamiment Institute, the same.

Sean Wilenz, Bruce Nelson, and Tim Gilfoyle each carefully read the entire manuscript and offered lengthy and trenchant criticism. I cannot thank each one of them enough for their suggestions and comments all of which strengthened this book. Tim Gilfoyle, in particular, made this a much more readable work and provided extraordinary support as a friend and colleague over a period of many years.

I have had the fortune of having the opportunity to work with one of the most highly esteemed presses and series in the field of American history. Many thanks to the editors and production team at the University of Illinois Press, especially to the director, Richard Wentworth, and to the manuscript editor, Rita D. Disroe.

I could not have completed this book without the financial and logistical aid I received from York College, both in the form of grants from the Faculty Enhancement and Research and Publication Committees and from the secretaries, work study students, and Dean. I was also fortunate enough to receive a grant from the Walter P. Reuther Library of Wayne State University.

Last, let me thank my family. For nearly two decades my father, Dr.

Allan Levy, and my stepmother, Maria Coia Levy, have provided the emotional support and love that helped sustain me through graduate school and after. Likewise, my sister Susan Levy Perry and my brother-in-law Dan Perry offered only encouraging words. For nearly as much time, my wife, Diane Krejsa, has done the same and more. She helped pay the bills when I still was not drawing a salary and moved with me, at considerable sacrifice, when I finally got a job. Most important, she has listened to me rehash this work more times than either one of us could ever count. I can truly say that without her this book never would have been published and I probably should share the title page with her. Let me also acknowledge my children, Jessica and Brian. When my daughter was born, I honestly believed that I had a shot at completing this book before she reached the age of one, and I certainly expected to complete it before Brian finished his first year. But now I can say, as they start to learn to read and write themselves, that I believe that in a strange indirect way, watching them mature has helped me mature as a scholar, writer, and certainly as a person. It is to them that I dedicate this book.

Introduction

Five minutes after noon on Friday 8 May 1970, about two hundred construction workers rampaged through New York City's financial district. Unlike workers of previous eras, who had come to Wall Street to attack the symbol of capitalism, this group directed its anger at the New Left and liberal politicians. Earlier in the day, hundreds of students from nearby colleges had gathered at Broad and Wall Street to demand the immediate withdrawal of American troops from Vietnam. Their protest was peaceful until the construction workers arrived. Marching behind a cluster of American flags, the "hardhats" descended on the protest from every direction. Brushing a small contingent of policemen aside, they pummeled longhaired youths with their fists and boots. After chasing away the rest of the demonstrators, the workers affixed an American flag to the statue of George Washington, located on the steps of Federal Hall, and then proceeded to City Hall. Along the way they chanted "All The Way, U.S.A" and "Love It or Leave It," tore down a Red Cross Banner from the gates of the historic Trinity Church, smashed windows at the nearby Pace College and assaulted passers-by. One victim Michael Berknap, a twenty-nine-year-old lawyer and an antiwar candidate for the state senate, was knocked to the ground and smacked on the side of the head. "Kill the commie bastard," the workers screamed while stiking him with their tools.[1]

The following Monday upward of two thousand workers and sympathizers staged a second noon-time pro-war march through Wall Street. By in large, this demonstration went peacefully, although a few bystanders were once again attacked. Nonetheless, the mood of the workers remained very ugly. Construction workers and longshoremen carried signs that displayed their disdain for students and Mayor Lindsay. One read "Don't Worry, They Don't Draft Faggots"; another called for impeaching the "Red Mayor."

Several days later it took the presence of a beefed up police force to avert another melee, this time between graduate business students, who had gathered in front of the Stock Exchange to protest against the war, and a force of construction workers and longshoremen. After the students departed to seek David Rockefeller's support for the peace movement, the workers took their place on the steps of the Stock Exchange and raised a banner that declared their support for the establishment and President Nixon's policies in Vietnam.[2]

Concurrently, New York City Building Trades Council President (soon to be President Nixon's Secretary of Labor) Peter Brennan proclaimed that local labor officials supported the worker's actions twenty to one. Brennan also announced that the council would sponsor a massive pro-war demonstration later that month. On 20 May, Brennan led sixty to one hundred thousand flag-waving patriots in support of President Nixon's recent invasion of Cambodia. Raymond Massaro, a twenty-five-year-old apprentice electrician, expressed the sentiment of many of the workers there. " 'This is my country,' " Massaro informed a *NY Times* reporter, "and I'm going to support it to the highest limit. I have a lot of friends that are over there being killed and I don't go for this [antiwar protest]." Regarding student dissent, Robert Romano, a forty-year-old general forman at the World Trade Center construction site stated: "I feel they have been with the silver spoon in their mouth too long and somebody has to take a hand in this to stop them, because if not, the country itself will come to ruins."[3]

Overall, the demonstration of the 20 May was an orderly and joyous event. But many viewed it with alarm. Cliff Sloan, for one, a freshman at the University of Michigan, where the Students for a Democratic Society (SDS) had been born at the beginning of the decade, remarked: "If this is what the class struggle is all about . . . there is something wrong here."[4]

Less than a week later, Brennan, along with twenty-one other labor officials, traveled to Washington D.C. to receive President Nixon's personal thanks. During a public ceremony, the trade unionists presented the President with a hardhat, labeled "Commander in Chief." Upon handing Nixon the helmet Thomas Gleason, president of the International Longshoremen Association (ILA), declared it was his hope that the hardhat would join the American flag as a symbol of "freedom and patriotism." President Nixon accepted the gift and informed them that their support had boosted the morale of American troops in Indochina.[5]

Because of the extensive news media coverage that the "hardhat revolt" received at the time, historians have focused on it in their writings on the 1960s. The violent rampage, the ensuing rally and the alleged public support of the National Guard at Kent State, have been interpreted to reflect both the relationship between the New Left and labor and the polarized state of America. The historian Irwin Unger, for example, contended that the events of May 1970 demonstrated the isolation of the student movement from Middle America. "It [New Left] has left the rest of America so far behind that it had lost all contact with national reality. Rather than winning the public to its vision . . . it had merely helped confirm the great social heartland and its allegiance to traditional decorum and deference."[6] This isolation, Unger added, grew out of the New Left's historical divorce from the Old Left. One-time socialist, Irving Howe, who befriended both prominent new leftists and trade unionists, concurred that the New Left had "no impact on such major institutions as the trade unions or such major social groupings as the working class."[7] Moreover, Howe, Unger, and others asserted that when the New Left and labor interacted, they did so antagonistically. Indeed, labor expert Arthur Shostak contended that the New Left had unwittingly pushed the "typical worker" into becoming "the most reactionary political force in this country."[8]

While some monographs have hinted at a more complex relationship, most general works on the 1960s or the post-World War II era have accepted the Unger/Howe/Shostak viewpoint.[9] William Leuchtenburg dealt with the relationship between the New Left and labor in only one section of *The Troubled Feast;* not surprisingly, he did so in his description of the notorious construction worker rampage.[10] *A History of Our Time,* a popular collection of essays on the postwar era, edited by William Chafe and Harvard Sitkoff, contained only one piece on the plight of the American worker, Richard Rogin's "Joe Kelley Has Reached His Boiling Point," that took as its subject a construction worker's rage with antiwar activists. "Inevitably, the social protests of the 1960s provoked a counter-response," Chafe and Sitkoff observed. "By the end of the decade a group dubbed by the media as the 'middle-Americans,' had rallied to the defense of the flag, traditional authority, and good manners."[11] Indeed, it is not an exaggeration to suggest that one of the most enduring images of the 1960s is that of construction workers assaulting antiwar demonstrators—meaning that the New Left and labor, or more grossly the youth movement and "middle America," were adversaries and adversaries alone.[12]

Clearly this perspective, as well as the generational analysis of the 1960s, has some value. Yet, like other theories that try to provide a simple understanding of a complex phenomenon, it falls short. It is at once too neat, uni-dimensional and ultimately ahistorical. By depicting the events of the end of the decade as representative of the whole, by portraying two of the most important social movements of the twentieth century as monoliths, by ignoring variation among themselves and over time, this interpretation misrepresents the decade, the New Left, and labor. In fact, the relations between the New Left and labor were far more complex than generally believed. Their relations must be assessed *historically,* as an unfolding of conflict and collaboration, never simple and always in flux.

In fact, in some ways the New Left was a child of organized labor, especially of the social activist bloc. Many of the original members of Students for a Democratic Society (SDS), for example, were directly related to or had personal ties to old leftists or trade union officials. In numerous instances, their relationship was symbiotic. Young leftists espoused the rights of workers within SDS while their parents and associates promoted SDS within labor circles. Building on personal ties, the New Left and labor collaborated in numerous fights against poverty and racial inequality, with funds and facilities serving as concrete commodities of exchange. Trade unionists provided the budding New Left with contacts and logistical and emotional support. More than once new leftists joined hands with striking workers and assisted in trade union organizing drives. Furthermore, in spite of differences over foreign policy, cooperation between the New Left and labor continued to grow through 1964, culminating with Mississippi Summer, spearheaded by SNCC and CORE and nearly a dozen Economic Research and Action Projects, led by SDS.

The New Left, however, did become critical of the labor movement by 1970. This antagonism emerged not because of *inherent* middle-class or antiworker bias, but rather due to much more historically specific factors. In particular, the rift that emerged between the two social movements was grounded in three important but external events: 1) the escalation of the Vietnam War; 2) the dramatic rise of Black Power; and 3) the blossoming of the counterculture. These events drove a wedge between the New Left and organized labor, as the former opposed the war, middle American culture and traditional liberal civil rights reforms, while the latter remained wedded, in general, to just the opposite. Differences over any one of these developments would have undoubtedly produced division. The conjunction of the three produced deep, unprecedented, and long-lasting antagonisms, many of which continue in some form today.

This said, in the midst of such turbulence, important cross-currents existed. New leftists collaborated with trade unionists in a variety of organizing drives. This was especially the case when labor organizations had an "independent" or "social activist" cast to them, or involved nonwhite workers; when labor's strategy involved mobilizing middle-class opinion actively in its behalf; when the employer involved in a labor dispute was a huge, unlovely conglomerate, a gigantic bureaucracy, or a university; and when labor battled against longer odds and tapped into the civil rights movement. The best example of this was the broad coalition of student activists, civil rights veterans, "bread and butter" and social activist unions that rallied behind the cause of the United Farm Workers. In addition, cooperation was prevalent, in the political realm, in enclaves of the New Left, such as Madison, Wisconsin, and Berkeley, California.

"Pro-labor" thought and "pro-left" discussion, on the part of the New Left and labor intellectuals, respectively, complemented these cross-currents. Much of this dialogue was shallow or artificial, simplistically touting old left lines about the revolutionary potential of the working class. But not all of it was. The journal *Radical America,* participants at the Socialist Scholars Conference, veteran activists like Stanley Aronowitz and Staughton Lynd, and budding labor historians and educators contributed new ideas or revived valued old ones on the nature of the working class and the history of labor that established a favorable context for collaborative endeavors.

In other words, the New Left's relationship to labor should be viewed dialectally. Cooperation was the main theme of the first half of the decade; confrontation was the main theme of the second half of the 1960s; and a synthesis or reconciliation of sorts appeared after 1970. Even though this synthesis remained hidden or overshadowed by real hostility between visible strands of both the New Left and labor, it would be remiss not to take note of it.[13] Indeed, if we are to arrive at a sophisticated understanding of one of the pivotal decades in American history, we must take note of both the sensational conflicts between the New Left and labor and the numerous instances of cooperation, especially on the local level, and we must pay as much attention to the developments of the first half of the sixties as we do to those of the latter half of the decade.[14]

Definitions: I have used the term *New Left* broadly. I consider the New Left to have been a historical movement that arose in the early 1960s, reached a peak in the mid–1960s and dissipated in the early 1970s. Most simply, the New Left was an uprising of students against the dominant policies and cultural mores of American society. More exactly, the New Left was an evolving movement or one in flux, that centered around the direct action civil rights protests of the early 1960s and the antiwar and black power movements later. Evidence of the emergence of the New Left included the birth and increase in circulation of left-leaning periodicals, such as *Liberation, Ramparts, Studies on the Left,* and *The Activist,* the specter of student protests, black and white, and the formation and revitalization of self-avowed left organizations, particularly SDS, SNCC and CORE.

I use the term *labor* broadly as well. Most broadly, labor means workers. But for methodological reasons, much of my research and discussion focuses on organized labor. I also use the term *social activist unions,* which consisted of 1) the core CIO unions, 2) a number of public employee and service unions and 3) a number of "old left" unions, some within the AFL–CIO, some independent.

One thing that set almost all the social activist unions apart from the rest of the House of Labor was that they sought to revitalize a generally moribund labor movement, to remake the Democrats into a truly liberal or Social Democratic party, and to move the nation's foreign policy in the direction of "detente" and demilitarization. This said, the social activist unions were not all cut from the same cloth. Some had been actively anti-communist in the 1940s and 1950s (such as the UAW); others became bastions for ex-communists and fellow travelers (such as Local 1199 and District 65); still others refused to bow to the whims of the red scare and were purged from the CIO for their behavior (such as the UE). As we will see, those social activist unions with ties to the Old Left tended to remain on friendlier terms with the New Left in the latter half of the 1960s than those who had purged themselves of communists. Yet, it would be misleading to suggest that the only unions that supported the New Left were old left ones, since this simply was not the case. In fact, in the first half of the decade, the two unions which had the closest association with SDS and SNCC, respectively, were the UAW and Packinghouse Workers (UPWA), both CIO unions that had abided by the Taft-Hartley Act's anti-communist provision. And not all unions and/or trade unionists who continued to cooperate with the New Left in the mid and latter 1960s were from old left stock, with the United Farm Workers being a case in point.[15]

1

We Shall Overcome: Labor and the Emergence of the New Left

On 28 August 1963, the heady idealism of the 1960s intensified at the foot of the Lincoln Memorial in Washington, D.C. Following a day of marching, singing, and speech-making, Martin Luther King, Jr., delivered his most memorable oration of his career. "I have a dream," King declared to over two hundred thousand protesters. "I have a dream . . . that one day . . . black girls will be able to join hands with little white boys and white girls and walk together as sisters and brothers. I have a dream," King exclaimed, "that one day . . . all God's children will be able to sing with new meaning 'My country 'tis of thee, sweet land of liberty, of thee I sing.' "[1]

King's speech provided a fitting climax to a day of protest and celebration, a day that had seen blacks and whites, young and old, students and labor unionists, militant and moderate civil rights activists join hands. Indeed, from its inception, the March on Washington epitomized the range of forces that had coalesced around civil rights by the summer of 1963. The lines dividing the different groups blurred. The motto of the March, "jobs and freedom," represented the two-pronged focus of the participants. The organizers personified the same: A. Philip Randolph, president of the Brotherhood of Sleeping Car Porters; Bayard Rustin, a life-long social democrat; Tom Kahn of the League of Industrial Democracy; Cleveland Robinson of District 65; and Norman Hill of the Congress of Racial Equality. The Southern Christian Leadership Conference, Student Nonviolent Coordinating Committee, CORE, United Automobile Wokers, National Association for the Advancement of Colored People, American Jewish Congress, National Council of Churches and Negro American Labor Council cosponsored the demonstration. The Students for a Democratic Society and other student-left groups chartered buses to the event. The demonstrators' songs illustrated the links between the labor and the civil rights movement, as thousands joined in revised versions of "Which Side Are You On" and "Hallelujah I'm a Bum," (this time entitled "Hallelujah I'm a Travellin'"). The banners and posters at the march reflected the unity of the day as well. For example, one group paraded behind a painted sheet that read: "Cambridge, Maryland, Student Nonviolent Coordinating Committee (SNCC) and United Packinghouse Workers of America, District 6." As representatives from each of the various cosponsors mounted the podium, the breadth of the movement became even more evident. A. Philip Randolph commenced the proceedings and Walter Reuther, John Lewis of SNCC and Martin Luther King Jr., presented the most memorable orations.[2]

Though some radicals deprecated the March—Malcolm X described the event as a "farce in Washington"—in general, the protest embodied the cooperative spirit of the time. The Longshoremen's newspaper described the march as a "remarkable show of Negro-White unity," in which one could "sense a rebirth a pride in the part labor played, historically and can play again." In spite of the "censorship" of John Lewis's speech, a SNCC staff member observed that "the March was a tremendous inspiration to the poor blacks from the Deep South. . . . It helped them believe that they were not alone, that there were people in the nation who cared what happened to them." SNCC stalwart Bob Zellner recalled that the presence of thousands of rank-and-file workers impressed him deeply. And SNCC's newspaper, the *Student Voice,* proclaimed that all who witnessed and participated in the March judged it "a success."[3]

Less remembered, although nearly as significant as the Great March, were a series of meetings that followed in its wake. In the last full week of September 1963, hundreds of packinghouse workers from all over the country traveled to Washington, D.C., to attend the "Civil Rights and Legislation Conference." Sponsored by the United Packinghouse Workers of America, one of the most progressive unions in the nation, the conference provided trade unionists, politicians, and black activists with the opportunity to interact and display their support for racial justice and equality. For several days the delegates heard civil rights leaders and friends of the movement call for close collaboration between labor and civil rights forces and passage of pending civil rights legislation. Monsignor George Higgins, a life-long ally of labor and a staunch supporter of racial reforms, brought the conferees to their feet with a rousing address praising activists who had taken to the streets and disparaging those segments of the labor movement that had been slow to endorse them.

Black comedian and a close associate of SNCC, Dick Gregory, reminded the delegates that the "Negro's" cause was also labor's cause. Commenting on the March on Washington, Gregory hinted that militants in the movement would welcome similar displays of support. "Never in the history of the world have that many people ever been able to come together with a three hundred year old gripe and [not] fight. That is strength. That is power."[4]

Fresh from a Plaquemine jail cell, where he had been when the March on Washington had taken place, CORE director James Farmer favorably compared labor's past with the civil rights movement's present and future. "In the thirties labor was on the streets; labor was accused of violating property rights. Today civil rights forces are in the streets and we are accused of violating property rights." Labor, Farmer asserted, had taught the civil rights movement how to use protest as a weapon. In the South, labor and civil rights activists faced the same foes. "The very same people who are anti-civil rights are the folk who are pushing for the so-called right-to-work laws. This natural alliance [between labor and the civil rights movement] should not be broken."[5]

Before they passed a resolution that commanded President Kennedy to send troops to the South to protect black "freedom fighters" and before they granted Farmer and Gregory $1,000 honorariums each (a hefty fee at the time), the packinghouse workers joined Farmer in singing an updated labor tune that had become the anthem of the civil rights movement.

> We Shall Overcome.
> We shall overcome.
> We shall overcome, some day.
> Oh-h, deep in my heart.
> I do believe.
> We shall overcome some day.[6]

Two months later, in the immediate aftermath of President Kennedy's assassination, over five hundred student activists attended SNCC's Jobs and Food conference in Washington, D.C. The gathering, SNCC's largest to date, was painstakenly put together by William Mahoney, a Howard University student and a member of SNCC's Nonviolent Action Group, and Lewis Carliner of the Industrial Union Department AFL–CIO. Keynote addresses were delivered by James Baldwin, the black author whose militant book *The Fire Next Time* had recently been published, Bayard Rustin, the organizer of the Great March, and long-time socialist Norman Thomas. The speeches mirrored those made at the Packinghouse Workers' convention. They emphasized that the movement needed to move beyond the issue of desegregation, that it had to focus on the economics of inequality.[7]

To enable the conferees to do so, Mahoney and Carliner had organized a series of special workshops generally headed by labor experts, such as Jack Conway and Stanley Aronowitz. In these workshops new leftists and trade union veterans discussed the interrelation of unemployment and racial segregation and considered different strategies for overcoming both. More generally, the workshops provided labor unionists with the opportunity to express and demonstrate their support for militant civil rights activism. For example, when some SNCC participants expressed dissatisfaction with Southern trade unionists, Carliner reassured them that labor "had a commitment to something greater" than the type of unionism SNCC had encountered, and that he along with like-minded officials would "use their sway in the labor movement to help SNCC." Many, if not most, of the SNCC delegates appeared moved by Carliner reassurances. One of them, Walter Tillow, wrote Carliner that he wanted to express his pleasure at being "part of the beginning of a genuine dialogue between the labor movement and SNCC." Others, such as James Forman and Stanley Aronowitz, cemented plans for working together in Danville, Virginia, and enlisting each other's aid in other locales.[8]

Several other parlays brought together blacks and whites, new leftists, trade unionists, and liberals. One meeting was devoted to the United Automobile Workers's Crusade Against Poverty. Another re-assembled the "coalition" that had staged the March on Washington. SDS, SNCC, and an ad hoc committee of veteran left-liberals sponsored a conference on poverty in Hazard Kentucky. Taken as a whole, these conferences represented the relationship of the New Left and labor in the early 1960s. They showed that both social movements were united in their desire to eradicate racial inequality and poverty. The conferences also revealed that both retained a faith in the perfectibility of American society and that both saw one another as necessary partners in effecting change. Moreover, the conferences demonstrated that whatever differences existed between the two movements they were outweighed by their common goals. Put another way, those who had united at the Great March on Washington believed that *they* could overcome.[9]

For the Students for a Democratic Society, the largest New Left organization of the decade, the most obvious connection it enjoyed with labor was via its parent organization, the League of Industrial Democracy.

(SDS had been known as the Student League for Industrial Democracy [SLID] until it changed its name to the Students for a Democratic Society or SDS in 1960.) Founded by Jack London and Upton Sinclair before World War I, LID was a standard-bearer of social democracy and the anticommunist left in the interwar period. After languishing in the 1950s, LID revitalized its ties to several social activist labor unions and an assortment of top trade union officials. In turn, SDS members gained exposure to labor issues and officials. For instance, in 1958, LID arranged a series of field trips for SLID to the Union Hall of the Seafarers. Following the visit, SLID members reported that the Seafarers were hardly a corrupt business union, as they had been pictured by congressional investigators and the press.[10]

SDS's connection with LID was not a mere coincidence. SDS's constitution explicitly described itself as LID's student branch dedicated to building a coalition of radicals and liberals around the goal of social democracy. Nor did SDS maintain ties to LID simply to retain its access to union funds. Some individuals joined SDS because of LID's reputation as an advocate of industrial democracy. Just as important, many members of SDS in the early 1960s shared LID's strategy of fostering a political realignment.[11]

LID was not SDS's sole link to labor. Several of SDS's key figures in its early years had indirect ties to labor via their associations with the Old Left. For example, Steve Max, whose father edited the Communist party's *Daily Worker,* drifted in and out of the youth branches of both old and new left organizations. Still other "red-diaper babies," such as Richard Flacks and Bob Ross, played key roles within SDS in its early years. Not suprisingly, most of these individuals tended to support the goal of realignment or forging a coalition of northern liberals, labor, and blacks within the Democratic party sans the Dixiecrats.[12]

For several SDS members, trade unionism was a family affair. The parents of two early SDS members, Sharon Jeffrey and Barry Bluestone, were top officials with the UAW. Jeffrey's mother, Mildred, was the community relations director of the International; Bluestone's father, Irving, was the administrative assistant to UAW president Walter P. Reuther. Sharon Jeffrey consistently pushed for establishing better ties with the UAW.[13]

While Sharon Jeffrey successfully prodded student activists to apply for labor funding, her mother and Barry Bluestone's father issued one favorable review of SDS after another to their superiors. In one case, Irving Bluestone contended that Bob Ross and SDS could be of "ultimate value to the liberal cause." Mildred Jeffrey went even further, describing SDS as "the most important student organization in the country." Both individuals endorsed SDS's proposals to fight poverty via its Economic Research and Action Projects, or ERAPs.[14]

Al Haber, SDS's first president, enjoyed similar ties to the labor movement. His father, William Haber, was a labor arbitrator, an active member of the Michigan Democratic party, president of ORT (a Jewish vocational/labor organization) and a personal friend of numerous labor leaders. One of Haber's first programs as SDS's leader was a boycott of Sears Roebuck & Co., which he charged denied blacks jobs and was breaking the AFL–CIO retail clerks' union. The Sears case, Haber hoped, would "bring to the fore the natural alliance of labor and the civil rights movement."[15] Still, several years later Haber wrote one of SDS's first manifestos, entitled "Students and Labor." The pamphlet argued that unions suffered from poor reputations on college campuses and called on SDS to educate students on the history and importance of labor unions. Simultaneously, Haber urged progressives within the labor movement to assert themselves.[16]

Like SDS, CORE benefited from personal and organizational ties with labor. Before dedicating himself full-time to CORE activities in the early 1960s, James Farmer moved in and out of the trade unions, including a stint as an AFSCME official. At another point, Farmer declined a position with the UAW. CORE community relations director Marvin Rich held a union position in the 1950s. Norman Hill worked alternately for CORE and the labor movement, ultimately ending up as an official with IUD, AFL–CIO. By the early 1960s, in fact, CORE's advisory board was stacked with presidents and vice-presidents of various unions, including AFSCME's Jerry Wurf, the IUE's James Carey, Walter Reuther, A. Philip Randolph, and the Teamster's Harold Gibbons.[17]

Berkeley, California's Free Speech Movement in 1964 revealed comparable connections between the Old and New Left. Bettina Aptheker, the daughter of the well-known communist historian Herbert Aptheker, Michael Rossman, the son of an old left family, and Barbara Garson, a former member of the Young Socialist Alliance, were part of FSM's Steering Committee. During rallies, FSM activists often sang old union songs. After the movement dissipated, many of its leaders helped form an American Federation of Teachers local for teaching assistants and sought to create a Free Student Union (FSU).[18]

While less well connected than SDS, SNCC enjoyed important organizational ties to labor, especially through the Highlander Folk School, which Myles Horton founded in 1932 as an experimental worker-oriented educational center. Before World War II, Highlander conducted workshops for trade unions and backed striking workers and the training of labor activists. Afterward it turned its attention to civil rights.[19] In

April 1960, for example, shortly after the Greensboro sit-ins, SNCC's founders Marion Barry, Bernard Lafayette, and John Lewis attended a Highlander conference entitled, "The New Generation Fights for Equality." There they learned several "freedom songs" that had been collected by Horton's wife, Zilphia, and Highlander's resident music director Guy Carawan, including "We Shall Overcome." At a later conference, SNCC members met several of Horton's labor friends, including Ralph Helstein. SNCC stalwarts, like Bob Zellner, a native southerner with no direct connections to the labor movement, departed knowing that "there were progressives in the trade union movement," an impression that stuck with him as the decade progressed.[20]

Ties between SNCC and labor were reinforced by the Southern Conference Education Fund. A spinoff of the Southern Conference for Human Welfare, SCEF was founded in the late 1930s by a collection of left-leaning southerners, including CIO activist Lucy Randolph Mason and educator Clark Foreman. SCEF's leaders Carl and Anne Braden published a steady diet of literature on the connections between black and white workers. They encouraged new leftists to organize around economic or labor goals. For example, with the help of trade union funds, SCEF paid the way for a succession of white field workers to work with SNCC.[21]

Still other incidental contacts linked the two movements. Stokely Carmichael, for one, had indirect ties to old left family members and friends. While in high school he befriended Gene Dennis, Jr., the son of Eugene Dennis, the top official of the Communist party in the United States. Subsequently he attended several old left summer camps and, upon enrolling at Howard University, joined the Nonviolent Action Group, a socialist-oriented affiliate of SNCC. Through NAG and his former old left friends in New York he spent some time helping the local branch of AFSCME organize workers in Washington, D.C.[22]

Even more important personal contacts with labor came via James Forman, SNCC's executive secretary. In 1960, Forman was a frustrated civil rights activist, making a living by teaching in the Chicago public schools. The same year he joined the Emergency Relief Committee to aid the Fayette County (Tennessee) Civic and Welfare League. (Forman had relatives in Fayette County.) Among those from whom Forman sought support was Sylvia Fischer, his colleague and the wife of Charles Fisher, Ralph Helstein's administrative assistant. Through the Fischers, Forman persuaded the Packinghouse Workers to back the Fayette struggle.[23]

After Fayette faded from the national scene, Forman continued to enjoy the UPWA's support. Helstein wrote a general letter of recommendation for Forman. In 1961, shortly after he started his new job as executive secretary of SNCC, the Packinghouse Workers sent the civil rights group $400 to bail Bob Zellner out of a Mississippi jail. A year later, SNCC received $1,500 from the union to aid its activists in McComb. In 1963, the UPWA granted still another $1,500 for activists in Georgia and Mississippi. Food was often sent along with Packinghouse money to these SNCC die-hards. SNCC leaders John Lewis and Stokely Carmichael even received college scholarship money from the union.[24]

Indeed, new leftists recognized the financial support it received from trade unions for what it was, a "concrete demonstration of partnership," to borrow James Farmer's words. In 1960, a UAW grant of $10,000 allowed SDS to hire Al Haber as its first full-time organizer. In turn, Haber and Tom Hayden energized SDS into the leading student left group in the nation. A year later, the UAW provided $5,000 worth of seed money for the Economic Research and Action Projects, which proved to be SDS's primary program. A second grant of $2,500 bolstered the ERAPs' treasury.[25] Still more UAW funds, as well as ILGWU and AFL–CIO money, flowed into SDS's coffers through the hands of LID.[26]

UAW leaders and the Industrial Union Department of the AFL–CIO supplemented SDS's finances by granting it access to their printing presses and meeting halls. In 1962, SDS used the UAW's summer retreat in Port Huron, Michigan, to write its manifesto, the "Port Huron Statement." The Packinghouse Workers printed thousands of copies of the document. Labor officials also lent their support to SDS's independent fund-raising appeals. On one occasion, IUD executive director Jack Conway urged his associates to contribute to SDS: "I have been especially impressed with the work of Students for a Democratic Society. This deeply committed group of young people who labored effectively in the civil rights struggle now seeks to extend their activities beyond civil rights issues into other areas." On another occasion, Walter Reuther praised SDS as "the vanguard student organization dedicated to the forces of progress in America."[27]

SDS hardly felt tarnished by labor money. Upon receiving a $5,000 grant from the UAW, Tom Hayden declared, "it is time to rejoice." SDS could use the money for all types of programs and there were "no strings attached."[28] Furthermore, the more money SDS received, the greater its appetite for labor funds grew. Following the receipt of one donation, SDS submitted proposals to the UAW and other unions for grandiose organizing schemes, staffed by student activists and paid for by liberal unions. Rennie Davis, for example, requested $76,450 for a program of community unions across the country. Similarly, Todd Gitlin asked the

UAW to contribute $12,820 to SDS to support a one-year campus development program, including the hiring of four field secretaries. While the UAW considered Davis's request beyond its means, both Walter Reuther and UAW secretary-treasurer, Emil Mazey, favored supporting Gitlin's plan.[29]

Like SDS, CORE received substantial financial support from the coffers of organized labor. Between 1961 and 1964, close to $40,000 originated from the ILGWU, Packinghouse Workers, District 65 of RWDSU, UAW, AFSCME and the Seafarers International. These donations allowed CORE to expand its direct action projects to a national scale. On several occasions the money saved CORE from financial disaster. A $5,000 grant from the UAW in the summer of 1961 bailed CORE activists from jail, leading Marvin Rich to declare that without the money the Freedom Rides could not have continued on a "systematic and organized basis."[30]

Lacking CORE's and SDS's direct connections to trade unions, SNCC initially found labor money harder to secure. Nevertheless, SNCC did not exist on the good will of poor tenant farmers alone.[31] The AFL–CIO, for example, provided the funds that allowed SNCC to convene its founding meeting. The United Electrical Workers (UE) and the west coast Longshoremen (ILWU) contributed seed money for a number of SNCC projects in the deep South. SNCC indirectly received labor money via joint projects with SCLC and CORE. Similarly, SNCC freedom riders and field workers in Mississippi benefited from bail money granted to CORE by the UAW. Some of this money came indirecty through the legal defense funds of the NAACP or SCLC. Yet both of these organizations were known to solicit donations from trade unions and other liberal sources by arguing that it would go to help SNCC.[32]

In the same years, the AFL–CIO's political arm, the Committee on Political Education, lent substantial financial aid to Voter Education Projects in the Deep South, many of which were staffed by SNCC and CORE members. COPE sent nearly all of this aid discretely or covertly, in part because it surmised that many southern locals would object to such aid. As a result, many new leftists in the South remained unaware of labor's helpful hand.[33]

SNCC's main labor benefactor was the UPWA, which for years had combatted the racial bigotry of many of Chicago's white workers. In January 1963, Helstein proposed that the union undertake a major program of support for SNCC, which would include guaranteeing subsistence to all of SNCC's field workers in the South. In his proposal, Helstein highlighted Forman's personal relationship with the union and the sacrifices that SNCC activists were making in the cause of freedom.

He also pleaded with his colleagues to remember their early days with the CIO. To build support for the program, Helstein instructed district and local leaders to bring SNCC members or "friends" before their members. On more than one occasion, Ralph Helstein proclaimed that SNCC deserved Packinghouse aid because it was not as good of a fund raiser as SCLC, CORE or the NAACP. While the UPWA never met the lofty goal of guaranteeing SNCC's livelihood, its contributions, along with those of many of its friends and allies, helped catapult SNCC into the forefront of the civil rights movement. By 1963, in fact, SNCC was raising over $300,000 a year from outside sources, more than even the NAACP.[34]

In the same time period, new leftists displayed their solidarity with the labor movement the old-fashioned way, on the picket line. When New York City newspaper workers went on strike in 1962, student activists Kim Moody and Ed Schiller proclaimed that it was incumbent upon SDS as a radical organization to display its solidarity with them. SDS national secretary Jim Monsonis concurred that it "ought to be an automatic reflex" for SDS to side with unions. Though some SDS members disagreed, most backed the strike, contributing to the union's strike funds and taking part in other supportive measures. A year later, University of Wisconsin students led by C. Clark Kissinger, a future president of SDS, organized sympathy protests and a boycott of a local Volkswagen dealership and garage that was being struck by the UAW. In New York City, CORE, SDS and Friends of SNCC supported strikes by District 65 of RWDSU and local 1199 against Lord and Taylor and Beth-El Hospital, respectively. In Oregon, Jeremy Brecher corralled Reed College students to serve as supporters of a local UAW strike. And SDS's Chicago chapter, in concert with the Packinghouse Workers, formed Jobs or Income Now (JOIN), a community union devoted to helping the underemployed and unemployed.[35]

Likewise, in San Francisco, officials from the Longshoremen's, Teamsters', Teachers' and several building trades' unions joined with CORE leaders and members of various student and peace groups to support civil rights. Among this local coalition's actions was a united protest against the Palace Hotel for its discriminatory and antiunion policies. This protest, in turn, served as the springboard for the explosion of student activism at U.C. Berkeley in the fall of 1964.[36]

Of all of these developments, those involving the fight for civil rights in the South proved the most important, because, for new leftists, the fight against racial inequality was the paramount issue. If labor had failed to express support for racial equality, agreement around other concerns would have been of little value. Labor displayed support for civil rights in enough instances to confirm the New Left's faith in cooperation and to make that cooperative relationship more real than imagined.

In the early 1960s, the *AFL–CIO News* and other labor papers consistently condemned segregation and praised the fight for equality. "Wipe Out Job Bias," announced one *AFL–CIO News* headline in the early spring of 1961; "Nation's No. 1 Moral Problem: Denial of Civil Rights," stated another. "The AFL–CIO is firmly and irrevocably dedicated to the proposition that all men are created equal. . . . We shall not rest until the God-given right is established in practice," the story below the headline explained. Independent "old left" unions went even further, admonishing the Kennedy administration for trying to temper black protest and commending the latter's use of direct action to obtain its ends. One *UE News* article proclaimed that the labor movement could relearn a great deal from the civil rights activists, including the "power of militancy." SNCC, SDS and CORE were aware of these stances, as they received a number of labor newspapers and through the reportage of *Guardian,* the primary left newspaper of the early 1960s.[37]

Moving beyond rhetoric, trade unionists expressed their support for specific civil rights demonstrations. Shortly after the sit-ins broke out, delegates to the North Carolina State AFL–CIO endorsed the students' use of "peaceful labor techniques such as the picket line, the sit-down and the consumer boycott for equal rights in public facilities." CORE chapters organized a coalition of labor, religious, and civil rights groups into sympathy strikes or picket lines at Woolworth's and Kress's in Los Angeles, St. Louis, and New York. The activism appeared infectious. Packinghouse Workers joined picket lines outside Woolworth's, with Ralph Helstein brandishing a sign that declared: "If you support Woolworth's Here, You Support Segregation In the South!" In New York City, the ILGWU alone "furnished as many as eight hundred pickets for a single afternoon," in the words of one appreciative CORE spokesperson. Even more impressively, some union members joined SNCC and CORE freedom riders on their journey through the Deep South.[38]

Front-line civil rights activists spoke before trade union leaders and rank and file to reinforce this support. SNCC stalwart Robert Moses detailed his experiences in Mississippi before a special committee headed by Eleanor Roosevelt, Walter Reuther, A. Philip Randolph, and Boris Shiskin, civil rights director of the AFL–CIO. On another occasion, in an open meeting of the UAW, Moses retold his story. Seizing upon Moses' descriptions of the hardships faced by blacks in the South, the labor presses reprinted his and others' testimony, reaffirming the virtues of organized protest. "The fight of people in the South to eat in a restaurant of their choice, to get the vote and to travel anywhere they please, is like the fight of labor for recognition, *and I'm talking about the strikes of the 1930s,*" chimed the UAW newspaper.[39]

It is questionable whether a majority of trade unionists initially favored direct action protest. Without a doubt, however, the percentage of workers who sympathized with the civil rights activists increased with each passing year. In 1963, when Birmingham authorities used water cannons to disperse nonviolent demonstrators, outraged Detroit fire fighters urged their international to "bend every effort," to halt the "assignment of firemen and fire equipment" to put down demonstrations in Birmingham. Similarly, San Francisco longshoremen cosponsored a rally in solidarity with the Birmingham demonstrators, in which up to 30,000 men and women participated, including ILWU president Harry Bridges and thousands of union members. Those in attendance contributed funds to the Birmingham freedom fighters, spoke in support of the protests, and called for "equality of opportunity in San Francisco" as well as in the South. Hundreds of trade union leaders and members sent letters and telegrams to President Kennedy demanding that he act in the cause of freedom. Walter Reuther wrote: "What is needed in the present crises is not half-way and half-hearted measures but action bold and adequate to square American democracies' performance with its promise of full citizenship rights and equal opportunities for all Americans." Even George Meany, who once bragged that he had never marched on a picket line, stated that he "would be the last one" to criticize King for "fighting for what I think is right."[40]

After Birmingham, labor unionists, moderate civil rights groups, and militant civil rights advocates continued to link arms. "Freedom Marches" took place across the country in the spring and summer of 1963. A Chicago march drew 10,000 participants; 25,000 men and women demonstrated in Los Angeles; between 100,000 and 250,000 individuals rallied in Detroit on 23 June 1963, with Martin Luther King, Jr., Walter Reuther and local black leaders in the lead. And in the largest and most dramatic demonstration in United States history, to that date, 250,000 individuals united for the March on Washington for Jobs and Freedom.[41]

The emergence of a variety of single-issue or local coalitions confirmed that new leftists and trade unionists were in a cooperative mood. The Student Peace Union, at the time the largest new left group, organized the very successful Washington Action, a nuclear ban protest of 5,000, with student activists, labor officials, and old leftists in the forefront. In turn, this core of activists successfully sparked a nationwide peace movement, which prompted President Kennedy to sign a nuclear test ban treaty. In Detroit, the Trade Union Leadership Council became a force in local politics and union affairs. The TULC consisted of black trade unionists, civil rights activists and a handful of leftist intellectuals. The TULC successfully supported the reform candidacy of Jerome Cavanagh for mayor, prompted the UAW to name two blacks, one a TULC member, to its executive board, and hastened the desegregation of the building trades. An impressed Bayard Rustin remarked: "I wish there was a TULC in every industrial city."[42]

A unique coalition emerged in Prince Edward County, Virginia, where the trade union movement and the New Left became virtually inter-changeable. There, sixty union teachers, joined by a contingent of Queens College students, established a "freedom school." Led by AFT officials Richard Parrish and Arthur Reese, the school provided black children with the education that they had been effectively denied since 1959, due to the decision of public officials to close the schools in protest against the *Brown* decision. Commenting on the AFT's participation, James Forman commended the union as a "colleague in the movement." The school was so successful that it served as a prototype for the freedom schools that were established in Mississippi in the summer of 1964.[43]

Alongside these symbols of unity, however, stood evidence of serious differences. Southern trade unions responded tepidly, at best, to the challenge of racial inequality in their own backyards. In Greensboro, the local AFL–CIO endorsed the sit-ins but did not form their own pickets around Woolworth's. In Jackson, Mississippi, state AFL–CIO president, Claude Ramsay, met privately with and supported Medgar Evers's organizing efforts, but did not challenge segregation in the state's locals. In Texas, AFL–CIO state chairman, Hank Brown, called for a massive movement of blacks, chicanos and working-class whites for labor and civil rights, yet did not break with the Democratic party that was tied to the large businesses of the region. And George Meany and the executive council of the AFL–CIO refused to endorse the March on Washington.[44]

Militant activists took note of Southern labor's relative absence from the front line of the struggle. SNCC members complained that suppos-edly progressive unions had allowed White Citizens' Councils to use union halls and cooperated in the Southern effort to defy the *Brown* decision. Gallup Polls and other surveys confirmed that white southern workers, unlike their northern counterparts, overwhelmingly opposed the goals of the civil rights movement.[45]

In the North, the record of craft unions, construction trades in particular, drew the wrath of civil rights supporters and was a constant reminder of the fragility of the New Left's collaborative relationship with organized labor. Surprisingly, two of the most serious attacks on the labor movement came from black leaders and organizations generally considered representative of the more moderate branch of the civil rights movement, and if they could not cooperate with the organized labor, then it seemed unlikely that the more militant New Left would. At the 1959 AFL–CIO convention, A. Philip Randolph publicly clashed with George Meany over the racial practices of a number of AFL–CIO affiliates. "Now!" Randolph exclaimed, "either we are for or not for segregated unions." Meany yelled back, "who in hell appointed you as the guardian of the Negro members in America?" Subsequently, in May 1960, seventy-five black labor leaders formed the Negro American Labor Council (NALC) to pursue the rights of black trade unionists, and in turn the AFL–CIO censured Randolph.[46]

In January 1961, the second break with the AFL–CIO occurred when Herbert Hill, representing the NAACP, submitted a report entitled "Racism within Organized Labor, 1955–1960." In the report, the NAACP charged the House of Labor with having "failed to eliminate the broad pattern of racial discrimination and segregation in many important affiliated unions." Besides condemning the craft unions, the report criticized the ILGWU, heretofore considered a liberal union and an ally of blacks. The AFL–CIO responded as it had to Randolph's charges. It claimed that the allegations were false and sought to pin the blame for them on Hill alone. For example, *Justice,* the ILGWU's newspaper, urged blacks to shun a split with its "labor allies," and to ignore the charges of one "irresponsible individual." Nonetheless, the NAACP pursued its charges of discrimination. For instance, it applauded a "finding" made by the New York State Commission for Human Rights that the ILGWU had acted in a discriminatory manner.[47]

These charges and countercharges spurred new leftists, many of them CORE members, to attack the discriminatory practices of specific local unions. In March 1963, James Farmer and Roy Wilkins led a rally of twenty-five thousand in Cleveland against discriminatory employment in the building trades. In the New York metropolitan area, local CORE chapters picketed construction sites in Harlem and Newark, demanding more minority hiring and greater access to apprenticeships in the building trades. Some labor leaders responded to these protests by arguing that employers, not unions, deserved the blame for discriminatory hiring practices. In fact, new leftists accused employers of discrimination and protested alongside labor unionists when the discrimination was blatantly the employer's fault. But employer discrimination did not stop new leftists from contending that labor unions shared the blame.[48]

Within a few years of their exchange, Meany and Randolph reconciled their differences. Meany went before the NALC and asked for a unified effort for racial justice. Shortly after, Randolph urged the AFL–CIO to restore the "historic negro-labor alliance" and the NALC officially called for an "alliance with union labor." Even though the NAACP continued to pressure the labor movement to abolish its discriminatory practices, it warmed to the AFL–CIO's plea that it renew their friendship.[49]

But did these apologies come in time? Public statements of reconciliation undoubtedly improved the spirit of unity. But they left unresolved the historic problem of the racially segmented labor market, within which the craft unions perpetuated discrimination by intentionally limiting membership in order to insure high wages. Employers historically divided workers by race, restricting certain jobs to whites and others to blacks. The exclusionary practices of numerous craft unions only reinforced such segmentation.

Sensing this unresolved dilemma, CORE and other new leftists retained their skepticism about the building and craft trades. CORE chapters continued to pressure these unions to hire more minorities and, in some cases, increased the frequency of their protests against discriminatory locals. Some CORE members became partial to separatism and extreme militancy, as espoused by Malcolm X, a sentiment that was anathema to most labor leaders. Likewise, a significant segment of the white student left developed a deep distrust of Meany, the craft unions, and of the ILGWU.[50]

Disagreements over foreign policy further compounded the New Left's misgivings about labor, especially the leadership of the AFL–CIO. Top labor leaders strongly backed America's cold war policies, with George Meany delivering one speech after another pledging labor's support "to fighting reds." In contrast, new leftists persistently challenged America's international role. Organized labor's and the New Left's conflicting views of Cuba typified their disagreements. American labor leaders applauded President Kennedy's policy toward Cuba, from the Bay of Pigs fiasco to the Cuban missile crisis; new leftists hailed the Cuban revolution and condemned the anti-Castro policies of the United States. Moreover, new leftists did not lose sight of labor's position. Writing for *Studies on the Left,* a prominent new left journal, Ronald Radosh traced the historical links between labor and America's anti-Soviet actions. He concluded that the AFL had supported an anticommunist policy since the age of Wilson. Sidney Lens extended Radosh's critique, giving organized labor a score of "near zero" in the realm of foreign policy.[51]

Despite these differences, most new leftists and labor leaders valued cooperation over confrontation. They did so for several reasons. First, neither saw one another as a monolith. New leftists understood that George Meany did not speak for the entire labor movement and trade unionists did not allow the antics of a few new leftists to color their perception of all of them. For instance, in the breath after he gave the labor movement a near-zero score on foreign policy, Sidney Lens paid tribute to UAW secretary-treasurer Emil Mazey for fighting for peace (Mazey delivered one of the keynote addresses at a major peace march in Washington). A month later, Dave Dellinger, who had been critical of the craft unions, heralded the formation of "Labor Action for Peace," a small group of dissenting trade unionists in New York City. After describing George Meany as a reactionary, Michael Munk praised the rank-and-file union members and numerous trade unions that supported the March on Washington.[52]

The personal ties between the New and Old Left undoubtedly assuaged the situation. Old leftists within the New Left, from A. J. Muste, editor of *Liberation* to the "red diaper babies" in SDS, brought with them the sophistication or background to allow the New Left to see the labor movement as varied. Similarly, trade union officials with familial connections to the New Left, presented the actions of the New Left in a good light.

Second, foreign policy was only a secondary or tertiary issue for the New Left in the early 1960s. Civil rights at home, not human rights abroad, remained the paramount issue. In the fall of 1963, SDS rejected a proposal to focus on foreign policy because it was "too remote from the basic interests of students." Instead, SDS expanded its fight against poverty, an effort that gained the support of the UAW and other unions. Obviously, SNCC and CORE shared SDS's emphasis on civil rights. (Not until 1965 would differences over foreign policy begin to outweigh domestic concerns.)[53]

Third, cooperation predominated in the early 1960s because the New Left believed it needed allies to bring about social change. Militants and moderates alike predicated their success upon convincing labor leaders and liberal reformers to prompt the federal government to act. As SNCC chairman Charles McDew wrote Packinghouse Workers' president, Ralph

Helstein: "We know that until a new push of forces—labor, progressives and students—unite to make our democracy real, the efforts of the segregationists . . . will forever block liberal legislation."[54]

Likewise, SDS's "Port Huron Statement" argued that only "genuine cooperation, locally, nationally, and internationally, between a new Left of young people and an awakening community of allies," consisting of campus activists, "labor, civil rights, and other liberal forces," could bring change. Indeed, even while SDS was critical of the AFL–CIO's contemporary course, it recognized the crucial role that labor had played in fostering liberal programs and sensed that leftists would have to revitalize it if they hoped to achieve more reforms. Thus, the "Port Huron Statement," rejected outright the theory that big labor was equivalent to big business. Though it had lost much of its idealism "its numbers and potential political strength, its natural interests in the abolition of exploitation, its reach to the grass roots of American society, combine to make it the best candidate for civil rights, peace and economic reform movements."[55] Or as SDS theorist Richard Flacks recalled twenty-five years later: "The Port Huron hope was not that a mass movement would make a revolution, but that a coalition spearheaded by a revitalization of organized labor, morally impelled by the civil rights movement, and aided by . . . students and intellectuals, could emerge."[56]

Labor unionists had their own reasons for cooperating with the growing New Left. After a decade of retreat, social activist unions were beginning to reassert their interests in progressive causes, including the drive for racial equality. (Some old left unions had never retreated but had been too isolated to be heard). When the civil rights movement emerged, they welcomed it as their own cause. Many trade unionists had joined the labor movement with an understanding that racial equality was a necessary precondition for economic and political equality for working men and women. As Emil Mazey proclaimed: "Discrimination and segregation are the twin tools of division, and the members, the working class, are those that suffer when we have division among us."[57]

Not exclusive of this ideological identification with the goals of black activists, trade union officials realized that there were pragmatic reasons for forging a coalition with the New Left. By allying with the disadvantaged and unorganized and supporting racial equality, labor improved its general reputation and discredited the claim that it was merely a special interest group. In addition, union officials discerned that support for the civil rights struggle would boost their drive to organize black workers in the South and please black union members in the North. For instance, COPE saw adding blacks to the voting roles as a precondition to trade unionism in the South.[58]

A core of UAW and AFL–CIO, IUD officials, whose influence was greater than their numbers, found both ideological and pragmatic reasons to linking up with the white student left. They sensed a lack of support among students and felt threatened, ironically, by what they saw as an increasing conservative presence on the college campus. McCarthyism had left a generation of students without much contact with traditional socialist groups and the conservative Young Americans for Freedom was making a concerted effort to recruit the so-called silent generation. To overcome the right-wing push, a core of trade unionists advocated reaching out to SDS. They saw the New Left as an auxiliary to liberalism. As Irving Bluestone explicitly argued, SDS helped counteract conservative efforts to win over young students and enabled students to make "connections with union causes." Potentially, Bluestone theorized, SDS could help unions organize workers on and around campuses.[59]

Cognizant of labor's desire for student support, SDS's leadership self-consciously promoted itself as labor's ally. For example, a Tom Hayden letter to Walter Reuther was replete with high-praise for labor; it contained none of the SDS leader's doubts about the AFL–CIO's shortcomings. "The need for creating different student attitudes toward labor and the American economy is imperative," Hayden wrote. "[The present] mood [is] disturbing, to those of us who believe that the labor movement remains the critical agency in the future advancement of democratic and egalitarian solutions to our economic troubles."[60]

Of course, anticommunism provided a potential stumbling bloc, with liberal unions seeing signs of "softness" on the part of SDS and SNCC. Some labor activists expressed concern with certain antiunion statement's of the original draft of the Port Huron Statement, which was the only draft they saw. Don Slaiman, civil rights director of the AFL–CIO, objected adamantly to what he perceived as the antilabor bent of the manifesto. Michael Harrington, a friend of several SDS leaders, agreed. Unaware that SDS had redrafted the manifesto, Harrington bitterly criticized SDS to the directors of LID. As a result, LID nearly forced Hayden and Haber to resign. In turn, not knowing that LID was acting on false information supplied by Harrington, SDS felt betrayed by LID and stood aghast with its obsession with anticommunism.[61]

Yet, these misgivings did not outweigh more positive feelings. LID and Harrington reacted much more negatively to the Port Huron Statement, in its draft form, than most union officials. LID and SDS did *not* split at this time. Last, for those who maintained doubts, UAW community relations director Mildred Jeffrey had a telling retort: "They [SDS] may be more radical than labor, they may ask searching questions, they may at times be critical of labor, but that's what we need."[62]

Given the gatherings of the latter months of 1963, trade unionists not only abided by Jeffrey's position toward SDS, it appears that they also followed her reasoning in regards to new leftists on the civil rights front.

2

Coalition Politics or Nonviolent Revolution

The years 1964–65 signified a high water mark in the history of American liberalism. Fears that President Kennedy's assassination would snuff out the progressive surge of the early 1960s quickly dissipated as President Johnson not only enacted Kennedy's programs but initiated even grander ones. On the racial front, President Johnson pressured Congress into passing President Kennedy's civil rights bill, without amendments. A year later, Johnson signed into law the Voting Rights Act of 1965. Johnson developed Kennedy's nascent antipoverty programs into a War on Poverty. Medicare, medicaid, and other welfare programs, all long-held liberal goals, were established virtually overnight. Moving beyond the traditional New Deal goal of economic security, LBJ called for the creation of a Great Society, whereby the federal government would help beautify the countryside, revitalize the cities and enhance the arts and sciences. Even the space program made great strides.[1]

In the same time period, the New Left came into full bloom. SNCC and CORE campaigned for racial equality in the heart of Dixie. SDS led a crusade against poverty in America's urban slums. And the Free Speech Movement erupted at the University of California at Berkeley, ushering in a wave of campus unrest that did not subside until the early 1970s.

This simultaneous flowering of liberalism and the New Left provided an opportunity for further collaboration between the New Left and labor and a test of the strength of their ties. Would labor continue to support the New Left's efforts now that it had achieved many of its long-standing goals? Or would the New Left, having grown in size and confidence, push for reforms that labor was unwilling to support? And even if labor offered aid, would the offers come with too many conditions or qualifications attached? And if this was the case, would the New Left seek to understand the reasons for such conditional support, maintain a dialogue with labor, or reject coalition in favor of revolution?

The heart and core of SNCC's and CORE's efforts and the civil rights struggle, in general, in 1964 was the Mississippi Summer Project. This imaginative and comprehensive "invasion" of the deep South, sent hundreds of volunteers, the majority of them white, many from elite families and schools, to the heart of Dixie, to test the Civil Rights Act of 1964 and to organize and educate poor blacks in the Delta and, to a lesser extent, poor whites on the Gulf Coast. "The Summer Project," in the words of Douglas McAdam, "reflected the liberal idealism so characteristic of America in the early sixties" including that of the "liberal/left coalition that [was] so much part of the progressive vision."[2]

While Mississippi Summer was primarily the creation of SNCC and CORE, right from the start it enjoyed labor support. Labor officials publicly endorsed the project. Edward P. Morgan, newspaper and radio spokesman for the AFL–CIO, for example, praised the more than a thousand college students [who] are expected to converge on Mississippi this summer to join the Negro fight for first class citizenship." Michael Quill, head of the TWU, hailed COFO's efforts and called upon President Johnson to send troops to Mississippi to "protect American rights."[3] Even stronger statements followed the disappearance of James Chaney, Michael Schwerner, and Andrew Goodman.[4]

Simultaneously, labor unions contributed funds to COFO, the umbrella organization in charge of the summer project. Large grants went to SCLC and NAACP, which as partners in the COFO project passed on the funds to the Mississippi volunteers. Social activist unions dispensed smaller grants directly to SNCC and CORE and helped pay for the legal costs of the project, such as the never ending need for bail money. Labor leaders also helped civil rights groups obtain additional money from liberal foundations.[5]

More significantly, trade unionists provided essential support for the Freedom Schools, one of the cornerstones of the summer project. Beginning in the winter of 1963–64, Norma Becker and Sandra Adickes, members of the United Federation of Teachers (the New York affiliate of the AFT) solicited endorsements for the schools from union leaders and the rank and file. They got Albert Shanker and Charles Coogen, presidents of the UFT and AFT respectively, to appeal directly to their members and to other labor leaders for aid. Coogen personally asked Harry Van Arsdale, president of the New York City Central Labor

Council, to join the UFT in sponsoring freedom schools. The AFT's magazine went further, urging locals and/or individual union members to "adopt a Mississippi Freedom School" by contributing one dollar a month out of their salaries for the project.[6]

In June, approximately sixty AFT members including thirty-five from New York City departed for Mississippi. They left with full knowledge of the dangers involved. Norma Becker observed that the number of inquiries from those who still wanted to volunteer increased following the disappearance of Chaney, Schwerner, and Goodman.[7] Many of them ended up in Hattiesburg, Mississippi, the flagship freedom school, where under the lead of Arthur Reese of the Detroit Federation of Teachers, they taught close to five hundred young Mississippians and tutored hundreds of novice teachers, mostly college students, on how to teach the three R's. (Several years later in Detroit Reese instituted a program in African American history based on material developed in Mississippi in 1964.)[8]

Even more importantly, labor activists played a decisive role in developing the Mississippi Freedom Democratic party's challenge to the "regular Democrats" at the National Democratic convention in Atlantic City, New Jersey. Joe Rauh, general counsel of the UAW and Vice President of the Americans for Democratic Action, encouraged COFO to make the challenge in the first place. "If there's anybody at the Democratic Convention challenging the seating of the outlaw Mississippi Democrats [regular party]," he informed SNCC leader Robert Moses in early 1964, "I'll help make sure that the challengers are seated." Soon after MFDP launched its challenge, Rauh introduced its leaders to influential Democrats who in turn promised to help them. Rauh and other lawyers, many of them paid with union money, advised MFDP on how to form a bona fide delegation; Rauh also wrote a detailed brief on the legitimacy of MFDP for submission to the credentials committee. Then, in Atlantic City, Rauh stridently argued MFDP's case: "And so, ladies and gentlemen, it comes down to some pretty fundamental things. . . . Will the Democratic Party stand for the oppressor or for the oppressed? Will we stand for loyal people, like those who testified, or the disloyal regular party."[9]

New leftists placed high hopes in Rauh and his labor friends. Both shared the belief that the time was ripe for reshaping the core of the Democratic party. As Kevin Boyle has argued, the idea of "realignment" was alive and well in the early 1960s. The UAW was animated by the goal of fostering a left-liberal Democratic party, equivalent to the British Labor party. COPE, the political arm of AFL–CIO, shared this objective.

And several of SNCC's stalwarts explicitly viewed the MFDP challenge as a first step in changing the Democratic party. For example, Cleveland Sellers recalled: "We were thinking far beyond Atlantic City. If our venture there was successful, we intended to utilize similar tactics in other Southern states, particularly Georgia and South Carolina." Sellers continued: "With the Dixiecrats deposed, the way would have been clear for a wide-ranging redistribution of wealth, power and priorities throughout the nation."[10]

MFDP's belief in realignment and in coalition was reinforced by the support it received from numerous liberal organizations. The Leadership Conference for Civil Rights, a coalition of liberal, labor and civil rights groups adopted a resolution calling for the "rejection of the Racist Mississippi Democratic Party." So too did the Americans for Democratic Action (ADA). The Church-Labor Conference, of San Francisco, sponsored an anti-Goldwater rally, where James Farmer of CORE, John Lewis of SNCC, and Ralph Abernathy of SCLC endorsed MFDP before thirty-five thousand cheering protesters, many of them members of the longshoremens' union. The Michigan Democrat party, a virtual arm of the UAW, supported MFDP's challenge too.[11]

The Republican party's nomination of the arch-conservative Barry Goldwater for president and the posture of Mississippi whites towards civil rights activists and their allies strengthened the links between the New Left and labor. Many if not most white Mississippians placed civil rights activists, labor organizers, and other leftists in the same boat. Historically, Mississippi leaders had treated labor and blacks with equal contempt. Bankers and merchants placed similar economic pressures on workers who joined unions and on blacks who showed any interest in the civil rights movement. Mississippi politicians had long records of opposing reforms in either field. As one Mississippian crudely stated: "There are three things in Mississippi that were in about the same category and the same danger: a union representative, a black, and a mad dog. A person with a gun in his hand would look at the three just about alike."[12]

Recognizing the animus of white southerners to organized labor, MFDPers turned this to their advantage. The Mississippi Project's statement of purpose endorsed unions and encouraged their growth. The Mississippi Freedom Democratic party's platform declared we need laws "guaranteeing labor unions the right to organize freely." Ed King, MFDP candidate for lieutenant governor, observed that the party consciously developed favorable views toward labor with an eye toward forging a future "alliance." Ed King's associate John Salter, who was driven out of

Jackson, Mississippi, by white supremacists, worked outside the state to garner support from trade unions and their associates.[13]

Meanwhile, in the North, SDS was busy trying to fight poverty on the grass roots level, via its Economic Research and Action Projects or ERAPs. The ERAPs grew out of a number of pilot projects conducted by local SDS chapters in 1963.[14] For example, in Chester, Pennsylvania, Swarthmore SDSers helped organize poor blacks from the surrounding industrial communities into a poor people's movement aimed at gaining full employment, improved housing and schools. Based on this experience Carl Wittman and Tom Hayden argued that SDS could enrich its relations with labor. "Certain unions, certain churches, certain regional organizers . . . are outstanding in character and program—and it is through the careful selection and identification of these groups that we will find vital sources of new power and support." "Making these bonds," Wittman and Hayden added, "is one of the most important horizontal organizing responsibilities before us." Few leftists disagreed, although some suggested that Hayden and Wittman placed too much emphasis on the potential of the poor and not enough on the more traditional proletariat.[15]

Even more so than with Mississippi Summer, labor's funding of the ERAPS solidified ties between the two movements. UAW money enabled SDS to staff eleven separate projects. The Packinghouse Workers, Machinists, Operating Engineers, Shoemakers and well known left and liberal intellectuals, who operated in and around labor circles—Brendan Sexton, Art Waskow, and A.J. Muste—donated money as well. Labor officials also provided ERAPers with contacts in the greater labor and liberal community. Jack Conway, director of the IUD, AFL–CIO, for example, urged his "friends" to help SDS "mobilize unemployed and poverty ridden workers." Irving Bluestone and Ralph Helstein furnished ERAPers with letters of introduction and recommendation.[16]

Just as SNCC leaders theorized that the Freedom Democratic party would have an impact on party politics well beyond Mississippi, SDSers contended that the ERAPs would effect poor and working people all over America. For example, Ray Brown argued that, contrary to prevailing views, an increase in the labor force, coupled with automation, a shrinking consumer market, and an inefficient defense economy spelled economic disaster. Thus, by establishing a foothold with the poor, he reasoned, SDS would be in a strategic position to rally the populace when the downturn occurred.[17] Many new leftists added that community unions, whereby workers were organized at their place of residence rather than at the point of production, represented the proper response to the modern economic scene. "Political questions [today] are thrown back into the community," not the work place, wrote James O'Connor. Unemployed and underemployed workers did not fit into trade unions. They lacked a trade and given the evolution of the economy would not get back into one. Collective bargaining, the mainstay of the labor movement, was irrelevant to them.[18]

While this argument contained an implicit critique of the labor movement for having failed to represent all workers, few new leftists drew the connection. They criticized craft unions for their restrictive policies but they did not dwell on the failures of industrial unions or the newly created public sector or white collar unions. Some SDSers even anticipated that the ERAPs would generate a relationship reminiscent of the past, with one activist claiming "that the once strong alliance between radicals and progressive unionists must and can be rebuilt."[19]

Indeed, this spirit of cooperation flourished up to SDS's invasion of the slums, as exemplified by the presence of numerous new leftists at labor meetings or conferences on poverty. On the special invitation of the UAW, over a dozen SDS members attended the union's Constitutional Convention in March, 1964. SDS and SNCC members, including Tom Hayden and Robert Moses, took part in the Intercollegiate Conference on Poverty in America at George Washington University from 24 to 26 April 1964. There they heard labor experts speak on the persistence of poverty in "affluent America." For example, Nat Goldfinger, Director of Research, AFL–CIO, Arnold Mayer, legislative representative of the Amalgamated Meat Cutters and Jack Conway, Director, IUD, AFL–CIO, led workshops which focused on strategies for overcoming this scourge.[20]

Building on contacts made at this meeting, and just before moving to the slums of Newark, Tom Hayden, with the help of Rennie Davis, rallied SDS and its "friends" behind a strike of the International Union of Electrical Workers (IUE) against an Essex Wire Company plant in Hillside, Michigan. Hayden and Davis argued that the strike was directly related to the persistence of poverty in America. The company hired one hundred unemployed workers from Appalachia and imported poor blacks as strikebreakers. The moderate Republican Governor, George Romney, sided with the company, protecting the plant with the National Guard. While a last minute settlement allowed the company to avert a demonstration organized by SDS, CORE and local labor and liberal forces, Hayden urged Ben Segal, IUE Director of Education, not to forget about the New Left.[21]

At about the same time that volunteers poured into Mississippi, the ERAPs began. Over one hundred students went to live in the slums of

Baltimore, Boston, Cleveland, Chicago, Hazard, Louisville, Philadelphia, Chester, Newark and Trenton. They exhibited an extraordinary amount of idealism and commitment. "Hardly anyone on the 'outside' can imagine the completeness of their transformation, or the depth of their commitment," wrote Andrew Kopkind. "They are not down there for a visit. . . . They are part of the slums, a kind of lay brotherhood, worker-priests, except that they have no dogma to sell."[22]

One of the better known projects was located in Cleveland, Ohio. In early June, eight volunteers, led by Sharon Jeffrey and Paul Potter, moved into their headquarters at 2909 Jay Avenue. No sooner had they unpacked their bags than they set out to learn more about the community, its make-up and concerns, and to contact various local liberal and labor organizations. On the morning of 24 June, the ERAPers met with Hank Eiban, an AFL–CIO and CORE official. In the afternoon, the ERAPers attended an emergency meeting on civil rights, regarding the disappearance of Schwerner, Goodman and Chaney. Later, a couple of ERAPers met with Sam Pollack and Frank Cimino of the local Meatcutter's Union, who welcomed the ERAP to the community, offered it the use of their library, mimeo machine, and an opportunity to raise some money by helping out on union picket lines. In the evening, Cleveland ERAPers umpired the neighborhood kids' baseball game. The following day the ERAPers spent most of their time knocking on doors. Afterwards Paul Potter, Ottie Fein and Kathy Boudin discussed the project's efforts. Two days later the ERAPers canvassed the neighborhood, analyzing its poverty and economics. The following Sunday was a day of rest. Some went to the beach; others went to church.[23]

Although these actions might appear tedious and a far cry from creating a radical social movement, they enabled ERAPers to learn a great deal about the concerns and backgrounds of the poor, and to adjust their plans accordingly. For instance, Cleveland ERAPers discovered that most of the poor in their community came from Eastern Europe, the South, or Appalachia. Interracial communities of poor people, one of ERAP's suppositions, did not exist. They also found that the poor felt more strongly about inadequate housing, recreation, and welfare benefits, than other liberal/left issues like voter registration. Ironically, the ERAPers did not develop a more clear sense of what the community expected in terms of jobs.[24]

Nonetheless, by the end of July, Cleveland ERAP's had breathed new life into a moribund welfare mothers association, organized a tenants' union and an unemployment council, and established a recreation group. The welfare mothers association, CUFAW (Citizens United For Adequate Welfare) was the most impressive of these. It planned a demonstration in which welfare mothers would demand a full set of clothes and school supplies for each child at the beginning of each school year. In later months, CUFAW circulated a petition demanding school lunches, participated in an AFL–CIO sponsored voter registration drive, and issued position papers on the food stamp program and the city's general poverty program, respectively. In February 1965, CUFAW mothers attended a "Community People's Conference," cosponsored by SDS, where poor people's organizations from all over the country discussed their grassroots' efforts. CUFAW's position paper urged the poor to organize and demand participation in existing "poverty" programs. The piece so impressed attending student activists that SDS reprinted it for distribution and sale.[25]

The Newark ERAP began much like Cleveland's. It tapped the Newark Committee for Full Employment and SDS friend Stanley Aronowitz for funding and logistical support. One of these leads resulted in a humorous internal report that warned volunteers "never to go to a trade union meeting with a pack of Camels in your pocket. They are scab cigarettes, and the whole affair can be grizzly." Like the Cleveland ERAPers, the Newark student activists soon found themselves consumed with developing their own organization and adjusting to the realities of the community. They encouraged local residents to drop into their Clinton Hill offices/living quarters and distributed leaflets announcing their willingness to help.[26]

Newark's ERAP stood out for its successful organization of block associations and for its ability to gain publicity. Jesse Allen, a Newark ERAP staff member, described one of the group's actions. "We called a meeting with the people and discussed our problems . . . We decided to go on a rent strike. . . . When the landlord came around for the rent we told them [sic] we're not paying." Eventually the landlord obtained an eviction order from the courts. But rather than back down, the students increased the stakes of the strike by picketing both the rented units and the landlord's Maplewood, New Jersey, home. Even though the judge never rescinded the eviction notices, the strikers continued to live in the building.[27]

Not all ERAPs enjoyed as much success in mobilizing the poor as those in Cleveland and Newark. As the unemployment rate dropped, the Trenton ERAP found it difficult to win the support of the poor around the issue of unemployment councils. A lack of standout leaders, such as those found in Newark and Cleveland, contributed to the Trenton ERAP's problems. The project in Louisville floundered and was discontinued. Those in Baltimore, Philadelphia, Chester, and Boston made some headway, but did not gain much publicity. With the help of the UPWA and several other local labor unions, Chicago ERAPers continued to organize underemployed and unemployed packinghouse workers, although the long-term impact of these efforts was insignificant in terms of new employment in the packing industry.[28]

The ERAP in Hazard, Kentucky, transcended the others because it involved more than a fight against poverty in *a* blighted area and since it allied SDS with other leftist organizations. Nestled in the heart of Appalachia, Hazard was synonymous with poverty. Michael Harrington's *The Other America* and Harry Caudill's *Night Comes to the Cumberlands* had emphasized that "affluent America" had passed the region by. Appalachia had never made a successful transition into the modern economy and increasing automation threatened to leave the area even worse off. Hazard was coal-mining country, and coal miners had traditionally suffered from hard and unhealthy work. New machinery or "automation" made matters even worse by reducing the number of jobs. Rather than offering the miners job training, mine owners took advantage of the situation by informing them that they had to keep down their wages. If they did not, the mine owners warned, they would either replace the men with machines or close the mines as uncompetitive. In addition, mine owners selectively closed down union mines and then turned around and leased the mines to nonunion operators. The miners were caught in a vicious circle. They needed better wages and conditions to pull themselves out of poverty. But, if they demanded too much, they would be replaced.[29]

Ultimately, Kentucky miners became so disgusted with conditions that they decided to stage public protests. Beginning in 1962, local miners sent out roving pickets to keep workers out and coal in the nonunion mines. This produced violent clashes with strikebreakers and all out war with mine owners, who hired armed security forces to protect their property. In the summer of 1963, Berman Gibson, the miners' local leader, and seven other miners, were arrested and charged with conspiring to blow up a railroad bridge. Their arrest brought the violence to an end but did not stop the insurgency. Calling the strike "unauthorized," the United Mine Workers refused to aid the defendants. Privately, union leaders contended that they could not afford additional legal costs that would come with a strike. Nonetheless, the miners persevered. The local populace rallied behind Gibson's trial and the insurgents successfully appealed for aid from outside sources.[30]

Immediately upon hearing of their plight, new and old leftists turned the Hazard strike into a cause célèbre. The *Guardian* heralded the miners in issue after issue in early 1963. Rallying behind the slogan

"Bring Christmas to Kentucky," left-leaning students from the New York City area and a smattering of small elite private colleges collected food and clothing for the miners. Phil Ochs, Judy Collins, and Ronnie Gilbert, of the Weavers, held a benefit concert for the miners at the Village Gate. The Militant Labor Forum invited Gibson to speak before its members in New York City. SNCC and CORE endorsed the miners' struggle and sent organizers to the region to help.[31]

Most significantly, new and old leftists, in concert with a handful of labor officials and activists established the Committee for the Miners (CFM) in March of 1963. Led by Stanley Aronowitz and Hamish Sinclair, CFM connected the miners with liberal lawyers such as William Ryan and Harry Caudill and raised money and publicized their cause.[32] For example, Hamish Sinclair and Arthur Gorson organized several tours for Gibson whereby he met a broad network of trade unionists, student leftists, and civil rights groups. A swing through Philadelphia introduced Gibson to SDS's Swarthmore chapter and presidents of locals of the ILA, UPWA, TWU, and Boilermakers. In New York City, Gibson and Sinclair met with an even larger contingent of union officials and student activists. The latter organized a "hootenanny" to raise funds for their honored guest from eastern Kentucky. Subsequent trips to Washington, D.C., brought Gibson into contact with Martin Luther King, Jr., Walter Reuther, and top officials of the International Brotherhood of Teamsters.[33]

In March 1964, CFM and SDS cosponsored a symposium in Hazard to discuss the region's problems. Over two hundred people attended, including at least twenty SDS members, representatives from SNCC, CFM, and ACFE (Appalachian Committee for Full Employment). Speakers presented papers on the general state of the American economy, the federal government's poverty program, the specific economic problems of eastern Kentucky and the history of the miners' struggles in the United States. Based in part on the papers presented, SDS decided to organize a special ERAP in Hazard, one that would directly commit it to an alliance with blue collar workers. CFM and SNCC cooperated in this venture.[34]

Indeed, many new leftists departed the Appalachia conference nurturing grandiose hopes. They perceived Hazard as a catalytic agent, one that could promote the marriage of the labor movement of the 1930s with the New Left of the 1960s. "Just as the coal movements of France, Belgium, England and other countries have been the heart of continuing movements for social change and democracy in their countries," wrote Robb Burlage, "so perhaps they [miners] can be at the heart of a *new movement* in America in the Sixties as they were the inspiration of the CIO in the Thirties." Implicitly, Burlage believed that the United States was not

that different from Western Europe. More explicit was Burlage's allusion
to the fact that the United Mine Workers, John L. Lewis in particular,
had sparked a labor movement committed to social justice in the 1930s.
If coal miners once played such a key role in the United States and
continued to stand in the forefront in Europe, why could they not do so
now in America?[35]

But dreams of altering life in Hazard and sparking a revitalized labor
movement dissipated in the face of the harsh realities of the region and
the different goals of the students, leftists, and the miners themselves.
Student volunteers found significant barriers in their way, from a repressive
local police force to an apathetic population. ERAPers Sally Susskind
and Chuck Koehler learned about the former soon after they arrived in
June 1964. Late one afternoon, the local sheriff arrested them and
brought them to police headquarters. After nearly twenty-four hours of
internment, Judge Babe Noplis warned them to clear out of town. Noplis
claimed that Koehler was a juvenile without any known means of
support and that Susskind was a "vagrant." The two were then released
without any formal charges being filed.[36]

ERAPers came to grips with community apathy more gradually.
Many of the local men and women who might have been of some help
were too consumed with Berman Gibson's trial to lend ERAP a hand.
When local residents attended ERAPs meetings, they rapidly lost interest because SDS did not offer solutions to their problems. Offering
solutions ran counter to SDS's goal of spurring the poor to help themselves.
Steve Max complained that careful guidance did not help because the
areas' natural leaders generally left the region as soon as they could.
"The problem is that there is nothing in the county to stay for and
everyone who is at all educated or in good health . . . leaves as soon as he
graduates high school."[37]

The unique structure of the Hazard ERAP, its joint sponsorship by
SDS and CFM, only made matters worse. Lines of authority were not
clear. Poor communication and jealousy exacerbated frustrations over
working with such an apathetic population. For example, after a summer of organizing, ERAPer Richard Rothstein accused CFM director
Art Gorson of isolating himself in an ivory tower, while SDSers struggled in the field. In a very nasty letter, Rothstein wrote: "I urged you in
August that if you really have any commitment to what you are doing, to
get out of that fucking office and into the field. . . . It is the assholes who
sit at a desk with a Committee for Miners signs staring them in the face
who can't see beyond the end of their noses." Gorson, needless to say,
did not reply.[38]

Another reason for SDS's irritation was the fact that local activists were more interested in bread and butter gains than catalyzing an interracial movement of the poor. Older miners, in particular, were worried about how they would survive their "golden years." When the United Mine Workers offered to re-enter the region, in an attempt to revitalize the local union, the Appalachia Committee for Full Employment responded with glee. Everette Tharp, one of Gibson's colleagues, informed CFM: "Everyone is so excited about the UMW drive to reorganize the miners that they have dropped everything." While neither CFM nor SDS publicly objected to ACFE's endorsement of the UMW, neither shared ACFE's enthusiasm about the development, especially SDS, to a degree because transforming America, not winning a decent pension fund, had been its underlying reason for getting involved in the first place.[39]

Put another way, the Hazard project was significant in and of itself and for the things it revealed about the New Left, its left-liberal allies and labor. It showed that they could cooperate but it also demonstrated the fragility of such collaboration. This was so, in part, because of the different ideological orientations of the participants. On the left stood SDS. It had noble intentions but a somewhat faulty analysis of the situation, especially its belief that the miners could and wanted to catalyze a much broader social movement. On the right stood the United Mine Workers and the mine workers. The union's and workers' goals ultimately remained concrete and their methods pragmatic. Somewhere in between lay the founders of CFM. They had a more accurate or mature assessment of the situation, yet they lacked SDS's drive or commitment to actively pursuing change. Initially, these differences did not get in the way of cooperation in Hazard. But in time they proved cumbersome and helped produce the collapse of the coalition.

———

Independent of Hazard, SDSers admitted that the ERAPs had not lived up to their expectations. Specific grievances, such as inadequate garbage collection, had not been effectively translated into building a more democratic and economically just society. Nor had the projects generated widespread publicity, especially in comparison to Mississippi Summer. Furthermore, the predicted economic downturn had not materialized; on the contrary, unemployment decreased and the war on poverty had begun to ameliorate the conditions of the slum dweller.[40]

Moreover, contrary to expectations, ERAPers experienced little sustained contact with labor unions and that which they did have was often unfavorable. In fact, Newark's ERAPers explicitly criticized trade unionists for reacting negatively to the demands of the block associations. "More surprising than the negative response from the city is the unwillingness of the small liberal circle in the city to accept the project and its implications," wrote Hayden and Wittman. "Since they had invited us to Newark, one would expect that the liberal community (ADA, CORE, the activist wing of the NAACP, some labor unions, community improvement groups) would be a major ally. But major reconsideration of this assumption has been forced by the course of events." Coming from two of the more influential SDSers (especially Hayden), this critique influenced the New Left's views of labor in general.[41]

Labor's reputation among new leftists was further tarnished by the experience that ERAPers had with local liberal Democratic political machines. Whereas conservative southern whites solidified ties between civil rights activists and trade unionists, liberal northern Democrats did just the opposite. When ERAPers encountered difficulties with local authorities, unions were assigned part of the blame, because they were a major player in local Democratic party politics. For instance, trade unionism in general lost favor with SDS every time the Chicago police harassed ERAP members since labor was considered a central part of the Daley machine and because policemen were viewed as part of the broad working class.[42]

The ERAPs, however, would *not* have had an adverse impact on the New Left's relationship to labor if events had taken a different turn in Atlantic City. Had labor unionists and other liberals fully backed MFDP, the ERAPs would have had a minimal effect. Indeed, the ties between the two movements probably would have been strengthened. But President Lyndon Johnson's heavy-handed politics and the fact that many liberals refused to challenge his decision to quash the MFDP, produced the opposite effect.

Insistent on retaining at least a facade of national unity and fearful of losing white southern support, LBJ presented MFDP with a "compromise," which included two at large seats at the convention and the promise of future reforms. LBJ presumed that this offer would placate the insurgents without offending the regular Democrats of Mississippi—who were required to pledge their loyalty to the Democratic ticket. (Typical of their ultra-conservatism, the Mississippi delegation rejected even this compromise.) Johnson did not personally make the offer to the MFDP. Instead, he worked through Hubert Humphrey, the expected Vice Presidential nominee. In turn, Humphrey pressured MFDP's allies Walter

Reuther, Joseph Rauh, Martin Luther King, Jr., A. Philip Randolph, Bayard Rustin, and Roy Wilkins, to prevail upon MFDP to toe Johnson's line. LBJ hinted that if the insurgents continued to press their challenge, he might nominate someone else for Vice President. Reuther, Wilkins, and Rustin, Humphrey supporters for almost two decades, saw the Minnesota liberal as their dream candidate. Hence, they felt compelled to compromise, urging MFDP to accept Johnson's offer. Reuther even threatened Rauh with the loss of his job as union counsel if he failed to go along.[43]

By MFDP's original goals, Johnson's compromise seemed at least a partial success. From the concept of a moral challenge and educational tool, the Freedom party had grown into a nationally known political movement with a legitimate voice. Yet, bolstered by their recent showing before the credentials committee and unable to forget their lifetime of repression, MFDP delegates refused to accept the offer. "We didn't come all this way for no two seats," declared Mrs. Hamer. The broader New Left fully supported this decision. More critically, the arguments of liberal allies, such as Rauh and King, who had initially supported the all-or-nothing demands of the MFDP, left them discredited in the eyes of the entire New Left. Some called Rauh and King traitors; almost all of the participants in the Mississippi project saw Reuther's actions as contemptible.[44]

The MFDP affair revealed generational differences between the New Left and labor. By the mid–1960s, the labor movement was wedded to the Democratic party. Lyndon Johnson's "great society," and the prospect of Barry Goldwater as president solidified the marriage. While Rauh and other labor unionists initially supported MFDP, they ultimately measured its worth against a whole other set of goals, formed over a lifetime. By 1964, Rauh and his associates had vested interests in the Democratic party, especially as it was constituted under Johnson. Endorsement of Johnson's "compromise" promised rewards elsewhere. In addition, organized labor was not about to risk returning the Republicans to power after only four years of Democratic control of the White House.

In contrast, MFDP did not and could not rest assured that fealty in this instance would pay dividends at a later time. Although most civil rights activists and white student leftists came from Democratic backgrounds, their allegiance to the party was less solid; it was not built on tangible experiences. Principle, not pragmatism, defined MFDP's political world. After all, a pragmatist would never entertain the challenge in the first place. New leftists could not measure LBJ's compromise against years of past relations and hence any advocacy of it became an anathema.

Moreover, SNCC had come to distrust the federal government, which it associated with the Democratic party, and the conclusion of the MFDP challenge merely confirmed this stance.

This said, Freedom Summer did not leave a simple legacy of betrayal and distrust as many historians have argued. For example, Milton Viorst contends that "Atlantic City ended the stage of history in which white liberals like Joe Rauh could walk hand in hand with blacks from every segment of the civil rights movement." Even more to the point, Viorst added: "The spirit of the March on Washington, always more fragile than it looked, had been *shattered* [my emphasis]." Rather, Freedom Summer, in combination with the ERAPs, was so broad and complex that it left an ambiguous legacy; it reinforced collaboration in some instances while producing new obstacles to cooperation in others.[45]

Viorst based his interpretation on remarks that new leftists made at the end of the summer, especially those made by SNCC leader Stokely Carmichael. He stated: "The lesson, in fact, was clear at Atlantic City. The major moral of the experience was . . . that, very specifically, black people in Mississippi and throughout the country could not rely on their so-called allies . . . to rely on the absolute assistance of external liberal, labor forces was not a wise procedure." Viorst and others also give much weight to SDS's concurrent disputes with LID, over the issue of anti-communism and unfriendly encounters that new leftists had with well-known social democrats.[46]

Yet, a more thorough examination of the evidence reveals that there were just as many new leftists who were not quite ready to advocate a separate course. They realized that cooperation presented both possibilities and limitations and determined to develop a more qualified or guarded strategy than they had in the past, not a separatist one. Without allies, new leftists observed, the MFDP challenge would not have evolved into a substantial challenge at the Democratic convention, in the first place. Moreover, as Dave Dennis, CORE's director in Mississippi, reasoned, it was incorrect to assume that liberal labor unionists would always be so tied to Johnson that the New Left could not depend upon them in other cases. "At this point, Walter Reuther depends heavily upon the Johnson administration. . . . At this convention, Reuther had to dance to the tune of the President. Because of certain ties that some of the civil rights leaders have with Reuther, they were forced to dance to his tune." Nevertheless, Dennis continued: "We're not saying that we should dissociate ourselves from the powers altogether, but we are saying that we should not ally ourselves to the extent that we cannot afford to go against their wishes."[47]

Similarly, Staughton Lynd observed that while Freedom Summer convinced some, like himself, to reject coalition, it did not have that impact on all of the New Left. "There is now going on within SNCC, and within the civil rights movement generally, a fascinating intellectual ferment," Lynd reported. In fact, "the need for broader alliances, uniting white and black, North and South, is conceded on all sides," he continued. "Some talk of a populist alliance between Negroes and labor, while others suspect the Administration of using the AFL–CIO bureaucracy to domesticate SNCC. There are those who think the Freedom Democratic Party can compel Democratic re-alignment and that every effort should be bent toward acceptance by the 1968 Democratic Party Convention. There are those, on the other hand . . . |who| think that the movement should keep clear of all suspect and subversive causes."[48] Put another way, while the New Left felt betrayed by labor, it did not reject collaboration, not yet.[49]

In fact, during the 1964 election, both SDS and MFDP supported LBJ, with the former sporting "Part of the Way With LBJ" buttons. More significantly, going into 1965 SDS leaders called for the ERAPs to continue to cooperate with trade unionists. Based upon a critique of his antiunion essay, Tom Hayden modified his stance, writing that ERAPers should join with younger aggressive unions such as local 1199 of the Health and Hospital Workers and District 65, RWDSU.[50] Likewise, in spite of Daley's harassment, JOIN continued to cooperate with local labor officials, with several JOIN participants going to work for the UPWA and several children of union leaders signing on with JOIN.[51]

Even more importantly, MFDP continued to seek and receive labor support after the 1964 election. In early 1965, the United Civil Rights Leadership, which included the International Union of Electrical Workers (IUE) and the ADA, endorsed the MFDP's attempt to unseat Mississippi's congressional representatives. Locals of several unions joined in writing a statement of support that was placed in the *Congressional Record*. The Leadership Conference on Civil Rights urged Congress to uphold the challenge.[52]

In addition, labor unions proclaimed that Atlantic City marked the last time that segregationists would be allowed to keep blacks out of the Democratic party. The *AFL–CIO News* declared that because of MFDP challenge "delegates will never be seated again if all voters, regardless of race . . . have not had the chance to participate fully." To insure that this was the case, a convention of the United Electrical workers listened to Ella Baker describe the history of MFDP's struggle and then passed a resolution endorsing the party's future efforts.[53] The UFT invited Fannie Lou Hamer and SNCC Freedom Singer to address its members. The Chicago Area Friends (CAF) of SNCC, headed by UPWA officials, held a "Mississippi Report Dinner," at which James Forman, Stokely Carmichael, Robert Moses, and Fannie Lou Hamer spoke.[54]

Last, there was the campaign in Selma in early 1965 that culminated in the mass march from Selma to Montgomery and the passage of the Voting Rights Act of 1965.[55] Regardless of SNCC's relationship to King during the Selma campaign, the struggle there signaled the high watermark of the civil rights movement and arguably the apex of the New Left's strength in the South. The winning of voting rights legislation was a giant step forward, one that southern blacks, many of whom had been directly and indirectly influenced by the direct action campaigns of SNCC, built on in the decades that followed. The march from Selma to Montgomery symbolized the distance that the civil rights movement had traveled in just a few years, as veteran activists walked through the heart of Dixie in defiance of the outspoken declarations of Alabama Governor George Wallace.[56]

During the march, veteran activists were joined by an extraordinarily broad array of supporters, including northern students, church groups, numerous CIO unions and, unlike previous demonstrations, members of the AFL–CIO executive council, building trades, old craft unions, and the Teamsters. The extent of labor's support—including that of the rank and file—was unprecedented for a direct action protest. As John Lavine, a Wisconsin newspaper publisher observed: "Never in our experience have [we] received such reaction from normally apolitical, nonemotional leaders of our community and "workingmen" alike."[57] In addition to expressing their solidarity with the activists in Selma, organized labor participated in massive sympathy rallies. For example, in San Francisco, even before the infamous attack on Pettus Bridge, thousands rallied for civil rights. Following the attack and the murder of James Reeb, marches took place in Washington, D.C., New York City, Chicago, Boston, Cleveland, Oakland, Philadelphia, Syracuse, New Haven, Detroit, San Francisco, Norfolk, Binghamton, Bakersfield, and St. Augustine.[58]

Surveys and polls confirmed that strong working-class sympathy for the civil rights movement existed. When asked how they felt toward "the recent showdowns in Selma, Alabama," manual workers responded two to one in favor of the demonstrators as opposed to the Alabama authorities. Two years earlier over 40 percent of the respondents to an NORC study who lived in either blue-collar suburbs or working-class ethnic communities had disapproved of the March on Washington. A Gallup poll found strong blue-collar support for Lyndon Johnson's civil rights efforts. Contrary to expectations, 59 percent of the surveyed professionals thought that Johnson was moving too fast in the "area of integration," while only 27 percent of manual workers expressed this opinion. In response to the same poll, only 9 percent of professionals and businesspersons stated that Johnson was not moving fast enough on integration, while 31 percent of manual workers thought he should be moving faster.[59]

In addition, many prominent labor leaders traveled to Selma to display their solidarity with the movement. Scores of them attended James Reeb's funeral; nearly as many joined the subsequent successful march from Selma to Montgomery. Reporting on the events, Oil and Chemical union representative Ray Davidson wrote: "All of us in the March felt good about it. We sang and chanted and felt like we were doing something right and maybe it was not very becoming of us but I think we felt better than the people on the curbs who stared at us in hatred"[60]

Throughout, the protesters demanded passage of a strong voting rights bill. Two days after the attack on the Pettus bridge, the LCCR sent a telegram to Johnson urging "immediate submission of voting rights." When Lyndon Johnson called for voting rights legislation, one labor union after another passed resolutions or sent telegrams to Johnson in support of the bill, including the Teamsters, IUE, ILGWU, UAW, ACWA, Machinists, Mine and Mill, National Maritime Union, Steelworkers, TWU, UPWA, and the United Rubber Workers. The Machinists' endorsement displayed the growth of labor support for the freedom struggle. Traditionally a conservative union, the Machinists had not outspokenly supported civil rights before 1965. Yet the union applauded the Selma demonstrators and hailed LBJ's stand on voting.[61]

Several explanations for labor's support can be offered. First, many trade unionists believed that the civil rights and the labor movement's foes were one and the same, especially in the South. As the labor presses observed, Sheriff Jim Clark's police force, which had brutally attacked activists in Selma, was first organized in 1958 as an "anti-labor" force, to "harass organizing efforts" by UPWA at R. L. Ziegers packing plant at Tuscaloosa.[62] Second, internal considerations played a role, as union leaders felt a need to placate black union members, whose numbers were growing rapidly. One way of doing so was to support the civil rights struggle. The International Longshoremen's Association, for instance, was involved in a series of complex contract negotiations and strikes (often wildcat). The union needed to appease black longshoreman in some manner in order for the existent leadership, disproportionately white and from the New York City region, to retain power. Third, one must consider the union leaders' and members' basic feelings of right and wrong. "We simply felt that we had to show our faces to testify which side we were on," reported Ray Davidson of the Oil and Chemical Workers. Like the nation at large, union members had been pushed by the left-wing of the civil rights movement. While they had not initiated the protests in Selma, they became converts to the cause when faced with the absolute tyranny that they revealed.[63]

But had the costs of victory at Selma been too high? And had the triumphant march come too late? Had the process of gaining victory, which included witnessing Martin Luther King, Jr., bow to the whims of the federal government and watching the nation become more outraged over the death of a white man (James Reeb) than it did over a black man (Jimmy Lee Jackson), undermined the coalition that won passage of the Voting Rights Act?[64]

To a large extent, the answer to all these questions was yes. Since its birth, the New Left had cooperated with trade unionists. During Selma, labor support was greater than ever before. The end result, the Voting Rights Act of 1965 was something that few imagined possible when the decade began. Put another way, throughout 1964 and early 1965, the New Left sought and received considerable labor support, especially from the social activist unions. Yet, just at the time that the nation moved to the left, the New Left grew exhausted with the strategy that had helped move it in the first place. Paradoxically, support produced growing doubts on the New Left's part about the virtues of cooperation. Many new leftists, saw the liberal reforms as too late in coming, insufficient and perhaps most importantly too costly in terms of what they took to acheive. Perhaps trade union leaders had difficulty understanding the New Left's anguish because so many of them had waited nearly a quarter century for such a moment, and they were not about to risk tampering with the reforms that were passed. Perhaps they also tended to feel that the New Left did not have an appreciation of the forces that liberals had had to overcome to acheive said reforms. Thus, the moment that appeared ready to produce a grand progressive coalition, gave rise instead to new types of confrontation.

Still, it would be too simple to claim that the spirit of cooperation died during the Selma campaign or that the New Left's relationship with labor lay shattered. If external events had not intervened, if the context had not changed, it is quite possible that the labor movement would have continued to move to the left and that injuries to its relationship to the New Left's relationship might have healed. SDS and other new left groups had not yet totally rejected the strategy of the "Port Huron Statement," namely acting as the moral conscious of liberal America, and probably would have had an impact upon liberal America had they continued such a strategy. Indeed, Selma suggested that even the Meany block of the labor movement could be affected. The ideological differences that appeared in Atlantic City, during the ERAPs, in Hazard and in Selma, were not so great that they necessitated confrontation. Nonviolent revolution was not the only possible product of the events of 1964 and early 1965. If not for a change in the external situation, the spirit of coalition might have prevailed.

3

Vietnam

In the spring of 1967, two generations of Reuthers, Bluestones, and Woodcocks gathered at the Bluestone's home for a Passover seder. Because of differences between the fathers and their children over the War in Vietnam, this year's annual get-together almost did not take place. But a last minute truce—a cease fire of sorts—was called, allowing the families to congregate, at least for a brief ceremony. Rather than reading from the Haggadah, Barry Bluestone and Leslie Woodcock, the children of Irving Bluestone and Leonard Woodcock, two of the top officials with the UAW, read speeches by Martin Luther King, Jr., and antiwar poetry from the World War I era. After they had finished, the mood was emotional. Some of the participants were almost in tears. At this point, Walter Reuther broke the truce. Unable to refrain from commenting on Vietnam, he felt compelled to defend his and the UAW's position. While admitting that the youths had made some good points, indirectly, about the immorality of war, he contended that the UAW's stance on Vietnam deserved further explication. The UAW, Reuther stated, had debated the war at length. Feelings ran high on both sides. "But because we have major negotiations coming up soon . . . there is a very strong feeling that this is not the time to break with the President on this issue." Leslie Woodcock fumed as Reuther completed his statement. Finally, she could not rein in her anger any longer. "You've said it! You've finally said it!" Reuther asked what she meant. "For fifty cents an hour extra in the pay envelope," she exploded, "you'll let thousands of Vietnamese and Americans die in the war." The normally gentle Roy Reuther came to his brother's defense. "That's not what Walter meant!" "Yes it is," Woodcock responded. "That's exactly what he meant."[1]

This quarrel epitomized the rift that developed between the New Left and labor over the Vietnam War beginning in 1965. Whereas in the early 1960s familial ties facilitated cooperation between the two—Irving Bluestone raising funds for the ERAPs; Leslie Woodcock working with the UPWA as part of JOIN; Walter Reuther endorsing SDS and champloning civil rights—the escalation of the Vietnam conflict fomented family feuds. And these feuds reinforced simmering but growing divisions between the New Left and labor. Even Passover seders were transformed into wartime morality plays. Dialogue, a mainstay of the New Left's relationship to labor in the early 1960s, began to disappear. Confrontation predominated.

From its birth, the New Left was critical of organized labor's foreign policy positions. Such differences, however, did not hinder cooperation between the two. A common desire to combat racial discrimination in the South and poverty everywhere took precedence over cold war disagreements.[2] Even during the 1964 presidential campaign, new leftists supported Lyndon Johnson, albeit skeptically, because he ran as the "peace" candidate, in contrast to his opponent, Barry Goldwater, who threatened to widen the war in Southeast Asia and to increase tensions throughout the world. But soon after his election, LBJ reneged on his peace promises, marking a watershed in the war and in the New Left's relationship to organized labor.

From the first air strikes, in February 1965, to Johnson's announcement of a suspension of the bombings, on 31 March 1968, most trade union leaders faithfully stood behind the President's policies, while new leftists condemned his actions. The day the United States began to bomb Vietnam, SDS called the war "hideously immoral," undeclared, and "self-defeating." The AFL–CIO executive council, in contrast, unanimously pledged its full support for the President's "energetic retaliatory measures to halt the communist acts of provocation and aggression." Several weeks after the bombings began, SDS sponsored an antiwar rally in Washington, D.C., where the New Left coalesced to protest against Johnson's Vietnam policy. In the following months, new leftists led antiwar teach-ins, organized demonstrations, and decried American intervention in Southeast Asia. At the same time, AFL–CIO President George Meany and individual unions, among them the Building Trades, Rubber, Steel, and Automobile Workers, proclaimed their support for Johnson's policy. And the National Maritime Union, led by Joseph Curran, sponsored a massive pro-war parade on Fifth Avenue in New York City, where on occasion workers scuffled with antiwar protesters on the sidelines.[3]

In December 1965, at the AFL–CIO's national convention in San Francisco, disagreements between new leftists and trade unionists exploded into open view. From the gallery, radicals shouted "Get out of Vietnam!" and "Labor fakers!" and demanded a debate on the war. In response, union delegates raised a chorus of boos and cries of "Get a haircut!" and "Go to Russia and debate." Simultaneously, George Meany pounded the lectern with his gavel and commanded the sergeant of arms to "clear these kookies out of the gallery."[4]

When Emil Mazey, secretary-treasurer of the UAW, defended the protesters' right to question the war, only one delegate seconded his statement. To the applause of the convention's delegates, Meany rebuked Mazey and Walter P. Reuther, Mazey's colleague, announced his support of Johnson's policy of "resisting communist aggression in Vietnam." After student activists were forcibly removed from the gallery, Reuther retorted that the "protesters should be demonstrating against Hanoi and Peking . . . [because] they are responsible for the war." The AFL–CIO delegates subsequently declared: "The labor movement proclaim[s] to the world that the nation's working men and women do support the Johnson Administration in Viet Nam." Gallup polls indicated that the statement accurately reflected the feelings of American workers.[5]

In spite of such actions, some antiwar leaders attempted to maintain a dialogue with labor. SDS members in Boston, for example, transformed their ERAP into an antiwar/prolabor project, passing out leaflets to workers and supporting strikes. SDS activists Kim Moody, Fred Epsteiner and Mike Flag explained that SDS had to orient itself toward American workers if it expected to change American society. Likewise, the antidraft organization the Resistance opposed student deferments because they smelled of class bias.[6]

The actions of a few unionists suggested that segments of the labor movement would be open to such entreaties. Trade Unionists for Peace, a small association of antiwar labor officials, centered in New York City, formed in the fall of 1965. It distributed leaflets to trade unionists that quoted labor officials and friends, such as Arthur Goldberg, in support of negotiations with Ho Chi Minh and peace in Vietnam. Three independent "old left" unions, the ILWU, UE, and the Mine and Mill workers, called for an immediate end to the war, with the Longshoremen pleading with the government to allow the Vietnamese to "determine their own destiny." And in Berkeley, old leftists within the American Federation of Teachers played a seminal role in establishing the Vietnam Day Committee, which organized some of the first antiwar demonstrations.[7]

With an eye toward maintaining the links between the student left and labor, the Committee for a SANE Nuclear Policy, commonly known as SANE, organized an antiwar protest in Washington, D.C., in November 1965. SANE hoped to exclude those who threatened the New Left's dialogue with labor. Communists were banned from attending, slogans were carefully monitored, and promotional literature was censored. SANE's efforts, however, went for naught. Pat Gorman, Emil Mazey, and Victor Gotbaum, top officials with the Amalgamated Meatpackers, UAW and AFSCME, respectively, withdrew their endorsements and plans to take part in the march. They did so, they argued, because new leftists planned to picket the White House, and they objected to any open criticism of the president. Furthermore, SANE was powerless to prevent militant activists from raising Viet Cong flags, chanting anti-American taunts or taking other inflammatory actions. For example, in a strongly worded address, SDS President Carl Oglesby declared the war a liberal affair, clearly indicting organized labor in the process, since it was considered a central part of the liberal coalition.[8]

Through 1966 and 1967, middle-class students constituted the vast majority of the antiwar movement. So-called umbrella organizations, like the National Mobilization Committee to End the War in Viet Nam, or MOBE, really represented only a limited segment of the population. This narrow inclusion became apparent at the 1967 Pentagon protest, which, unlike the March on Washington of 1963, which had attracted a diverse coalition of participants, was primarily a white student affair. Well-known adults gained headlines but they did not constitute a significant percentage of participants. African Americans—more publicly opposed to the war than any other group and constituting a large part of the local populace—were largely absent. In effect, the Pentagon demonstration symbolized the class and racial limits of the antiwar movement, reaffirming the movement's image. In 1968, the student revolt at Columbia University and the violent demonstrations at the Democratic National Convention in Chicago, only reinforced this public impression.[9]

More important, such demonstrations highlighted those aspects of the New Left that labor found most objectionable. Rather than seeing a utopian vision of the future, as with the ERAPS, or a living example unity, as with the March on Washington, trade unionists saw disorder and infantile nihilism. The Garment Workers' newspaper described the Pentagon demonstration as "VIOLENT, ILLEGAL, VULGAR." Dissent was an American right, the newspaper added, but the protesters were "straining the nation's tolerance." At the ensuing AFL–CIO convention, union officials in near unanimity reaffirmed their support for Johnson, blasted "hate peddlers . . . as a threat to America" and urged union members to "reject extremists."[10]

In addition, as the antiwar movement grew more militant, labor leaders increasingly red-baited it. Joseph Curran argued that agents financed by "Moscow and Peking" were using the antiwar movement, just as they had attempted to use the labor movement in the past. "The communist influence can very easily be seen by the fact that they show no desire to protest the aid from Communist countries that fuels the war." Trips by prominent new leftists to North Vietnam, such as Tom Hayden and Staughton Lynd, augmented these views. Shortly after Lynd, Hayden, and communist historian Herbert Aptheker returned from Hanoi, several of the building trades called for an increased devotion of Americans to South Vietnam and compared antiwar dissenters to strikebreakers.[11]

Meanwhile, revelations of the AFL–CIO's ties to the Central Intelligence Agency only tarnished labor's reputation in new left eyes. In May 1966 Victor Reuther, director of the UAW's International Affairs division, claimed that Jay Lovestone, head of the AFL–CIO International Affairs division, had gotten the AFL–CIO and several international unions to participate in numerous covert operations sponsored by the CIA. For instance, the intelligence community had used the AFL–CIO's international affiliates as fronts to oust communists from the labor movement in Europe and Latin America. Victor Reuther acknowledged that the UAW had once participated in such clandestine operations, but now felt compelled to speak ot against them.[12]

Several leftists expanded on Reuther's charges. Sidney Lens outlined the AFL–CIO's cooperation with the American Institute for Free Labor Development in Latin America, including the latter's single-minded pursuit of an anticommunist policy. In both articles and a book, Ronald Radosh further described the AIFLD: "A close working relationship exists between the State Department, AID, the CIA and the AFL–CIO," Radosh wrote. The AFL–CIO, CIA–State Department nexus, he continued, was a central aspect of America's cold war policies. Even though Victor Reuther condemned Lovestone's "obsession" with anti-communism, Radosh observed that UAW officials too had purged communists from the Union's ranks and had accepted CIA funds in order to build anticommunist unions in Europe. "Like George Meany," Radosh concluded, "[Walter] Reuther completely accepted the premise of Cold War foreign policy. The CIA was viewed as merely another institution which extended funds for legitimate purposes." (In later years, new left exposés of CIA infiltration of the National Student Association and the American Congress of Cultural Freedom, two prominent liberal organizations, added to its disgust with liberalism in general.)[13]

Labor officials and rank and file further distanced themselves from the antiwar movement by participating in boisterous pro-war rallies. On 14 May 1967, for example, Thomas Gleason, president of the International Longshoremen Association led a 7½ hour pro-war parade down

Fifth Avenue in New York City. Thousands of longshoremen, sailors, teamsters, carpenters, motion picture mechanics, and other workers marched alongside, many adorned with jingoist signs, such as "MY COUNTRY RIGHT OR WRONG." Others chanted "burn Hanoi not our flag." Gleason boasted that ILA members had "beat up young war protesters and draft card burners," adding that, "we hope they keep it up because we will just desecrate their ranks, if they have enough soldiers." While most labor leaders avoided such brazen proclamations, they neither repudiated Gleason nor condemned a "vigilante mob against citizens—who rightly or wrongly—were invoking the American tradition of protest," to use James Weschler's words.[14]

The respective reactions of the New Left and labor to Martin Luther King, Jr.'s declaration against the war in early 1967 illuminates the divisive impact of the war. In the first half of the decade, King attracted a variety of participants into a broad coalition for civil rights, including the New Left and organized labor. He acted as a "vital center," to use August Meier's words. In its first issue after King's Riverside Church proclamation, however, the *AFL–CIO News* excerpted a pro-war speech by Massachusetts Senator Edward Brooke, the only black in the U.S. Senate. Brooke claimed that King was over his head in criticizing the president's "foreign" policy. The ILGWU reprinted Brooke's speech and another by NAACP head Roy Wilkins, which attacked civil rights leaders who thought that they could serve their people at home by involving them in disputes over foreign policy. ILGWU vice president William Ross left the traditionally liberal union's stance in no doubt: "Dr. King was wrong in thinking that by subordinating civil rights to international affairs in some mysterious way he will help the cause of integration.... You can not go against the policy of your country and expect to aid civil rights!" Even the once militant and isolationist United Mine workers, which admitted it did not "pretend to have any firm opinion about the war," called King's opposition "wrong."[15]

In sharp contrast, the New Left welcomed King's public opposition to the war. *Ramparts* reveled in its exclusive and authorized publication of King's "Declaration of Independence from the War in Vietnam." The *Guardian* described King's speech in glowing terms. CORE leader Floyd McKissick declared: "I'm glad to have him with us." MOBE touted King as the keynote speaker at its 22 April antiwar demonstration in New York City. And in the months following the April protest, King toured college campuses drawing large crowds of antiwar protesters.[16]

The many arenas of disagreement between labor and the New Left raise a difficult question: why was organized labor's attack on the antiwar movement so strident? At least four answers come to mind. First was political pragmatism. Labor's endorsement of Johnson's foreign policy was inextricably linked to LBJ's prolabor domestic policies. Labor shared Johnson's vision of the Great Society. It considered Johnson's foreign and domestic policies to be equal parts of the liberal agenda to extend democracy and prosperity. Criticizing the president's foreign crusade, labor feared, could jeopardize the domestic one. Johnson had done more for liberals "than any other president since Roosevelt," declared ILGWU official Gus Tyler. How could they consider abandoning him?[17]

Second was economics. Most labor leaders assumed that the war would *not* cut into the Great Society. They could have both guns and butter. As New Deal economist Thurmond Arnold informed trade unionists, "there is no reason why we cannot carry our international burden and at the same time promote economic progress at home." Indeed, many assumed that the war was good for the economy and thus for the labor movement. A declining unemployment rate, from 5.7 percent in 1963 to 3.6 percent in 1968 along with a jump in hourly earnings for blue-collar workers confirmed this view. So too did the rise in trade union membership, from 18.2 million in 1965 to 21.8 million in 1973.[18]

Third was ideology or foreign policy. AFL–CIO leaders had a long history of supporting America's Cold War policies, including some but not all of the social activist unions. In the 1960s, this translated into protecting South Vietnam from communist invasion. We back the policy of "guarding the nation's [South Vietnam's] independence"; stated various branches of the House of Labor. We favor the "current policy of insuring against Communist military victory while holding forth the hand of negotiations."[19]

Undoubtedly George Meany and Jay Lovestone, AFL–CIO director of Foreign Affairs, both hardened anticommunists, went beyond this view. Lovestone envisioned rolling communism back. Meany had moved his way up the AFL ladder by becoming a specialist on foreign affairs with a hawkish attitude toward the Soviet Union. Even during the 1930s and World War II, he touted an anti-Soviet line, and during his tenure as president of the AFL–CIO he committed approximately one-fourth of the federation's funds to anticommunist unions around the globe.[20] Yet it remains unclear whether the majority of labor leaders shared Lovestone's and Meany's stance. Like most Americans, trade unionists supported the Cold War in the abstract. But limited evidence suggests that aside from articulate and highly visible officials, such as Gus Tyler, they saw the

Vietnam War within the qualified framework of protecting the free South from the invading North at a minimal cost to the domestic agenda. Furthermore, their support for Johnson's policies rested on the assumption that victory was in sight and that democracy was viable in South Vietnam.[21]

Indeed, as Nelson Lichtenstein has suggested, by the early 1960s the UAW and other liberal unions were growing increasingly critical of the rigid anticommunism as represented by Meany. They favored a thaw in Soviet-American relations, recognition of China, and a decrease in the defense budget, akin to detente as it developed in the early 1970s. However, such thoughts rarely cracked the public's image of labor as single-mindedly anticommunist and pro-Vietnam, personified by George Meany's staunch support of the president. This view resulted partly from Meany's insistence that he would not tolerate dissent on the war. To avoid a public clash with Meany and with President Johnson, Reuther himself as well as several other top labor officials muted their opposition to Johnson's policies.[22]

A fourth factor was culture. The images of the antiwar movement, specifically its association with the counterculture, antagonized labor. The antiwar movement's style offended trade unionists as much as the former's opposition to the war. In the minds of labor leaders and the rank and file, drugs, promiscuity, long hair, and burning the American flag were inextricably linked to the New Left's opposition to the Vietnam War. As workers who assaulted antiwar demonstrators proclaimed: "Get the hippies, get the traitors." Or as longshoreman Eric Hoffer put it, he stood for "traditional values" and against "absurdist America . . . LSD and happenings." Even trade unionists who disapproved of Johnson's policies found it difficult to link arms with the antiwar movement because of its countercultural bent. Lawrence Spitz, a leader with the Steelworkers said that he could not prod his members to sympathize with individuals who "wore the flag on the seat of their pants."[23]

———

Rather than reach out to trade unionists, the New Left took note of labor's barbs and increasingly coupled its opposition to the war with criticisms of the war's supporters, including the labor movement and the working class. This criticism was especially directed at the social activist unions of whom the New Left expected better. For example, through most of 1965, Sidney Lens remained faithful to organized labor, yet he criticized some of its particulars. In December 1965, however, Lens railed at the American labor movement. Meany's stance was predictable, wrote Lens, but Reuther's "total support" signified the loss of vision within organized labor. "Men like Reuther once talked of the injured and the oppressed. But now lose their tongues over the killing of three-year old babies by American grenades or the napalming [*sic*] of old people." Likewise, Staughton Lynd argued, "I think if we are honest one must conclude that western workers don't much care about the underdeveloped world. They have been 'bought off.' "[24] And Marvin Garson, a Free Speech Movement leader, expressed a similar view, although in a less sophisticated manner: "The next time some $3.90 an hour AFL type workers go on strike for a 50 cents raise, I'll remember the day they chanted 'Burn Hanoi, not our flag,' and so help me I'll cross their fucking picket line."[25]

In addition, the New Left increasingly saw labor as part of the establishment, or more theoretically as a partner of corporate liberalism. This ideological drift away from the old left faith in the proletariat drew on arguments made by several independent radicals of the 1950s and 1960s, namely C. Wright Mills, Herbert Marcuse, and William Appleman Williams. New leftists argued that America was dominated by sophisticated business leaders and conservative labor unionists who cooperated with each other to the benefit of themselves and the detriment of unorganized minorities and the Third World. Even though Mills never considered labor as part of the power elite, the New Left did, with Ronald Radosh contending that collusion between labor and corporate America could be traced to the early years of the twentieth century. The labor movement had learned, Radosh argued, that it would prosper at home if it supported American adventures abroad. Paradoxically, in making this argument, the New Left also drew on the thoughts of various liberal theorists who otherwise it rejected. Daniel Bell, for one, had contended that American capitalism had overcome class divisions and that class issues had ceased to be central to American politics.[26]

Years later Radosh expanded on the significance of this intellectual turn: "If we needed proof of our theory that liberal America was the real enemy, Vietnam came along to provide it. . . . We responded with hostility to the suggestion that communists might be the enemies of freedom," Radosh wrote. "In this struggle, the communists were our progressive allies, and the anticommunists [including social democrats like Irving Howe, Michael Harrington, and Norman Thomas] our reactionary enemies. We saw any kind of anticommunism as a mask for counterrevolution and we sided with the anti-imperialist revolutionaries of the Third World."[27]

Some new leftists and trade unionists, however, viewed America's polarization with horror, including Sidney Peck. A sociologist at Case Western Reserve and co-chair of MOBE, with a background as a labor activist, Peck challenged the confrontational philosophy of the militant wing of the antiwar movement. "Super radical actions" did not end the war and only alienated potential antiwar support. The movement needed to regain a "profound confidence" in the ability of the average person to recognize that the war was wrong. Directly rebutting the tactics of the Pentagon and Chicago demonstrators under the lead of Jerry Rubin and Abbie Hoffman, Peck added that the antiwar movement "cannot be built on gimmicks or theatrics"; it had to be based on a working relationship with "our fellows in the shops and offices, at the universities, and factories and in our neighborhoods."[28]

Peck's faith in building a mass movement rested to a degree on the appearance of antiwar sentiment within labor itself. Even though AFL–CIO leaders continued to staunchly defend the Vietnam War, a small but growing cluster of labor officials dissented. Standing between the mainstream of the labor movement and the New Left, these labor unionists for peace were unable to reverse organized labor's position or gain much notice until after the Tet offensive. But by establishing a base of opposition, they created space for other doubting trade unionists to operate and they undercut the image promoted by Meany and the mass media that labor unanimously and uncritically supported Johnson's policies.[29]

Several labor unions and officials had criticized the escalation of the war from its inception. In March 1965, Local 1199 of the Hospital Workers condemned the bombings of North Vietnam. David Livingston, president of District 65, RWDSU, called for a return to common decency. The Negro American Labor Council demanded peace. And Teamster vice-president Harold Gibbons criticized the U.S.'s intervention in both Vietnam and the Dominican Republic. Yet, this dissent came largely from fringe left unions and officials who had disagreed with the AFL–CIO's staunch anticommunism since the late 1940s. Much of this opposition remained unorganized and unpublicized, and hence insignificant.[30]

This slipshod attitude began to change in early 1966 with the formation of a special trade union division of SANE. Several New York City labor leaders with old left backgrounds, including Henry Foner, David Livingston, Leon Davis, and Sam Meyer, founded the division. On 3 May 1966, 173 union officials from thirty unions in the New York metropolitan area held the organization's first official meeting. They met again in

November, with the addition of several prominent midwestern labor leaders: Emil Mazey of the UAW, Patrick Gorman of the Meatcutters, and Frank Rosenblum of the Clothing Workers. Shortly afterward, sister chapters were established in the Midwest, Los Angeles, and San Francisco.[31]

Those who joined were appalled by the war's brutality. They disagreed with the predominant view that the United States could afford both guns and butter. They abhorred the polarization taking place in America, in particular the alienation of youths and blacks, and predicted that the nation would lose a whole generation of productive Americans if the war did not end soon. Old left unions, which had been critical of America's Cold War policies since their inception, constituted an important core of this group. But they did not comprise the whole. Individual labor leaders from anticommunist unions, such as Frank Rosenblum, and mavericks like Harold Gibbons, added breadth and legitimacy to SANE's trade union division, as did SANE's sponsorship itself.[32]

In November 1967, the trade union division of SANE metamorphized itself into a new organization, the Labor Leadership Assembly for Peace. Hopeful of gaining the attention of disenchanted veterans, the assembly held its first meeting on Veterans Day weekend. LLAP attracted 523 labor leaders, from fifty international unions and thirty-eight states. Assembly leader Frank Rosenblum announced that the group primarily hoped to demonstrate that the labor movement did *not* "monolithically" support the war. Secondarily, to encourage more labor officials and workers to speak out, the assembly argued that dissent was not unpatriotic. Shortly after its first convention, LLAP took part in various demonstrations, most notably one in Chicago, where Martin Luther King, Jr., spoke, and the Vietnam Veterans Against the War made one of their first appearances.[33]

The emergence of the Vietnam Veterans Against the War signified an additional if different source of antiwar sentiment among labor. Whereas the Labor Leadership Assembly for Peace represented dissent from the top down, the VVAW symbolized dissent from the bottom up. Vietnam Veterans were drawn disproportionately from manual, sales, and clerical workers. Though slightly less working class than Vietnam Veterans in general, close to 50 percent of those who participated in VVAW protests came from manual labor families, less than 30 percent from professional or managerial ones. Their vociferous condemnation of the war, indeed, simply the sight of antiwar veterans, with the accouterments of the counterculture, presented a shocking contradiction to older workers who were led to believe that only spoiled upper- and middle-class students opposed the war. Furthermore, returning veterans affected the

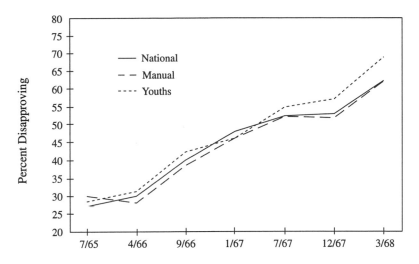

Figure 1. Disapproval of Johnson Administration Handling of Vietnam

views of their families. As John Helmer has shown, 70 percent of the parents of members of Vietnam Veterans Against the War changed their attitude toward the war, moving to more dovish positions.[34] (Independent of the VVAW, some black veterans joined this working-class opposition to the war. Although unorganized, they constituted a potential radical mass among the ranks of labor.)[35]

George Meany belittled the emergence of trade unionists for peace. He ignored antiwar veterans and red-baited dissenters. From the podium of the AFL–CIO convention in 1967, he insisted that the over five hundred labor officials who attended the Labor Assembly for Peace's convention represented only a tiny portion of organized labor and suggested that they were dupes of the communists.[36] Yet Gallup and Harris Polls cast doubt on Meany's arithmetic. From 1965 through 1967, the public's support for Lyndon Johnson's policies slowly diminished. Disapproval climbed from 27 percent in July 1965 to 52 percent in July 1968 (see figure 1).[37]

Then came the Tet offensive. By overselling the success of the war, Johnson set himself up for the backlash that followed. His optimistic claims rang hollow in spite of the ability of American and South Vietnamese forces to turn the offensive back. Not only did Johnson's popularity plummet but also the number of doves drastically increased. Moreover, American workers' attitude toward Johnson's policy shifted along with the general public. Contrary to the stereotype of "hard hats" as hawks, virtually every survey demonstrated that at any given time manual workers were just as likely to oppose the war as were youths, the archetypal doves.[38]

A shift in the political context contributed to labor's dovish turn. In about a year's time, the war changed from a liberal Democratic affair to a conservative Republican one, while simultaneously metamorphosing into a prolonged struggle in which America no longer seemed destined to win. Nixon's public stance, of peace with honor, was an acknowledgment of this. To the extent that labor had supported the war because of its commitment to the Democratic party, it was no longer so bound. In so far as workers favored the war because they saw it as limited and winnable their commitment became considerably more problematic.[39]

The spread of antiwar sentiment among the ranks and leadership of labor clearly influenced the New Left. Stanley Aronowitz, for one, argued that the Chicago meeting of the Labor Leadership Assembly for Peace "was the most important antiwar expression by sections of the trade union movement." Similarly, articles in *Liberation* and *Ramparts,* traced the devastating affects of the war on working Americans. As Mrs. Betty Rucker, the wife of an electrical lineman and mother of a Vietnam War fatality told a interviewer, "There's just no sense to it. Just slaughter. A lot of young kids going over there to get killed for no reason at all. . . . They tell us we're fighting communism. . . . If the South Vietnamese want to fight, let them fight their own battles."[40]

For a segment of the New Left, not only did greater sympathy for the working class emerge, so too did the sense of the need for allies. "Almost everyone in the anti-war movement recognizes that students alone do not have the power to end the war," read one leaflet jointly authored by SDS's Labor Committee, the International Socialists, Columbia Student Mobilization Committee and Columbia Young Socialist Alliance. Since several of these organizations were branches or fronts for old left organizations, their pro-worker stance was somewhat predictable. Yet, not all of them were. Moreover, several of these old left groups, most notably the Young Socialist Alliance, or YSA, were able to recruit many newcomers to their ranks by touting their strategy of building alliances with workers.[41]

Given the media depiction of the New Left as unanimously antilabor, any sort of reconciliation might have been impossible to achieve if some new leftists had not already poised themselves to renew friendly relations. Yet, Sidney Peck and several other activists had done just this. In 1967, with the help of a number of trade unionists and veteran new leftists, Peck had established the Cleveland Area Peace Action Coalition. Using CPAC as a base, Peck, along with Sidney Lens and Fred Halstead, steered the antiwar movement, especially MOBE, in a more conciliatory direction. In July 1969, for example, CAPAC sponsored a series of national antiwar conferences to which it invited a broad array of participants, student leftists, veteran pacifists, and dissenting unionists. Indeed, CAPAC administrator and one-time labor lawyer Jerry Gordon drafted the call to the conference with an eye toward attracting workers.[42]

Peck's effort clearly bore fruit as SDS, Student MOBE, SNCC, CORE, and nearly a dozen top labor officials attended the summer meeting. The presence of dissenting unionists allowed UAW Ohio Regional director Leo Fenster to claim that the labor movement was waiting to be organized. The breadth of the participants also prompted the group to make plans for staging a series of massive nonviolent demonstrations, most notably the Moratorium and New MOBE.[43]

Jerome Grossman originally conceived of the Moratorium as a nation-wide or general strike. Antiwar leaders Sam Brown and David Hawk liked the idea but feared that the term *strike* would alienate middle-class supporters. Thus they decided to call it a "moratorium." Whatever its name, the demonstration held on 15 October 1969, was the largest in U.S. history. (Labor historians might even consider the Moratorium as the single largest general strike.) It attracted a broad array of Americans, including a substantial contingent of labor officials. In New York City, forty trade unions endorsed the protest. Sam Meyer, president of UAW Local 259, led a candlelight vigil in New York City's Central Park; his West Coast colleague, Paul Schrade, officiated at a massive rally at the University of Southern California. In Detroit, Douglas Fraser, Grady Glenn, and Myra Wolfgang, representing the UAW and Hotel and Restaurant Workers, demanded peace before tens of thousands of demonstrators.[44]

A month later, the New MOBE sponsored two massive protests. Between 500,000 and 800,000 Americans rallied in Washington, D.C., another 125,000 to 250,000 in San Francisco. Students predominated but vast numbers of nonstudents protested as well. Union officials Harold Gibbons of the Teamsters, Frank Rosenblum of the Clothing Workers, Patrick Gorman of the Meatcutters, Leon Davis of Local 1199, David Livingston of District 65 and the Alliance for Labor Action endorsed the demonstration. Gibbons and Livingston delivered keynote addresses. As hundreds of thousands sang that afternoon, all they wanted, was to "give peace a chance." True, there were some exceptions to this spirit. Several thousand new leftists split from the main rally to mount a more militant protest, but even they railed at the connections between labor's foes and America's major war contractors.[45]

The Vietnam Moratorium and New MOBE demonstrations provided the basis for an even broader antiwar movement. Contemporary surveys showed widespread discontent with the war. A poll of the Chicago region revealed that 59 percent of the respondents wanted the United States to withdraw from Vietnam by December 1970, while 19 percent favored departing as soon as the Vietnamese could carry the burden. Only 20 percent favored the present course or wanted to increase military pressure. Most important, polls showed that dove sentiment was not confined to students or youths. Votes on antiwar referendums reaffirmed that union members and minorities exhibited a great desire to end the war. In the fall of 1970, Detroit residents overwhelmingly passed a referendum calling for immediate withdrawal (63 to 37 percent), with labor unionists and blacks constituting the backbone of the antiwar vote.[46]

To counteract expanding antiwar sentiment, President Nixon unleashed Spiro Agnew and expanded covert operations aimed at debilitating the Left. The vice-president juxtaposed Nixon and the protesters; he called the former a supporter of "our heroes" and the latter a "breed of losers" who attended elite universities and waved Viet Cong flags. Agnew's diatribes drew attention away from the war and prodded George Meany and other AFL–CIO officials to characterize the antiwar activists as spoiled, unpatriotic, and disingenuous. For instance, in an article that appeared in the *AFL–CIO News,* John Roche proclaimed that radicals cared little about the war, that they used it to satisfy personality quirks. In other words, Agnew's campaign successfully tore at the antiwar movement. Yet, just as the movement seemed on the verge of disintegration, Nixon resuscitated it by ordering the invasion of Cambodia.[47]

Organized labor did not support Nixon's policy of widening the war, Meany's statement and the May 1970 Wall Street rampage notwithstanding. Scores of labor leaders joined student activists in decrying the American invasion. Teamster Vice President Robert Holmes viewed it as "a form of deceit which the American people will not accept." AFSCME stated that "no further blood and resources be wasted." Scores of union presidents sent telegrams to President Nixon condemning his latest action, with Walter Reuther writing: "We must mobilize for peace rather than wider theaters of war." (This was Reuther's last public statement as he died in an airplane crash shortly afterward.)[48]

In addition, trade unionists joined hands with new leftists in public protests against the expansion of the war. Labor officials participated in an emergency anti-Cambodia demonstration on 9 May 1970, in Washington, D.C. Still other union leaders endorsed the protest but did not attend. On May 21, the Coalition of Peace, a student-labor group headed by AFSCME Local president Victor Gotbaum, sponsored an antiwar rally in New York City. Although smaller in size than the previous day's pro-war demonstration (twenty to fifty thousand vs. sixty to one hundred thousand) it showed that labor and the New Left were willing to openly unite in opposition to the war. Unionists also participated in the March Against Racism and Repression, held in Georgia in memory of students killed at Jackson State. Leonard Woodcock, the new UAW president, told the mourners that he intended to follow Reuther's lead. District 65's leader, Cleveland Robinson, seconded Woodcock's declaration. Subsequently, a very large contingent of trade unionists attended CAPAC's Emergency Conference against the Cambodia-Laos-Vietnam War. (Approximately one-fourth of the two hundred sponsors represented labor.) Whereas the Wall Street rampage, or Black Thursday, as it became known, and the subsequent displays of support for Nixon were lead stories in the national media, collaborative efforts between the New Left and labor received little attention.[49]

Regardless of the contemporary misrepresentation of the events, the assault of 8 May and ensuing pro-war demonstrations should not be interpreted solely as evidence of worker support for the war and disfavor of the antiwar movement. First, not only workers took part in the large pro-war rally. Second, local contractors encouraged the expression of pro-war sentiment and evidence suggests that a right wing organization with business funding helped organize the assault in the first place. (One investigation even showed that workers did not have pay docked for time missed while participating in either event and some contractors even offered cash bonuses for participating in the rampage and rally.) Third, polls found that a majority of unionists disapproved of the rampage of 8 May, with Lou Harris finding that 53 percent of union members "condemned the hard hat action," while only 30 percent approved.[50] Fourth, follow-up interviews with participants in the assault found contradictory and unclear motives. As one IUE official stated, "I would say that the majority were opposed to the decision to go into Cambodia. They feel the students should have a right to dissent." They were "not against demonstrations . . . not against the students," remarked another worker. In other words, differences over the war were not the sole cause of the infamous rampage. Frustrations over wasted tax dollars, a challenge to endeared cultural values, fear of unemployment, and a declining standard of living helped produce the outburst. (During 1970, 30 percent of all New York City construction workers were unemployed at some time. In the same period, inflation reduced wages to 1965 levels.)[51]

Perhaps because they understood that Black Thursday did not mean that workers favored Nixon's latest move, pro-war labor leaders played on workers' economic fears to encourage them to rally around Nixon's policy. The day after Nixon announced the invasion of Cambodia, CWA president and long-time hawk, Joseph Beirne, declared that the war actually helped workers economically; he added that the war's end, particularly if it happened quickly, would be devastating. "The effect of the war . . . is to keep an economic pipeline loaded with a turnover of dollars because people are employed in manufacturing things of war." This crude defense of the war was consistent with labor's general belief that war was good for the economy, a view that seemed valid until the latter part of the 1960s but that became less tenable as unemployment and inflation mounted in the early 1970s.[52]

More important, the events of May 1970 may have served as a catharsis to pent up anger. No more actual confrontations between workers and antiwar activists took place. The following spring, antiwar groups organized massive protests. In New York City, local labor leaders, the Vietnam Vets Versus the War, and student activists sponsored a memorial rally for the Kent State dead. This time the Building Trades Council did not organize a pro-war rally. CAPAC's third national antiwar conference, held in the fall of 1971, attracted an even broader spectrum of trade unionists than its first two. Furthermore, by the fall of 1971 Gallup Polls showed that 61 percent of all respondents favored pulling out of Vietnam by the end of the year, with union households adopting this view more than any other group except racial minorities.[53]

The formation of Labor for Peace in early 1972 affirmed the polls' finding. Larger than its predecessors, it gained the endorsement of well-known labor leaders and entire trade unions. One thousand trade unionists representing thirty-five international unions from thirty-one states attended its founding convention. They did not debate the merits of Nixon's policy, as they were unanimous in their disapproval. Instead they considered calling for a general strike against the war.[54]

The growth of antiwar labor sentiment not only accelerated the eventual withdrawal from Vietnam it produced a sympathetic view of the labor movement on the part of large segments of the New Left. Tom Hayden recalled that he altered his conception of radicalism in late 1971. "My idea was to go to the mainstream. . . . The Movement had gotten itself isolated at the very moment that large numbers of people were ready to be mobilized." Jeremy Brecher argued that May 1970 marked a "sea change in the attitudes of American workers," citing examples of workers warmly greeting antiwar protesters at factory gates. "The labor movement as a whole is breaking out of its conservative integration into the American status quo and becoming more militant," added Brecher, and he urged fellow leftists to take advantage of this change. Along these same lines, long-time antiwar activists increasingly couched their appeals in terms that spoke directly to working-class concerns. Staughton Lynd and his wife Alice, for instance, urged new leftists to organize workers from the bottom-up. And numerous new left journals published articles sympathetic to the plight of the American worker.[55]

In other words, ultimately Vietnam had a contradictory impact on the New Left's relationship to labor. Coming on top of the MFDP affair, the ERAPs, and Selma, it initially drove a wedge between the two social movements. It turned a fragile relationship into a confrontational one. For example, the war intensified the labor movement's "Americanism," and thus exacerbated its concerns about the New Left's softness on anticommunism. This increased concern was especially the case for the Meany block of the labor movement. Likewise, the war, since it was directed by a liberal Democrat, heightened the New Left's distaste for liberalism in general, including labor. This was especially true among new leftists who had few links to the Old Left or House of Labor. Yet the continuation of the war also prodded a segment of the New Left to recognize the futility of confrontation and simultaneously compelled segments of the labor movement to consider an alternative course to President Johnson's policies in Southeast Asia. Richard Nixon's assumption of the presidency reinforced this development.

This said, before Vietnam became something that could actually bring the New Left and labor together, other developments, often associated with the war, widened the rift between them. Put another way, even though it has become common to single out Vietnam as the event that polarized America in the 1960s, with the Wall Street rampage symbolizing this polarization, a more careful analysis compels one to develop a more complex view of the decade. While Vietnam, on its own, drove a wedge between the New Left and labor, it was not a powerful enough force to widen or maintain the rift. Only the concurrent emergence of Black Power and the flowering of the counterculture, could do this.

4

Black Power

In the late spring of 1966, representatives of the Maryland Freedom Union met with Jerry Menapace, an official with the Meatcutters Union, to discuss an organizing drive that MFU had initiated in the Baltimore area. MFU had been formed earlier in the year by several CORE veterans who sought to organize poor, largely black and Hispanic workers into an independent and militant union. A number of MFU's founders enjoyed good relations with several social activist trade unions and unionists, including Menapace. They had worked together in various struggles for civil rights in Baltimore and elsewhere. During the meeting, Menapace stated that he would support MFU's efforts as long as it respected or followed certain procedures. Most important, the Maryland Freedom Union would have to recognize the jurisdictional claims of all AFL–CIO unions. It could not practice "dual unionism." If MFU agreed to these procedures, Menapace would support it.[1]

One MFU spokesman, who probably did not understand what Menapace meant by the term *dual unionism,* responded that black activists considered the Meatcutters a "good" union. He added that MFU would not challenge Menapace's union. However, he continued, MFU refused to guarantee that it would not raid the jurisdictions of other unions.[2]

While MFU's refusal to pledge itself to respect the jurisdicitions of AFL–CIO unions disturbed Menapace, he was much more upset by what followed. As he related to Abe Feinglass, president of the Meatpackers: "These two CORE leaders told me quite mater-of-factly that they do not intend to accept white liberals in positions of leadership in their movement . . . that Negroes cannot continue to accept their patronage." Yet, Menapace incredulously added, they still wanted liberal money! To make matters worse, a MFU spokesman informed Menapace to his face that he was not "a true friend of the Civil Rights Movement."[3]

Exactly what happened next remains unclear. Based on an examination of an exchange of letters with Abe Feinglass, it appears that Menapace decided to continue to work with civil rights groups, despite MFU's rebuke. Yet, shortly after Menapace's meeting with MFU, Walter Reuther threatened CORE (at the time MFU's parent organization) with a loss of financial aid, if it did not get out of the union business. Regardless of whether or not the Menapace meeting with MFU actually triggered this development, MFU was compelled by CORE's director Floyd McKissick to officially disassociate from CORE, and MFU's members tended to blame Menapace for this.[4]

Shortly after the Menapace-MFU meeting, the president of the *Afro-American*, a respected black-owned newspaper headquartered in Baltimore, invited a variety of civil rights activists and allies to a discussion of the general racial situation in the region. His hope was to soothe tensions through dialogue. At this meeting, an AFL–CIO official raised the issue of MFU's practice of dual unionism. CORE official Lincoln Lynch retorted, "MFU is a response to the failures of organized labor." John White, head of the Baltimore branch of the National Alliance of Postal and Federal Employees, an independent black union, seconded Lynch's assertion. In other words, CORE, which had once enjoyed close relations with many trade unions, was coming to the defense of a practice that was anathema to the labor movement. The labor officials at the meeting could not accept this claim. While they recognized that labor had its faults, they were not about to jettison one of their basic operating principles for the sake of unity. Thus, rather than assuaging tensions between labor and the militant wing of the civil rights movement, the meeting left the two groups angrier with each other than before.[5]

In many ways, MFU's feud with Menapace and the labor movement in Baltimore represented the impact that Black Power had on the New Left's relationship to labor. Even though MFU, itself, was not a black nationalist group, it was influenced by black nationalist ideas and feelings and was a branch of the broader New Left. Like Black Power itself, the emergence of the MFU revealed and caused a widening rift between the New Left and labor. It symbolized the move of the civil rights movement into the urban North, which in turn raised the issue of racism within liberal unions.

Contrary to popular belief, labor's response to the emergence of Black Power was not backlash. Rather, most labor leaders reasserted their faith in liberal ideals and policies and in many cases actively fought backlash within their ranks. Yet, rather than appeasing the New Left, this development only aggravated tensions because many new leftists had begun to see liberal programs and ideals as insufficient and outdated.

The New Left especially felt this way when it came to problems faced by urban blacks in the North, problems that the urban disorders of the latter half of the 1960s brought to the fore. These riots, in the New Left's perspective, demonstrated the need for radical measures, not more liberal reforms. And many new leftists could not understand how liberals could simply reassert their liberal beliefs in the face of such riots—riots that liberal intellectuals had taught new leftists were not supposed to take place, in America, in the first place.

Not only did the labor movement consider the New Left's criticism of its call for more reforms underserved, it felt that leftists should quietly appreciate or commend the labor movement for standing firm, for refusing to succumb to backlash. Perhaps if the Vietnam War had not already begun to drive a wedge between the two movements, this development might have taken place; militant blacks and social activist trade unionists might have arrived at an understanding of each other's position and maintained a dialogue. But given the concurrent escalation of the war and the emergence of the counterculture, such an understanding did not develop. On the contrary, the size and severity of the rift only worsened.

Not long before Menapace's meeting with MFU, liberals in Baltimore as well as nationwide had been in a celebratory mood. With Johnson's landslide victory in the fall of 1964, they predicted an era of unequaled progress. The swift passage of the Voting Rights Act seemed to confirm that a new era had dawned. Unemployment was low. The economy was growing at a robust pace. Even though he lacked John F. Kennedy's charisma, President Johnson had energized the nation with his calls for eradicating poverty, beautifying the countryside, and renewing America's cities.

Liberals assumed, however, that henceforth change would come through "normal" political channels, that the era of mass demonstrations in the streets had passed. Even life-long socialist Bayard Rustin, who had served as an adviser to Martin Luther King, Jr., student leftists, and the labor movement, argued that the movement had to change its tactics. In his seminal article, "From Protest to Politics," Rustin claimed that the 1964 elections was a turning point in American history. It was not merely a reaction against "Goldwaterism." Rather, it signified "the expression of a majority liberal consensus," and by liberal Rustin meant a left-of-center group.[6]

Not long after Rustin's article was published and just five days after

President Johnson signed the Voting Rights Act, however, the ghetto of Watts, Los Angeles, erupted into flames, leaving the liberal's sense of fulfillment and Rustin's dream of a new coalition buried amid the rubble. While Watts and subsequent riots did not create Black Power—not until July 1966 did Stokely Carmichael popularize the term—the riots symbolized the foundations of the Black Power movement. They portrayed the pent-up rage felt by millions of blacks, for whom the early civil rights movement had little effect, except, perhaps, to raise their expectations. This rage sprouted from a society pervaded by racial discrimination and social and economic inequality, manifested most explicitly by police brutality, poor housing, inadequate schooling, restricted economic opportunity, and a culture dominated by whites.

The different responses of the New Left and labor to Watts and the subsequent riots were telling. In general, labor responded to the riots with dismay and horror. The "nightmare world of slums where rats abound and old-fashioned stoves ward off winter in Dickens-type squalor," caused the riot in Detroit, reported *UAW Solidarity*. Abusive police and pervasive discrimination added to the problems that plagued blacks, explained Steelworker president I. W. Abel. (Abel was a member of the Kerner Commission that President Johnson appointed to investigate the riots.) Or as AFL–CIO spokesman Edward Morgan put it, for many of America's blacks the American dream was a "nightmare." Even more stridently, a special Packinghouse Worker task force concluded that the riots were the product of a people against colonial-like conditions.[7]

Notably, the destructiveness of the riots did *not* lead labor leaders to call for radical measures. On the contrary, they insisted that riots proved the need for strict enforcement of existing civil rights programs and additional reforms. Labor unionists especially made this point following the failure of the federal government to pass fair housing laws in 1966 and 1967.[8] Indeed, rather than assuming part of the blame, trade unionists held southern reactionaries and conservative politicians responsible. As the Retail Workers contended, shabby tactics in the Senate, including filibuster, which blocked open housing and other civil rights legislation, provided fuel for the fire.[9]

In several instances, trade unions went beyond speaking out or lobbying for more reforms in Washington, D.C. The UAW and other social activist unions sponsored the Watts Labor Community Action Project, which sought to bring "constructive political and social reform" to the region. Many of the same union leaders threw their support behind SCLC's community union project. In Newark, the IUE sponsored "Brotherhood Conferences," whereby they invited veterans of the civil rights movement, such as Aaron Henry, and local activists, such as

Robert Curvin, George Richardson, and Mae Massie to voice their concerns. IUE members from the Newark area also joined black militants and the Reverend Ralph Abernathy in the Poor People's Campaign in Washington, D.C. No sooner had the Detroit riots ended then Walter Reuther pledged the "volunteer aid of 600,000 UAW members in removing the scars." Even though this particular proposal "turned to smoke," in Sidney Fine's words, Reuther's ideal of rebuilding the city in the wake of the riot served as the foundation for the New Detroit movement.[10]

Many unions also remained active in the drive to integrate schools. The Berkeley local of the AFT spearheaded the desegregation plan in that city. Other local AFT chapters sponsored conferences on racism in education. At one Detroit conference, teachers and activists, including CORE's Floyd McKissick, advocated the introduction of courses in African and African American history, partly with the aim of raising black self-esteem. New York City teachers implemented this recommendation when they formed "freedom schools," in the midst of their own strike in 1967.[11]

In contrast to labor, which expressed its dismay with the riots and used them as an occasion to reassert its faith in liberalism, the New Left tended to view the riots from a symbolic perspective. Rather than see them as a terrible waste of life and property, they viewed the uprisings or rebellions—the New Left did not even like using the word "riots"—as a sign that the revolution was imminent. Put another way, what counted most was not the destruction of the riots themselves but the message of the uprisings, that black Americans were angry and willing to act on their anger. For instance, in 1967, CORE's Floyd McKissick and SNCC's H. Rap Brown both traveled to Detroit in the immediate aftermath of its disorders. Rather than shed tears over the loss of life and property, they celebrated the "rebellions" and sought to direct black anger into an organized and militant direction. Or as the Reverend Albert Cleage, a leading local black militant, put it: the uprising was simply a "dress rehearsal" for a much grander revolution.[12]

Julius Jacobson, a friend of the radical black activists, added that trade union condemnation of the violence of the riots confused the issue. Labor mistook the victims for the perpetrators. Blacks, not the police, constituted the bulk of dead and wounded. Furthermore, the call by social democrats for blacks to withdraw from the streets marked a significant reversal in tactics. In the middle of World War II, Jacobson reported, A. Philip Randolph and Bayard Rustin defied the patriotic call for unity when they organized March on Washington Movement. Jacobson also could have observed that in planning for this protest, Randolph defended black separatism. Similarly, James Boggs contended that Black

Power really reflected an adoption of labor's tactics. Just as workers fought for greater control of the factories in which they worked, Boggs wrote, "blacks must struggle to control, to govern the cities" and communities in which they lived.[13]

The reasons why new leftists responded to the riots in this manner are manifold. Even before Watts had exploded, SNCC and CORE were engaged in a search for a renewed sense of purpose. Already they were questioning the value of integration, nonviolence, and coalition. The riots only soured them more on these ideals and hastened their espousal of Black Power.[14]

Black militants rejected integration, not just because efforts to integrate schools and neighborhoods had failed, and with white flight from urban centers, would continue to fail. More important, militants challenged the value of integration or assimilation for the first place. Why should blacks want to assimilate regardless of feasibility? As long as integration remained a one-way street, Stokely Carmichael and others asserted, it was a demeaning objective. "The concept is based on the assumption that there is nothing of value in the black community and that little of value could be created among black people. This reinforces, among both black and white, the idea that 'white' is automatically superior and 'black' is by definition inferior."[15]

Black Power advocates also expressed doubts about the specific goal of desegregating historically segregated trade unions. Drawing on the experience of his father, who was a construction worker, Stokely Carmichael commented that even in cases where blacks fought to gain admission to conservative craft unions, they found, once inside, that these unions were corrupt and unconcerned with the rank and file. Moreover, due to the sacrosanct rule of seniority, blacks were still the first to be laid off when cutbacks took place. And now, as "good" union members, they were no longer afforded the opportunity to challenge their dismissals because such protest was seen as antiunion, rather than antisegregationist.[16]

Perhaps the most important black militant to focus on the labor issue was James Haughton. Although he never advocated all of the particulars of Black Power and never became a key player in the New Left, Haughton influenced both movements. A long-time foe of the segregated construction trades in New York City and a founding member of the Negro American Labor Council, in the latter 1960s, Haughton broke with moderates, such as Randolph, to join forces with a wide range of black militants. Haughton argued that the labor movement had "lost all vestige of the dynamic force it once used to be." Blacks could not depend on Reuther or other one-time darlings of the left to regenerate or revitalize the House of Labor. Rather, blacks had to develop their own mechanism for addressing the needs of the black worker.[17]

In fact, the notion that liberal unions were the primary foe, that they had betrayed blacks, or in the least that labor had misled them into expecting something better, was a prominent theme among many radical black and white intellectuals. Having once vested faith in the CIO as a potential savior for the black working class, they railed at the failure of the labor movement to overcome white racism. For example, Robert Allen, an editor for the *Guardian* wrote: "Union leaders, once militant fighters for social change, have no program other than a panicky defensive reaction to the challenge of automation and deindustrialization. . . . Pleas to labor leaders to organize the jobless go unheeded. . . . Labor leaders increasingly stress the need for protecting members. The unemployed are seen as a great mass of potential strike breakers . . . ready on a moment's notice to . . . upset the wage scale for which unions have so bitterly fought."[18]

Stokely Carmichael and Charles Hamilton in their seminal work, *Black Power,* presented an equally sharp critique of the labor movement. Based on the House of Labor's history and contemporary action, they vigorously rejected Rustin's call for coalition. Historically, they argued, the AFL set its sights on bread-and-butter objectives at the "exclusion of broader goals." While the CIO initially "signaled a slight change" from the AFL's pure and simple trade unionism, it too never "seriously questioned the racist basis of society." (Carmichael and Hamilton cited V. O. Key and Selig Perlman to substantiate this point.) To make matters worse, they added, labor unions had proven treacherous friends to blacks. With the passage of the Wagner Act the general status of black workers declined, they argued. AFL craft unions "deliberately excluded black workers." Carmichael and Hamilton added that unions preferred to take care of their own at the expense of unorganized black workers. The authors quoted extensively from the arch-conservative *National Review* to support their points. While this did not mean that they were inaccurate, it suggests the length to which Black Power advocates were willing to go to criticize labor. Carmichael and Hamilton also asserted that organized labor had found blacks politically "expendable," and that labor's growth was closely interrelated to the United States' imperialistic exploitation of the nonwhite Third World, a view similarly uttered by several white new leftists.[19]

Of the various Black Power groups, the Black Panther party had the reputation as the most fervid antiwhite organization. Yet, it was the Panthers who presented the least critical view of the labor movement of all of Black Power groups. The Panthers touted a modified Marxist-

Leninist line that called for forging a class-based movement. "The Black Panther Party stands for revolutionary socialism with all people," declared a Black Panther party communique. "Employed or unemployed, workers must unite," wrote Panther leader Bobby Seale. The BPP even saw a role for blacks and whites joining together inside community and labor unions as long as whites supported Black Power goals, such as community control of the police and an end to American imperialism.[20]

But Panther rhetoric, sensationalized by the media, insured that it would gain few allies within labor, leadership, or rank and file. Shortly after the Panthers arrived at the California state captitol building adorned with rifles and bullets (a la Pancho Villa), George Meany wrote A. Philip Randolph that Carmichael's claim that Black Power did not denote violence was ridiculous. "I've got news for Mr. Carmichael, the reputed author of the Black Power slogan," Meany declared. "The Negro goons who go on racist rampages know exactly what Black Power means. To them it means the chance to go on a spree of violence with a testimonial as a 'freedom fighter' for a cover."[21]

In addition, the authenticity of the Panther's commitment to an alliance with white workers was always dubious. The BPP most ardently advocated coalition during a short-lived alliance with remnants of the Communist party. Antiwhite and anti-middle American rhetoric, especially the Panthers' depiction of policemen as pigs, often undercut or at least obscured the Panthers' more subtle positions. And even if Panther leaders preached a neosocialist position, their appeal remained strongest among young inner-city blacks who were much more interested in the Panthers' bravado, street gang image, and notoriety than in class alliances.

Not surprisingly, labor leaders found Black Power's attacks on their liberal ideals dismaying and offered their own critique of Black Power, as they understood it. Foremost, trade unionists condemned Black Power's alleged advocacy of violence. "You and I agree that extremism is the antithesis of democracy and extremism by advocates of justice for America's minority population cannot be countenanced any more than extremism by advocates of white supremacy," wrote George Meany to A. Philip Randolph. Only the attainment of racial justice through the "democratic process" deserves commendation. Likewise, an *AFL–CIO News'* cartoon showed a jury of black labor leaders proclaiming both the Klan and "black supremacists" guilty. By having a group of black trade unionists read the unfavorable verdict, this cartoon had the double affect of equating Black Power with a fringe group, previously condemned by the house of labor, and challenging the legitimacy of Black Power. Still another cartoon, published widely by the labor press, displayed a baseball bat with a fist around it labeled white supremacy. Above this white fist was a black fist labeled Black Power. The bat was labeled violence and the cartoon entitled, "The Game Nobody Wins."[22]

Labor spokespersons lashed out at Black Power's separatist schemes, such as black capitalism, as well. On different occasions, trade union officials labeled black nationalism "dangerous," "divisive" and "anti-democratic nonsense." Black nationalism or separatism ignored the history of upward mobility in America, as well as the economic impossibility of building minority "islands" of capitalism, declared one labor official.[23] Indeed, labor maintained the counterattack through the latter half of the 1960s, insisting as late as 1973, that trade unionism, not Black Power, was acting in the best interest of the black masses. In making this argument, AFL–CIO representatives contended that blacks were assimilating into the mainstream and that they were beginning to make progress. In fact, between 1961 and 1968, black unemployment dropped from 11.7 percent to 3.9 percent, average income rose, and the number of blacks graduating high school was also on the rise.[24]

Even labor leaders who understood that Black Power did not stand for violence or race supremacy advised blacks to drop the slogan because most Americans did. J. C. Rich, editor of the *Hat Worker* explained: "The advocates of black power are doing damage to their own cause by provoking retaliation from whites." Or, as others put it, while more aggressive action on the federal government's part might be necessary, attacks on the value of integration only played into the hands of conservatives who sought to undermine the gains of recent years.[25]

Whereas personal contacts had facilitated cooperation between black activists and trade unionists in the first half of the sixties, the exact opposite proved true in the latter half of the decade. Rather than producing a mutual respect for one another, personal contacts between representatives of both movements resulted in even greater mistrust. For example, in the summer of 1967, UAW official John Lopez attended a Black Power convention in Oakland, California, where, among other things, Stokely Carmichael delivered a blistering attack on liberals and whites. The tenor of the entire conference left Lopez horror-stuck. As he wrote to his boss, William Oliver (one of a handful of black UAW officials), Ron Karenga, a member of US, a Black Power group based in LA, delivered "the most bitter anti-white speech I had ever heard." Karenga called for the use of " 'any force necessary to obtain freedom,' " So too did Black Panther member Bobby Fields. The latter "was very dramatic and said in part—you must have shotguns, hand grenades, rifles, pistols and dynamite." In addition, Lopez wrote, Fields proclaimed that "the gun is the only form of power that the white Honkies recognize. Tell them what you want and if you don't get it blow up their railroads . . . the whole damn power structure until we get what we want."[26]

Before Lopez's visit, Walter Reuther considered resigning from CORE's advisory board. But he had not done so. Lopez's hands-on report convinced Reuther to change his mind, in spite of CORE director's Floyd McKissick's personal appeal that the UAW not be misled by "bigots" who sought to destroy the civil rights movement by misrepresenting Black Power.[27]

One of the main ways that labor displayed its disapproval of Black Power was by either directly cutting funding to civil rights organizations that advocated separatism and violence (in reality self-defense) or by encouraging liberal friends to do the same, although they did not need too much encouragement. In a period of five years, from 1965 to 1968, SNCC and CORE watched their income from outside sources drop from $637,736 and $677,785 to $25,000 and $210,000 respectively. Even the United Packinghouse Workers, one of the strongest supporters of the civil rights movement, cut aid to CORE and SNCC. In contrast, the revenues of the NAACP and the National Urban League skyrocketed in the latter 1960s. From 1965 to 1970, the NAACP saw income from outside sources jump from $388,077 to $2.66 million. The National Urban League's operating budget rose from $1.8 to $14.54 million.[28]

Partly in recognition of labor's fealty, many moderate black leaders reaped praise on the AFL–CIO. "If anybody thinks I am not as angry as the most angry black man in this country, you misread me," exclaimed Urban League president Whitney Young before a convention of autoworkers. Yet, Young continued, my anger reaffirms my insistence on more reforms, not separatism. Vernon Jordan, Young's more militant successor, continued this tradition with a speech before the 1971 AFL–CIO Constitutional Convention in which he described the AFL–CIO as "the home of some of the most progressive elements in American life" and the "deserving beneficiary of the loyalty of black workers." Labor leaders returned the favor by going before the members of SCLC, the NAACP, and the National Urban League to reiterate their support for civil rights.[29]

Bayard Rustin and A. Philip Randolph played a particularly important role in defending the labor movement and broadcasting its commitment to liberal ideals. Predictably, Rustin claimed that Black Power was

an ideology of frustration. It offered destructive rather than constructive solutions to problems that black militants correctly identified. "Now, my friends, I am opposed to the concept of black power," Rustin declared at an American Federation of Teacher's luncheon, shortly after the term gained notoriety. "I am opposed to slogans which lack content. I am opposed to slogans which tend to separate those who must be brought together." Despite certain problems in the building trades, labor was the "only organization" with a coherent program for eradicating poverty and racism that sprung from poverty. One-tenth of the population can not solve the nation's economic and social problems, Rustin insisted. Only a coalition of forces, consisting of blacks, labor, and liberals could succeed. In a speech before the AFL–CIO's 1969 Constitutional Convention, Rustin further rejected the Black Power position by invoking the words of labor's old friend, Woody Guthrie, declaring, "I'm sticking to the union."[30]

Likewise, Randolph told a convention of steelworkers: We must have "discussion rather than violence in solving problems faced by Negroes." He lambasted separatism as another form of segregation, which if accepted, would give white reactionaries free reign to bring back Jim Crow. For those who charged him with hypocrisy, for condemning separatism considering his stance during the WWII March on Washington movement, Randolph responded that he had opposed black nationalism since his youth. "As I opposed Marcus Garvey, so will I continue to oppose any movement that would substitute escape and withdrawal for democratic struggle." Randolph described black nationalism as an understandable "ghetto people's defense and offense mechanism against persecution, insult, oppression and poverty." Yet, he maintained, it remained counterproductive. In contrast, Randolph asserted that the NALC had sought to eradicate the basis for black nationalism by forming a coalition of black trade unionists within an integrationist framework.[31]

The fact that the House of Labor utilized black leaders to voice its criticism of Black Power deserves special attention. In one respect, it displayed labor's insecurity over its image with black workers. Faced with a growing minority constituency and intertwined with an expanding black electorate within the Democratic party, trade union leaders feared being called racist. Labor felt it could not see its claim to the title of representative of the black worker jeopardized. This was especially true for the traditionally progressive industrial unions, such as the UAW, UPWA, and ILGWU, whose nonwhite membership skyrocketed in the 1960s. Coupled with these pragmatic concerns, it should be acknowledged that more than a few labor leaders joined the labor movement because it promised more than better wages for organized labor. Even as trade union issues came to dominate the daily agenda, they maintained their hopes of rekindling their youthful dreams of creating an integrated brotherhood of workers. The civil rights movement rekindled these dreams; they felt that they were good allies in the fight for racial equality and, to a certain extent, felt betrayed by blacks who now berated them as enemies to the movement.

Ironically, in the early 1960s the AFL–CIO had clashed with those blacks who now came to its defense. It had blocked Rustin from speaking at SNCC's convention, because it considered him too radical. At the same time Meany had publicly quarreled with Randolph. Nonetheless, by the latter half of the decade the AFL–CIO gladly allowed Rustin and Randolph to speak for it.[32]

This development was due partly to the degree to which the context had changed. While the rhetoric of Black Power advocates exaggerated the faults of the social activists, the basic critique had more than a grain of truth to it. The postwar labor movement believed that it was possible to expand opportunity, to allow blacks to move up the social ladder and to assimilate into the mainstream, without having to sacrifice any of its own relatively recent gains. But radicals sensed that this view conflicted with reality. The Gomperian view of "more" for everyone, rather than redistribution of wealth or an alteration of the relationship between capital and labor, might mesh with an expanding economy. But it did not address the problems that black workers faced in a stagnating or declining one.

Perhaps because they were the first to see and feel the structural changes that were beginning to affect the economy, perhaps because they were already beginning to lose the jobs that they had only recently gained, black workers and black youths were the first to critique the Gomperian and liberal view. Put another way, since black workers were already feeling the impact of economic restructuring that would sweep across America in the 1970s and 1980s, since they worked in the plants first affected by automation, layoffs, and an increase in the speed of the line, which one Black Power group derisively labeled "niggermation," they proved receptive to Black Power's criticism of liberalism. Ironically, the social activist unions, which had stood at the front of the fight for civil rights and economic reform, bore the brunt of the Black Power critique because they were the unions that were most susceptible to the structural changes taking place. In contrast, the construction unions that had the worst records on civil rights were less affected by structural changes and thus escaped part of Black Power's wrath.[33]

An examination of two specific clashes, the first in Detroit, involving DRUM and the League of Revolutionary Black Workers and the UAW, and the second, in Ocean Hill-Brownsville, between local militants and the AFT, illuminate the divisive impact of Black Power. Both affairs pitted local activists imbued with the spirit of Black Power against traditional liberal unions, allies of the civil rights movement in the first half of the decade; both incidents resonated throughout the broader labor movement and New Left, exacerbating tensions resulting from the war, the counterculture and Black Power in general.[34]

In the wake of the Detroit riot, black autoworkers, outraged with conditions in the plant in which they worked, Chrylers' Dodge Main, in Hamtramck, Michigan, formed the Dodge Revolutionary Union movement, or DRUM. DRUM emphasized that in recent years the pace of work had increased sharply, not nearly as fast as wages, and that industrial accidents were mounting as a consequence. The union's apparent lack of concern with dangerous work conditions led DRUM to lambaste it as racist. While blacks had leveled charges of racism at companies and conservative craft unions for years, this was the first time that the UAW became the focus of such accusations. DRUM substantiated its charge by noting that 95 percent of the foreman, 100 percent of the plant supervisors, and 90 percent of the skilled tradesmen, all less dangerous and better paying jobs, were white.[35]

DRUM's rise inspired similar black caucuses in other auto plants in the Detroit region, including ELRUM, in the Eldon Avenue Gear and Axle Plant, and FRUM, in the Ford Motor Plant. Like DRUM, ELRUM and FRUM denounced the union and company as racist and focused on the "unfavorable conditions of blacks" inside the plants. In 1968, the caucuses joined together to form the League of Revolutionary Black Workers, a self-described Marxist-Leninist organization that sought to combine black nationalism with a class perspective.[36]

DRUM and the league picketed union locals and the International's headquarters. For instance, it demonstrated outside a UAW convention, which the union had convened, ironically, to consider seceding from the AFL–CIO. But DRUM's pickets forced it to adjourn.[37] DRUM and the league also challenged the top leadership in union elections, running slates against the regular or incumbent candidates. These campaigns brought to the fore another of the league's main complaints, that in addition to being underrepresented in the skilled trades, blacks rarely held positions of power within the union. Majority black locals had few if any black officials; the International had only token black representation. In one case, DRUM candidate Ronald March won a plurality of votes but lost in the run-off when the International mobilized a large contingent of retired workers, largely Polish Americans, in favor of the "loyal" slate. The International appealed to these older workers by warning that DRUM would reduce their retirement benefits.[38]

Just as Black Power gained adherents by railing at local authorities, namely the police, and the intolerable conditions of the ghetto, perpetuated by liberal governments, militant black autoworker caucuses gained support by emphasizing terrible work conditions and the maliciousness of plant authorities, especially that of foremen and local union figures. In other words, while its long-range goal was "the complete social transformation of society," the league's strength lay in addressing the particular grievances of black workers inside the plants and their union.[39]

Like the broader Black Power movement, the league utilized a revolutionary rhetoric that spoke of the need for smashing imperialism and racism. This rhetoric proved very attractive to the broader New Left, black and white. Wayne State's SDS chapter and the national office of SDS endorsed the radical black workers' struggle. The support of the former allowed John Watson, Mike Hamlin and Luke Tripp, of the league, to take control of Wayne State's student newspaper, the *South End,* which they used to publicize their cause. Likewise, independent new left magazines released one article after another in praise of the DRUM and the league. For example, one article by Eric Perkins, which appeared in *Radical America,* announced that the league displayed that "the American labor movement is now a memory." At the same time, Perkins claimed that the emergence of the league suggested that the black working class might be the "vanguard for the social revolution."[40]

Union leaders did not take the emergence of DRUM or the league lightly. Local 3's magazine, *Battleline,* described DRUM as "a racist, communist group, which was attempting to destroy the automobile industry through internal subversion." The executive board of the International sent a special letter to approximately three hundred thousand members in the Detroit area. It argued that the radical black autoworkers stood for "the complete separation of the races" and the "tactics of violence, fear and intimidation." Emil Mazey, often considered one of the most progressive officers of the International, added that the league was a bunch of "black fascists."[41]

Indeed, the entire House of Labor rallied to the UAW's side. This despite the fact that the UAW and the AFL–CIO were involved in a bitter feud, one that culminated in the UAW leaving the federation.[42] The explanation for such solidarity rests in the labor movement's fear that the league was not an isolated development. In fact, the latter years of the decade were replete with black worker protests against unions almost all of which received new left support.

For example, following a spontaneous walkout by autoworkers at Ford's plant in Mahwah, New Jersey, in early 1968, in response to the harassment of a black worker by a white foreman and the refusal of the union to intervene, black militants in the plant formed the United Black Brothers, or UBB.[43] When the company refused to punish the foreman for insulting black workers on the line, the UBB staged a slowdown and sick-in. To strengthen its position, UBB called for and received help from both radical blacks and whites. Local black nationalists, many of whom had come to the fore during the riots in Newark, championed the UBB. Fresh from their campus revolt, a contingent of Columbia University SDSers led by Mark Rudd crossed over the Hudson River to offer a hand. Even though they had little knowledge of the particulars of the protest, they were determined to display their solidarity with the black militants and opposition to the liberal union. In response, the union red-baited the UBB, claiming that student radicals had fomented the dissent due to an agenda of their own.[44]

The rise of the league and other black worker caucuses coincided with the Ocean Hill-Brownsville affair in New York City. This clash pitted black community activists against the New York Teachers Union (UFT–AFT), long considered an ally of the cause of civil rights, and probably even more than the league revealed and reinforced the rift between the New Left and labor. The UFT had played an active role in Mississippi Summer. Albert Shanker had a long record as a supporter of progressive causes as did many of the union's middle level officials. Sandra Feldman, for example, who was the UFT's field representative in Ocean Hill-Brownsville, was a member of Harlem CORE, a veteran of the "Route 40" Freedom Rides and a volunteer during the March on Washington. In fact, Feldman believes that she was sent to Ocean Hill-Brownsville because of her progressive reputation and connections to the civil rights movement.[45]

Like its better-known counterpart in Manhattan, Harlem, Ocean Hill-Brownsville, of Brooklyn, suffered from extremely poor education. Various efforts to reform the schools failed to reverse the decline in educational achievement. White flight to the suburbs undermined desegregation efforts. Hence, local black activists and educators in Harlem and Ocean Hill-Brownsville demanded that the New York schools abandon the goal of integration in favor of "community control." In so doing, the activists combined a traditional reaffirmation of the value of neighborhood schools with the Black Power ideal of racial liberation. Diane Ravitch explained: "They saw the school not just as a place to transmit skill and literacy, but as *the* main institution which might generate a new sense of self-worth and community among blacks." Or as Rhody McCoy, who became superintendent of the Ocean Hill-Brownsville district put it: "The schools were not there to teach skills . . . but to prepare a learning environment where youngsters would be educated." This entailed caring less about performing well on standardized tests and more about critical thinking. In putting forth these views McCoy drew heavily on the thoughts of Malcolm X, the ideological father of Black Power.[46]

The United Federation of Teachers initially supported the project in Ocean Hill-Brownsville. But cooperation eroded rapidly once the local activists took control of the school district's governing board and started making decisions that affected jobs and the curriculum. Union teachers argued that they were not offered a fair chance to participate in the schools' governance. Community activists countered that many of the teachers responded intransigently to change.[47]

The conflict exploded into the open in May 1968, when the Ocean Hill-Brownsville governing board ordered the involuntary transfer of thirteen teachers and five principles out of its district. The UFT protested that the teachers had been fired without due process as required by contract. Feldman remarked: "From the point of view of the union, it was a totally basic issue. . . . You're talking about nineteen people who were told in effect: 'You haven't got jobs anymore. . . . The Union really had no choice." Hence, it called a strike which lasted most of the remaining school year.[48]

The governing board, however, saw the dispute differently. It insisted that the teachers had not been fired but rather transferred to other New York City school districts, in accordance with their contract. As Rhody McCoy observed, the issue was really white control, not union control. When school resumed in the fall, the AFT called a citywide school strike to win reinstatement for its members. The strike forced hundreds of thousands of students to stay home. Union members and black activists heckled each other across picket lines and held separate marches in the streets.[49]

Not surprisingly, the entire New York political and intellectual community entered the frey. Local black community activists and their new left supporters claimed that the union's actions demonstrated its tradi-

tional autocracy. One black activists declared: "The current issue . . .
with the union is clearly one of old time boss politics. Mr. Albert
Shanker has handled himself in a manner reminiscent of the traditional
Union Boss." His were the callous actions of a power broker who would
"do everything possible to prevent us from really ever controlling the
education of our children."[50]

The UFT countered that it was a young progressive union that
historically had fought for the rights of all workers and that it too had
only just won basic rights. Most important, the teacher's union reiterated that due process, the essence of democracy, was their main concern.
Or as Shanker proclaimed: "The issue is . . . will we have a school system
in which justice, due process and dignity for teachers is possible, or will
we have a system in which any group of vigilantes can enter a school and
take it over with intimidation and threats of violence."[51]

When the UFT charged the governing board with anti-Semitism, the
divisions between the New Left and labor widened further. Among the
anti-Semitic remarks attributed to those allied with the Ocean Hill-
Brownsville groups was a poem read by Leslie Campbell, a teacher at
Junior High School 271. The poem read: "Hey Jewboy, with the yarmelke
on your head / You paleface Jewboy, I wish you were dead." UFT
officials and supporters also pointed to an offensive statement made by
an unidentified CORE spokesman: "If a black teacher says that Hitler
killed three million Jews and he's told six million, then Hitler was a
better man."[52]

The Ocean Hill-Brownsville governing board and its supporters
adamantly denied charges of anti-Semitism. The Reverend C. Herbert
Oliver, for instance, one of the founders of the project, recalled that the
ACLU as well as Jewish leaders in the district paid for an advertisement
in the *NY Times* that straightforwardly stated: "This is not an anti-
Semitic governing board." Oliver also noted that several Jewish teachers
continued to work within the district.[53]

Most new leftists shared Oliver's position. They did not see anti-
Semitism as the issue nor did they feel that the teacher's union was
acting in good faith. For instance, in a lengthy piece that appeared in
Ramparts, Sol Stern labeled the AFT's strike "a case study not only in
middle-class racism but in the degeneration of a once exciting union."
The union had run the gamut from social activist unionism to pure
bread-and-butter unionism. It no longer fought for workers at large;
instead the teacher's union acted as a protector of its middle-class
status.[54] Moving beyond words, local student radicals crossed picket lines
or scabbed to keep the Ocean Hill-Brownsville school running. They
defended their actions by claiming they were in the "vanguard of a

grassroots movement in the ghetto which would end the exploitation of the poor and oppressed."[55]

One reason that Ocean Hill-Brownsville galvanized the New Left was that the notion of community control dovetailed with its long-standing ideal of participatory democracy. Since the beginning of the decade, the New Left had called for a more decentralized and responsive political system that would involve the grass roots in the decision-making process. Like the Mississippi Freedom Democratic party, the New Left perceived the governing board of Ocean Hill-Brownsville as an example of the previously voiceless demanding a say in their lives.

Another reason for the white New Left's position was its romantic view of Black Power. More so than blacks themselves, white radicals tended to believe the rhetoric of the Panthers and other black militants. They found in it proof that a revolution was imminent and thus a rationale for their own militancy. This was tragic to the the extent that it hindered the New Left from trying to understand labor. It quit listening, because it did not see a reason to do so. Action or confrontation was necessary, but not dialogue. Indeed, throughout the Ocean Hill-Brownsville affair, labor leaders insisted that the radicals' charge that the labor movement opposed democracy was unfounded. The AFL–CIO defended the UFT on the grounds that the strike was simply a defense of "job security and the right of due process." A. Philip Randolph and a group of Negro Trade Union Leaders argued that they supported the concept of decentralization, but only within a "framework which includes due process, or substantial investment of financial resources and a genuine commitment to quality integrated education." Similarly, a coalition of New York intellectuals, headed by Michael Harrington, emphasized that the teachers' union should not discard time-honored worker rights.[56]

Considering the national scene, it was not surprising that the New Left viewed these statements as a ruse or as a sophisticated attempt to hide the real issue. As many new leftists saw it, the dispute in Ocean Hill-Brownsville was over who would have power, which included the power to control the education of black youths. For instance, Herbert Hill posited that as long as Albert Shanker controlled the educational process, he could and did restrict the range of acceptable discourse.[57] Hill substantiated this claim by reviewing an AFT reader on the introduction of African American history into the schools, officially entitled *Lesson Plans in Afro-American History.* Even though the publication of the reader represented a seeming concession to radical demands for a relevant education, Hill demonstrated that it was not. The union issued the reader only after Shanker censored its contents. Among the deleted sections was the Kerner Commission statement that the nation was

moving toward two separate societies, one black and one white. Perhaps
even more tellingly, Hill added, Shanker reduced the size of the sections
on Malcolm X and Frederick Douglass in favor of an enlarged section on
Booker T. Washington. Gone from the revised lesson plan was Douglass'
famous dictum that: "Those who profess to favor freedom yet deprecate
agitation, are men who want crops without plowing up the ground. . . .
Power concedes nothing without demand."[58]

Shanker's defenders warned that the New Left was overly enamored
with the notion of community control. They argued that the New Left
assumed that decentralization of power alone would somehow resolve
societal problems. Without adequate resources, decentralized school
districts were severely limited in the types of reforms they could enact.
Moreover, union insistence on certain fundamental rights, such as "due
process," grew out of the long-standing political and theoretical notion
that all power poses a threat to individual liberty and that certain rights
have to be protected from majority rule. Observing that the goal of
decentralized education received support from the far right as well as
the left, A. Philip Randolph emphasized the dangers inherent in extol-
ling local or "home" rule without individual protection. "If due process
is not won in Ocean Hill-Brownsville," Randolph rhetorically inquired,
"what will prevent white community groups from firing black teachers
or white teachers with liberal views? What will prevent local Birchites
and Wallacites from taking over?"[59]

The New Left tended to ignore or downplay this issue, in part because
they saw liberalism as an even greater threat than the far Right. Indeed,
they tended to feel that a revolution was imminent and that there was
little difference between the far Right and liberalism. Both black and
white new leftists had moved from a position in favor of fostering
coalition with liberals to one of confrontation. Paradoxically, some new
leftists even viewed right-wing backlash as a welcome sight. They argued
that Wallace's strength in the North confirmed the bankruptcy of
liberalism. They also assumed that the New Left could win the support
of alienated workers, in other words Wallace's supporters, in the wake of
liberalism's collapse.[60]

To labor's credit, it did not adopt a reactionary stance, such as that
espoused by Wallace. Labor leaders and black moderates insisted that
liberal policies had improved the lot of the black masses and would
continue to do so in the future. They maintained that black nationalism,
even if emotionally appealing, would fail to alleviate the woes of poor
blacks. Yet labor too somewhat misjudged the situation. They did not
clearly see how vulnerable liberalism was and thus responded to the
New Left's attacks with counterattacks. Indeed, perhaps the most signifi-

cant and tragic part of the emergence of Black Power was that it prodded both the New Left and labor to adopt unrealistic views of their times. Black Power fed the New Left's belief that a revolution was imminent. It also redirected labor's attention from its traditional foes, on the right, to new ones on the left. This was readily apparent in Ocean Hill-Brownsville, as the two traded punches like two boxers in a championship fight. Before either movement stopped confronting the other, the New Right had emerged the victor. Ironically it did so to a large degree by presenting liberals and new leftists as interchangeable, both equally responsible for society's troubles and turmoil.

5

The Counterculture

In its original form, the protest song "Which Side Are You On?" as written by Florence Reese, featured the brutality of Harlan County's mine operators, especially J. H. Blair:

> They say in Harlan County
> There are no neutrals there
> You'll either be a union man
> Or a thug for J. H. Blair.

In 1961, James Farmer and Freedom Riders revised the tune, focusing on their new foe, Mississippi governor Ross Barnett.

> They say in Hinds County
> no neutrals have they met
> You're either for the Freedom Ride
> or you 'tom for Ross Barnett.

In 1962, the Albany movement made Chief Pritchett the antihero of its version of the song. And a year later Birmingham demonstrators satirically singled out segregationist governor George Wallace:

> I heard that Governor Wallace
> Just up and lost his mind
> And he bought a case of Man Tan
> And joined the picket line.

In all of the different renditions, the chorus brought the same rhetorical rejoinder: "Which side are you on, boy? Which side are you on?"[1]

At the same time as new leftists in the South were singing "Which Side Are You On?" left-leaning students in the North were flocking to coffee houses where they listened to Joan Baez, Bob Dylan, and other "guerrilla minstrels," to borrow Wade Hampton's terminology. These performers drew on a tradition of protest that was intertwined with the labor movement. Bob Dylan, for example, heroized Woody Guthrie, the balladeer of the Old Left. He came to New York in the early 1960s to visit Guthrie who was slowly dying in a rest home in nearby Morristown. His early songs displayed his affinity for Guthrie and more broadly the cultural continuity of protest movements, running from Wobbly balladeer Joe Hill, through Woody Guthrie and Pete Seeger.[2]

Taken together, these developments revealed that in the early 1960s, the New Left's cultural leanings did not alienate it from labor. On the contrary, a strain of folk culture, especially folk music, played a special role in bridging the gap between the two. Civil rights protesters relied heavily on folk tunes to rally the local populace and to maintain their spirits in the face of repression. Often they sang updated versions of old labor tunes that invoked a message of solidarity. "We Shall Overcome," the anthem of the early civil rights movement, had been a prominent labor tune in the 1940s. The CIO Food and Tobacco Workers sang it on the picket line, where Zilphia Horton, song-leader of the Highlander Folk School, first heard it. In turn new leftists learned it from Guy Carawan or from Pete Seeger and other folk singers who visited HFS. Other labor songs that civil rights activists revised and updated included: "We Shall Not Be Moved"; "Hallelujah I'm a Travellin," from the Wobbly's "Hallelujah I'm a Bum"; "The Movement's Moving On," from "Solidarity Forever," itself from "John Brown's Body"; and "Freedom Train a 'Comin," from "Union Train a Coming." At the same time it was not uncommon to hear peace protesters in the North sing "Where Have All the Flowers Gone" or various anthems made famous by Peter Seeger and other balladers of the Old Left.[3]

By the late 1960s, however, the cultural leanings of the New Left had taken a dramatic turn. Instead of serving as an intergenerational vehicle of unity, culture became a source of antagonism or discontinuity. The blossoming of rock music, long hair, sexual promiscuity, and drug use, symbolized perhaps by Bob Dylan's turn to rock music at the Newport Jazz Festival in the fall of 1965, signaled the break with an earlier tradition of protest. (Another symbolic break came at U.C. Berkeley in 1966 when antiwar protesters broke from singing "Solidarity Forever" and started to sing the Beatle's "Yellow Submarine," a song that many felt touted the use of psychedelic drugs.) The counterculture of the latter 1960s rejected the cultural authority of the Old Left. New leftists poked fun at "folk" in general and folk tunes in particular. Directly and indirectly new leftists criticized the values and culture of middle America, of which labor was part. In place of middle-American culture they adopted the counterculture, which was not only different from the Old

Left's folk culture, but which was anathema to the bulk of the House of
Labor.[4]

For example, new versions of "Which Side Are You On?" appeared,
which unlike those of the early 1960s denigrated the labor movement.
One version turned the song on its head. Instead of J. H. Blair, AFL–CIO
president George Meany was asked which side he was on:

> George Meany was a worker
> But he ain't no worker no more
> Instead he helps the Government
> To stir up hate and war
> Which Side Are You on George?
> Which Side Are You on?

One other version of the same song did not explicitly challenge the labor
movement, but by so distorting the lyrics it ridiculed the labor imperative of the Old Left:

> My father owns a drugstore
> He's in the bourgeoisie
> And when he comes home at night
> He brings a drug to me
> Which drug are you on, boys?
> Which drug are you on?[5]

In fact, the counterculture probably antagonized workers more than the
New Left's politics. Its symbols—long hair, drugs, permissive sexual
mores, informal and unkempt clothing—united politicized youths with
apolitical members of their generation but antagonized older Americans;
it increased the size and solidarity of the antiwar and black power
movements while alienating workers. Labor leaders and the working
class came to share a common view of the New Left that identified
radical politics with deviant cultural behavior. They associated the
counterculture with opposition to the war in Vietnam and militant black
politics and came to distrust new left politics as they were repulsed by
new left culture.

Conversely, the New Left's estrangement from middle- American
culture exacerbated its divorce from the House of Labor.[6] New leftists
disdained America's outer-directed orientation, its mass consumerism
and homogenized culture, and they considered the American worker
the consummate middle American. Some working-class youths, turned
new leftists, displayed a subtle anger with the Old Left and to a certain
extent the labor movement for selling out. As they saw it, the Old Left
and labor movement were guilty of accepting the "postwar deal," whereby

Americans produced and consumed more and more goods, lived in increasingly look-a-like homes, and accepted more mundane and less fulfilling jobs, all in exchange for better wages that allowed them to buy even more of the same. Put another way, the New Left came of age enjoying the benefits of abundance, yet rejected its birthright as insufficient.

The counterculture was even more divisive because labor leaders had a great deal of difficulty fathoming its critique. They felt that they were being blamed for having succeeded. Having come of age in an era in which poverty was a reality of life, trade unionists were not about to jettison their material gains for some utopian vision of a more fulfilling, less alienating life, especially when the New Left's utopia transgressed some of the oldest and most sacred sexual and racial taboos. Conservative politicians and opinion makers added to the divisive impact of the counterculture by skillfully playing on its infantile and escapist side, rather than examining its broader critique of mass society.

But why the shift? Why were new leftists attracted to the counterculture? Why didn't they build on the Old Left or folk culture? Most simply, folk culture ultimately proved inadequate to the urges and needs of the New Left, particularly those under thirty. The New Left perceived alienation as the main problem, not exploitation or material depravation. While some old leftists focused on the alienation of work and the need to alter the ownership of production, or called for exchanging alienating work for more and more hours of leisure, new leftists maintained that the workplace or the economic sphere were secondary and that leisure-time in itself did not provide authenticity. Indeed, they argued that in modern American society leisure in itself was alienating. The key was to "liberate" the individual, or to link the personal and the political. Political changes would have to take place alongside personal ones or even possibly personal changes would have to precede political ones. As Theodore Roszak, who coined the phrase "counterculture" wrote: "There is a revolution coming. . . . It will not be like revolutions of the past. It will originate with the individual and with culture, and it will change the political structure only as a higher act."[7]

Such a vision, even if not fully articulated, had been part of the New Left since its birth. The "Port Huron Statement" announced that SDS sought to create a "meaning in life that is personally authentic." Mario Savio in his famous "End of History" address, delivered during the Free Speech movement, implored his fellow students to combat the depersonalized society that they faced. "America is becoming ever more the utopia of sterilized, automated contentment . . . for which American students now prepare. . . . This chrome-plated consumers' paradise would have us grow up to be well-behaved children. But an important minority of men and women coming to the front today have shown that they will die rather than be standardized . . . and irrelevant." In the same vein, Eldridge Cleaver, the cultural minister of the Black Panther party, declared: "I had to find out who I am and who I want to be, what kind of man I should be, and what I could do to become the best of which I am capable." Yet it was not until the mid–1960s that this vision, when coupled with several external developments, such as that in the rock music world, became manifest.[8]

Insight into the nature and development of the counterculture and its break with the past can be garnered through a brief examination of the life and work of beat poet Allen Ginsberg. Ginsberg was a transitional figure in the history of the left. Along with other beat artists he helped give birth to the counterculture. Unlike many other beats, however, he became part of the New Left, taking part in various antiwar protests and acting as a mentor and inspiration to numerous political and cultural rebels during the 1960s (and after). Ginsberg grew up in the political and cultural milieu of the Old Left. His father, a Russian emigre, was a socialist and a poet. His mother was a communist—she once headed a local chapter of the CPUSA. Both lived a somewhat bohemian life, especially his mother, and knew several prominent radical-artistes, such as Max Eastman.[9]

As a youth Ginsberg attended communist-run summer camps, learned left-wing songs, like "On the Line," and campaigned for a labor candidate for congress. When he departed for Columbia University in the early 1940s, Ginsberg dreamed of serving the working class, perhaps by becoming a labor lawyer. Yet, for a variety of reasons, he soon found this dream, which was a combination of old left dogma and his parents' goal of social mobility, unfulfilling. His homosexuality, of which he became consciously aware while in college, only left him further estranged from both mainstream America and the Old Left. Neither allowed him to transgress the sexual norms of American society. Hence, Ginsberg began experimenting with a variety of alternative lifestyles. He sought to experience life in a way that would be personally meaningful.[10]

Ginsberg's and the beats' rebellion against normative behavior did not represent an explicit rejection of the Old Left or of the working class. Yet it did signify an implicit critique of the old left vision of serving the working class—of becoming a labor lawyer. In Ginsberg's estimation, America was in the need of a spiritual revolution. For him, chanting mantras or taking drugs was just as political or revolutionary an act, if not more, as joining workers on the picket line. Clearly the relative affluence of the 1950s, which allowed workers to become middle American in their lifestyle, contributed to Ginsberg's turn away from his parent's faith in old left doctrines. But just as clearly, Ginsberg felt that all Americans, including poor and exploited workers, were in need of something more than merely better material circumstances. As he told an interviewer in 1963: "Somebody has got to sit in the British museum again like Marx and figure out a new system, a new blueprint. Another century has gone, technology has changed everything completely, so it's time for a new utopian system."[11]

While neither Ginsberg or his fellow beats retreated to the British Museum—Ginsberg journeyed to the Far East to study different eastern religions—several philosophers were attempting to meet Ginsberg's challenge of developing a new philosophy. Most notably, Herbert Marcuse argued that society artificially perpetuated repression. In a society of scarcity, such repression served a purpose. But in the present system it merely upheld the ruling class's dominance. In both *One Dimensional Man* and *Eros and Civilization,* Marcuse called for a "great refusal," that is, a rejection of repression and traditional taboos by the people. By unleashing eros (which many read as sexual desires) individuals could achieve a fulfilling or less alienating life.[12]

Paul Goodman, another of the New Left's mentors, likewise railed at the dehumanizing nature of American culture. He explicitly attacked the American dream as long as it was defined as more and better consumer goods. If the ultimate reward for hours of work on an assembly line, or some other mundane job, was just a bigger refrigerator or automobile, Goodman argued, it was self-evident why so many youths "dropped out."[13]

Robinson Lillienthal, son of a Jewish survivor of Nazi Germany, a Quaker, and later a SDS radical at Reed College, provided a less sophisticated explanation of the advantages of the counterculture. Paralleling Marcuse's and Goodman's contention that American culture left individuals with a sense of void, Lillienthal found rock music and drugs enthralling, especially on a gut or emotional level. Like Allen Ginsberg, he waxed laconic about the Wobblies, the Scottsboro boys, or other old left icons, but these traditions could not compare to the exhilaration that the counterculture offered. They simply did not address the personal part of the revolution that the New Left sought.[14]

In his semiautobiographical examination of the 1960s, Abe Peck, editor of the major underground newspaper the Chicago *Seed,* offered a similar appraisal. "Born in 1945," nearly twenty years after Ginsberg, Peck recounted, "I'd grown up in a working-class Bronx neighborhood that assumed Judaism, the Democratic party, and college. My dad routed trucks and pushed skids in a book bindery. Mom cooked great roast chicken." Like Ginsberg's parents, they were immigrants who, in Peck's words, "wanted their son to do well in the Promised Land of America." Peck graduated from Bronx Science High School and New York University. But then, in 1965, as he put it, he found himself without a job or a girl. To avoid being sent to Vietnam, he joined the Army reserves and found himself splitting time between the Eleventh Special Forces and the fledgling hip scene on the Lower East Side. Life consisted of the "Army and the counterculture," Peck recalled. "It was no contest which lifestyle I liked better."[15]

From 1965 on through the early 1970s, Peck devoted himself to the cultural and political revolution. He rejected traditional values, lifestyles, and society. While his parents wanted him to use his education to escape the material deprivation they had known, he lived like a bohemian in a barren tenement apartment in the very neighborhood that poor Jews had struggled to leave behind. Besides being more fun, Peck chose this alternative route because it was "a chance for me to get back at parents, government, cops, society, culture, you name it," to explicitly reject the American dream as middle America defined it.[16]

Jerry Rubin, who along with Abbie Hoffman symbolized the marriage between the New Left and the counterculture, similarly displayed his estrangement from the values of his working-class parents.[17]

> I am a child of Amerika. If I'm ever sent to Death Row for my revolutionary "crimes," I'll order as my last meal: a hamburger, french fries and a Coke. . . . I collected baseball players' cards when I was a kid and wanted to play second base for the Cincinnati Reds. . . . My father drove a truck delivering bread and later became an organizer in the Bakery Drivers Union. . . . My mother had a college degree and played the piano. . . . I dropped-out of the White race and the Amerikan nation. I dig being free. I like getting high. I don't own a suit or tie. I live for the revolution. I'm a yippie! I am an orphan of Amerika. Fuck Amerika.

While differences existed between the New Left and counterculture, most Americans, including labor, perceived them as the same. Before the term *hippie* became prominent, labor leaders commonly used the word "peacenik" in their diatribes against student activists. This demonstrated their conceptualization of two distinct movements, the beatniks and the peace movement, as identical. Writing for the *American Federationist,* Tom Kahn, a one-time SDS member, and director of LID at the time, explicitly joined the two, stating that "more and more," SDS was being "taken over by hippies and yippies." Photographs that accompanied Kahn's article bolstered his argument. One showed a young man with shoulder-length hair and a tie-die shirt protesting in the streets of Chicago. Joe Kelley, a construction worker in New York City, observed that peace protesters, Viet Cong flag waving youths, long-haired boys, and naked girls were a single entity. Kelley's fellow workers, who went on an anti-antiwar rampage in New York City, expressed the same opinion, screaming: "Get the Hippies. . . . Get the Traitors." The *NY Times* observed that long-haired men were singled out for assault by these same workers. Similarly, well-known longshoreman/writer Eric Hoffer lashed out against disruptive youths. In his own words, workers stood for "horse sense, traditional values and honest sweat-making labor," and against "absurdist America . . . LSD and happenings."[18]

Even television shows, movies and popular writings on the working class reinforced such negative attitudes toward new left culture. Archie Bunker, the lead character in the popular show, "All in the Family," first aired on 12 January 1971, was the consummate blue-collar worker who hated long-haired youth protestors. Archie railed against his "egg-head" son-in-law Mike, who according to Archie, wasted his time in college protesting against the Vietnam War and paraded around in long-hair. The movie *Joe,* focused on a foundry worker who despised "liberals, blacks, dissenters and hippies." Even if Archie and Joe were the creations of Hollywood and not real workers, select evidence suggests that workers identified with what they saw on the television and movie screens and perhaps even modified their behavior to conform to it.[19]

Moreover, media versions of new leftists and workers reinforced divisions between the New Left and labor. After all, in the latter part of the 1960s, American workers and new leftists rarely met directly. The antiwar and black power movements remained largely abstract movements to working men and women. They entered working-class homes and communities primarily through the media or popular culture. Most demonstrations took place on college campuses or in city centers, such as the mall in Washington, D.C, or on Fifth Avenue in New York City, not in working-class neighborhoods. Urban riots struck closer to working-class communities, but generally remained contained within minority ghettos. Thus worker attitudes toward the politics of the New Left were inevitably fairly inchoate.[20]

This is not to argue that the antiwar movement and Black Power did not affect workers. But the counterculture was slightly different in that it directly entered working-class homes or threatened to do so. All American parents during the 1960s and early 1970s had to face the cultural changes that were taking place. Millions of youths listened to rock 'n roll music, experimented with drugs, new hair styles and clothing, and freer sexual behavior.

Some studies have argued that upper middle-class and middle-class youths were more receptive to the counterculture than working-class youths. William O'Neill contended that the counterculture created a greater cleavage between social classes than it did between generations, in spite of the much heralded "generation gap." "In Middle America especially, it was hated and feared," O'Neill wrote. "The result was a national division between the counterculture and those adults who admired or tolerated it—upper middle-class professionals and intellectuals in the Northeast particularly—and the silent majority of workers and Middle Americans who didn't."[21]

Yet, a more careful analysis of the poll data reveals that even if they were not originally receptive to the counterculture, by 1971 white working-class youths adopted views more in line with their age cohorts than with their parents. O'Neill based his argument largely on a Daniel Yankelovich study conducted for *Fortune* in 1969. Two follow-up studies, one by Jeffrey Main for *Fortune* and the other by Yankelovich himself, found that by early 1971 youths of all classes were increasingly calling for a change of values, a position not shared by their elders. "Parents disagree widely with their children on matters of sex, religion, dress, patriotism and so forth," wrote Main. Differences over cultural attitudes, as opposed to political ones, were becoming more marked with each passing month, concluded Yankelovich.[22]

At the same time statistical studies demonstrated an increasing antipathy for the counterculture, or at least its symbols, among the populace at large. Nearly all polls showed that long hair, drugs, advocacy of sexual freedom, and rock 'n roll music polarized Americans. A 1968 Gallup poll asked if America was "getting better or worse off in terms of morals?" Eighty-one percent of the manual workers who responded stated that morals were getting worse; only seven percent felt morals were improving. Professionals and businessmen, white-collar workers and farmers had only slightly less pessimistic views. A 1971 Roper study found that Americans considered drug abuse to be the nation's "number 1" problem, more than the war in Vietnam, racial tensions, or the

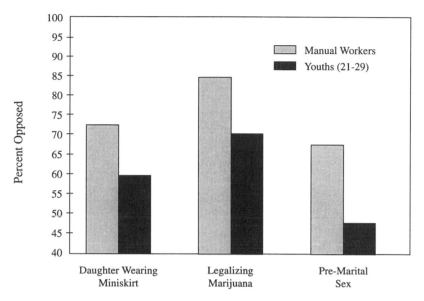

Figure 2. Divergent Mores and Values

economy. Only youths deviated from this view. While activists touted drugs as conscious-raising instruments—John Sinclair stated that "LSD brought everything into focus . . . until we started eating all the acid we couldn't figure out what was happening"—most Americans perceived drugs as physically and psychologically dangerous. In 1970, while a majority of union members opposed Nixon's bombing of Cambodia and the rampage of construction workers in New York City, a whopping 80 percent opposed legalizing marijuana. A study of attitudes toward the miniskirt revealed a similar trend. Manual workers and parents did not think that their daughters should wear one; youths found the new fashion much less offensive (see figure 2).[23]

Moreover, even if working-class youths were not attracted to the counterculture, working-class parents feared that their children would be attracted to it in the near future. The fact that thousands of working-class youths entered college for the first time in the 1960s only increased their fears. So too did a changing occupational structure that insured that a substantial number of the sons and daughters of the working class would not move into the trades of their parents.[24]

What O'Neill and other commentators who emphasized the working class's dislike for the counterculture may have sensed was that while the middle and upper class disapproved of the counterculture they did not articulate their feelings with as much vehemence as the working class.

The former felt secure enough to withstand the counterculture's onslaught against traditional values. Indeed, enough proved willing to flirt with some deviant or bohemian behavior to lead well-respected commentators to believe that they approved of it.[25]

In contrast, older workers were insecure about their social and material status. Inflation, structural changes that they did not understand, and the civil rights and sexual revolutions threatened to undermine their way of life. As a result, George Fackre observed, to overcome an otherwise alienating life, workers fell back upon their family, ethnic community, religion, and fraternal societies. Culture and family provided a "balm for his woes" generated by an impersonal workplace. While the New Left agreed that society was alienating it deplored the call for a retreat to traditional values. The New Left wanted to throw out the baby with the bath water. To overcome alienation, it proposed transforming American culture.[26]

The counterculture's critique of materialism and hard work amplified labor's negative reaction to it. Even as material conditions improved in America, workers continually faced the threat of slipping back into poverty. Memories of the Great Depression augmented their fear of not having adequate food, clothing, or shelter, not to mention health care or education. Yet the counterculture denied the necessity of work and mocked materialism. As viewed by the mass media, hippies withdrew from consumer society, lived from hand to mouth like gypsies and called on the rest of America to join with them in their rebellion against the worship of material goods and the boredom of routine work. Rather than struggling to get ahead, the counterculture promoted dropping out. "Screw work," announced Jerry Rubin, "we want to know ourselves." Or as Abbie Hoffman put it: "We must abolish work and all the drudgery it represents."[27]

Labor spokesman responded that this philosophy stank of elitism. As the *AFL–CIO News* declared, new leftists never had to work for a living and continued to live off their parents. "They have all 'had it made" in economic terms." The Teamster paper expressed the same view in a defense of the collective bargaining emphasis of trade unions. "There is too much immediacy to human needs in the past and the present to prove the Hippies are wrong. . . . Ask most wage earners if recent . . . gains have been meaningless." And ILWU president Harry Bridges, a long-time radical who joined with the New Left in its condemnation of the Vietnam War, lambasted student radicals for depicting trade unionists as "well-fed, affluent . . . fat cats." "I don't know any rich workers," exclaimed Bridges. And those labor officials who had begun to enjoy some security had fought for what they had.[28]

Whereas past bohemian and/or radical movements had rebelled against the mediocrity of American society and culture, they tended not to fault labor. They focused on the predominance of greed and materialism among the upper and middle classes, not the working class. They assumed that the working class did not share the materialism that the middle class worshipped. In turn, bohemians often sought to overcome America's cultural incipience and the oppression of workers at the same time. For example, in the early twentieth century, Greenwich Village radicals rejected the genteel tradition of the upper and middle classes and fought to replace it with a socialist society.

But the New Left was different. Since activists of the 1960s did not consider workers oppressed, especially organized ones, they did not perceive traditional socialism as an adequate response to America's problems. "Marxism is irrelevant to the U.S.A., as irrelevant as Capitalism," proclaimed Abbie Hoffman. I care more about the Marxism of Groucho than Karl, chimed Jerry Rubin.[29]

Indeed, when asked to compare the Greenwich Village radicals of the early 1900s to the New Left, Max Eastman, founder of the *Masses,* the avant-garde magazine of the earlier era, singled out the latter's absence of a socialist bent as the major difference. "The bohemian wing of the bourgeois, sons and daughters of the well-to-do, have no real class affiliation and no alliance with the working class," Eastman noted. "The mood of militancy is the same . . . and so is the general rejection of convention. But many of today's youths are caught up on trivialities."[30]

While the elitism of the counterculture offended labor leaders and workers, the symbols and images that prominent new leftists heralded outraged them. Images and symbols had grown tremendously in importance in modern America. Television and glossy popular magazines had the knack of taking a few visual images or phrases and casting them as the essence of the New Left. Children of the first generation of television, many new leftists had learned the techniques of communicating through media and reasoned that they could recruit others to the New Left by exploiting the powerful symbols of rock 'n roll and drugs. Proper use of symbols, they figured, would unite apathetic and politicized youths, or the heads and the fists, as Lawrence Leamer has called them. As Jerry Rubin observed, in reference to the significance of long hair, it "tells people where we stand on Vietnam, Wallace, campus disruption, dope.

We're living tv commercials for the revolution." In contrast, Rubin added that "young kids identify short hair with authority, discipline, unhappiness, boredom, rigidity." While some politically inclined new leftists criticized Rubin's and Abbie Hoffman's reliance on symbols and images, with the Progressive Labor party taking the extreme position of disdaining all forms of cultural deviance, this fact escaped the notice of labor.[31]

By the end of the decade, opening political rallies with rock music or making radical remarks at rock concerts became common fare. In so doing, new leftists attracted normally apolitical youths to their demonstrations, indoctrinated audiences already committed to the counterculture, but not necessarily to radical politics, and added to the solidarity of the youth movement. At Woodstock, for example, the superstar English band the Who disdained songs with a political message in favor of escapist music. But Crosby, Stills, Nash & Young, Joan Baez, and Country Joe and the Fish placed politicized music at the center of the countercultural event of the decade. The latter's rendition of "Feel Like I'm Fixin to Die Rag," which followed the famous "FUCK" cheer, for a moment, transformed an escapist concert into an antiwar protest with the following words:

> One, two, three
> What are we fighting for?
> Don't ask me, I don't give a damn
> Next stop is Vietnam.
> And it's five, six, seven
> Open up those pearly gates.
> Well it ain't to late to be wondering why.
> Whoopee we're all going to die.

Media coverage of the concert, which highlighted scenes of naked men and women and clips from Country Joe and the Fish's famous song, reinforced the public's image of the counterculture and the New Left as one in the same.[32]

The significance of symbols and style became especially apparent during several campus rebellions during the latter part of the 1960s. For example, at Columbia University radicals occupied University buildings because of the school's gym and defense research policies. But, once inside, they concentrated at least as much on developing "beloved communities" as on the university's policies. One study of the Columbia revolt observed that those who occupied University buildings "shared the 'commune' spirit." Students reveled in the "collectivism" of their revolt. One participant recalled, "Everything belonged to everybody:

the building was 'liberated.'. . . Couples slept together in plain view, nobody cared. . . ." Shortly before the New York City police violently cleared the protesters from the buildings, campus chaplain William Starr married two of the radicals. The groom wore a Nehru coat; the bride was adorned in white dungarees and tennis shoes. After exchanging vows, Starr declared them "children of the new age."[33]

Yet, whereas the radicals celebrated the "groovyness" of the revolt, older socialists and much of the rest of America viewed the students' antics with disdain. Daniel Bell, for example, emphasized that the demonstrators literally trashed the main administration building, wantonly destroyed professors' research notes and took infantile pleasure in using swear words. "Don't underestimate the relationship between litter and liberty at Columbia," Bell wrote. "Until last Tuesday . . . students paid rent, kept house rules and took exams. Then the rebels arrived. . . . They ransacked files . . . plastered walls . . . raided the administrative offices (the psychological equivalent of robbing your mother's purse)."[34]

Likewise, a study of a student uprising at the University of Southern California revealed that the cultural aura of the protest became at least as important as any overt political statements or stances, to both the participating students and diffident public. In a word, the demonstration was a big "trip." The trip was fanciful and liberating to the demonstrators but frightening and disagreeable to most working and adult Americans.[35]

The sexual connotations of so many of the counterculture's symbols made them that much more threatening. Long hair, drugs, and rock 'n roll music either truly challenged the traditional relationship between the sexes, or were perceived as clashing with them. Long hair did not mesh with the "proper" image or role of men. Parents even wondered if their sons were gay. Drugs lowered inhibitions and according to drug gurus, such as Timothy Leary, improved sex, to the delight of youths but to the chagrin of their parents. Rock 'n roll did much the same, especially the raucous songs of the Rolling Stones.[36]

One can only imagine parents' reaction to Janis Joplin. They could insist that their own daughters were not like her. But in reality, Joplin's childhood resembled that of millions of American girls. She grew up in Port Arthur Texas, a hard-working and insulated oil town. She had few peculiar habits, belonged to the slide rule and art clubs and earned decent grades. But by 1968, Joplin was a wild woman, a rock 'n roll star, who wore long frizzy hair, beads and bracelets, wire-rimmed glasses, and slinky clothing. She became a drug addict and flaunted her sexuality. True, Elvis Presley's contortions had raised similar fears in the 1950s, but Americans more easily absorbed his bad boy image, and the pronounced sexuality of a man, than they did Joplin's affront to a women's "proper" place.[37]

Indeed, surveys and polls demonstrated that American workers were terrified by the cultural challenges embodied by Joplin. A 1972 Gallup Poll of Minnesotans found overwhelming unfavorable attitudes toward homosexuals and pornography among every subgroup except students. Seventy-one percent of the public in the same year felt that family life was in deep trouble. And thirty-two percent blamed drugs or permissive attitudes toward sex as the single greatest reason for the demise of the family. Twenty-nine percent blamed the family troubles on permissive parents. Indeed, fifty-two labor press editors who attended a special conference on the "generation gap," asserted that "today's youth problem has come about because of the breakdown of the once bounding family structure," as well as the disappearance of community.[38]

Black radicals, who had their own set of cultural symbols, sent shock waves through the labor movement as well. John Lopez's critical report on the Black Power Convention in Oakland began with a description of the bizarre Afro hair styles and clothing of those in attendance. Clenched black fists affronted labor's assimilative sensibilities. Jimi Hendrix's psychedelic rendition of the "Star Spangled Banner" seemed crazy, if not unpatriotic, to those accustomed to hearing the regular version of the song before a baseball game. And the championing of interracial sex sent working-class (and professional) parents into a frenzy. A mere 2 percent approved of interracial dating in a 1968 poll. The same sample of individuals overwhelmingly felt that blacks unfairly faced discrimination.[39]

Put another way, one of the things that made the counterculture so divisive or explosive was that it reflected and reinforced the collapse of racial and sexual segregation. Previously confined to "colored" radio stations and "uptown" music halls and dives, rock became the "new generations'" sound. Along with rock music, youths dabbled into drugs, like marijuana, which had existed for years but rarely crossed the boundaries of the black ghettos. The introduction of the birth control pill for commercial sale, in 1960, allowed women to escape from the worry of unwanted pregnancy and to openly engage in free sexuality (or at least approve of such practice). "Free love" became the countercultural equivalent to "Freedom Now!" or "Out Now!" The popular slogan "Make love not war" depicted the link between New Left politics and the counterculture. In sum, new leftists championed behavior that had been previously confined to blacks or placed off limits for women. Tearing down racial and sexual taboos, advocates of the counterculture proclaimed, would produce licentious results for all.[40] Yet, rather than seeing these developments as portents of liberation, most working-class Americans responded with fear and clung to their traditional values.

In fact, not only did they cling to their traditional values, American workers championed their own set of symbols, most notably the American flag. Nothing angered them more than attacks on the American flag by antiwar activists. As journalist Thomas Williams discovered while writing a feature story on construction worker rampage in May 1970, the workers were "not pro-war" or against demonstrations, or students. They simply wanted "the flag of the United States of America to be respected. . . . It is the flag that matters most, the palpable symbol of what he wants his country to be." The Carpenter's Union put this even more strongly:

> In this period of public protest it seems fashionable for the immature and the rebels in our midst to burn draft cards and deface flags, in public defiance of . . . the "masses" "the Establishment" or whatever else the wild-haired far-leftists care to call those of us who don't grow beards, dream in LSD or flake out in marijuana smoke. So-called artists drape models in the nation's banner . . . protesting American intervention in Viet Nam. . . . The Flag is the visual representation of the nation as a whole, and no one should be allowed to desecrate that emblem. The bantlings should be invited to try their hands at desecrating a communist flag inside China and see how long they would keep their necks . . . literally! . . . In this 190th anniversary of Flag Day, we urge all to rally round the flag in its time of distress.[41]

Workers also had their own set of pro-American songs, such as "Green Beret" and "Okie from Muskogee," which unlike the antiwar tunes, heralded the flag, the family, and manliness. Not suprisingly, new leftists were nearly as offended by these symbols as workers were of theirs.

A brief examination of the 1968 Chicago riot and reactions to it sheds further light on the importance of culture. The significance of Chicago was not accidental. New leftists and old guard Democrats recognized its symbolic importance. In the center of Chicago stood Mayor Richard J. Daley, the last of the great urban-machine bosses with his ethnic working class and trade union base. In David Farber's estimation, Daley stood for politics as usual—stability, loyalty, protection of property, and law and order. The most visible representatives of Daley's machine were the police, termed the *blue meanies* by some new leftists. In the New Left's eyes the police personified all that it detested. They were

dehumanized, detached, and latently repressive. In contrast, Daley saw
the police as representatives of the people and the New Left as a media
creation that received undue attention at the expense of the plain folk in
the wards.[42]

By the time the convention took place, Hubert Humphrey's nomination was a foregone conclusion. Hence, the battle between Daley and
the New Left was not over political particulars but rather over images.
Yippie leaders Jerry Rubin and Abbie Hoffman initiated the call for
protests, announcing they would hold a "Festival of Life" as opposed to a
"Festival of Death." They believed that they could make a revolution by
simulating a revolution that looked like fun. The simulation would play
to the mass media and through the mass media it would be made
available to apolitical youths. Realizing that victory could not be won
through a vote of the delegates, Chicago protest coordinator Rennie
Davis proclaimed the "MOBE battle plan is to raise cain outside the
convention hall." Challenging Daley to unleash his police, Tom Hayden
declared that sustained protest would " 'delegitimate' the Democratic
party." The Yippies added that they "wanted the tear gas to get so heavy
that the reality was tear gas" so as "to create a situation in which the
federal government and the United States would self-destruct." In a
moment of bravado, which hinted that the activists had begun to believe
their own threats, Dick Gregory forewarned that unless racial conditions
improved he would "make it possible for the Democratic party to hold
its convention here [Chicago] only over my dead body." And Black
Panther Bobby Seale showed up in the midst of the demonstrations to
notify authorities that "in any revolutions developing out of the Chicago
gathering," blacks would carry guns.[43]

The coordinators of the Chicago protest enjoyed their greatest success when they made an entirely symbolic threat. Before the convention,
Rubin and Hoffman warned that they were going to dump LSD into the
city's water supply. Even though they never had any intention of carrying out this prank, Chicago authorities took them seriously. In general,
however, Mayor Daley did not wince over the New Left's threats. He
knew he had the superior forces. His objective was theatrical as well. He
wanted to show to the nation that mainstream America was still in full
control, that law and order reined.[44]

George Meany's vision mirrored Daley's. "We in the AFL–CIO have
the utmost faith in the United States, in the American political system,
and in the ability of that system to meet any and all challenges," Meany
declared shortly before the convention. In contrast to the New Left,
Meany concluded, "We are unashamedly devoted to the American
system." Aptly summarizing the significance of Meany's stance, James

Gannon of the *Wall Street Journal* wrote, "George Meany is staking the future of the AFL–CIO on the gamble that 'old politics' is not dead."[45]

In terms of numbers, Chicago was one of the smaller demonstrations of the latter half of the 1960s. (More people attended Chicago White Sox games that week than demonstrated in the streets.) But that was not the image that Americans received on their television screens, and in their newspapers and magazines. Rather, Americans witnessed a showdown, a bloody melee and ultimately a rout of the New Left by the Chicago police.[46]

Despite their wounds, most new leftists figured that the Chicago campaign was successful. Having correctly predicted that Daley would unleash a rein of terror, they assumed that the public would side with them. As one-time SDS president Carl Davidson wrote: "The message [still using mass communication terms] of the week was of an America ruled by force. This was a big victory." Likewise black activist Julius Lester reported that the demonstration was "reminiscent" of the early civil right's protests, inducing that it had forced liberals to re-evaluate "how much [more] they can continue to work within the system."[47]

Just as important, new leftists concluded that they had won the support of working-class youths in Chicago. At one point during the demonstration a scruffy motorcyclist volunteered to act as Jerry Rubin's body guard. "Damn, I've got a genuine biker [meaning working-class youth] who's been radicalized," thought Rubin. Not until after the convention did Rubin learn that the biker was an undercover police agent. Indeed, a year later SDS organized another round of protests in Chicago. Advertised as SDS's "Days of Rage," these protests saw small groups of militants rampage through the streets of Chicago, smashing store windows, taunting police and jamming up streets. Like the earlier protests, the objective of these was symbolic as well, to impress working-class youths that new leftists were tough or macho, an image that they assumed would gain the new left working-class support.[48]

Yet, the New Left misinterpreted the impact of the confrontations in Chicago. While it saw victory, harder evidence depicted defeat. An overwhelming majority of Americans felt that Daley had not used excess force; 75 percent of the public rated the protestors negatively. This included a majority of respondents who felt that the Vietnam War was a mistake. Numerous qualitative studies conducted in the aftermath of Chicago substantiated the poll data. As one social scientist observed: "No matter how the average American may feel about the war in Vietnam, there is one thing which he is likely to feel certain and strong about. This is his opposition to strikes, demonstrations and other forms of protests." And there is absolutely no evidence that the "Days of Rage" protests won the New Left any working-class support.[49]

The symbols that activists emphasized contributed to their failings. In addition to defiling the flag, Chicago protesters extensively used the word "pig" to describe the police. This tactic backfired. Rather than striking a respondent chord it served as a constant affront to the working class and as an example of the protesters' prejudices. "Although most student 'radicals' in the sixties would deny that they were engaging in middle-class elitism against the term, workers clearly recognized it for what it was," stated Andrew Levison. "The word 'pig' has always been an upper-class insult to deride the poor, based on the image of pigs as living in filth, eating slop, and being tremendously fat." (As one apprentice electrician once told this author, he despised rich people who lived on Madison, Park and Fifth Avenue, who forced him to use the service entrance, and did not allow him to use their bathroom and treated him as if he were some pig.) Not only did the use of the term *pig* provoke police violence, it antagonized millions of Americans who, even if they felt that the police response was excessive, considered it an understandable reaction to the protesters' elitist taunting.[50]

Thus, while new leftists tried to present themselves as opponents of the establishment, workers saw them as part of the elite. From the point of view of a Polish television watcher on Milwaukee Avenue on the Northwest side of Chicago, wrote Sidney Verba, "the long-haired militants and their faculty are every bit as much a part of the Establishment as are the presidents of corporations. . . . Someone like David Dellinger [one of the leaders of the Chicago protests] with his Yale degree [was] very much an Establishment personage." Or as Joseph Epstein observed, "In the eyes of, say, a sixty-year-old, Czech-born, Cicero homeowner, a wage worker and a union man, America must seem a place recently gone quite mad—and become quite threatening. My God," Epstein concluded, "such a man feels, is nothing any longer valued in this country—not family, not church, not hard work, not the law, nothing! Easing himself into a chair before his television set or unfurling his newspaper, he has in recent years seen and read about universities aflame; children pumping their bodies full of drugs . . . women, blacks, homosexuals making strident demands in abusive language. . . ." To make matters worse, these extremists had their defenders within the establishment, in the mass media and so-called institutions of higher learning.[51]

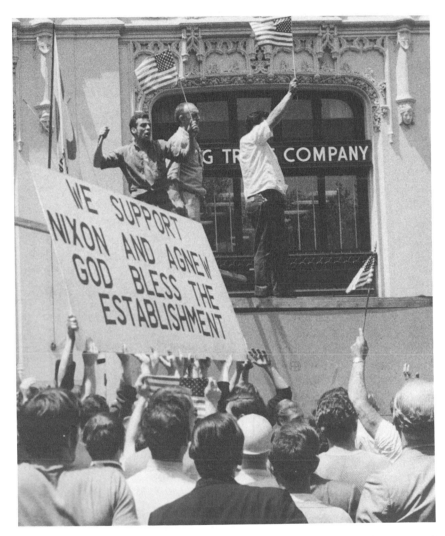

"Construction Worker Demonstration," New York City, 9 May 1970. Reprinted by permission of the *NY Times.*

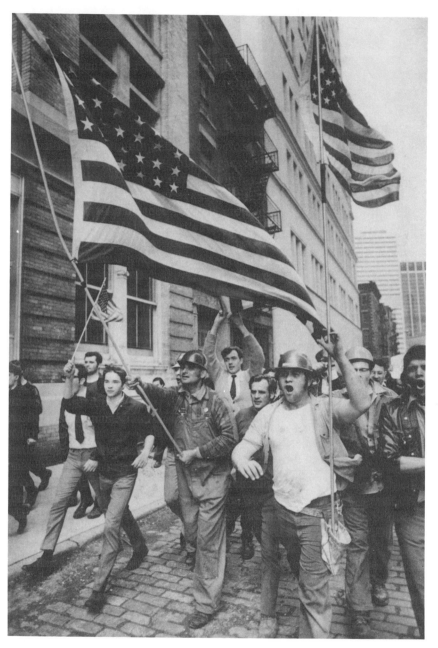

"Marching Construction Workers," New York City, 9 May 1970. Reprinted by permission of the *NY Times*.

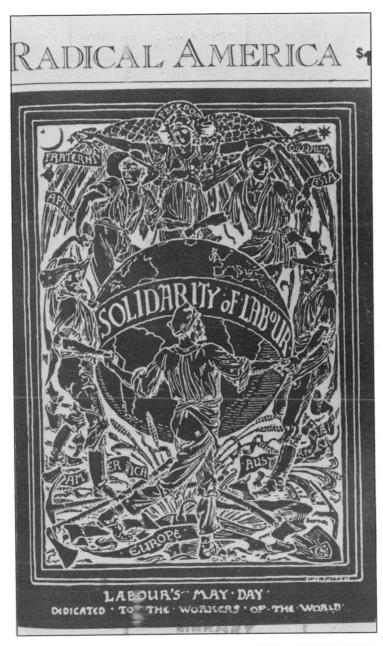

Cover from *Radical America*, 5:3 (May-June 1971). WHi(X3)48512-48515. Reprinted by permission of the State Historical Society of Wisconsin.

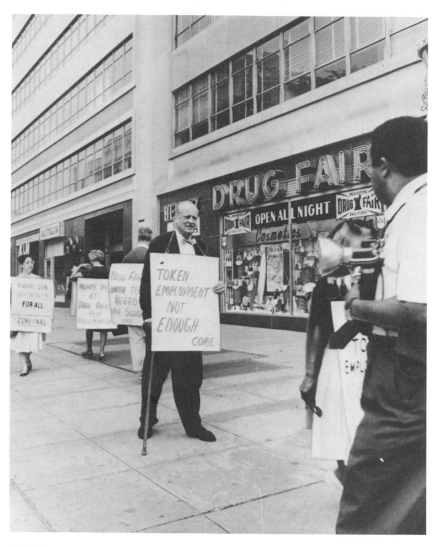

Boris Shisken, AFL-CIO civil rights director, on picket line organized by CORE and the Nonviolent Action Group of SNCC, Washington, D.C., 21 July 1962. Reprinted by permission of the George Meany Memorial Archives.

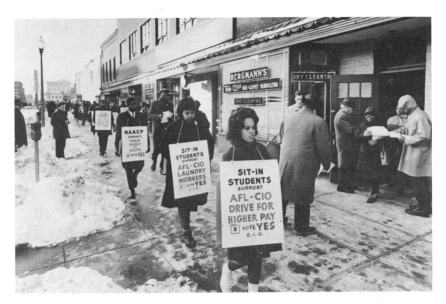

"Organizing Together." Civil rights and student activists aid AFL-CIO in organizing drive in Washington, D.C. Published in the AFL-CIO IUD Bulletin, 1964. Reprinted by permission of the George Meany Memorial Archives.

United Farm Workers organize pickets of students and labor outside of the Department of Defense, in New York City, to protest shipment of grapes to Vietnam, 18 October 1969. Reprinted by permission of the George Meany Memorial Archives.

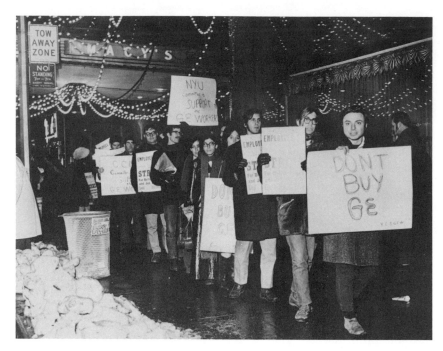

College students picketing outside Macy's, New York City, as part of consumer boycott of General Electric, *AFL-CIO News,* 17 January 1970. Reprinted by permission of the George Meany Memorial Archives.

The Game Nobody Wins, *AFL-CIO News,* 19 August 1967. Reprinted by permission of the George Meany Memorial Archives.

The underground papers of the 1960s were the most clear-cut link between the more narrowly defined political New Left and the counterculture. They contained information of interest to both and embodied the connection between the two. If the papers had a single vision, it was of a radical youth culture that stood for Black Power, free love, rock 'n roll, drugs, and peace. As the *Berkeley Barb,* one of the best known underground papers wrote: "Hippies are more than just people who walk down Haight Street with beads, bells, long hair, stoned on drugs. They are a concept, an act of rejection, a militant vanguard, a hope for the future."[52]

Unlike their predecessors, such as the *Masses* or the *Daily Worker,* the underground papers of the 1960s showed little concern for the working class. They presented neither favorable views of labor nor tried to sell copies to working men and women. Liberation New Service (LNS), the wire service for the underground newspapers, did not "even try to get into the hearts and minds of the white working class," stated underground newspaper historian Lawrence Leamer. When and if underground presses published articles and/or photographs relating to blue-collar life, they usually presented a mocking view. For example, the cover of one issue of *Rags* showed a photograph of a hard-hat worker, who resembled Ed Norton, a blue-collar television character on "The Honeymooners." The worker smiled like an idiot and stared off the page like someone from another world. The accompanying headline read: "The Hard-hats are Watching."[53]

While the editorial viewpoint of the underground press was antilabor, their editorial boards were not overwhelmingly middle class. On the contrary, many of the leading underground papers were founded and run by individuals with significant ties to the Old Left and/or working class. The founders of two of the most influential underground newspapers, the Los Angeles *Free Press* and the *Berkeley Barb* were Arthur Kunkin and Max Sherr, respectively. Kunkin, a one-time tool and die worker, wrote for various Trotskyist Socialist Worker party newspapers, including a stint as the business manager of the *Militant,* before starting the *Free Press.* Scherr was a union organizer before publishing the *Berkeley Barb.* Hence, it is incorrect to argue that the middle-class origins of the New Left accounted for its disdain for the working class as revealed in the coverage of the underground press.[54]

The lack of comment on the counterculture by the the labor press presents the historian with a methodological dilemma. While labor's papers commented frequently on the Vietnam War and Black Power, they ran remarkably few stories on the counterculture. Most often stories on the counterculture appeared in the papers of traditionally left unions, which were generally sympathetic to the New Left. For instance, the *UE News* insisted that labor needed to listen to the complaints of the young, especially those concerning their estrangement from society. The editors of the United Rubber Workers' called for its members to "tune in" to the concerns of the young. AFL–CIO spokesman Edward Morgan contended that the counterculture was part of the traditional rebelliousness of youth and that workers should seek to understand, though not condone, LSD trips and the like. And District 65's paper explained that long hair represented simply a new fad, just as crew cuts had. There was nothing intrinsically wrong with it. Jesus Christ, William Shakespeare, and the American revolutionaries wore their hair long. District 65's newspaper even quoted the public relations director of the Barber's Union, George Boozer, praising the new fashion. "The new long hair requires more frequent shampooing and conditioning and more care in general." In other words it was good for business.[55]

Yet these declarations had a hollow or false ring. Hidden in each was a desire on the part of the union officials to explain a thoroughly confusing phenomenon to themselves and the rank and file. Furthermore, each piece contained comments that hinted at a repressed or subconscious fear of the counterculture. Morgan fretted over the sexual identification of the hippies. District 65 hoped that long hair was just a change of fashion rather than a manifestation of a broader critique of societal values. George Boozer qualified his favorable comment on long hair by adding that the Barbers Union condemned "hippie style" long hair because it rejected the value of appearing well-groomed. And the *UE News* worried that the youth rebellion would lead to an undermining of the union itself by its new members.[56]

The sparsity of explicit comment on the counterculture, especially when juxtaposed to developed positions on the war and civil rights, hinted at its volatility. Paradoxically, labor spokespersons focused on those aspects of the New Left that they felt capable of combating. Labor officials were accustomed to lobbying in the halls of congress for certain domestic and foreign policies. But they did not know how to respond to a movement that called for personal liberation, that, in Jerry Rubin's words, threatened to "steal their kids" through the enticements of long hair, drugs and rock 'n roll. This fear partly explains the virulence of the remarks that labor made about the counterculture when it did explicitly comment on it.[57]

––––––––––

Despite these antagonisms, it would be an oversimplification to depict the counterculture solely as an anti-working-class phenomenon. While it demonstrated some of the New Left's estrangement from labor, the counterculture contained utopian strains that hoped to liberate workers as well as youths. A few activists, for example, sought to create new art forms with the objective of uniting disaffected youths with the working class. Julian Beck, for one, organized the Living Theater with the goal of transforming it into a medium for the masses, one that would challenge American capitalism in its themes and form. "Theater has to stop being a product bought and paid for by the bourgeois." With the Living Theater workers would "take over the means of production . . . and turn them all into factories of . . . love and the extended mind." The San Francisco Mime Troupe and to a lesser extent the street theater group the Diggers had similar objectives.[58]

In some respects, rock 'n roll music, in the late 1960s, became a means for uniting middle-class radicals with working-class youths. John Lennon, for one, turned away from his early ditties and psychedelic music and returned to his working-class roots. "Give Peace a Chance" was more like "We Shall Overcome" than "Lucy in the Sky with Diamonds," which had celebrated the trip so offensive to working Americans. The former was an anthem of harmony, that reached out beyond those youths who were already radicalized. In Wade Hampton's estimation, "Give Peace a Chance" was one of the "classic organizing songs in the protest tradition [that] includes Ralph Chapin's 'Solidarity Forever' and Florence Reese's 'Which Side Are You On.' Similarly, 'Working Class Hero,' in Lennon's own words, aimed at "people like me who are working class . . . who are supposed to be processed into the middle class."[59]

In an insightful piece, labor spokesperson Gus Tyler even suggested that the counterculture might in time serve as an agent for bringing workers and new leftists together. While Tyler denounced much of the counterculture as little more than elitist delinquency, he recognized that an increasing number of working-class youths were attending college. Although Tyler claimed that these youths shared his disgust with the "revolutionary" antics of a minority of activists, they were, Tyler had to admit, attracted to aspects of the counterculture. Rather than bemoaning this fact, Tyler suggested that the sons and daughters of industrial wage workers be used as a means to bridge the gap between labor and the New Left. Working-class youths in college could serve as the "core of a progressive coalition that reaches into both the leftists and the conservative (especially) trade union wings."[60]

In part, People's Park stood as an attempt to do this. In the spring of 1969, a group of Berkeley radicals, led by ex-mechanic Michael Delacour, *Barb* writer Stew Albert, an assortment of hippies, atypical professionals, and community activists decided to turn an unused piece of property, owned by the University of California, into a "People's Park." At their own expense and on their own time, local residents came to the barren piece of land and planted trees and grass, built a play area, served free food and held music festivals and carnivals.[61]

On 15 May 1969, U.C. Berkeley chancellor Heyns ordered Berkeley police to "retake" the park. Officers swept the area and guarded construction workers who rapidly raised a chain link fence around the property. Local officials also readied the riot squad and the national guard to defend the site. One-time SDS president and Berkeley resident at the time, Todd Gitlin, recounted the scene. "That night, Governor Ronald Reagan sent three thousand rifle-bearing national Guardsmen into Berkeley. From a 'liberated zone' Berkeley was converted into occupied territory." In spite of the show of force, Berkeley activists persevered. For days they battled in the streets for control of the park and the community in general. Before the fight was over, James Rector lay dead, one of the first casualties of the northern student movement.[62]

Heyns justified "retaking" the park on the grounds that the property belonged to the University. Berkeley radicals countered that the property belonged to the people by right of "usership" and contended that the University's claims of ownership ignored the fact that the State had taken the land from the Indians in the first place. (The invocation of Indian symbols and rights was a prevalent theme in many new left arguments. It was part of its attempt to see itself in noble terms, as defenders of the downtrodden and as spiritually opposed to the forces of materialism.)[63]

To those involved, People's Park depicted the conjunction of radical politics and the counterculture. It sought to liberate both from repression; the park represented "soulful socialism," the beginning of a "free man's nation." The park embodied the vision of brotherhood: free music, greenery, and love. Yet, during the confrontation, the activists lost sight of their utopian vision of reaching beyond the youth community. Even though several local labor unions decried the use of excessive force, the vast majority of state residents supported Reagan's and Heyns' response. Just as in Chicago, new leftists could not believe that the public supported the excessive use of force, which included tear-gassing the city and the fatal shooting of a Berkeley resident. As a result, People's Park left the New Left further isolated from the working class than before.[64]

Not surprisingly, various conservative political figures cut their teeth in the battles of the 1960s. Ronald Reagan and Edwin Meese both took hard-line stances toward the rebellions in Berkeley, U.C. Santa Barbara, and elsewhere. Reagan and Meese especially emphasized the nihilism of the youth revolt. They championed the traditional family and proper decorum, as opposed to the orgies, communes, and defiance of law and order. For instance, in a 1966 campaign speech, Ronald Reagan focused on the countercultural aspects of a fund-raiser held by Berkeley radicals. The event, according to Reagan, highlighted rock 'n roll music, rhythmic and sexual dancing, and psychedelic light shows so appalling they he could not even describe them in detail. In other words, if it was a confrontation that the New Left wanted, then conservatives would lay down the welcome mat. However, in so doing conservatives shrewdly blurred the distinctions between the New Left and liberals. Their objective was not the preservation of the "establishment" but the introduction of a new political order, and if they could use the New Left to damage liberalism they would do so.[65]

Perhaps in a different context, the goal of turning an unused property into a community park or garden would engender different results. But to a large degree, because of the different generational orientations of the New Left and labor and the explosiveness of the symbols of the counterculture, attempts to reform American culture in line with working-class needs failed. Antagonisms fostered by the Vietnam War and Black Power intertwined with those generated by the counterculture to produce a deep rift between the two social movements. By in large, labor unionists lost sight of their own struggles with police and other state authorities. They dismissed student grievances as unauthentic and defended their own liberal agenda. Simultaneously, new leftists exaggerated the well-being of workers and their own sense of oppression. Long hair, drugs, sex, and rock 'n roll became the problem, or the solution, depending on which side one was on. Both movements underestimated the strength of the New Right and opted for confrontation rather than cooperation. Indeed, it was not until the New Right had gained national power, in the 1980s, that either movement fully understood that they had to cooperate if they were to thwart the New Right from implementing its conservative agenda and if they were to protect the reforms of the 1960s, which they had fought for together in the first part of the decade.

6

Debating the Labor Question

In mid June 1969, student radicals gathered in Chicago to attend SDS's annual national convention. Their numbers displayed the New Left's phenomenal growth. Ten years earlier SDS was unknown. Its convention attracted only a handful of people and its membership was below one thousand. In contrast, in 1969 SDS's convention attracted over two thousand and its membership stood at upward of one hundred thousand and was growing. Moreover, polls showed that the public considered student unrest to be the nation's number one problem, more so than the war or urban revolt. Yet, ironically, SDS was on the verge of collapse.

The immediate cause of SDS's demise was its debate over the "labor question," or more precisely over the nature of the working class, and stance or position that the organization should adopt toward it. On one side of the debate stood the Progressive Labor party (PL), a Maoist group within SDS that had maintained an old left position throughout the 1960s. On other side stood the national leadership of SDS, known as the National Office or NO, which, itself, was held together only by its opposition to PL.

While PL had enjoyed little influence through most of the 1960s, toward the end of the decade its position within SDS was enhanced tremendously by a combination of internal and external events. The assassination of Martin Luther King, Jr., and Robert F. Kennedy and, most important, the May 1968 uprising of students and workers and France gave PL a big boost. The latter, PL argued, proved that student leftists allied with industrial wage workers could act as an agent for radical change. Put another way, PL contended that the French uprising showed the correctness of its old left strategy.[1]

Not long after the French uprising, PL proposed that SDS adopt an all-encompassing plan known as the "worker-student alliance" (WSA). According to this strategy, students would consciously foster a proletariat revolution. This included forming a Student Labor Project, whereby students would obtain jobs inside factories in order to radicalize workers. PL also viewed the WSA as a tool for educating students on the exploitation of the proletariat.[2] While such a plan would have won few converts in the early 1960s, the revolutionary aura of the latter years of the 1960s along with PL's decision to operate as a tight-knit caucus, which allowed it to take advantage of SDS's decentralized character, provided the faction with the opportunity to vie with NO for leadership within SDS at the 1969 convention.

The national leadership of SDS responded to PL's plan by developing one of its own, known as the Revolutionary Youth movement, or RYM II. Developed by Mike Klonsky, RYM II (itself a revised version of an earlier program known simply as RYM), suggested that SDS could recruit workers in a more subtle manner than that proposed by PL. Rather than metamorphosing SDS into an auxiliary of the proletariat, RYM II called for SDS to recruit working-class youths into a revolutionary movement by organizing at community colleges, high schools, and other nonelite institutions. This, Klonsky claimed, would allow SDS to ultimately reach the traditional proletariat—through their children—but at a the same time it would permit SDS to focus on its traditional constituency, namely students.[3]

SDS's debate over the correct theoretical line toward the working class produced one more main faction, the Weathermen, or Weather Underground, and one more plan. In "You Don't Need a Weatherman to Know Which Way the Wind Blows," this group, like RYM II emphasized the role that youth would have to play in a revolution. Although unlike either RYM II or PL, the Weathermen stressed the international nature of the struggle and the need for physical confrontation. Seeing themselves as the American Viet Cong, part of a guerilla army committed to staging a worldwide revolution, the Weathermen, in their own jargon, proposed living the revolution, engaging in sporadic bombings of various public and private facilities and rigorous programs of self-criticism.[4]

In contrast to PL, the Weathermen rejected old left ideology as simplistic and anachronistic. Weather theory argued that white workers enjoyed "white skin privilege," meaning that they were bought off. Trade unions were seen as one of the pillars of the corporate liberal state and a potential component of fascism. This said, the group's emphasis on action suggested that the Weathermen were interested in recruiting young workers to the movement. Through "macho" behavior, the Weathermen believed, these young workers could be convinced to relinquish their white skin privilege. As Weatherperson Cathy Wilkerson recalled (with regret), the Weathermen sought "to reach white youth on the basis of their most reactionary macho instinct." They were "intellectuals playing as working-class toughs."[5]

To bolster their cases, the various sides or factions linked themselves with an assortment of other new left groups and goals. For example, the NO allied itself with the Black Panther party and lambasted PL for its opposition to black nationalism. At the 1969 convention, members of the Black Panther party officially condemned PL as racist and counter-revolutionary. Each side also highlighted its particular position on the Vietnam War and the counterculture, with PL adopting the most doctri-naire or old left views. To win converts, delegates at the convention resorted to sloganeering. With the aim of highlighting PL's lukewarm support for the North Vietnamese, NO forces chanted "Ho Ho. Ho Chi Minh." Seeking to emphasize their communist roots, PL's contingent countered, "Mao Mao. Mao Tse-Tung." (Some in the crowd amusingly chimed "Let's Go Mets.")[6]

Rightly fearing that SDS was on the verge of a schism, a group of delegates started to sing. Throughout the 1960s, they figured, music had proved to be a force for unity. Perhaps it could be so again. Yet, rather than singing "We Shall Overcome," "Give Peace a Chance," or another new left anthem, they sang the old labor tune "Solidarity Forever." It was unclear whether all of the delegates even knew the words. Regard-less of whether they did or not, their choice of songs revealed that nearly everyone wanted to display their political correctness on the labor question.[7]

Even this tactic, however, could not forestall the inevitable. After another round of sloganeering and caucus meetings, the NO expelled PL from SDS. In response, PL declared itself the real SDS. The Weather-man sided with the NO and then broke from it in opposition to the revisionist nature of RYM II. While all of these factions claimed to have the correct line on the labor question, none of them made significant inroads among the working class. Nor did they reach either a working-class audience or a select group of influential labor intellectuals. As Charles Demby, a life-long radical autoworker wrote: "What workers will not respond to are those who are out to lead or direct them. They have seen enough of that. . . . They won't ally with student radicals who see workers as muscle, but not reason." Yet, this was exactly how many student radicals envisioned workers: as the soldiers in their revolution-ary army.[8]

In short order all of these factions became meaningless fringe organizations, and many of their ideas evaporated with them. SDS became a shell of itself. Nonetheless, these developments should not mislead us into thinking that the New Left never had any meaningful thoughts on labor question. In fact, theoretical or intellectual investigations into the nature of the working class and its radical potential, or what I have termed the labor question, were central to the New Left's development and to its relationship to labor.

To understand the New Left's thoughts on labor, we must first briefly examine the intellectual foundations upon which they were built. Simply stated, the New Left inherited an anticlass perspective; it assumed that class struggle and class structure were essentially irrelevant to the modern American experience. Contemporary social theorists described workers as satisfied, labor as bureaucratized and complacent, and class conflict as anachronistic. Daniel Bell, for one, proclaimed that "workers, whose grievance were once the driving energy for social change, are more satisfied with the society than the intellectuals."[9] By portraying America as a pluralist, affluent, and consensual society, John Kenneth Galbraith, Arthur Schlesinger, Jr., Robert Dahl, and others bolstered Bell's claim. Daniel Boorstin, Richard Hofstadter, Louis Hartz, and others added historical weight to the argument.[10]

Even independent leftists, who otherwise disagreed with liberal or consensus thought, offered similar interpretations. Many of these independent leftists, or "forefathers" of the New Left, had roots in an earlier left-labor tradition. A. J. Muste, for one, was active in the labor struggles of the 1920s and 1930s. He helped found the Brookwood Labor College in the 1920s and headed the American Workers' party in the 1930s. Similarly, Sidney Lens, a cofounder, with Muste, of *Liberation*, participated in union-organizing drives as late as the 1950s.[11]

Though never a member of the Communist party nor a trade union official, C. Wright Mills began his academic career by writing a series of favorable articles on trade unions for the new journal *Labor and Nation*. In one article, Mills called upon other intellectuals to study "every aspect" of union behavior, with the goal of finding out where the "left" is going and "where we want to go." In the spring of 1948 Mills reported enthusiastically on the UAW's constitutional convention for the left-liberal journal *Commentary*. "To see them is to realize that the union is their creature. . . . Underlying their collective need is a common denominator: the basic psychology of the 'wobbly,'" he added approvingly. Mills's early interest in labor culminated in his book *The New Men of Power*, first published in 1948. The work compared the AFL and the CIO and discussed the public's views of union leadership. It came to some ambiguous conclusions. For example, Mills displayed a growing cynicism toward labor leaders, critically comparing them to Theodore Dreiser's "country girl in the city, [who] often became the whore of power." Yet, Mills concurrently asserted his faith in the rank and file and in the labor intellectual, writing, "The union made intellectual are a vanguard; they can turn the unions into vanguard organizations."[12]

The young Herbert Marcuse had roots in the tradition of a left-labor alliance as well. As a young intellectual in Germany, he briefly belonged to the German Spartacist league. In his writings, he concentrated on the works of Hegel and Marx, trying to "read Marx's notion of labor back into Hegel." In one of his earliest essays, "The Foundation of Historical Materialism," Marcuse agreed with Marx that the essence of man was to be found in his labor, and like Marx he predicted that workers would rebel against their alienating situation.[13]

Similarly, the young Paul Goodman displayed an interest in labor, though with a twist. Along with his brother, Percival, he advanced a vision of a decentralized capitalist society in which home, work, and community were integrated. In some ways, Goodman's ideal community approximated the town in the pre-industrial era, in which the artisan producer stood at the center of activity and human concerns counted more than economic ones.[14]

But it was not the young Mills, Marcuse, or Goodman that the New Left inherited in the early 1960s. Rather, it absorbed the works that the forefathers wrote in the late 1950s and early 1960s. These works presented an unfavorable view of labor. Like liberal intellectuals, Mills, Marcuse, and Goodman asserted that workers had gained material benefits and would continue to do so in the near future. They cast the labor movement as increasingly bureaucratic and conservative. And they concluded that neither workers nor trade unions would serve as the engine for radical change, a central premise of the Old Left. For example, in *The Marxists,* published in 1963, Mills launched a frontal assault on the Old Left's faith in labor, or the *labor metaphysic,* as he termed it. Wage workers had not and would not serve as agents for change, Mills declared. Historically, "wage workers in advanced capitalism have rarely become a 'proletariat vanguard,' they have not become the agency of any revolutionary change of epoch."[15]

The historian William A. Williams went even further, contending in *Contours of American History* that the labor movement had evolved into one of the pillars of corporate capitalism. And Herbert Marcuse turned the traditional Marxist position on its head, positing that Americans no longer lived in a world dominated by need. Scarcity was no longer relevant to our world, Marcuse wrote, though the assumption of scarcity was "artificially perpetuated in the interest of preserving the system of domination." Since neither the working class nor the labor movement could see beyond the myth of scarcity, the left could not depend on either to "throw off the yoke" of modern repression.[16]

This does not mean that the forefathers constructed an exclusively anti-working-class intellectual foundation. While commenting unfavorably on labor's material conditions, they also wrote sympathetically about the psychological discontent of American workers, their alienation, and repression (as opposed to oppression). Paul Goodman, for one, wrote that "our abundant society is at present simply deficient in many of the most elementary objective opportunities and worth-while goals that could make growing up possible."[17]

An assortment of other independent leftists, from those associated with the Catholic worker movement to Socialists of various strains, writing for such journals as *Dissent* and *Monthly Review,* kept alive the notion that the working class was not content or economically secure. A handful of doctrinaire Marxists, such as Philip Foner and Herbert Aptheker, published a steady diet on the proletariat, black and white, which was available to younger leftists.[18] In time, some new leftists would draw on these thoughts to bolster their own theories on alienation and the labor question. But initially, they did not.

But if workers would not serve as the agents for change, who would, and by what reasoning? If Marx's predictions and theories were inaccurate, to whom should the New Left turn for direction and a better understanding of its own rebellion? Clearly, liberal thinkers were of little help. Was it possible that the New Left could develop its own radical theory, that it could serve as a surrogate proletariat? Or as SDS leader Carl Oglesby wondered:

> In view of modern radicalism's unchallenged doctrine that the revolution is to be made by the army of industrial labor, how does the new radical dare to proceed (putting it mildly) in the conspicuous absence of that army. . . . Does the white middle class New Left constitute the embryonic beginnings of a class-for-itself? Does it embody the beginnings of an identifiable historical practice which can neither be transferred to another class nor abandoned nor permanently defeated? Or, on the contrary, is the movement merely the suds, the effervescing of a globalized class war in which the West plays the role of capital and the entire neocolonial South that of labor, and whose basic features therefore differ only in scale from the class conflict of the nineteenth century?[19]

In the first half of the 1960s, an influential collection of new leftists flirted with the idea of forging an interracial movement of the poor as a replacement for a working-class movement. The poor, with the help of student activists, new leftists posited, whether white or black, northern or southern, rural or urban, would act as the agents for change. In place of trade unions, which were becoming increasingly anachronistic because of automation, new leftists called for building community unions. Built from the bottom up, these unions would empower the underemployed and unemployed and pave the way for a reinvigorated left-liberal coalition.[20]

Some new leftists, however, challenged the idea that the poor could serve as the surrogate proletariat. "Assuming that the poor can be fully organized and will become fully conscious of the need for radical politics, by themselves they must remain impotent," the editors of *Studies on the Left* proclaimed. "There are not enough of them, nor do they command sufficient resources to constitute a political force that can win power."[21] As an alternative, the editors of *Studies* suggested that the time was ripe for the revival of a new radical political party, akin to the Socialist party of the early part of the twentieth century. The poor would comprise part of such a Party, but so too would other components of the population, including dissident labor unionists.[22]

Social democrats connected to the social activist wing of the labor movement dismissed both community unions and the idea of reviving the Socialist party. Instead, social democrats asserted that the time was ripe for forming a broad coalition of liberals and leftists. Bayard Rustin most forcefully made this argument in "From Protest to Politics." Michael Harrington, ILGWU official Gus Tyler, Irving Howe, and others reiterated Rustin's argument.[23]

While a coalition of Social Democrats seemed a viable alternative, it never won the support of the New Left, in part because of the escalation of the war in Vietnam and the emergence of Black Power and the counterculture. In the summer of 1965, in a piece in *Liberation* magazine, which counted Rustin as one of its coeditors, Staughton Lynd lambasted Rustin and the idea of coalition. Coalitionism "is a posture which . . . mutes criticism of American imperialism so as to keep open its channels to the White House," declared Lynd. "And men like Rustin will become the national spokesman who sell the line agreed on behind the doors to the faithful followers on the street."[24] New Left intellectual Ronald Radosh echoed Lynd's critique, characterizing Rustin as a "toady of fascism." (Approximately twenty years later Radosh personally apologized to Rustin for his "arrogance" and Rustin genuinely accepted his apology.)[25]

Social Democrats unanimously came to Rustin's defense. David McReynolds, Tom Kahn (as of 1965 the director of LID), Irving Howe, Michael Harrington, Norman Thomas, August Meier, Jack Newfield, and Murray Kempton claimed that Lynd's attack was personally motivated and that it went beyond the pale of civilized discourse. Separately, Howe went on an intellectual rampage against the New Left, attacking it for its romantic support of the North Vietnamese communists and for its sophomoric and nihilistic countercultural tendencies. The New Left, Howe contended, cared more about style than it did substance. It sought to shock and to outrage rather than to effect change.[26] Perhaps Howe and other social democrats hoped that such diatribes would bring the New Left to its senses. But if this was their hope they proved ill-founded, since they tended to reinforce division rather than mend it.

———

As America polarized in the mid–1960s, the New Left's search for a surrogate proletariat took on a new direction and tone. Militant and action-oriented men and women took the place of the early leaders of the New Left, many of whom had connections to the Old Left or the House of Labor. In turn, novel new left theories on change and labor appeared, almost all of which emphasized the role of new leftists themselves at the expense of the traditional proletariat. Poor and organized workers received less attention, except when race rather than class became the animating concern. Meanwhile, social democrats and their labor friends watched with horror as their dreams of building a progressive movement disintegrated. (In later years they would lament that they were born too late to be part of the social movements of the 1930s, but too early not to have learned its lessons. They were condemned for being critics during the 1950s, when criticism was out of fashion, and "left-liberals" in the 1960s, when radicalism came into vogue.)

Not surprisingly, radical black students took the lead in moving the New Left to its next stage of development. As the most exploited group, suffering from both colonialism and racism, they claimed that African Americans occupied an objectively revolutionary place. They were in the vanguard of a worldwide struggle against the Mother Country and accordingly should be granted leadership status by the New Left in America. We are a colony within the Mother Colony in solidarity with other colonial/imperial subjects, Black Power spokespersons declared. Or as Julius Lester, a SNCC member and prolific writer observed: "At the present time the world is polarizing into West (white) versus everybody else (colored, black, yellow) and the war in Vietnam is only a rehearsal for what the U.S. must do if it is to protect its interest in Latin America, other parts of Asia, Africa and at home."[27]

The cornerstone of this theory was that African Americans were historically super-exploited, thereby sharing a racial and economic bond with the Third World. During slavery, so the argument went, blacks provided the surplus wealth on which America was built. As the United States became an industrial power, African Americans continued to play a strategic role. To paraphrase the League of Revolutionary Black Workers, blacks had "finally got the news" that white capital came from their blood, sweat and tears, from the colonial and antebellum plantations to the more modern steel forges, slaughterhouse yards, and automobile assembly lines.[28]

Even though much of this analysis rang with Marxist-Leninist familiarity, most Black Power advocates insisted that race, not class, defined their status. "Racism, for black people in this country, is far more important than exploitation," exhorted Stokely Carmichael, "because no matter how much money you make in the black community, when you go into the white community you are still a nigger."[29] Or as James Forman recalled, his mere use of the word Marxian brought the following rejoinder from another black militant: "But Motherfucker, Marx was not a black. . . . He was a white writer." To those who claimed that blacks were part of the American tradition and thus had a basis for cooperation with whites, William Melvin Kelley replied:

> Is it still necessary, in 1968, to discuss the differences between the two peoples, African and European, who inhabit the United States? I thought everybody accepted these differences . . . between James Brown and Elvis Presley . . . Willie Mays and Mickey Mantle. . . . Please Sir, we are different sir. Our ancestors came from Africa, yours from Europe. Our ancestors did not want to come to the United States. Yours did.[30]

Black Power theorists drew sustenance from the outburst of third-world revolutions that took place in the 1960s. The overthrow of European colonial powers coupled with the success of the Viet Cong lent credence to the idea that a revolution of nonwhites could succeed. Black radicals traveled to Africa, Latin America, and Asia to meet with "freedom fighters" and their new revolutionary heroes, such as Fidel Castro, Ho Chi Minh, and Kwame Nkrumah. Armed with the rhetorical support of these leaders, black militants touted themselves as part of a worldwide struggle. "We got brothers in Africa, we got brothers in Cuba, we got brothers in Brazil," declared Carmichael following one of his tours. This alleged support was particularly important in refuting Bayard

Rustin's and A. Philip Randolph's claim that black nationalism was an impractical panacea. By allying with their brethren of the Third World, black militants turned Rustin's and Randolph's argument on its head. Simply stated, when counted with nonwhites around the globe, African Americans constituted a numerical majority; whites were the minority.[31]

Black Power advocates also validated their theory by pointing to the blackening of America's cities and the wave of rebellions that broke out in them during the mid–1960s. The latter demonstrated the willingness of urban blacks to take a revolutionary stance; the former revealed the latent strength of the African American community. If organized, militants could transform the ghettos and the southern blackbelt into bastions of political strength. At bare minimum, blacks could take control of their communities simply by exercising the vote.[32]

While Carmichael and other Black Power advocates drew widespread support from all wings of the New Left, most white new leftists retained a tinge of uneasiness with the third-world/black nationalist analysis. And even if most of the white New Left did not go so far as to openly reject the Black Power perspective, it felt compelled to develop an alternative vision, one that would rationalize its own role and explain how it could replace the industrial wageworker as the agent for change.

As early as the Free Speech Movement in Berkeley, Mario Savio posited that students were oppressed. The system that denied blacks basic rights controlled their lives as well. "The battlefields [the South and the University] may seem quite different to some observers," Savio declared, but "the same rights are at stake in both places." Or as another FSM participant stated: "The events at Berkeley should be . . . an impetus to American radicals to finally kick the labor metaphysic and drop the vulgar Marxist belief . . . that men must be hungry or unemployed or discriminated against to participate in radical political action."[33]

Out of FSM and subsequent campus uprising grew the notion of student power. Student radicals would serve as the primary agents of change, not as adjuncts to other people's struggles. A core of activists theorized that the *multiuniversity,* a term coined by U.C. Berkeley chancellor Clark Kerr, objectively stood at the center of society. Universities provided society with its essential goods and services. They maintained the war machine, fed the corporate world and cultural apparatus, and socialized students into accepting the status quo. "What we must see clearly is the relation between the university and corporate liberal society at large," wrote one-time SDS president Carl Davidson.

"Our educational institutions are corporations and knowledge factories. What we have failed to see in the past is how absolutely vital these factories are to the corporate liberal state." Since universities depended on a compliant student body to function, activists could upset the system simply by refusing to cooperate. If students organized into a modern-day Wobbly movement, a "One Big Student Union," in Davidson's words, they could topple society. Advocates of the student power theory added that the growth of the student population augmented their power. It made students numerically more significant and simultaneously alienated them from their schools.[34]

The Columbia University uprising in the spring of 1968 bolstered the student power idea. Both student radicals and the Columbia administration saw their actions as a microcosm for a larger revolt. Students no longer held to a "narrow conception" of themselves as a "privileged class asking for inclusion in the university," wrote a euphoric Tom Hayden. Rather, they held a much broader sense of their role. They were "taking an international and revolutionary view of themselves in opposition to . . . imperialism." And they expected, rightfully so in Hayden's estimation, for their uprising to spread to other campuses around the globe.[35] Or as Mark Rudd, one of the leaders of the Columbia revolt contended, the confrontation forced people to choose sides, either for the university and "the interests they represent," namely corporate and imperialist America, or with the Left and the "interests of humanity."[36]

Black student radicals tried to blend the ideas of black and student power. Like white students they sought to link their campus situation to the outside world—imperialism, racial, and class inequity. Yet, they did so separately. At college campuses across the country they demanded a more relevant education and a greater say in university administration.[37]

The insular nature of college life added credibility to the student power idea. The media sensationalized university disturbances and student radicals avidly watched the news and read the papers for stories that confirmed their own importance. New Left Notes even ran a column entitled: "We Made the News Today Oh Boy," which tracked the ability of the New Left to gain headlines. Academic scholars added to the students' sense of self-importance by churning out scores of treatise on the so-called generation gap, including works by Lewis Feuer, Daniel Bell, Zbigniew Brezinski, Bruno Bettelheim, Alvin Toffler, Seymour Martin Lipset, and Irving Howe.[38]

A number of radicals, however, wondered how students could ever lead a mass rebellion. Even if one admitted that students occupied a strategic place in society, they simply were not a large enough social grouping, or class, to lead a revolution. And even if students could force people to choose sides, how could they guarantee that the masses would choose the right side?[39]

One solution to this dilemma, some new leftists contended, was to modify or broaden the student power idea into the larger category of youth power. Students could lead a revolt not as students per se, but as members of the postwar generation commonly known as baby-boomers. "The essential class for the perpetuation of the existing economic system is not the young," explained John and Margaret Roundtree in the *International Socialist Journal,* the organ of a Trotskyist offshoot. "The young occupy the critical work-places; they man the war machines and the idea factory. They absorb by their own sacrifices the surplus which the irrational economic system can not dispose of."[40]

New leftists found support for this idea wherever they looked. Youths led the civil rights movement. They sparked the antiwar movement and campus rebellion. And even more broadly, youths were building a counterculture. In recent years, "an entire culture . . . began to distinguish youth," declared Yale law professor Charles Reich. "As it did the message of consciousness [specifically revolutionary consciousness] went with it. And the more the older generation rejected the culture, the more the fraternity of the young grew up." Or as Theodore Roszak argued, youths were the new comrades; they had replaced the industrial proletariat as the "social lever" for revolutionary change.[41]

Yet another segment of the New Left found the category "youth" too loose or vague. As some of them noted, many well-known activists were not even a part of the baby-boom generation, defined as those born since World War II. Hence, this group proposed still another replacement for Marx's proletariat, the "new working class." Dave Gilbert, Bob Gotleib, and Susan Southern argued that "class most simply refers to who controls (and who does not control) the means of production." Hence, the modern working class consisted of those individuals who shared a lack of control over the means of production but who performed society's essential functions. This group of technocrats, engineers, and key service workers was a class in and of itself.[42]

Two French Socialists, Andre Gorz and Serge Mallet, who wrote extensively on changes in the occupational structure of postindustrial society, provided much of the meat for this theory. In works that several key new leftists read, Gorz and Mallet emphasized that advanced capitalism was generating its own new nemesis: a new proletariat. Just as nineteenth-century industrial workers lost control over their lives to the capitalist owners of the means of production, the new working class was losing control over "what to produce; how to produce it, or for what market to produce." Both old and new working classes were commodities, bought and sold on the open market by capital. Neither controlled the means of production and both were alienated from the workplace. They were cut off from the products that they produced and did not gain a sense of fulfillment from their work or leisure. Furthermore, expounded Mallet, the new working class occupied a strategic place in society. Their position was analogous to that of skilled manual workers in a less developed economy. Through its own contradictions, capitalism was creating a new radical agent, one that could shake society simply by withdrawing its labor.[43]

In 1967, SDS leaders Carl Davidson and Greg Calvert translated the idea of the new working class into official new left dogma. In February of the same year, SDS convened a special conference at Princeton University at which Calvert presented a paper entitled, "In White America: Radical Consciousness and Social Change," in which he candidly observed that the New Left's main concern since its inception had been its search for a constituency, "for an agent of social transformation, for the 'revolutionary class.' " The search began with the realization that the Old Left analysis had proven faulty. It ignored the transformation of modern capitalism and failed to acknowledge the incipient signs of reactionary class consciousness of the proletariat. To make matters worse, Calvert posited, the Old Left accepted the myth that students were part of the middle class.[44]

But, Calvert insisted, students were not middle class; they were "not small independent producers" (petit bourgeois). Even if it did not presently suffer from classic economic oppression and deprivation, the new working class was oppressed by a poverty of spirit. It suffered from alienation at work and in leisure. The new working class had lost control over its life. However, Calvert continued, campus revolts and union drives among white-collar workers revealed that the new working class was awakening to its subordinate position and would refuse to accept its newfound status. "America is beginning to break up," Calvert proclaimed. "The myth of the great American middle class is crumbling!"[45]

In addition to benefiting from a nice Marxist tone, the new working-class theory surpassed the student power idea by more clearly defining the role of radical students after they left the university. Political ideals learned in college would be passed down to the workplace. Today's engineering, science, social science and humanities students were tomorrow's technocrats, bureaucrats, teachers, and managers. Accordingly, the role of student activists remained the same. Students could remain in college or graduate school and the New Left could retain its college campus focus armed with the knowledge that university uprisings served as training grounds for future revolts against society at large.[46]

Yet, the new working-class theory had an Achilles heel. Unlike the student, youth or Black Power ideas, it did not translate into a nice revolutionary cry. Activists like Abbie Hoffman and Jerry Rubin could not package the new working-class theory into a sexy message that sold well when played on television. It did not conform to the demand for a militant ideology; it was not confrontational enough for the revolutionary situation that the New Left presumed it was in. In addition, its stature within SDS rested to a large degree on the ascendancy of Calvert, not a widespread understanding of the theory itself. Consequently, it remained vulnerable to attack, especially ones mounted by well-organized factions, such as the Progressive Labor party, which saw the new working class as a direct repudiation of its own neoclassic Marxist theories. Moreover, when compared to the theory of third-world liberation, it was difficult to maintain that well-paid technocrats, even if alienated, shared the same degree of oppression as peasants or America's ghetto residents.[47]

Hence, in 1968 when the leadership of SDS changed, the new working-class theory fell out of favor. When the heroes of the Columbia revolt and other self-proclaimed revolutionaries assumed power, they dismissed Calvert's thoughts as revisionist ideology. Black militants who insisted on the primacy of the colonized in the impending revolutionary struggle lent support to these attacks. Even Carl Davidson, who initially supported the new working-class theory as a more sophisticated version of student power, sided with Mike Klonsky and Bernadine Dohrn who led the charge that Calvert had manipulated SDS into accepting the theory in the first place.[48]

While SDS ultimately collapsed in the process of debating the correct line on the working class, the broader New Left continued to probe the labor question. Indeed, one of the most significant by-products of the radical ferment of the 1960s was the emergence of numerous centers of independent leftist thought, which ultimately found an audience within labor circles. Journals, such as *Radical America,* conferences like the Socialist Scholars conferences, and left college campuses and communities provided the milieu in which new leftists maintained a vital dialogue on the nature of the working class, the subject of agency, and other related topic. In fact, this dialogue refutes the argument that the middle-class nature of the New Left and/or its emphasis on personal politics predetermined its trajectory. Moreover, the nature of this dialogue suggests that the New Left actually expanded the theoretical boundaries of the discussion of labor and, in turn, provided the context for renewing and improving ties to labor and vice versa.[49]

One of the most significant contributors to the dialogue on the labor question was Herbert Marcuse. In *One Dimensional Man* and a series of essays, Marcuse scrutinized advanced industrial society. While he agreed with much of the new working-class analysis, indeed can be seen as one of its progenitors, Marcuse retained a more critical edge to his theory than younger new leftists who touted him as their philosopher king. With an eye to cultural and psychological determinants, as well as material, Marcuse posited that the new working class was repressed as much as it was exploited. Advanced capitalism had created consumers, not producers, who sought gratification. But modern society had evolved in such a way as to demand that individuals deny their sexual and libidinal desires. This contradiction lay at the base of the new working class's alienation and plagued the traditional working class as well. Nonetheless, Marcuse continued, advanced capitalist society had constructed powerful cultural constraints that limited the new working class from becoming conscious of its own repression. Hence, a revolution was not imminent.[50]

Less famous than Marcuse, though perhaps as influential, was Stanley Aronowitz. Along with Sidney Lens, Aronowitz carved out a niche within the New Left as its resident labor expert. From the pages of the *Guardian* and other left journals, he offered constructive comments on the labor movement and the working class. While Aronowitz would later contend that the labor movement could not be regenerated, as of the latter 1960s he held a more ambivalent position. He staked out a middle ground. Without acting as a a labor booster, Aronowitz defended it from those who would write it off. He dismissed PL's argument that the American worker was a step away from revolutionary class consciousness and the Weatherman's contention that they enjoyed "white skin privilege." For example, Aronowitz approached the formation of the Alliance for Labor Action as a phenomenon deserving new left attention, even offering the guarded remark that the split within the House of Labor was a "signal for a new alliance."[51]

The development of vibrant and independent left thought on labor became even more apparent with the birth of *Radical America* in 1967. Initially an autonomous arm of SDS, (as part of SDS's Radical Education Project), *Radical America* supplanted *Studies on the Left* as the most important theoretical and semischolarly leftist journal, after *Studies* ceased publication. *Radical America* tried to combine the best of the old with the best of the new. It contributed to the dialogue on Socialist theory by examining the history of radicalism in America and reaching out to unaligned intellectuals and a broad audience of activists. In so doing, it explicitly hoped to fill a void on the New Left, namely a lack of knowledge about past radical movements and a lack of theory. As

Radical America's editors put it, they accepted the mission of unburying America's radical past from layers of liberal consensus analysis. If new leftists had forgotten or never known about American radical traditions, the editors felt they could rectify the deficiency.[52]

Radical America published articles on the IWW, the Socialist party, the Southern Tenants Farmers' Union and excerpts from American radicals, such as Daniel DeLeon. In addition, *Radical America* presented pieces, indeed entire issues, on the role of popular and working-class culture, gender differences, the relationship between the Third World and the economically advanced world, and the militancy of young workers, worldwide. One of its founders, Paul Buhle, later admitted that the journal did not achieve its lofty goal of providing the theory that would direct the imminent revolution. Nevertheless, it built a permanent legacy. The fact that over twenty-five years later *Radical America* was still around testifies to its achievement. As Paul Berman wrote on the fifteenth anniversary of the magazine: "It helped set a tone for a generation of historians and intellectuals, who have spread these ideas to many more people than ever see the magazine."[53]

Other journals, institutes, disciplines, and conferences, added to the debate on the labor question. Inside academia, a core of labor and social historians, including Herbert Gutman, Jesse Lemisch, and Alfred Young gained an important toehold, out of which would grow a much larger revision of American history. They inspired a generation of historians, sociologists, and other experts to dig deep into the American past to unearth a tradition of collective action and community strength on the part of working people. In the study of literature, law, economics, and other social sciences a similar revision of the existing canon took place. Writing in 1982, Bertell Ollman and Edward Vernoff proclaimed: "A Marxist cultural revolution is taking place in American universities. More and more students and faculty are being introduced to Marx's interpretation of how capitalism works (for whom it works better, for whom worse), how it arose, and where it is tending."[54] Even if Ollman and Vernoff exaggerated the extent of the revolution, no one could challenge their claim that American education had undergone a considerable change since the late 1950s when Marx or nearly any study of class had disappeared from the college campus and curriculum.

In the South, several SSOC (Southern Student Organizing Committee) veterans ended up working for *Southern Exposure,* which, like *Radical America,* dedicated itself to unburying the tradition of dissent. A special issue of *Southern Exposure,* published in 1974, entitled "No More Moanin': Voices of Southern Struggle," analyzed past labor battles, such as the UAW's sitdown strike in Atlanta in 1936 and the textile workers' uprising in Gastonia in 1929. *Southern Exposure* also paid homage to several lesser-known southern activists, such as Claude and Joyce Williams.[55]

Root and Branch, a short-lived but influential journal, subsequently republished in book form, did much the same. Like *Southern Exposure* and *Radical America,* it examined the history of workers in America. *Root and Branch* reported on the current labor scene, highlighting various rank-and-file revolts. It introduced readers to obscure theories of working-class control, such as those of Anton Panocek. Lastly, like *Radical America* and *Southern Exposure, Root and Branch* presented a critical view of the AFL–CIO and labor leaders, while at the same time promoting a favorable view of the working class and the centrality of its struggle in the past, present, and future.[56]

Discussion of the labor question also prospered at the Socialist Scholars Conferences, held annually between 1964 and 1969. Open to anyone who considered themselves a Socialist, and attended by a wide variety of individuals, the conferences clearly depicted the intellectual ferment that had developed in the 1960s alongside the revolt in the streets. During the height of the cold war, radical intellectuals had remained isolated and depressed. The growth of the New Left prompted older leftists to escape their isolation, and the Socialist Scholars Conferences provided them with a forum for exchanging ideas. At the conferences, younger Socialists came into contact with veteran leftists. For example, Paul Sweezy, Irving Howe, Christopher Lasch, Stanley Aronowitz, Tom Hayden and Abbie Hoffman, and SNCC militant Ivanhoe Donaldson were among those to present papers at one year's conference. An even more eclectic group of individuals listened to their presentations or mulled in the halls. While the discussions did not produce consensus, nor significantly influence the militant wing of the New Left, they did stimulate dialogue.[57]

One key topic addressed by the conferees was the supposed demise of the proletariat. Commentator after commentator observed that industrial workers had not played their prescribed role. "A consensus is emerging among Marxists themselves that the industrial proletariat is no longer a potentially revolutionary force," stated Martin Nicolaus. Why? Because, as Nicolaus explained, the past was worse than the present, and the future promised to be a bit better.[58] Several other conference participants, old and young, bolstered Nicolaus's prognosis, with Irving Howe suggesting that Socialists should quit seeking a revolutionary agent.

Another issue of concern was put forth by Christopher Lasch, a young leftist scholar who gained notoriety through his attack on the

American Congress for Cultural Freedom. He bemoaned less the state of the proletariat than that of the history of American radicalism. American culture had failed to generate a radical political tradition, Lasch postulated. "Every serious thinker on social questions has had to start almost from scratch, because the conceptual schemes available to him are so primitive as to be useless for the purpose of critical analyses." Lasch, who assumed that the working class was not materially deprived, added that leftists had to escape the economic myopia of the Old Left; they had to turn to the study of culture and politics.[59]

One of Lasch's colleagues, John Cammet offered a less pessimistic view of this subject. While Cammet agreed with Lasch's disapprobation of America's past, he reasoned that leftists could turn the absence of an American radical tradition to their advantage. Rather than despair, Cammet suggested that the lack of a tradition and an a priori agent for change freed the New Left from past mistakes and cumbersome legacies. Quoting another colleague, John Cowley, (Cammet, Lasch, and Cowley all wrote for *Studies on the Left*) Cammet stated:

> Precisely because the American socialist movement is one of the most backward and feeble in the world . . . it possesses what Veblen called the 'advantages of the borrower,' the possibility of utilizing the most advanced concepts of the European Left without inheriting the dead weight of the past under which European socialism must labor.[60]

Cammet identified Antonia Gramsci as the key thinker from whom the New Left should borrow. Gramsci, according to Cammet, criticized both trade unions and Socialist parties (especially as political entities) as negative forces. He argued that both reacted against capitalism but failed to serve as positive forces for a revolution. Both were restricted by their relations with the bourgeoisie; both accepted "the rules of the game" and capitalist laws. And thus both were "incapable of embodying a positive revolutionary movement." According to Cammet, Gramsci shared the New Left's faith in participatory democracy. "Gramsci was unyielding on the question of absolute representation," and considered absolute democracy, or participatory democracy in new left terminology, as an alternative to trade unions and politically oriented Socialist parties. In sum, Gramsci offered a sophisticated view of culture and political economy and a new means for defining the role of the working class and the intellectual.[61]

Several leftists responded favorably to Cammet's paper or, more specifically, to Gramsci's ideas. In a rave review of Cammet's *Antonio Gramsci and Italian Communism,* Marxist historian Eugene Genovese declared that the left owed Cammet "an immeasurable debt of gratitude for introducing Gramsci," to them. Gramsci's thought, in Genovese's estimation, represented the "maturation of Marxism and its restoration to the high level of its founders. . . . it exposes the degeneration of much that has passed for Marxism in our day." Gramsci moved away from the crass determinism and economic reductionism of many self-proclaimed Marxists. He expanded the concerns of the Socialist intellectual to include the role of culture and politics as well as economics. Gramsci's writings provided important insights on the nature of the working class, giving a boost to those who wanted to define the proletariat as a relationship rather than as an economic category. Yet at the same time, Gramsci retained a prominent role for the traditional proletariat in any radical movement; he did not write them off as bourgeois imperialists.[62]

Many at the conference did not share Genovese's enrapture with Gramsci. But the fact that a debate was taking place was more significant than the substance of the debate itself. In a nutshell, this was what really mattered. Even though SDS disintegrated various segments of the New Left persevered. While new leftists did not reach a consensus on the definition of socialism nor arrive at a plan for a revolution, they maintained an open and vibrant dialogue on the labor question. And, as became evident at the Socialist Scholars Conferences and in various radical journals and books, they examined new and interesting theories and gave Socialist thought, in general, a big boost. Furthermore, Social Democrats allied with the labor movement, like Michael Harrington and Gus Tyler, participated in this dialogue. In turn, this provided new leftists with the opportunity to renew links with the labor movement itself.[63]

Although here we must be careful not to exaggerate. As noble as the intentions of those who continued to probe the labor question were, they shared a certain unrealistic view of their times with the most starry-eyed radicals of SDS. They tended to see themselves in a revolutionary situation and were often animated by the belief that they were constructing the theory that would accompany if not pave the way for "the revolution." Such a stance, however, insured that they would have little chance of forging lasting ties with labor in America, leaders, or rank and file. Indeed, no evidence exists that suggests that labor favored revolution. They favored continued reform not radical change. Put another way, until new left theorists shed their belief that a revolution was possible or even desirous their theories would retain a false ring. Only when they reconciled their noble desires for a more perfect society with realistic assessment of their times could their theories establish the basis for forging lasting ties with labor, either as a whole or significant parts, thereof.

This said, the New Left's debate of the labor question, regardless of its impact on its relationship with labor, reveals how important labor was to the New Left in the first place. Many new leftists, from Stanley Aronowitz to Greg Calvert, spent considerable time and energy pondering the nature of the working class and the New Left's proper stance toward it. They did not consider labor to be irrelevant and, at least in their minds, were not cut off from it as numerous commentators have claimed.

7

Organizing the Unorganized

For over fifty years a variety of groups sought to organize migrant farm workers. Before World War I, the IWW valiantly struggled for better wages and conditions in the fertile fields in California. In the 1930s, the Communist party did the same. And in the 1950s, AFL–CIO officials initiated sporadic campaigns to unionize those who picked much of the produce that Americans consumed. Each one of these efforts generated an array of heroic tales, from John Steinbecks's *Grapes of Wrath* to the CBS film documentary, "The Harvest and the Shame." Yet, none of them achieved their goals. Indeed, as the 1960s dawned, migrant farm workers faced just as depressing conditions as they had a half-century before.

This all changed rapidly with the emergence of the United Farm Workers of America under the leadership of Cesar Chavez. Beginning with a strike against California's wine grape growers, in 1965, and then spreading to other fruit and vegetable producers, the UFW fought and overcame their adversaries. Indeed, by the end of the decade, the UFW had staged the largest consumer boycott in modern American history and had won a union contract for its members.[1]

Without a doubt, the United Farm Workers of America owed much of its success to the backing it received from an extraordinary coalition of supporters. As the union's newspaper *El Malcriado* reported shortly after farm workers struck at Delano in 1965: "Priests . . . student groups . . . Mexicans, Filipinos and Negro groups . . . [and] other poor workers" united behind them. Some came in person; others sent aid, letters of support, or their prayers. According to Dick Meister and Anne Loftis, these outsiders "flocked to the vineyards from all over California with money, food, clothing and new ideas, tactics, influence and technical skills the farm workers lacked." They transformed the strike into "a worldwide cause—a civil rights movement with religious overtones."[2]

Civil rights groups and individual veterans of the crusade for racial equality in the Deep South were among the first to back the farm workers. The *Movement,* SNCC's newspaper, exuberantly described the National Farm Workers of America, the UFW's predecessor, as "somewhere between a movement and an industrial union" and commanded all activists to support its efforts. CORE leader George Wiley and SNCC officer Elizabeth Sutherland jointly urged their "friends" to back the farm laborers. In the fall of 1965, CORE and SNCC volunteers rushed to Delano to teach the strikers the practice of nonviolence. At approximately the same time individual civil rights activists, many of them fresh from struggles in the Deep South, made their way to the San Joaquin Valley in California. (Some white activists did so because they were no longer welcome within SNCC.) Marshall Ganz, for one, a Mississippi summer volunteer, joined the farm workers movement in the fall of 1965. Ultimately he became a member of the union's executive board.[3]

Student radicals joined the crusade just as quickly, with University of California at Berkeley students and the union developing a special relationship. In the fall of 1965, Berkeley students set up tables on campus and canvassed the community to solicit aid. They established ad hoc groups to coordinate their efforts and invited union organizers to speak on campus. At one rally, UFW president Cesar Chavez addressed thousands of supportive students. While he described the horrid work conditions that farm workers faced and the brutality of the growers, the students collected $2,000 and a truckload of food on behalf of the union. In the spring of 1966, Berkeley radicals joined farm workers in the last leg of the latter's Delano to Sacramento pilgrimage. From the steps of the state capitol, Chavez thanked them for their demonstration of solidarity. Later that summer, Berkeley activists organized a summer labor project which, like the Mississippi Summer project of 1964, placed student volunteers in the field alongside exploited workers.[4]

In centers of radicalism and on campuses that had been largely untouched by the movement, students rallied behind the UFW as well. University of Wisconsin activists organized marches and demonstrations in sympathy with the UFW with as much zeal as they campaigned against the war. Daniel Ortiz, a Lincoln, Nebraska student, wrote Chavez that he planned to organize a new chapter of SDS around the specific goal of helping the farm workers. (He found the orientation of the National Office of SDS out of touch with most of his fellow Cornhuskers.) Similarly, University of Florida student activists worked with the Industrial Union Department of the AFL–CIO and the Packinghouse Workers to organize a separate UFW chapter.[5]

Trade unions quickly endorsed the farm workers' strike too. The

Teamsters and Longshoremen, for example, refused to ship nonunion goods. Unions that worked in related fields, such as the Retail Clerks, Packinghouse Workers, and Seafarers, helped man the picket lines, lent their facilities to the farm workers and provided food, clothing and money. The AFL–CIO voted to give the NFWA "100% support." Subsequently, Walter Reuther and UAW western regional director Paul Schrade rushed to Delano to inform the strikers of organized labor's decision. "This is not your strike, this is *our* strike," Reuther told a rally of hundreds of farm workers. Reuther presented Chavez and Larry Itlong, the leader of AWOC, with a check for $10,000, divided equally between the NFWA and AWOC. After speaking, Reuther and Schrade joined Chavez, Itlong and hundreds of other farm workers in a march through the streets of Delano. In defiance of a court order against demonstrating, Reuther triumphantly hoisted a NFWA sign, emblazoned with the word "Huelga" and the NFWA's symbolic black eagle, high above his shoulders. (Chavez later credited Reuther with bringing the strike national attention.)[6]

After winning an unprecedented union contract from several vintners, the farm workers turned to the more arduous task of winning recognition from table grape growers. Their success depended on staging the most successful consumer boycott of the postwar era, perhaps in all of U.S. labor history. The boycott transformed hundreds of thousands of Americans into union allies; it united the very same groups that were otherwise bitterly divided.[7]

The AFL–CIO executive council immediately endorsed the effort. Labor papers advertised their support and individual unions posted proboycott broadsides in union halls and passed out leaflets at union meetings. All across the country labor leaders and rank-and-file union members and their families set up pickets and refused to purchase goods from stores that carried the forbidden fruit.[8]

Concurrently, SNCC and CORE volunteers followed shipments of grapes across the country and alerted local organizing committees when nonunion goods arrived in town. SDS chapters organized boycott committees on college campuses and led demonstrations against scab grapes. In Boston, SDS, SNCC, and CORE members staged a "Boston Grape party," dumping crates of grapes into the Boston harbor. Not to be outdone, Berkeley students staged a sit-in at Sproul Hall to demand compliance with the boycott. When the university arrested the participants, over three thousand students congregated in Sproul Plaza to demand their release.[9]

The boycott in New York City epitomized the coalition, with radical students, conservative trade unionists, and liberal politicians overcom-

ing their differences to cooperate for the farm workers' sake. Sam
Kushner writes:

> It was there that taxi drivers, who had probably never before met a
> farm worker, marched in picket lines with campesinos who never
> before had encountered the cold winter in New York, let alone ride
> in a taxi. It was also in New York that one of the most incongruous
> relations developed—between the farm workers and the Seaman's
> Union, headed by Paul Hall. This union, one of the most conserva-
> tive in the nation, provided living quarters for farm workers from
> Delano, furnished them with transportation and made accessible
> offices out of which the strikers operated.[10]

At one New York City demonstration Cesar Chavez, Mayor John
Lindsay, New York Central Labor Council president Harry Van Arsdale
Jr., Congresswoman Bella Abzug, Congressman Edward Koch and Construction Union leader Peter J. Brennan led a crowd of housewives,
antiwar activists, trade unionists and others in chants of "Huelga" and
"Boycott." Just a few years later Brennan would defend construction
workers who beat up antiwar demonstrators. On another occasion, in
1968, black leader Percy Sutton, feminist Gloria Steinem, labor leader
Morris Iushewitz and columnist Jimmy Breslin asked demonstrators to
boycott the supermarket chain Gristedes, simply because it carried
nonunion grapes. New Yorkers responded with fervor. Not only did
Gristedes' revenues decline, but throughout the city grape sales plummeted
95 percent.[11]

The boycott in Chicago revealed a similar pattern. In what was
otherwise one of the most polarized cities in America, trade unionists,
civil rights workers, student leftists, antiwar activists, and an assortment
of reformers united to win a decent life for migrant workers. The
Chicago Citizens Committee to Aid the Delano Farm Workers counted
as its members union leaders, such as Charles Coogen, Murray Finley
and Ralph Helstein, new leftists, such as Richard Flacks, Bernard Lafayette,
Lee Webb and Jesse Lemisch, and Chicago civil rights activists, such as
Al Raby.[12]

Considering the divisive effects of the Vietnam War, Black Power,
and the counterculture, why did student radicals, Black Power advocates,
trade union officials and rank-and-file members join together? What led
them to cast aside their differences? What made the farm workers special?

First, the farm workers engendered unity because they were visibly
and excessively exploited. Farm workers toiled long hours performing
arduous physical labor, for rock-bottom wages, lived in dilapidated
shacks, were constantly on the move, and had few chances of escaping

their plight. Radical students who disdained supposed middle-class workers had no qualms about supporting impoverished ones. As one leaflet read:

HAVE YOU EVER WORKED
- for an average of $1,307 a year?
- surrounded by poisonous chemicals all the time?
- in a job where there are no fringe benefits, no medical insurance and no pension plans?
- in a job that isn't covered by minimum-wage laws, unemployment compensation, or laws allowing collective bargaining?
- the people who pick your fruits and vegetables do![13]

Union leaders stressed the same theme.[14]

Ironically, large growers did not deny these charges. Instead, they reasoned that substandard conditions justified the extension of the "bracero program," which allowed Mexican nationals to come to the United States on temporary work visas. Begun during World War II when farmers faced a labor shortage, the bracero program continued until the mid–1960s. Intense lobbying efforts by the growers, who argued that U.S. citizens would not work under prevailing conditions, enabled the program to continue for two decades beyond its original purpose.[15]

Second, Chavez and the union tapped into the upsurge in racial pride that abounded in the 1960s. By casting themselves as representatives of "La Raza," the farm workers emphasized that their struggle was more than just a fight for union recognition but for minority rights as well. This emphasis strengthened the union's ties with chicanos, many of whom had never worked as farm laborers. It solidified links with black activists who viewed the United Farm Workers as comrades in the worldwide liberation movement against racism and imperialism, and it advanced their standing among white student radicals for whom minority empowerment was a paramount objective.[16]

Third, the farm workers gained support by implying that they symbolized an even broader crusade for justice and equality, known as "La Causa." While the definition of La Causa varied, it included the claim that the farm workers were an extension of the early civil rights movement, part of the antiwar and ecology movements and, most broadly, the cutting edge of all progressive causes.[17] Student activists who had misgivings about rallying around a simple drive for union recognition, flocked to this one. To them, wrote Paul Jacobs, a veteran leftist who had written a seminal and critical work on labor in the early 1960s, the UFW provided "a new source of hope."[18]

Paradoxically, some union leaders clung to the farm workers movement not because it symbolized their progressive present but because it reminded them of their more militant past. Participating in the farm workers movement signified that "they still had a heart . . . a militant spirit," stated AWOC head Larry Itlong. As Walter Reuther remarked while marching in Delano, "I haven't felt like this in years." Chavez's and the UFW's commitment to nonviolence swelled the sympathizers' ranks. Martin Luther King, Jr., for one, designated Chavez a patron saint in the nonviolent crusade, "a living example of the Gandhian tradition with its great love for social progress and its healing spiritual powers."[19]

Fourth, just as southern white supremacists, like "Bull" Connor, had engendered unity among new leftists and labor in the early 1960s, so too did the clumsy actions of the UFW's foes. Large growers opposed the UFW at every step. They hired goons to beat up picketing workers, sanctioned the John Birch Society's red-baiting of the union, and prodded conservative members of the California Senate Committee on Un-American Activities to conduct an investigation into the alleged communist ties of the NFWA. When these heavy-handed tactics failed, agribusinesses hired public relation firms to run a consumer rights campaign, with conservative politicians, such as Governor Ronald Reagan and presidential candidate Richard Nixon boasting that they had probably eaten more grapes in 1968 than ever before. When all of these actions failed, growers resorted to signing sweetheart contracts with the corruption-riddled Teamsters. Yet all of these tactics backfired, as new leftists, labor, and liberals, redoubled their efforts.[20]

Of course, tensions existed between the collaborators. George Meany, the consummate business unionist, worried about the AFL-CIO's commitment to such an unusual labor organization, one that called itself La Causa and La Raza. Meany even asked William Kirshner, the AFL-CIO official in charge of organizing the farm workers, whether the UFW was really a trade union. Meany also expressed his concern about the UFW's performance, observing that the AFL-CIO had contributed thousands of dollars to the union with little to show in return. At the same time, new leftists questioned the propriety of allying with Meany and the AFL-CIO, postulating that the House of Labor would co-opt the farm workers and transform La Causa into a bread-and-butter union. Chavez himself feared that the AFL-CIO would restrict his freedom and the farm workers' militancy.[21]

Nonetheless, the divergent groups continued to cooperate. In spite of his concerns, Meany extended funds and an offer of a union charter to the farm workers. Chavez openly accepted the AFL-CIO's backing and offer because he believed that organized labor could provide more in terms of pragmatic support than it could take away in terms of militancy. Unprepared to abandon the farm workers just because they operated under the AFL–CIO banner, the New Left extended the grape boycott and its interaction with Chavez.[22]

In the same years as the Farm Workers fought for union recognition in California, other workers campaigned for better wages and conditions across the country. Many of these efforts occurred in traditionally hard to organize industries, especially in the South. Relatively good economic conditions produced a context favorable to labor organizing. The civil rights movement galvanized many workers into action, especially black workers. In some instances, veteran civil rights activists or student leftists led the organizing campaigns. For instance, one union drive was a direct outgrowth of the Mississippi Summer Project of 1964. In January 1965, poor cotton workers, farm laborers, and tenant farmers, many of whom had participated in freedom schools and the Mississippi Freedom Democratic party, including Fannie Lou Hamer, formed the Mississippi Freedom Labor Union. By the summer of 1965 the MFLU had enlisted over twelve hundred workers from eight Delta counties. At harvest time, the union called a strike that gained the additional support of approximately three hundred skilled tractor operators. As the *NY Times* observed, the MFLU signified the first attempt to organize southern farmhands since "the abortive sharecropper uprisings of the Thirties and Forties."[23]

MFLU defined its goals in terms that fused class and race appeals; it joined the tactics of trade unionism and the southern civil rights movement. "Wake up and think. We as Negroes should want to be equal and get high wages," read one leaflet. "Please join the union because if you are not in the union you just aren't anywhere." Like the southern civil rights movement, the MFLU prodded the federal government to enforce the law, namely the payment of the federal minimum wage of $1.25 an hour (Mississippi farm workers earned about $3.00 a day), disbursement of federal farm subsidies to tenants, not just to landowners, and enforcement of the Wagner Act.[24]

From its inception, the MFLU built upon and sought additional support from the New Left. SNCC and CORE heralded the union as the "economic arm of the revolution." Several SNCC veterans, including Robert Analavage, joined MFLU in the field. *Southern Patriot,* SCEF's newspaper, championed MFLU as one of the "most significant developments" in the nation. Activist Liz Shirah added that the cotton workers' strike represented an important turn to economic concerns.[25]

Yet, unlike the UFW, the MFLU's stike collapsed, partly because new left and labor support never blossomed. Consumed with their own internal debates, SNCC and CORE did not commit themselves fully to this organizing drive. The white student left focused its attention on campus affairs and the Vietnam War. As in the past, the AFL–CIO extended only minimal aid to migrant farm workers in the Deep South, with Claude Ramsay, state AFL–CIO chief, counseling against rushing to MFLU's side, because, in Ramsay's estimation, there were simply too many underemployed and unemployed farmers in the region to win. He added that some of MFLU's supporters were opportunists who "don't have the welfare of the people at heart."[26]

Yet MFLU did not disappear; instead it metamorphosed into a poor people's movement in the Delta. Aided by the Delta ministry, an off-shoot of the National Council of Churches, MFLU staged a series of protests to demand economic relief. First it occupied Greenville Air Force Base. Then it conducted a pilgrimage and set up several symbolic encampments, known as "Strike City," "Mud City," "Tent City" and finally "Freedom Village," in Mt. Beulah. It settled on the last location about the same time as James Meredith was shot. While SNCC used the Meredith shooting as the chance to broadcast its message of Black Power, the transformed MFLU developed cooperative workshops and a self-sustaining community. In time, several MFLU members gained political power, including Owen Brooks, who secured a post as an administrative aide to Mike Espy, the first black congressman in Mississippi since Reconstruction.[27]

Still another union drive took place among migrant farm workers in Texas. Inspired by their brethren in California, Texas farm laborers struck for better wages and conditions. They immediately gained the support of the UFW. Texas state AFL–CIO officials, led by state federation president Hank Brown, organized demonstrations in sympathy with the migrant workers, including one of twenty thousand in front of the state capitol. The AFL–CIO executive council and constitutional convention endorsed the Texas organizing campaign. Numerous labor papers published articles and photographs that graphically depicted the repression of the Texas workers at the hands of the Texas Rangers. Even George Meany issued pleas for aid. Student and civil rights activists joined the Texas struggle with 250 students from eleven colleges organizing a four-hundred-mile march. New left journals championed the Texas struggle, with Doug Adair reporting that the Texas farm workers strike had broadened into a social movement that was "sweeping through all of South Texas." As a result of these actions, John Spragens, Jr., announced that the movement's call had changed from "Freedom Now" to "Huelga."[28]

Migrant farm workers in Florida also sought to form a union. Like their comrades in California and Texas, they gained the support of student leftists and union officials. The Southern Student Organizing Committee, an ally of SDS and SNCC, played an especially prominent role in helping them organize. SSOC member Tommy Martin led a strike of about two thousand migrant workers in Belle Grade, Florida. For his efforts, he was slugged in the face by a local labor contractor and arrested for disturbing the peace. (The case was subsequently dismissed.) Nan Guerrero reported that these efforts paved the way for a successful farm workers' union in the state. By February 1967, she claimed, over twenty-five thousand workers had signed union cards. Even though she exaggerated her numbers, her point should not be dismissed. Considering the barriers to organizing migrant workers, even a few thousand union enrollees was a considerable achievement.[29]

Meanwhile, in the birthplace of the student civil rights movement, Greensboro, North Carolina, and in other nearby college towns, student and black activists rallied behind textile and campus workers who sought union recognition and better wages and conditions. At first, many of these workers doubted the value of their new advocates. They felt uneasy with radical students and questioned the depth of their commitment. This was especially true for workers who lived in small, isolated and provincial "company towns," such as Haw River, North Carolina. In such communities, the only contact they had with students was through the local media, which, in the words of one activist, convinced them that most students were "beatnik Communists—or worse yet—civil rights workers." But, by shaving their beards and persistently offering their services, student activists earned these workers' trust. For instance, small meetings between textile workers in Haw Mill and students and the continual presence of the latter on the picket line reinforced the workers' faith in their new allies. Workers even started to visit various regional campuses to recruit student support.[30]

Workers were not the only ones who had to overcome their provincialism. Students had to do so as well. Especially in the South, where trade unionism had been historically weak, labor was not seen as a natural constituent by campus activists. As Anne Schunior, a senior at North Carolina University simply put it: "A lot of students I talk to don't like unions." The student newspaper at North Carolina University concurred: "What business do students have in a labor dispute?" Direct and indirect contact with workers, however, convinced a substantial number of students that they had "plenty" reasons for involving themselves in a labor dispute. "For what's involved," declared the student newspaper that had posed the question, "is the bringing of some members of North Carolina's textile industry—kicking and screaming, if necessary—across the threshold of the 20th Century."[31]

Exposés of financial connections between industrial powers and southern universities fortified this view. They allowed student activists to see union drives as part of a larger battle for power against multinational corporations and the war machine. For instance, one exposé revealed that Duke's board of trustees was stacked with the heads of textile, tobacco, and financial corporations, all of which had long antiunion records and supported other conservative causes.[32]

Two examples of collaboration were the strike against a Levi Strauss plant in the Blue Ridge Mountains and the attempt of Duke University nonacademic employees to gain a union contract. The former allowed SDS to make a significant symbolic move. "Levis have been the 'uniform' of the college students, the civil rights worker, the young and the hippie," proclaimed Sam Shirah, a veteran southern activist. "We are asking you to show your support for the 400 brave women on strike in Blue Ridge by giving up your uniform." Chapters in New York City, New Orleans, and Atlanta responded by staging "strip-ins" of blue jeans.[33]

Likewise, when Duke's employees went on strike, student activists utilized a variety of tactics or techniques that they had developed in campaigns against the war and racial inequality. They held mass demonstrations, vigils, sit-ins and conducted an intensive investigation into the corporate ties of the university. Future historian Sara Evans captured the objective of many involved in the latter campaign, writing, "A union victory at Duke will be a symbolic victory over entrenched southern anti-unionism and university paternalism."[34]

———

Much of the support for southern workers came from a loose collection of southern white students who had joined the civil rights movement in the early 1960s. Though most of them were not of working-class background, and unlike many of SDS's founders did not have old left or labor ties, they felt a need to organize poor blacks and whites around economic goals. Many were influenced by W. J. Cash's idea that the South was a special segment of the nation, historically exploited by the North. They also felt that neither SNCC nor SDS could organize southern whites, since they were either too militant or lacked an adequate base outside of the North.[35]

To give voice to their views, this groups established the Southern Student Organizing Committee. SSOC held its first organizing conference in Nashville, Tennessee, in the spring of 1964, where it elected civil rights workers Sue Thrasher and Gene Guerrero as executive secretary and chairman, respectively. At the same time, SSOC laid plans for a larger convention following Mississippi Summer. Among those who attended either the Nashville or ensuing Atlanta conventions were Howard Romaine, Sam Shirah, Ed Hamlet, Bob Zellner and Dottie Miller, Cathy Cade, and Casey Hayden. Nearly all of them had been influenced by Carl and Anne Braden, Jim Dombrowski, and Myles Horton, all persistent advocates of forming an interracial movement of working people.[36]

Shortly after SSOC was formed, Peter Brandon, a TWUA official and a long-time supporter of SNCC and SDS, recruited Guerrero to organize textile workers in the Carolinas. Though Guerrero was skeptical about the commitment of national labor unions to such an effort, Brandon convinced him that the Textile Workers Union permitted its locals enough freedom to make the drive worthwhile. The fact that one of the targets of the TWUA drive was the Cone Mill plant on the Dan River, outside Danville, Virginia, the location of one of SNCC's greatest confrontations, also influenced Guerrero's decision to join the campaign.[37]

Typical of student activists who allied with the labor movement, Guerrero maintained a militant posture. He called for an all-out strike against the mills, rather than a series of small job-actions as recommended by seasoned union officials. When union officials refused to follow his strategy, he grew impatient. Ultimately, he left the Dan River campaign but not the union, turning his attention to organizing workers at a much smaller plant owned by the National Spinning Company in Whiteville, North Carolina. There, he organized a freedom march from Whiteville to Wilmington," which he hoped would garner additional outside support.[38] Though he failed to win a union contract, his efforts were not fruitless. As was the case in Danville and at Duke University, the employer was forced to raise wages and make other concessions. Moreover, in years to come, activists built on the momentum developed in these early drives to win breakthrough contracts.[39]

In April 1966, SSOC held a "Student and Labor Conference" in Durham, North Carolina. The conference built on increased interest in economic issues and the students' admitted desire to know more about organized labor. Without muting their criticism of the labor movement, the activists saw the conference as a mechanism for establishing deeper ties with labor, which in turn would lead to more joint projects. Among those who attended were SDS veterans, Jim Williams and Robb Burlage, labor activists, Peter Brandon and Norman Hill, and several younger southern activists, including Sara Evans and Harry Boyte. The participants paid special attention to the possibility of combining student and

labor resources in southern organizing drives. Many of the conferees left
the meeting with the feeling that it was both "desirable and feasible" to
cooperate. Robb Burlage even argued that union organizing provided
SSOC with "the best potential" for establishing a link between Negroes
and poor whites," which was essential to the goal of democracy and
social justice in the South.[40]

Shortly after the conference SSOC established the Southern Labor
Action movement. SLAM's manifesto described itself as an auxiliary or
support group for strikes or organizing campaigns already in existence
and as a promoter of worker-student alliances, particularly on college
campuses. "We believe that the southern worker is beginning to move
and that his developing movement should be supported and projected.
He needs to feel a part of something bigger than the narrow union to
which he belongs. We therefore formed SLAM for the purpose of
dramatizing and projecting a movement that is already growing in the
hope that it will develop and flourish."[41] Through its contacts with SDS
and SNCC, SSOC brought in Pete Seeger to conduct a benefit concert
for the Levi's strikers. When this strike collapsed, SSOC members transferred their attention to a similar effort against Farrah's.[42]

In time, internal divisions, of the type that plagued SDS and SNCC,
tore SLAM apart. Progressive Labor, the Revolutionary Youth movement and other smaller factions of the New Left battled for control
of SSOC and its labor organizing arm. As a result, most of SSOC's
founding members left SSOC. But they did not eschew the ideal of
organizing workers. Many of SSOC's founders remained in the South;
they congregated in and around Atlanta and the underground newspaper the *Great Speckled Bird*. Several of SSOC's other founders established *Southern Exposure*. Both publications, but especially the latter,
maintained an interest in the history and contemporary struggle of
working people.[43]

Like other white, native southern civil rights veterans, Bob Zellner,
dedicated himself to the labor cause, although he did so independently
of SSOC. Partly due to his contact with Myles Horton and the Bradens,
partly because SNCC left him with no other role, and also because of his
analysis of inequality in America, Zellner determined that organizing
workers was the next logical step in the drive to attain a more just
society. With the help of SCEF and some unions, Zellner and his wife
Dottie formed GROW, Grass Roots Organizing Workers. Initially conceived as an auxiliary of SNCC, GROW ended up as an independent

project, staffed primarily by veterans of Mississippi Summer, and the southern civil rights movement.[44]

Zellner's first major effort was in Laurel, Mississippi, among wood-workers at a local Masonite plant. The company had precipitated a bloody strike (the workers called it a lockout), most likely as part of a larger strategy to break the union. In order to divide black and white workers, the company fed rumors that the union was run by Klansmen (a rumor that was not entirely unfounded). But Zellner was not deterred. His relatives had once been members of the KKK. Moreover, he figured that the workers were in desperate need of support.[45]

With the help of an introduction provided by state AFL–CIO head Claude Ramsay, Zellner and his two colleagues Jack Minnis and Rob Analavage went to meet the local union leaders. Fearing that they might not be received warmly, the three synchronized their watches and agreed to leave, no matter what, at an appointed time. Escorted down a dark hallway into a dimly lit room, the first glance they got of the union's leadership was of twenty large white men sitting around a table. The local president, J. D. Gallagher, introduced them one by one, ending with Herbert Ishie, a notorious Klan enforcer or executioner. Ishie, who was built "like a tree trunk," in Zellner's words, held a big black box, which he occasionally opened and out of which the GROW organizers caught a glimpse of something dark, blue and metallic, presumably a gun. Drawing on years of experience as an organizer, Zellner swallowed his fear and announced: "Hi, my name is Bob Zellner and this is Jack Minnis and Bob Analavage." With typical GROW candidness he continued, "and we all work for SCEF. . . . we used to be on the staff of SNCC . . . and we have all been arrested . . . and we've been charged with criminal anarchy . . . called communists and nigger lovers." Ishie had not drawn his revolver yet. "But we are interested in the strike and know you are having a hard time and we have come to see if we can be of any assistance." Silence followed. Zellner added, "otherwise we'll be glad to leave." In a barely audible aside to his friends he added, "if we can." Still silence. Suddenly, the notorious Ishie burst out: "Well we don't give a shit who you are, we need help from whoever the fuck we can get it." Thenceforth it was "off and running" in Zellner's words. GROW developed a strong relationship with the local woodworkers and ultimately with the large Gulf Coast pulpworkers.[46]

Other civil rights veterans who followed Zellner's footsteps included Sam and Liz Shirah, Mike Higson, and Walter Tillow. A member of SNCC since the spring of 1963, a manager of the Atlanta office and an organizer of the MFDP challenge, Tillow was one of the main propo-nents of bridging the gap between the New Left and labor just as the two were drifting apart. He departed SNCC's 1963 "Jobs and Food Conference" determined to build a network of sympathetic contacts within the labor movement.[47] With the help of Myles Horton and the Bradens, Tillow convened a conference of southern civil rights activists and labor people in early 1965. The meeting, which took place at Highlander Center, attracted a wide array of individuals, including Bob Maxwell, Charles Koehler, and John Perdew, veterans of the White Folks, Hazard, and Southwest Georgia projects, respectively, as well as a dozen lesser-known Mississippi activists and labor officials. Though he could not attend, Teamster Vice President Harold Gibbons extended his support. "Warmest greeting to the conferees at the Student Nonviolent Coordinating Committee Labor Conference. . . . It will only be through the continued development and community of purpose that labor and the civil rights movement will forge a new America based on freedom and social justice." The conferees discussed labor law, economics, organizing tactics, and other related topics. Afterward, participants wrote Tillow that they were glad to have taken part in the meeting and hoped there would be more.[48]

It remains difficult to gauge the impact of these various conferences and individual efforts. Nevertheless, they displayed that a coalition could be built. Even though neither labor unions nor the New Left expanded precipitously in the South in the 1970s or 1980s, they did grow gradually and came to affect the economic and political scene. Even if they fell short of achieving the lofty goal of transforming the South, even if the millennium did not come—given the enormous odds against organizing unions, from centuries of racism to antilabor legislation—this new dialogue was an achievement nonetheless. Moreover, even though change was slow in coming, on occasion it could emerge with revolutionary fervor, and each time it did it affirmed the potential of all the other local struggles. Such was the case of the sanitations workers' strike in Memphis, Tennessee, in the late winter and early spring of 1968.

In 1963, T. O. Jones had begun an organizing drive among Memphis's predominantly black sanitation workers. In 1964, the sanitation workers affiliated with AFSCME—local 1733. The union received emotional, tactical, and some financial support from a handful of AFL–CIO locals, such as the Retail Clerks, and from civil rights groups, most prominently a coalition of black ministers, many of whom belonged to the NAACP. As the union gained strength, Jones routinely demanded union recognition from the city as well as better wages and conditions. The city refused to accede to these demands.[49]

A change in the structure of the city government and the election of a new Mayor, Henry Loeb, however, set off a chain of events that dramatically altered the situation. Loeb was a fiscal conservative who called for trimming the city budget. This included some cost-cutting measures involving the collection of garbage. Though not aimed particularly at Jones and his union, these actions aggravated relations with it. For instance, on 1 February 1968, two black sanitation workers were crushed to death while on the job. The sanitation workers blamed the deaths on a recent change in the work rules and a malfunctioning and improperly safe-guarded garbage truck, the by-products of recent cuts. Coming on top of years of friction with the city, the deaths provided the spark or the occasion for calling a strike.[50]

Civil rights groups, especially black ministers led by former SNCC leader, James Lawson; local NAACP leader, Benjamin Hooks; and Maxine Smith, a veteran of the sit-ins and freedom riders quickly endorsed the sanitation workers' walkout. Much of the local labor movement, including Memphis's AFL–CIO and Tennessee's state labor federation, did so as well. The Committee on the Move for Equality, or COME, an umbrella organization, was formed to direct sympathy protests. AFSCME immediately sent in veteran organizer P. J. Ciampi. National president Jerry Wurf followed. The union leaders held contentious meetings with the mayor and other city officials in which they demanded recognition and a dues' checkoff. The city refused to allow for either. Indeed, even when Wurf offered a compromise, one that allowed for the checkoff to come through the credit union, Loeb, who was an adamant opponent of public unions and a paternalist when it came to blacks, refused to budge.[51]

Reminiscent of the struggles of the early civil rights movement, local leaders threatened to protest until the jails were overflowing. Sanitation workers and sympathizers held daily marches from the black community to city hall. Rhetorical battles erupted during city council meetings, in the Mayor's office and in the press (the two major city papers were initially adamantly antiunion, though the local black press was much more sympathetic to the sanitation workers' cause). Following one heated exchange with the city council, COME led a march on downtown. The protest was peaceful until poorly trained and frustrated police officers wantonly attacked the crowd with mace and billy clubs. Even conservative ministers and federal civil rights authorities were injured in the melee. Younger black activist, some of whom belonged to a local neoblack nationalist organization, known as the Black Organizing Project (BOP), of which the radical Invaders were members, were outraged by this attack and hinted that they would turn to more militant tactics if the strike was not resolved peacefully.[52]

Still, Loeb refused to negotiate in good faith, insisting that public employee union's were illegal. Consequently, local activists arranged for national figures to come to Memphis, including Jesse Jackson, Hosea Williams, Roy Wilkins, and Bayard Rustin. Jerry Wurf reported financial support from unions around the country. Martin Luther King, Jr., accepted James Lawson's invitation to speak. In so doing, King emphasized that the strike stood as a prototype for his upcoming Poor People's Campaign in Washington, D.C. Other local ministers made plans to bring in SNCC militants Stokely Carmichael and H. Rap Brown, or as activist put it, "anyone that would be able to lend support to the strike."[53]

King's presence galvanized the entire black community of Memphis behind the sanitation workers and gained the strike national attention. Moreover, King's appearance provided the civil rights movement with a new objective—gaining economic rights for black workers through unionization. Even the *Wall Street Journal* recognized the significance of this aim: "A powerful Negro coalition has risen from the garbage of 'America's Cleanest City.' . . . Negroes have found a weapon in a sanitation workers strike that may be picked up elsewhere by civil rights militants." Black workers, the *Journal* pointed out, comprised a large percentage of the public employees in the South. And in the strike, blacks were discovering a goal that could be transferred to other cities, southern and northern, one with which the black and student left and trade unionists could cooperate. As some local ministers stated, the sanitation workers strike marked just the beginning. First, the sanitation workers would fight for union recognition. Other black workers would follow. Finally blacks would wage a consolidated struggle for economic equality.[54]

In reality though, Memphis blacks had to overcome internal divisions, similar to those found elsewhere between young militants, like the Invaders who disdained nonviolence, and moderates such as the SCLC. The rift in the black community became apparent in the midst of a massive protest march led by King. Less than half-way to its goal of city hall, the march disintegrated into looting and street-fighting. In response, King immediately turned the march around. Although a major riot was averted by King's action, his reputation was seriously tarnished. Both local and national officials and the mass media suggested that he was responsible for the violence and that he no longer enjoyed the respect of the black masses. The media and local officials also insisted that King announce a "cooling-off" period.[55]

Rather than acceding to this demand, King reaffirmed his commitment to the sanitation workers' strike. As he put it, their struggle marked a turning point; it was a confrontation that could not be avoided.

"Something is happening in Memphis [and] in our world," King informed an overflow crowd at the Mason Temple on the stormy night before his assassination. "The masses of people are rising up. And wherever they are assembled today, whether they are in Johannesburg, South Africa, Nairobi, Kenya, Accra, Ghana, New York City . . . or Memphis Tennessee, the cry is always the same. We want to be free!"[56]

If the second march had taken place, King probably would have successfully overcome the divisions within Memphis's black community and provided an alternative to confrontation. SCLC had carefully involved the Invaders in the planning of such a march by turning them into marshals. Since labor unionists and new leftists had trained their eyes on the events in Memphis, they very well may have mimicked it. In other words, a second march might have led the New Left and labor to cast aside their differences. Once again King would have served as a "vital center." Still other developments, namely President Johnson's decision not to seek renomination and Eugene McCarthy's and Robert F. Kennedy's startling showings in the primaries, might have reinforced this shift.[57]

Yet, a second successful march did not take place because King was assassinated. In place of a new spirit of cooperation, confrontation received another boost. Eldridge Cleaver declared that King's assassination "killed a dream"; Stokely Carmichael added that "now there won't be any other Negro leaders who will tell his brothers not to burn cities." Numerous activists fell into utter despair, joining in the riots that swept across the nation. Pointing to King's opposition to the war, they claimed that liberals were hypocrites for pretending to honor King on the occasion of his death.[58]

Nonetheless, King's assassination did not solely feed the fires of discord. While the nation convulsed in violence, Memphis activists recommitted themselves to winning economic justice for the sanitation workers through nonviolent struggle. A number of activists staged a sit-in at the Mayor's office. Others attended community "talks," which brought together COME veterans with opponents of the union. Most important, even before King was buried in his grave, tens of thousands of Memphis blacks, joined by national union and civil rights leaders, student activists, black militants, including the Invaders, staged another mass march. They strode arm in arm to city hall where they demanded immediate union recognition and a contract that met the sanitation workers' demands. Joan Turner Beifuss offers this description: "Eight abreast came the marchers. . . . In the front rows were well-known SCLC leaders; Walter Reuther . . . Albert Shanker . . . anti-war hero Dr. Benjamin Spock, Harry Belafonte . . . Ossie Davis. . . . As in Selma, there were men from the race and civil rights divisions of the national religious

denominations; the AFL–CIO civil rights division officials were there."
Cesar Chavez, rank-and-file unionists from all over, student activists
from LeMoyne and Southwestern College and most important the sanitation workers themselves marched. Behind the scenes Bayard Rustin
attended to the nitty gritty details of the protest, just like he had in
1963.[59]

At the rally that followed the march, Coretta Scott King inquired:
"How many more must die before we can really have a free and true and
peaceful society?" Reverend Ralph Abernathy proclaimed: "Nobody
gonna turn us around!" Jerry Wurf declared that "as a white trade
unionists, I say to you . . . that so long as we shall live we shall not forget
our struggle to be men, our struggle to stop being 'boys,'. . . we will not
go back to work!" And Walter Reuther pulled a $50,000 check out of his
pocket to give to Local 1733. (P. J. Ciampi and T. O. Jones ripped it out
of his hands before he had the opportunity to renege on his commitment.)[60]

Within a week, even as violence and shouts of revolution continued
to gain headlines, Mayor Loeb and the city government recognized the
sanitation workers' union and acceded to its demands for a dues checkoff and better wages and conditions.[61] Moreover, the Memphis strike
catalyzed other strikes, including one involving poor black health care
workers, members of Local 1199 of the Hospital Workers, in Charleston,
South Carolina, in 1969. The hospital workers gained the support of
SCLC, the AFL–CIO, and new leftists.[62]

And Charleston was only the best-known post-King assassination
union drive. In Charlotte and Chapel Hill, North Carolina, for example,
black workers made new strides in their struggle for dignity and decent
wages. Indeed, based on her study of this effort, Karen Sachs argues that
King's assassination marked a turning point. Afterwards, AFSCME
Local 77 consciously channeled student and community anger into
support for campus workers. Students and workers participated in sit-ins
and vigils and set up picket lines, all aimed at pressuring the university
into recognizing the union. Hundreds of local white union members
supported the strike as well. "It was a beautiful sight to see," stated
kitchen worker Shirley Rice, and a far cry from the claim that King's
dream had died.[63]

Not only did civil rights and student activists take up the union
mantle, in some cases the House of Labor displayed signs of having
adopted new left means. The Industrial Union Department (IUD),
AFL–CIO, established several of its own community unions. The rationale and structure of these organizations echoed those of SDS. The
most effective community union, was developed in Chicago's Lawndale
projects under the joint sponsorship of the Chicago Area Industrial

Union Department and SCLC. Charles J. Chiakulas, an old-time labor radical and James Bevel, a SNCC and SCLC activist, headed the effort. (Martin Luther King's forays into Chicago were related to Bevel's work with the Lawndale community union.) Sharon Jeffrey, one of the original SDS members and co-leader of the Cleveland ERAP also became involved. Several other SDS veterans, including Richie Rothstein, Nanci Hollander, Robert Ross and to a lesser extent Paul Booth and Rennie Davis, allied themselves with CCCO, the umbrella organization of all the Chicago community projects. In Chiakulas's words, the community union built on a tradition of labor and movement cooperation that first emerged in Montgomery and climaxed in Selma. In addition to addressing the needs of the poor, the Lawndale movement sought to serve as a model for others to follow.[64]

Of course, these organizing drives among poor workers could not compete for the nation's attention with massive antiwar protests, urban uprisings, and the counterculture. But they did build a bridge (or kept one erect) between segments of the New Left and labor. They acted as a cross-current to the main current of confrontation. Moreover, they symbolized that the labor movement was still alive, that it was not stagnant. In fact, union membership grew from 18.1 million to 20.7 million during the 1960s. Much of this growth took place in the public sector and among white-collar and minority workers. Obviously, labor's growth paled in comparison to its record during the 1930s and early 1940s. Yet compared to what took place in the 1970s and 1980s, the House of Labor was quite healthy. Perhaps it was the New Left's subconscious sense that labor could be made even more dynamic that attracted it to collaborate in various local affairs. Regardless of whether this was the case, the New Left's participation in these organizing drives set the stage for further collaboration on the labor front.[65]

8

Solidarity on the Labor Front

In early 1969, Local 1–561, of the Oil, Chemical, and Atomic Workers of Richmond, California, declared a strike against Standard Oil of California. Fearing for its property, the company obtained a court order limiting the number of pickets that the local could assemble outside its factory gates. The union countered by calling for outside help. Among those to respond favorably to this call were radical students from San Francisco State. Leaving behind their own protests against their university, they traveled across the San Francisco Bay to march on the oil workers' picket lines. Concurrently, fellow Bay Area radicals heralded the strike and invited OCAW labor leader to speak at campus rallies. The National Office of SDS followed suit, announcing a nationwide boycott of Standard Oil. In return, oil workers joined students and teachers in protests against San Francisco State. G. T. Jacobs, secretary-treasurer of Local 1–561 of OCAW, described the events as "the dawning of a new era" and predicted that "the old spirit of solidarity and identification with progressive social causes that characterized the historic movement of organized workers for justice and equality was being revived." A rank-and-file oil worker offered a more mundane assessment of the situation: "When I came out here [picket line] before day light, I felt very good to see those students; the more the better. The goons don't come out when they are here, and the cops are too busy chasing them around to bother us." The *Guardian* echoed Jacob's appraisal of the situation, claiming that the strike demonstrated that "workers and students can cooperate together on a principled and militant basis." The radical paper emphatically added: "Alone the student movement can raise hell. Together with the working class it can raze governments."[1]

Far overshadowing the Standard Oil action was a strike against General Electric, which began in October 1969 and lasted through the winter. Like the Oil strike, it stood in stark contrast to the traditional picture of the New Left as an adversary of labor. Not since the CIO had

expelled the UE following World War II, had the labor movement
displayed such unity and received such wide support. In a short period
of time, GE workers gained the support of the AFL–CIO, independent
unions, and nearly every strand of the New Left. The AFL–CIO executive council hailed the strike as a cause for all trade unionists and
created a special strike fund for the GE workers (initially this fund did
not cover the independent UE). Independent unions, most importantly
the UAW and ILWU, made similar pledges.[2]

Given General Electric's record in the field of labor relations, this
support was especially impressive. Since the late 1940s, GE had prac-
ticed a strategy known as "Boulwarism." Named after Lemuel Boulware,
who headed GE's labor relationship department from 1946 through
1961, Boulwarism stood for a strategy whereby GE played the UE and
IUE off against one another. Boulware offered "take it or leave it"
contracts to each union, to the detriment of the workers, who earned
less money than comparable workers in other industries. Bouleware
kept labor costs down, and GE experienced no national strikes during
his tenure.[3]

With only a partial understanding of "Boulwarism" and the history of
the IUE–UE split, new leftists rallied behind GE's foes. Stanley Aronowitz
expressed the opinion shared by many new leftists that the strike presented
a "unique opportunity for the left." It gave radicals "a chance to make
the connections between corporate responsibility for imperialism and
war and the malevolent hypocrisy of this corporate leader and the
conspiracy against American workers' living standards and job conditions."
Even those who disdained Progressive Labor took up its chant: "WAR-
MAKERS, STRIKEBREAKERS, SMASH GE!" Local SDS chapters (many of
them controlled by PL) and unaffiliated campus radical organizations
joined the pro-GE crusade. Students contributed money, food, walked
on picket lines, and voiced their support of the strike in a variety of
ways. For example, scores of demonstrators at the massive New Mobe
antiwar rally, left the main site of the protest to demonstrate outside of
the Department of Labor in support of the GE workers.[4]

Actions in the Boston area exemplified the spirit of solidarity that
Aronowitz envisioned. Students from MIT, Boston College, Holy Cross,
Harvard, Northeastern, and Boston University participated in various
types of anti-GE actions. On 30 and 31 October, MIT activists along
with a contingent of UE workers from GE's Ashland, Massachusetts
plant, held a large anti-GE rally, at which they sang old labor songs such
as "Solidarity Forever," and "Union Maid." After the rally a segment of
the activists established a picket line to block a GE personnel recruiter
from conducting interviews on campus. Holy Cross radicals did likewise.

When Holy Cross's school administration responded by suspending four black and twelve white students, the Black Action Committee—comprised of sixty black students, the entire black student body, along with about forty white students—packed their bags and left the campus. This so embarrassed the administration that it rescinded the suspensions and announced a moratorium on GE recruitment on campus.[5]

Even more sensational protests took place at Boston University where the GE strike set the student body and the school administration at odds for the entire school year. In mid-November, approximately fifty BU radicals, representing the BU PL–SDS/WSA and the independent BU Action Group, held a prostrike rally at the center of campus. Afterward, a number of activists marched over to the school auditorium to disrupt a previously scheduled speaking engagement by Herbert H. Meyer, GE's national vice-president in charge of personnel. When the students arrived, a BU dean emerged from the auditorium to read a court injunction that barred eight specifically named students and unnamed associates from taking "any activity which could disrupt the normal functioning of the university." The students defiantly ignored the order, forcing the dean to request the police to enforce the injunction. A bloody melee followed. A few days later a group of strikers from UE local 205 in Ashland expressed their unity with the BU radicals by distributing leaflets on campus that thanked the students for their support and welcomed them as allies in the movement. One leaflet rhetorically asked, are "there some connections between the General Electric Company, University Administrators and police departments?"[6]

Rather than squelching the protest, the presence of police on campus and the arrest and suspension of students aggravated the situation. Whereas in December 1969 the Progressive Labor movement constituted the main contingent of proworker new leftists on campus, with only about 150 students protesting against on-campus recruiting by GE, by the end of February, 1970, 10,000 students, out of a student body of 17,000, participated in a peaceful strike against the university. In the interim, BU activists conducted a sit-in, called for a boycott of all GE goods by the university, and marched on picket lines at GE plants in Lynn and Ashland, Massachusetts.[7]

One interesting by-product of the strike involved the nascent feminist organization Bread and Roses and female GE employees. The two groups conducted special conferences on the exploitation of women workers and the history of women in the labor movement. The conferees discovered that 80 percent of the work force at GE's plant in Ashland was female; yet, out of eleven hundred total female employees, only fifty-five earned as much as any of the male employees, and none of them made as much as the all male high-skilled trades. Such findings led local activists and employees to push for special increases for female employees. The conferences also established a foundation for future cooperation between various Boston Area women's collectives and female workers.[8]

The protests at Boston University demonstrated that the Progressive Labor party, which had taken over SDS in the fall of 1969, served as the nuclei for new left support for GE workers. As an adherent to an old left line, PL reflexively supported the strike just as it had others throughout the 1960s. Yet, it would be incorrect to characterize the New Left's support of the GE strike as PL controlled. A broad array of activists allied with GE workers, including many who found PL's dogmatism repugnant and counterproductive. They did so not because they felt that the GE strike fit the PL's line of forging a worker-student alliance, but because they believed that the GE workers deserved support, regardless of PL's strategy or role.

One of the main reasons for this attitude was that the UE was an atypical union. Throughout the 1960s, it maintained especially friendly relations with the New Left—supporting SNCC, opposing the war, and hiring several one-time SNCC and SDS veterans in the mid–1960s on a special student-labor project, including Walter Tillow. Indeed, even before the strike took place, UE leader James Matles called for an alliance between students and workers. Furthermore, the strike engendered considerable support simply because it was against GE, which, as the protesters emphasized, was a pillar of the military-industrial complex.[9]

The New Left's collaboration with the IUE and the AFL–CIO was built on a shakier foundation and developed more gingerly. Several weeks after the strike began, the AFL–CIO bargaining unit disavowed SDS's "sympathetic" actions. "We resent and reject any attempts by outside groups to exploit the cause of the GE strikers for the advancement of their own political or ideological aims." The IUE discouraged local activists in Syracuse, Louisville, Philadelphia, and Bridgeport from picketing, although the largely black Newark local welcomed student and black leftists to their side. As the strike lingered on, however, the AFL–CIO began to warm to new left support. The *AFL–CIO News* drew parallels between the GE struggle and student unrest. Previously the labor press had discussed the two movements as completely distinct phenomenon. Donald Slaiman, civil rights director of the AFL–CIO, addressed the National Student Association's convention with the aim of gaining its support for the GE strike. Although Slaiman qualified his plea for student help by renouncing "opportunistic" radicals, it seemed clear that he hoped the NSA would use its contacts with left-leaning students to bolster the strike. (The NSA was not a new left organization, but by 1970, it consisted of many individuals who could bridge the gap between liberals and radicals.)[10]

A month later, the AFL–CIO's guarded position gave way to an even more favorable view, with the labor press carrying stories on pro-GE actions at Holy Cross, BU, and Rutgers. These stories came without editorial qualifications and often were accompanied by photographs of long-haired students on an IUE picket line—suggesting that maybe there was something good about the hippies, after all. In fact, the caption of one photograph appreciatively announced that the strike had spurred youth to "do their thing."[11]

Ironically, the enthusiasm of some new leftists waned as labor warmed to its participation. Uncertainty over whether to support the entire labor movement, segments of the House of Labor, or just the rebellious rank and file lay behind this development. The Progressive Labor party made clear that it supported the rank and file but not the UE or IUE. Not surprisingly, PL termed the final settlement of the strike a sellout.[12] But most new leftists, even while sharing PL's skepticism of the labor movement, held a more positive position. They emphasized the achievements of the strike: the militancy of the workers and the cooperation of labor and the Left. For example, the *Old Mole,* an underground paper published in Cambridge, Massachusetts, argued that the strike had provided the basis for the emergence of a New Left among white workers.[13]

Hardly any time passed before another major strike erupted. In mid March 1970, 200,000 postal workers in the New York City walked off the job. Representing nearly 30 percent of the 750,000 national membership, they faced very long odds. Their strike violated federal law and a court injunction. President Nixon accused the strikers of being unpatriotic and mobilized federal troops to move the mail. In addition, the strikers disobeyed their national union leaders who called for them to return to work for a cooling off period.[14]

The strike continued, in part, because of the support that it received from new leftists. Despite their own sectarian disputes, they heralded the postal workers as their newfound heroes. Most new leftists were enthralled by the postal employees defiance of the law; they gushed at the possibility that the strike would bring corporate America to a halt and championed the militancy of the rank and file. " 'Even as President Nixon said the issue of the postal strike 'is the survival of government based on law,' large numbers of postal workers defied federal law . . . and even the mobilization of federal troops," wrote Free Speech Movement veteran Jack Weinberg. The response of the government to the walkout replicated its reaction to Watts, Chicago, and Santa Barbara (site of a recent confrontation between students and police), to call out the army, wrote the *Old Mole*. "The army can sometimes put down a rebellion, but it can't move the mail," the paper added. "The postal strike is the biggest forward surge for the workers movement since the post-World War II strike wave," chimed the *International Socialist*. "The power of working people to bring society to a halt . . . has been made clear to every person in the country."[15]

The postal strike attracted the support of almost every faction of the New Left because each one could find in it a different cause or possibility. The strike was a direct outcome of the war, explained some. President Nixon claims the government cannot afford to grant postal employees a wage hike, but what he really means, Weinberg asserted, was that he could afford to spend $80 billion a year on the war and defense but refuses to pay a living wage to government employees who have seen their salary shrink in real terms due to war-bred inflation. (The highest salary for a postal employee with twenty years seniority in 1970 was $8,500.) Other new leftists found the strike crucial because it represented the growing militancy of the rank and file, especially young and black workers, many of whom had found jobs in the postal service.[16] For still other new leftists the action displayed that the working class was shedding its conservatism as economic conditions changed. As the underground newspaper *Helix* observed: "This is the rise of Nixon's silent majority and they are finding out who there enemies are . . . for Nixon is worried about inflation and his solution is apparently to screw the worker." Even relatively moderate new leftists saw the postal strike as pregnant with significance. "If one reflects on the meaning of the postal strike, really it is more of a revolutionary act than the many protest demonstrations and activities that have occurred in the past few years," wrote one moderate activist. "I say more revolutionary because rank-and-file workers with an obvious stake in the solvency of the government that employs them dared to do the forbidden . . . [and] because they did not hesitate to put an immediate stop to the most vital communication network in the country."[17]

But without the support of other federal workers or their national union the postal workers could not afford to stay out indefinitely. Hence, just as the strike became a new cause célèbre, it came to an end. Still, new leftists maintained that the strike ended in victory because it produced a wage hike. Moreover, they saw the strike as an omen of things to come. Surely, one radical journal theorized, "workers in private industry will see that if the lowly postal workers can move in a massive manner even in the face of anti-labor laws, then they can do the same," especially since the conditions that gave rise to the strike, inflation and poor working conditions, remained.[18]

The resumption of college classes in the fall of 1970 coincided with the next big national walkout: four hundred thousand autoworkers at General Motors. It was the UAW's first confrontation with the giant automaker since 1946. Even though many activists were extremely suspicious of the auto union, most factions of the New Left supported the strike because almost all of them agreed that GM symbolized the worst of America. GM was a gargantuan corporation, the largest in the world. With greater assets than most countries, GM epitomized institutionalized racism and imperialism. Underground newspapers exposed the company's ties with South Africa, where black autoworkers earned approximately one-sixth their white co-workers' wages and faced the racist contempt of white South African managers. Other new left presses focused on GM's enormous defense contracts. Still others highlighted the fact that GM exported jobs abroad and instituted dehumanizing work conditions on the assembly line, just so it could make ever greater profits.[19]

Though the New Left unanimously abhorred GM, it remained divided over whether it should cooperate directly with the UAW or operate independently. Those with a strong countercultural penchant or ties to black nationalism tended to portray the union as useless. "GM, Ford and Chrysler are not the only ones who are uptight," declared *Rising Up Angry.* "The leadership of the UAW is pretty freaked out too. . . . For these militant brothers and sisters (striking workers) have seen through the game of racism and cop outs."[20] At the same time, other new leftists, with deeper ties to the Old Left, such as Art Kunkin of the *LA Free Press,* and those allied with the International Socialists, an offshoot of the Trotskyist Socialist Workers party, adopted a bit more favorable stance. They argued that autoworkers had to organize on a shop floor level to pressure the International to return with a worthwhile contract, one that included: "a steward for every foreman," and "made line speed and production quotas negotiable issues, with ratification by the ranks." When UAW's leaders returned from the negotiating table with a contract lacking these guarantees—even though it did restore a cost of living agreement (COLA), lost in 1967—this segment of the New Left proclaimed that the UAW's leaders were rotten to the core. However, they did not go as far as those on the extreme left, who wrote off the rank and file as well.[21]

A third, more prolabor position was staked-out by a core of veteran new leftists who had broken with SDS. The best example of this group was one-time SDS leader Paul Booth. Booth coordinated student support for the strike with the full sanction of the UAW and Alliance for Labor Action. Like other leftists, Booth highlighted GM's nastiness. But unlike other new leftists, Booth touted the UAW as a bulwark against reaction. "It is necessary to distinguish between those elements of organized labor who are genuinely pro-Nixon and all that he stands for (overt racism, militant anticommunism, repression of dissent and worker militancy . . .), and those elements that are at least anti-Nixon and his program." In a manner that harkened back to the cooperative spirit of the early 1960s, Booth added: "A UAW victory strengthens the anti-Nixon—in its broadest sense—forces in the country; a UAW defeat, like the union defeat in 1946 GM strike, weakens the anti-repressive forces, and substantially undermines the position of workers in general and, indirectly, of the student left."[22]

Giving meaning to his views, Booth organized close to two thousand students in the Chicago region in support of the union. Twenty workers and four hundred University of Illinois students picketed GM job interviewing in Urbana/Champaign. Similarly, Jim Kosik, Booth's fellow strike-support coordinator in California, arranged for UCLA law students to provide free legal advise to the strikers, organized a benefit concert with Arlo Guthrie and Joan Baez (with the help of UAW official Paul Schrade) and encouraged the Black Panther party to support strikers at a UAW local in Freemont. Slightly less successful student support groups emerged at Wayne State, University of Michigan, Michigan State, Rutgers University, and Newark State.[23]

What accounted for the different new left positions? As suggested already, those new leftists with the weakest links to the labor movement in the first place continued to distrust the union hierarchy the most. In contrast, those with deeper ties to the Old Left or labor leaned toward some form of cooperation. Along with several other old guard SDSers, including Lee Webb, Steve Max, John Fuerst, Nat Stillman, and Jim Williams, Booth retained ties to the labor movement throughout the sixties. He worked temporarily as research director for the United Packinghouse Workers, was active in the National Conference for a New Politics, helped develop the School of Community Organization in Chicago (an extension of JOIN and SCLC's activities in the city), worked for the Labor Workshop, and edited *New Directions in Labor,* a newsletter that covered the Labor Workshop's affairs.[24]

Booth and several of his fellow activists even entertained the possibility that top labor officials would clandestinely support their effort to build a middle level rank-and-file movement. After all, Steve Max wrote Booth, "the labor folks are all unhappy that there is no one from the youth to carry on in the labor movement." As top leaders from the AFT, Meatcutters, and ILGWU told him, Max continued, "there were no socialist youth to carry on the socialist tradition in the labor movement." Given the fact that the labor movement could expect massive retirements in the near future, Max argued, new leftists had the opportunity to take these jobs away from those low level officials who had joined the movement simply for the money.[25]

Another new leftist whose position somewhat paralleled Booth's was Staughton Lynd. Born in 1929, the son of two famous sociologists, Lynd had been a prominent new leftist for years. In the late 1950s and early 1960s, he joined the editorial boards of *Liberation* and *Studies on the Left*. Upon receiving his Ph.D. in American history from Columbia University in 1961, he went to work at Spelman College, an all black women's college, in Atlanta, Georgia. There he advanced the cause of the burgeoning civil rights movement. In the summer of 1964, he directed the Mississippi Freedom Schools. From 1965 through 1969, Lynd redirected much of his attention to the Vietnam War. He attended early teach-ins and demonstrations, helped organize the Resistance (the leading draft resistance association), journeyed to North Vietnam, and wrote numerous articles and books about the war.[26]

Before the New Left burst upon the public scene, Lynd had flirted with the Old Left. As a young historian, he had displayed an interest in class issues and briefly belonged to the Trotskyist International Socialist League and the Socialist Workers party. By the mid–1960s, however, he had grown disenchanted with both the Old Left and labor. In a seminal debate with Bayard Rustin, Lynd proclaimed that workers no longer served as agents for substantial change and admonished intellectuals who refused to criticize the liberal labor movement.[27]

Yet, as the New Left became more violent and the economy took a downturn, Lynd renewed his interest in labor issues and the working class itself. In 1969, his article "Guerilla History in Gary" suggested that "radical scholars should begin to collect oral histories of 30s rank and filers." This led to the publication of *Rank and File,* a collection of the personal histories of fifteen working-class organizers, including pieces on leaders of contemporary insurgent movements. The book's introduction read:

Now American working people are stirring again. They are beginning to question foremen and corporation executives whom they did not elect, and union officials who have lost touch with their membership. The group which took part in the cultural revolution of the 1960s are moving into the work place. Blacks have become a majority in many automobile plants and steel mills, students have graduated and taken jobs in white-collar bureaucracies, veterans are returning from Vietnam, women have gone out to work in larger numbers than at any time since World War II. A new restlessness is evident.[28]

Lynd also wrote numerous theoretical essays promoting socialism with an American twist, namely an emphasis on participatory democracy. He suggested that American radicals should base their affiliation with workers on noneconomic problems, on alienation and the lack of control. In "Prospects of the New Left," Lynd expanded on these thoughts. "So far as I can see . . . the best spot for a radical in a union is to a hold low-level local office (as a griever, committeeman, or whatever) but at the same time to be active in grass-roots organizational forms outside of the union structure," possibly around issues such as pollution, which affected both workers and the surrounding community. Practicing what he preached, Lynd worked for the Chicago Organizing School and eventually obtained a law degree, so that he could provide legal counsel to workers in the depressed steel region.[29]

Another veteran new leftist who adopted a similar stance was Kim Moody. Though he disparaged the contemporary state of the House of Labor, Moody retained his long-standing interest in some form of workers' movement. In place of the Old Left's faith in trade unions, Moody called for the creation of a neosyndicalist system in which workers had the power to make and enforce contracts. Like the Labor Workshop, he suggested that the New Left construct parallel structures, whereby workers would organize independent shop floor committees, interconnected with other industries and regions. These committees would free workers from the restraints of union bureaucracies and establish the basis for "union democracy and . . . workers' control." In essence, this plan wedded participatory democracy with the spirit of solidarity of the early CIO.[30]

The renewed interest of segments of the New Left in labor reached new heights in 1972 with the Lordstown strike. To the New Left this walkout epitomized the intersection of several developments and verified several of its theories: its faith in the rank and file, the importance of working conditions, and the radicalization of the young and blacks in America. Staughton Lynd spoke for many when he called the Lordstown strike a rebellion against "arbitrary authority and the lack of respect for human rights in the capitalist workplace." Clearly "a parallel between the student revolt of the sixties and the young worker revolt of the seventies," existed, wrote James Green, one of the cofounders of *Radical America.* Moreover, as the strike involved a challenge to the nation's largest corporation and its new showpiece plant, considered by many to be America's response to growing foreign competition, it became doubly important. "On both sides," contended Ted Farrow, "the Lordstown plant is a sort of laboratory. . . . It offers us a trial run of the class struggle of the '70s."[31]

At Lordstown, GM had sped up work in order to increase productivity. This strategy fit nicely with President Nixon's economic policy of cutting costs in order to compete with the Japanese and Western Europeans. Ostensibly, it did not produce inflation nor necessitate layoffs. As in the past, the UAW did not challenge the corporation's control of the means and use of production. However, the unusually young rank and file, who averaged twenty-four years of age, refused to comply. First they sabotaged production to the point where the assembly line had to be halted; then they walked out. *Workers Power,* one of many small new left periodicals that covered the strike, asserted that "GM's vanguard plant has turned out to have a vanguard workforce."[32]

Lordstown took on even greater significance as rank-and-file movements sprouted in the steel, mining, and trucking industries. As John Hillinson hinted, "There are plots being hatched in the bathrooms and crosshairs etched on the necks of foremen in a thousand Lordstowns." The mine workers' challenge was given a boost by a Ralph Nader report that UMW president Tony Boyle had misused union pension funds and collaborated with management for his own self-aggrandizement. Jock Yablonski, a member of the UMW executive board, declared his candidacy for the presidency of the UMW, pledging to make Boyle account for his actions. Boyle countered by highlighting his long-standing association with John L. Lewis. (Lewis died shortly before the election.) UMW dissidents rallied behind Yablonski nonetheless. In the election Boyle gained a victory, winning 75,680 votes to 43,307. Even though he lost, Yablonski, who termed the election the most dishonest in labor history, noted the narrowness of the margin (it was the closest election in UMW history) and vowed to carry on his fight. Clearly, Boyle was concerned about this pledge. A few weeks after the election, on New Years Eve, 1969, Yablonski and his family were shot to death in their home.

Subsequently, Boyle was found guilty of conspiracy to murder and was forced to relinquish his leadership to union dissidents.[33]

Disenchanted steelworkers built a similar movement called RAFT. As with the UMW, the rank-and-file challenge came to the head with an attempt to unseat the union's entrenched leadership. Ed Sadlowski, who quickly became a favorite of new and old leftists alike, promised more union democracy and militancy if elected.[34] Other dissident movements arose among independent Steel haulers in the Midwest, Teamsters in Los Angeles and the Midwest, and among the Oil and Chemical Workers Union and teachers. The Teamster revolt in Los Angeles prefigured a rank-and-file movement, which, with the help of the federal government, ultimately unseated the union leadership in the early 1990s.[35]

Perhaps the most impressive collaborative effort took place in Madison, Wisconsin, with the birth of the Teaching Assistants' Association. Indeed, the TAA represented a marriage of the New Left and labor. It symbolized a reconciliation of differences and the transformation of the New Left, at least in one locale, into a trade union itself.

Madison had been a center of the New Left since its birth. *Studies on the Left* originated among University of Wisconsin graduate students, as did *Radical America.* University of Wisconsin students supported the civil rights movement and actively demonstrated against the war, the draft, and numerous other causes. Protest peaked in a massive student strike aimed at Dow Chemical recruitment on campus in 1967, and activism remained high well into the 1970s. Madison also generated a large countercultural community, centered on Mifflin Street, and various ultraleft groups.[36]

In the Spring of 1966, in the midst of campus-wide antidraft sit-ins, thirty-five teaching assistants met to discuss the war and the impact that it had on them as teachers. At the time, the university complied with a federal policy that ranked students for the draft by their academic grades. Antiwar TAs were put in a bind by this policy since they were responsibile for determining grades. If they complied with the policy, they would be fostering the war effort. But, if they did not comply, they faced the prospect of losing their jobs, which in turn might force them to drop out of school. The teaching assistants argued that determining who should go to Vietnam was not a legitimate part of their job responsibilities. Such a stance, and the discussion that led to it, raised the teaching assistants' consciousness about other work-related grievances and laid the foundation for the formation of a teaching assistants' union, called the TAA.[37]

Throughout the latter part of the 1960s, TAA acted more like a new left organization than a union. For instance, during the DOW strike of October 1967, it called for a walkout of TAs, not over a work-related issue but rather over the war. Nonetheless, as time passed, it tried to combine political activism with bread-and-butter unionism. In addition to supporting various causes it issued a monthly newsletter and initiated departmental organizing. The University bolstered the TAA's cause when it expelled and thus fired a TA who was one of the DOW sit-in leaders. The firing highlighted the lack of a grievance procedure, informal hiring, firing, and rehiring policies.[38]

While the existence of poor working conditions gave the TAA a means to increase its membership, it was not until January 1969, that it sought recognition as the contractual representative of all teaching assistants at the Madison campus. Another student strike, this one regarding the demands of the Black Student Association, sparked this turn of events. A pending piece of legislation, which threatened to raise the tuition of out-of-state TAs, further convinced TAA that the time was ripe to launch a massive organizing drive.[39]

By the middle of the spring–1969 term, the TAA had signed up nineteen hundred members, well over one-half of those eligible. Subsequently, TAA leaders, accompanied by officials of AFSCME and the AFT, met with the chancellor to demand recognition. Not suprisingly, he rejected their demands, although he established a burdensome procedure whereby the union could hold a collective bargaining election. Much to nearly everyone's surprise, the TAA overcame the technical barriers that the chancellor had placed in its way. The union even gained support from traditionally conservative TAs in the schools of engineering, agriculture and the various science departments. By winning recognition, the TAA became the first teaching assistants' union in the country.[40]

Yet the battle had only just begun. For almost a year, the union fought to convert union recognition into a favorable contractual agreement. The struggle culminated in the early months of 1970 with a five-week strike. Madison TAs remained remarkably solid throughout the walkout. A supportive student body and numerous labor unions aided the TAs. The labor unions, for instance, refused to cross the TAA's picket lines. Only when the university won an injunction declaring the strike illegal were the campus unions forced to quit giving such overt support. Less than a month before Madison erupted in antiwar protests, sparked by the invasion of Cambodia, a contract was signed. TAs won four-year job guarantees, a grievance procedure and a health care plan.[41]

The TAA's formative years reflected many of the trends evident in the larger New Left. It was a concrete manifestation of the reconciliation that was taking place between segments of the New Left and labor. In justifying the formation of their union, the TAA drew on the theories of the "new working class." It argued that teaching assistants should organize because they were workers who suffered from harsh working conditions just like those experienced by blue-collar workers. "Is there real difference between ourselves and the man in the factory?" inquired one TAA pamphlet. "We will be fired for showing incompetence. . . . We have no control over the manner in which our job is to be performed."[42] TAA organizers also insisted that a concern with working conditions, such as a grievance procedure, was compatible with promoting a radical ideology.[43]

The TAA's initial ambivalence toward the labor movement prevented it from affiliating with the AFL–CIO at first. But as concerns about the AFL–CIO diminished, it became only a matter of time before it did.[44] In fact, by 1974, the only real debate among TAA members concerned not whether to join a national union but which one, the NEA or the AFT. One anti-AFT TA noted that signing on with the AFT meant joining forces with George Meany, "the same kind of dinasauer [*sic*] that should have become extinct at the same time Richard Daley . . . should have become extinct." The same member also warned against allying with Albert Shanker, of Ocean Hill-Brownsville fame. But as other TAs argued, these objections paled in comparison to the advantages of the AFT. Hence, in February 1974 the TAA affiliated with the AFT, AFL–CIO.[45]

Subsequently, the TAA became a progressive force within the AFT and the Wisconsin AFL–CIO. TAA representatives sought passage (unsuccessfully) of a resolution that would have forced the AFL–CIO to disaffiliate from the American Institute for Free Labor Development, a CIA associate. Locally, the TAA spearheaded the Teamsters for Democracy movement. It cosponsored antiwar resolutions at various labor conventions. Moreover, the TAA served as a training-school or entrée into other unions. Bob Muehlenkamp, one of the founders of the TAA, became a prominent member of local 1199 of the Health and Hospital Workers Union. Other TAA veterans bolstered the forces of the progressive wing of the labor movement in the state of Wisconsin.[46]

The willingness of the New Left to ally with workers was paralleled by a diminishment in labor's hostility toward the New Left. Labor papers carried more and more articles with a favorable slant on student activists.

In the *American Federationist,* for example, Tom Kahn observed that a high percentage of students had participated in some form of campus activity related to the labor movement, such as helping farm workers or supporting GE workers. Kahn added that the prospects for forging ties with students looked good. A piece in *UAW Solidarity* substantiated Kahn's findings, commending new leftists for paying more attention to labor's struggles. Similarly, the UFW's newspaper, *El Malcriado* pronounced that "students have been among the most important allies in the struggle of the farm workers since the strike began."[47]

A series of meetings at Harvard University, in 1970, attended by a number of traditionally progressive labor leaders, left-leaning professors, and student leaders confirmed that relations between segments of both movements were improving. Nobel laureate and antiwar veteran Dr. George Wald initiated the conferences. In the spring of 1969, Wald put out feelers for forging a student-union coalition. Wald argued that the repression faced by leftists represented only the "coating on the pill," which when looked at more closely signified "an attack on the working man." There were many similarities between workers and students, Wald declared. The Nixon administration was engaged in a divide and conquer strategy that would ultimately come to hurt labor if it did not fight back. UAW stalwart Victor Reuther, concurred. "There are people in this country trying to divide workers from students. It is as cold and calculated a strategy as the southern strategy, but there are no two groups that have more in common than working people and students."[48]

Among those who participated in Wald's conferences were the UAW's Leonard Woodcock, the Teamster Harold Gibbons, ACWA's H. D. Samuels and Joseph Potofsky, RWDSU's Cleveland Robinson, and Abe Feinglass of the Meatcutters. Faculty representatives included Wald, Noam Chomsky, Fred Shurman, Seymour Melman, and Sidney Peck. Student leaders included David Ifship, John Rodriguez, Ron Eachus, and Frank Greer. With Wald presiding, the group discussed ways in which the academic and labor communities could cooperate. UAW official Nat Weinberg put forth his view: "You are articulate. . . . we have the members. Lets put our assets together." Wald observed that "cooperation between academics and labor . . . would give the academic community what it most lacks; a base in the outside community." The conferees drafted an official resolution agreeing to establish "a national coalition for political and social cooperation," in which labor leaders pledged "membership support" and academics promised "brain power and student cooperation." The conferees also elected an executive committee of nine, three from faculty, unions and students to carry out this directive.[49]

One tangential by-product of this meeting and others like it was the growth of labor education. New leftists, either veterans and/or newcomers, joined with trade union officials and/or rank-and-file workers to develop a variety of projects. In-house schools for union stewards staffed by new leftists sprang up. So too did labor colleges for apprentice and journeymen building tradesmen. For example, the Midwest Academy, comprised primarily of veteran radicals, such as Steve Max and Heather Booth, consciously sought to link different activists from labor unionists to student radicals in an educational setting.[50]

Even before the women's movement took off in the latter half of the 1960s, women's rights activists, especially those affiliated with the labor movement, were actively involved in efforts to prod the federal government to combat sexual discrimination in the workplace. Estelle Peterson, a life-long labor activist, first with the Amalgamated Clothing Workers and then with IUD, AFL–CIO, served as JFK's and then LBJ's Assistant secretary of labor and as director of the Women's Bureau. From this top-ranking post, she pressured President Kennedy to sign the Equal Pay Act of 1963 and to establish and then support the Presidential Commission on the Status of Women (PCSW). As head of the same, she steered the commission away from a debate on the ERA (a debate she saw as divisive) and toward an investigation of discrimination as faced by women workers, such as unequal pay. The PCSW did not signify the emergence of the women's movement, nor did the statewide and federal commissions that succeeded it. But, the PCSW planted a seed of change that grew in the latter half of the decade.[51]

At approximately the same time as the PCSW examined sexual discrimination in the workplace, Virginia Senator Howard Smith proposed an amendment to the Civil Rights Bill of 1964, whereby sexual as well as racial discrimination would be outlawed. Smith was not a closet feminist. He proposed adding the amendment on sexual discrimination with the aim of killing the entire civil rights bill. Like many others, Smith presumed that a ban on sexual discrimination would deter northern conservative and moderate politicians, who otherwise might have favored civil rights legislation, from voting for the bill. Indeed, Peterson, along with several other liberal women's rights activists, opposed Smith's amendment, not on principle, but because they did not want to be blamed for the defeat of civil rights legislation, which they strongly favored. But, to the surprise of many, several congresswomen, along with a handful of female labor lobbyists, including Caroline Davis of the Women's Department of the UAW, gained passage of the Civil Rights Act of 1964 with the antisexual discrimination amendment (Title VII) intact.[52]

Paradoxically, this unexpected victory dealt a short-term blow to these very same women's rights activists. Enforcement of Title VII came slowly, if at all. This led numerous feminists, many of them members of the recently formed National Organization for Women, to demand passage of the Equal Rights Amendment. But NOW's endorsement of the ERA angered many of those who had fought for Title VII in the first place. Historically, trade unions had opposed the ERA, as had many liberal women, because they saw it as a threat to protective labor legislation. Though less convinced of this than their male union counterparts, women labor officials tended to follow their union leads in opposing NOW's endorsement of the ERA. One direct by-product of this disagreement was that NOW lost its first permanent office, in the UAW's headquarters in Detroit. In addition, female labor activists who had played a prominent role in establishing NOW, tempered their support for the organization. And if labor women could not reconcile themselves with NOW, the chance that trade unions could unite with the emerging radical wing of the women's movement seemed minimal.[53]

This radical wing was directly tied to the New Left. It was made up of many women who had participated in SNCC's struggles in the Deep South and in various antiwar and campus demonstrations. In the latter half of the 1960s, these radical feminists distinguished themselves from NOW by calling for a decentralized women's movement (NOW was very hierarchical), voicing their concerns in a militant fashion (as opposed to within traditional political channels), and focusing on personal politics, such as issues that involved sexual definition (rather than those of the workplace). One by-product of the rise of the radical feminist wing of the women's movement was that it further radicalized the New Left, leaving it further estranged from labor.[54]

Yet, this division was not permanent. By the early 1970s, many segments of the women's liberation movement, turned their attention toward labor, especially the concerns of working women. Concurrently, women within the labor movement, influenced by the women's movement, displayed a feminist bent. "Pressure began to build for changes in the union's traditional outlook toward women," Ruth Milkman writes, "Women's caucuses . . . began to emerge . . . [and] there was an upsurge in female labor activism." The feminist spirit also influenced thousands of women workers outside of the House of Labor, further ripening the conditions for collaboration.[55]

The formation of the Coalition of Labor Union Women, in 1974, represented one such form of cooperation. In her opening remarks before CLUW's approximately three thousand female union delegates, Addie Wyatt, of the Meatcutters, stated that when people ask "why are union women getting together?" I say, "Women everywhere else are doing it. It's time we did." CLUW president-elect, Olga Madar, a long-time official with the UAW, added that CLUW demonstrated that "fewer and fewer union women will be saying we are not women's libbers," from now on.[56] Numerous radical feminists from outside labor's ranks attended the conferences. (By CLUW's by-laws they did so as observers. Only trade union members could attend as voting members.) In general, their reports on the convention were very favorable. Jo Freeman, for example, praised CLUW and applauded those feminists who had awakened to the concerns of working-class women.[57]

Yet, not all feminists held this view. The radical wing of the women's movement, in particular, criticized the founders of CLUW on several issues, most importantly, the latter's narrow membership rules. Radical feminists argued that CLUW was cutting itself off from thousands of working women who were outside of trade union folds for no fault of their own. *Radical America* even contended that CLUW had been formed in order to control the militancy of women workers.[58]

CLUW's founders scoffed at such charges. Patricia Cayo Sexton, a veteran of the labor movement, defended the trade union focus of CLUW and railed at those who cast issues of personal or sexual freedom, such as abortion and lesbianism, as equivalent to economic concerns. At the same time, however, Sexton showed that she was not adverse to fostering better relations with feminists, as long as they would accept the female trade union insurgency on its own grounds.[59]

If CLUW depicted an uneasy alliance, the formation of 9 to 5 displayed a more solid marriage. Established in 1973 by veteran new leftists, 9 to 5 sought to organize or, in the least, facilitate the organization of female office workers in the Boston area. In so doing, the founders drew on techniques prominent in the women's liberation movement, such as "consciousness raising" sessions and dramatic public protests. The organization 9 to 5 also utilized traditional trade union methods and fought for bread-and-butter goals, such as better wages and working conditions. In 1975, it affiliated with the Service Employees International Union—receiving a special charter that allowed it to organize all women office workers in the Boston area. SEIU president John Sweezy explicitly acknowledged the degree to which the women's movement and labor movement had allied, declaring that the local was to be run "for women and by women who understand their problems."[60]

Nor was 9 to 5 alone. Across the country female collectives raised the consciousness of women workers and provided resources to women workers who sought to organize. Former new leftists, as workers, became organizers and long-time female wageworkers allied themselves with middle-class feminist groups. For example, in the San Francisco Bay area, in an organizing drive among clerical workers at Highland General Hospital in Alameda County, feminist Kay Eisenhower worked hand-in-hand with Cathy Tuley, a rank-and-file hospital worker.[61] Feminist writers lent support to such endeavors and encouraged all women's rights advocates to emphasize the concerns of working women.[62]

In other words, overall the growth of the women's movement both strengthened and weakened their relationship. The emergence of the women's movement amplified the New Left's critique of liberalism in general and the House of Labor in particular. For example, the women's movement raised the New Left's consciousness of the labor movement's historical failure to organize women workers and the relative paucity of women in leadership positions within existing trade unions. Yet, at the same time, this failing or fault provided new leftists and labor unionists alike with one of the best opportunities they had to collaborate. This became especially apparent as women rights activists turned their attention to economic issues and as women in the workforce and labor movement felt the impact of the feminist insurgency of the late 1960s and early 1970s.

In sum, by building on local organizing drives and on the theoretical ponderings of the intelligentsia, significant segments of the New Left came to support traditional blue- and pink-collar workers and to a lesser extent large national unions in the very late 1960s and early 1970s. Even if labor unionists initially retreated from this show of solidarity, they tended to accept and encourage it as time passed. Furthermore, in certain enclaves of student radicalism, such as Madison, Wisconsin, the New Left and the labor movement merged. There, student radicals transformed the theory of the new working class into a reality, gained the support of the local labor movement and ultimately affiliated with the AFL–CIO. This is not to ignore the very real antagonisms between segments of both movements, as revealed via the rampage of construction workers on Wall Street or the antics of the Weathermen. But an accurate understanding of the New Left and labor in the 1960s must recognize the complexities of the times. Polarization was not the only order of the day. Rather it coincided with a renewed interest in collaboration. Put another way, the years 1969, 1970, and 1971 witnessed a dramatic surge in the number of strikes and hours lost to work stoppages. In 1970 alone the United States experienced fifty-six hundred work stoppages or about 62 million lost man-days, more than in any year in over a decade.[63] These figures include strikes against some of the largest industries and most essential sectors of the economy, for example, General Motors, General Electric, AT&T, the railroads, and the post office. While most of the work stoppages concerned only trade unionists and management, some of them served as arenas for renewed cooperation between the New Left and labor. They displayed the New Left allying with traditional blue-collar workers against the pillars of corporate America. They showed that segments of the New Left and labor were reconciling their differences. And even if a new alliance was not forged, a detente, of sorts, was in the making.

9

Testing the Political Waters

Throughout the 1960s, electoral politics acted as an arena in which trade unionists and new leftists interacted and tested one another. Should they cooperate? Should they endorse or support the same candidate? Seek similar programs and campaign together against a common foe, even if in disagreement over particular issues? Every four years the beat of American history repeated itself. And each time, regardless of past experiences, the two movements flirted with the ideal of coalition, and with near predictability, each election produced greater not less antagonism. At least that was the pattern through the late 1960s. Then, signs of a new pattern emerged. In numerous instances, segments of both movements forged coalitions. Especially in enclaves of the New Left, left-leaning candidates gained the support of both the New Left and labor. Blacks, who conservatives and moderates alike labeled radical extremists, were elected to congress, state, and federal offices on the backs of the civil rights movement and labor. Veteran new leftists campaigned for local offices and won with the support of student radicals and trade unionists. And then, in 1972, George McGovern challenged the New Left and labor to reconcile their differences, to coalesce around his candidacy for the presidency of the United States. The Weathermen and other far left organizations denounced the idea of voting for a liberal candidate. Similarly the AFL–CIO refused to endorse their party's nominee. Still others contended that it was imperative to support a bona fide antiwar candidate. Throughout the fall of 1972, the different sides put forth their case for voting or not voting for McGovern. Put another way, as the sixties came to a close, the New Left and labor tested the political waters. Many jumped in, but others remained ashore in hope of a more perfect day.

The 1960 election set the stage for those to follow. John F. Kennedy, who was the darling of neither the AFL–CIO nor the nascent New Left, boosted the hopes and confidence of both movements. With JFK's election, labor had a friend in the White House, and as his term proceeded, the New Deal coalition (perhaps without the South) grew stronger. George Meany, Walter Reuther, and other labor leaders enjoyed greater access to the presidency than they had since FDR, if indeed ever. Kennedy charmed ethnic Americans, especially Roman Catholics who otherwise were drifting toward the Republican party. Moreover, despite his timidity on civil rights, Kennedy became an icon in the homes of millions of working-class blacks. The spirit of the Kennedy Era, his challenge to do something for America and the disadvantaged abroad, raised the New Left's sights too. Yet, when the president and Congress did not deliver significant civil rights legislation, failed to protect southern activists and, threatened world peace, the New Left grew disillusioned with him.[1]

Nonetheless, even while the New Left drifted away from Kennedy, the arena of electoral politics retained its potential as a point of collaboration. The Kennedy Administration encouraged civil rights militants to focus on voter education and registration, garnering liberal support for such endeavors. After some debate, SNCC and CORE activists took the bait. The Mississippi Freedom Democratic party was a direct outgrowth of a seed planted by the Kennedy Administration and it represented the New Left's limited willingness to participate in the political process.[2]

What seemed a point of agreement, however, proved one of departure. The logic of voter registration prodded the New Left to invest much time and hope in MFDP. Prominent figures associated with organized labor played a key role in getting the New Left to mount a challenge at the Democratic National Convention in 1964. Hence, when Lyndon Johnson, with the seeming complicity of labor and other supposed liberal allies, squashed MFDP's challenge, the New Left felt betrayed. Subsequently, the New Left tended to regard electoral politics, especially within the confines of the two major parties, very circumspectly. Some even called politics a form of co-optation, or in one activists words, "a waste of time."[3]

But it would be wrong to infer that the New Left completely wrote off politics. Segments of the New Left continued to try to use the political system, albeit skeptically. Yet, paradoxically, the first segment of the New Left to reenter the political arena with the possibility of cooperating with labor was that which had been most directly affected by Lyndon

Johnson's heavy-handed politics at Atlantic City, namely civil rights activists who remained in the South after Selma. When Stokely Carmichael first popularized the term *Black Power* he emphasized its political meaning. As he told blacks in Greenwood, Mississippi, "the only way we can change things in Mississippi is with the ballot. That's black power." And on the last leg of the "James Meredith March," in Jackson, Mississippi, Carmichael reiterated that Black Power meant "the vote." "It's the right to control your own vote, to fire the police who uses tear gas and brutalizes you." While the mass media lost track of this aspect of Black Power, Southern black activists did not. On the contrary, they made it the mainstay of their movement in the latter half of the 1960s on through at least the 1980s.[4]

Evidence of the intersection between Black Power and electoral politics emerged even before Carmichael uttered the term. In Lowndes County, Alabama, SNCC helped establish the Black Panther party and in Atlanta, Georgia, Julian Bond, one of the founders of SNCC, undertook a grass roots campaign for the Georgia House of Representatives. Bond emphasized his opposition to the War in Vietnam and his support for further civil rights legislation. He sided with those who felt blacks needed to unite politically. "There's nothing wrong with people voting as a block," he claimed during the campaign. "Every other ethnic group has gotten together . . . and now its time for the black vote to rise up." While Bond opposed becoming a "mistress" of organized labor, he clearly recognized that blacks should "declare itself in the interest of laboring people." The bulk of the black populace was working class and thus any bona fide black politician would have to address labor issues. In turn, this would provide the basis for entering into alliances with white workers and trade unions.[5]

Simultaneously, MFDP carried on a battle for political power in Mississippi. Following the summer of 1964, MFDP continued to build political bases in the black community, especially in the Delta. They did so with a separatist bent, organizing around the ideal of racial solidarity and independent of the "Regular" Democratic party. Other liberal Mississippians, black and white, led by Charles Evers, brother of the slain Mississippi hero Medgar Evers, Aaron Henry, one of the founders of MFDP, and Claude Ramsay, head of the state AFL–CIO, concurrently built a black-white coalition within the Democratic party. Initially, these two blocks, like the New Left and liberals on the national level, opposed one another. (Both also opposed the Regular Democrats of the state.) A meeting organized to gain the support of the Young Democratic Club epitomized the depth of the antagonism between the two. Stephen

Lawson describes the scene: "The meeting ended in shambles. [Hodding] Carter (one of the reformers) staged a walkout with his allies ... and sniped at the FDP's antiwar pronouncements with a resolution condemning advocacy of draft evasion as 'an ideology foreign to the spirit of Americanism.'" FDP spokespersons responded that the "reformers" disdained grass roots politics, the essence of democracy."6

Nonetheless, in 1968 the MFDP, NAACP, Young Democrats, Prince Hall Masons, Mississippi Teachers Association, and state AFL–CIO combined to form the "Loyal Democrats" with the purpose of unseating the Regular Democrats at the national convention in Chicago. While confrontation reigned in the streets, Aaron Henry, Charles Evers, Fannie Lou Hamer, and Hodding Carter, led the campaign to oust the Regulars from their seats. This time they were successful as the Humphrey, McCarthy, and uncommitted camps on the credentials committee overwhelmingly, eighty-four to ten, accepted their argument that the Regular Democrats discriminated against blacks and were not loyal to the national party and thus did not deserve recognition.7

Four years later, without a credentials fight, a similar coalition, pledged to George McGovern, consisting of FDP veterans and reformers, represented the state at the Democratic convention. This time, Aaron Henry, who had headed the MFDP's ticket in 1964, chaired the state's Democratic party and served as McGovern's state campaign manager.8

Outside Mississippi, most black electoral efforts focused on developing strong bases in majority or near-majority black communities, either very rural areas or urban ghettos, neither bastions of organized labor, yet comprised of laboring people. In instances in which organized labor became an issue the results were mixed. Daniel Powell, AFL–CIO COPE director in the South, took pride in labor's endorsement of Barbara Jordan and Andrew Young, who became the first blacks from the South to be elected to the House of Representatives since Reconstruction. But COPE did not support Charles Evers in his campaign for governor of the state of Mississippi. Relations between trade unions and black politicians or office seekers were best in urban areas in the border states where labor had at least some base. For example, in St. Louis, William Clay received strong support from CORE and the Municipal Employees Union—he had been an official with both—in his successful campaign for Congress. Marion Barry, the first national chairman of SNCC, moved his way up the political ladder in Washington, D.C., from school board, in 1971 to Mayor, in 1979, with labor's endorsement. Parren Mitchell gained the backing of black activists and organized labor in his campaign for Congress in Maryland. And Maynard Jackson became mayor in Atlanta, with the ardent support of AFSCME.9

Several mayoral campaigns in the North provide a further measure of the relationship between the New Left and labor in politics. While few new leftists ran for office, several prominent mayoral candidates received support from new leftists, spoke the language of Black Power and the antiwar movement and in some cases channeled the interests and efforts of the New Left into electoral politics and away from the streets. For instance, Amiri Baraka (Leroi Jones), a self-proclaimed revolutionary, actively campaigned for Ken Gibson for mayor of Newark, and joined with Mayor Gary Hatcher and Julian Bond in organizing the Gary Convention of 1972. Manning Marable has characterized this gathering as "the largest black political convention in U.S. history." It attracted a broad array of black activists, from revolutionaries to integrationists, directing their attention to electing blacks to office.[10]

Another example of cooperation involved Richard Hatcher's campaign for Mayor of Gary, Indiana. Of all the major black politicians to come to power in the late 1960s, Hatcher was probably the most respected by black militants. Well before the Gary Convention, Hatcher received the enmity of regular Democrats for refusing to repudiate black militants. Hatcher's primary opponent in 1967, Mayor Martin Katz, described him as "a radical extremist and advocate of black power." John Krupa, local chairman of the Democratic party demanded that Hatcher denounce "specifically by name Martin Luther King Jr., Stokely Carmichael, . . . Joan Baez, H. Rap Brown and Marlon Brando." In response, Hatcher issued a weak denunciation of violence while upholding his right to associate with whomever he wanted. In 1967, despite such attacks, Hatcher defeated his regular Democratic and Republican foes. It was an unprecedented event. As Alex Poinsett observed: "Considering that Indiana's citizens voted . . . in 1850 to exclude blacks from settling in their state, considering that Indiana has long been a Ku Klux Klan stronghold, considering that segregation was not officially abolished until 1949, the election of a black mayor . . . was . . . revolutionary."[11]

Hatcher owed his victory first and foremost to the votes of working-class blacks, steel workers, slaughterhouse workers (like his mother), and casual laborers. He also garnered enough white votes, many of them steel workers, to put him over the top. Most notably, he received the strong support of the largest union in the city, the United Steel Workers of America. In his inaugural address Hatcher directly thanked USWA local head Joseph Germano for his help and made a "special plea" for organized labor to join him in reversing Gary's deterioration. Germano responded enthusiastically. "I believe," he said, that "we are on our way to that day when we recognize men for what they are . . . not for how they talk . . . not for where they come from . . . not for the way they worship God . . . and not for the image in which God created them. The election of Richard Hatcher . . . will stand as an historic milestone. . . . Our union believes in Richard Hatcher . . . the United Steel Workers of America pledge to him our hearts and our hands."[12]

Subsequently, Hatcher appeared as a keynote speaker at the Steelworkers' National Convention. Once again he thanked the union for its support. "At the time, there were many reasons why the leadership of the Steelworkers should have stayed out of the election," Hatcher informed the union delegates. "But they stood up for principle. They stood up for what was right." Even though a segment of the white workers in the city continued to oppose Hatcher with vehemence, with a steelworker leading an unsuccessful drive to have a white section of the town secede, Hatcher continued to pursue white, working-class votes and his popularity among them grew, as evidenced by his landslide victory for reelection in 1971.[13]

Another example of cooperation came in Madison, Wisconsin. There, Paul Soglin, a twenty-four-year-old graduate student who had developed a reputation as a leading Madison activist, determined to run for alderman after deciding that the size of the New Left in the community provided activists an opportunity to obtain political power. Running in the Eigth Ward, a predominantly student district, he won fairly easily. Once in office, Soglin expanded his base by working with rather than against party regulars to enact progressive legislation. At the same time, he maintained his radical base by identifying himself with various leftist causes.[14]

In 1971, Soglin ran for mayor on a populist platform: he promised to provide more services to the poor and lower taxes on the middle class. Even though he lost, he did well enough to lend credibility for a future campaign. In 1973 Soglin ran again, this time successfully, with labor support proving crucial. Shortly before the runoff, Soglin spoke on a special radio show sponsored by Madison's building trades. For one-half hour he answered questions posed by the president of the construction unions. His responses completely allayed labor's fears about his supposed left-wing lunacy, as charged by his opponent, and won him the endorsement of Madison COPE. In 1975, Soglin was reelected, with the help of solid majorities in the working-class wards.[15]

Soglin justified working within the political system by arguing that "the full liberal program has not yet been realized." Leftists would be best served, he asserted, by forming coalitions with liberals and pushing them to the limits of their convictions. This position resembled the reasoning of early civil rights activists with a new twist. In the early 1960s, new leftists influenced regular Democratic politicians from the outside. Soglin's victory showed that new leftists could attain positions of power themselves and then act as a progressive force from within the Democratic party. Or as radical sociologists Philip Altbach and Dennis Carlson argued: "one segment of the activist left has found a way of working successfully within the political system without abdicating most of its beliefs."[16]

In Berkeley, another enclave of the New Left, the political arena resembled that in Madison. As early as 1966, *Ramparts*' editor, Robert Sheer, had run for Congress in the Berkeley area and barely lost. A number of local activists followed his example, some successfully, including Ronald Dellums. Dellums was born in the ghetto of West Oakland, served in the Marines, went to Merrit College, the same school that Huey Newton and Bobby Seale attended, and then received a B.A. and M.S.W. from San Francisco State and U.C. Berkeley, respectively. In the mid–1960s, Dellums headed poverty programs in the ghettos of San Francisco and developed a following among Berkeley new leftists. They persuaded him to run for city council, which he did successfully, in 1967. As a council member, Dellums fought for benefits for the elderly and poor, supported student protesters in their battle for People's Park, and earned a reputation as an independent radical. Like Soglin, Dellums proclaimed his radicalism while retaining his faith in the political process. He rejected the politics of despair, asserting that violence intimidated most Americans and that it, not working within the political system, was the real "cop-out."[17]

In 1970, Dellums ran for a seat in the House of Representatives. In the primary he faced Jeffrey Cohelan, a six-term incumbent with a staunch liberal record. (Cohelan had the only 100 percent ADA rating in Congress.) Dellums emphasized that Cohelan was "out-of-step" with his district on the Vietnam War and ran on his record as a friend of students, minorities, senior citizens, and workers. He won 55 percent of the vote. After the primary, conservatives harangued Dellums as a part of "the lunatic left wing." Vice-President Spiro Agnew called Dellums an "out-and-out radical" and accused him of being close friends with Eldridge Cleaver, Huey Newton, and Bobby Seale of the Black Panthers. Republican opponent John Healy went even further, characterizing Dellums as a "creature of the Black Panthers."[18]

Such claims were not entirely unfounded. A study of black power in Oakland suggests that earlier political efforts by the Black Panther party, including Bobby Seale's unsuccessful campaign for mayor, had sown the seeds for Dellums victory and for the election of a series of black mayors in a city that heretofore had been ruled by conservative whites, like Oakland *Tribune* publisher, William Knowland. Dellums, indeed, attended affairs with the Panthers and refused to disassociate himself from them. In return, Panthers and their sympathizers got out the vote for him on election day.[19] Ironically, many political experts, paid little attention to his primary campaign, theorizing that by tapping into the left insurgency on the East Bay, Dellums had succeeded too well. By outflanking Cohelan on the Left, the experts reasoned, Dellums insured that he would be swept away in a wave of political backlash from the right in November.[20]

These predictions, however, proved unfounded. Dellums not only held onto his student and minority base but he also mended fences with Cohelan's traditional supporters, most important with local and national labor unions. Indeed, Dellums increased his margin of victory, winning nearly 60 percent of the vote. In endorsing him, COPE, the political arm of the AFL–CIO, called his race one of the most important in the country. A large collection of local unions, ranging from the Longshoremen to the Building Trades, contributed substantially to his treasury. *The Dispatcher* praised Dellums for his antiwar record and steady support for the United Farm Workers and described his campaign as a "critical contest" that would determine the "balance of power."[21] Over the next two decades Dellums lived up to his reputation as a radical while retaining his broad base of support. One might even argue that Dellums originated the rainbow coalition.[22]

Still another candidate for higher office who fused segments of the New Left and labor was Shirley Chisholm. A long-time community activist from the Bedford-Stuyvesant area of Brooklyn, Chisholm shared much of the New Left's distrust of the Democratic and Republican parties. However, as she put it, in reference to Black Power, she refused to channel her frustrations into a politics of despair that depended on violence, inflated militant rhetoric, or the formation of a third party. Rather, she pursued a middle course of building a local alliance of minorities, the young, feminists, and poor workers and then branching out to form a coalition with the regular Democrats, "including George Meany."[23]

Ironically, Chisholm's first race for Congress, in 1968, pitted her against nationally known civil rights leader James Farmer. Both candidates promoted the standard goals: more jobs, housing, and education. Both opposed the war in Vietnam and endorsed community control of schools. Chisholm distinguished herself from Farmer in two ways. First, she depicted Farmer as an outsider—Farmer lived in Manhattan—while simultaneously emphasizing that she had been born, raised and educated in the Bedford-Stuyvesant area of Brooklyn. Second, Chisholm attacked Farmer for his independence from the two main political parties. Farmer ran on the Liberal party line and refused to differentiate the Republican party from the Democrats. In contrast, Chisholm ran as an insurgent Democrat. She voiced her differences with Democratic party regulars (who had opposed her in the primary), but she remained committed to cooperating with the liberal segments of the party in the long run. This strategy bore fruit as she gained the endorsement of the New York State AFL–CIO in the general election. Moreover, while in Congress she worked with labor lobbyists to win passage of legislation that protected female workers.[24]

Chisholm brought to the campaign and to the political arena in general a new or additional factor. She was a feminist and to a certain degree she embodied a challenge to which both the New Left and labor had to respond. She showed that feminism, an offshoot of the New Left, would concern itself with electoral politics. She told a convention of feminists that "women are becoming aware, as blacks did, that they can have equal treatment if they will fight for it. . . . In particular, I am certain that more and more American women must become involved in politics."[25] Indeed, Chisholm's ultimate significance lay more with her symbolic value, as a representative of feminism and the black insurgency, than with her actual political positions, which turned conservative in the latter part of the 1970s.

Without a doubt, feminist goals, from the ERA to abortion and maternity rights, stirred up the political pot. And though the women's rights and labor movements did not initially unite around most of these goals, the potential for cooperation always existed. For example, in 1970, shortly after the UAW endorsed the ERA, the stage was set for collaboration between feminists and labor. The Women's Department of the UAW established the Network of Economic Rights, a coalition of women's rights activists dedicated to the passage of legislation that prohibited economic and sex discrimination, including the ERA. Along with NOW and other feminist organizations, NER lobbied for the ERA on a state-by-state basis. In addition, NER helped establish Labor for Equal Rights Now, which itself organized mass marches and parades in support of the ERA. One such protest brought together thousands of labor women and one-time student and civil right activists on the steps of the capitol building in Richmond, Virginia—one of the fifteen states that had not ratified the ERA.[26]

Furthermore, by 1974, many radical feminists and trade union women had joined NOW, which itself focused much of its attention on a variety of political endeavors. NOW supported left-liberal candidates, such as Bella Abzug and Barbara Mikulski, and lobbied for women's rights legislation in Congress, such as a Chisholm sponsored bill that amended the Fair Labor Standards Act to include domestic workers. Labor unionists also joined with feminists in filing suits against sexual discrimination in the workplace.[27]

This is not to suggest that the emergence of the women's rights movement produced some form of grand coalition between the New Left and labor in the political arena. Initially the women's rights movement reinforced divisions between the New Left and labor and added new points of disagreement. But in the long run the issue of women's rights provided a bridge between the New Left, radical feminists, and mainstream liberals, including organized labor and unorganized workers.

Soglin, Dellums, Chisholm, and others showed that activists running on left-leaning platforms could succeed in politics in certain locales and forge coalitions with labor in the process. However, their victories did not answer the critical questions: Could politics serve as a point of collaboration on the national level? Could the New Left and labor overcome their animosity built on the war, Black Power, and the counterculture to support a candidate who ran on a left-liberal platform? And if not, why not?

The debacle of Atlantic City topped by the historical developments of the mid–1960s seemed to foreclose the possibility of collaboration in a national election. An attempt to build an alternative political movement via the National Political Conference in 1967 collapsed in failure, and NCUP, as it was known, reached out to only the most progressive wing of the labor movement. Yet, to almost everyone's surprise, for a brief moment in 1968, a window of opportunity for collaboration opened, and the polarization so evident everywhere one looked almost disappeared.

Until 31 March 1968, President Johnson served as a focal point for both movements. To new leftists, LBJ personified the war in Vietnam and the ogre of corporate liberalism, with one of their favorite slogans being "Hey, Hey, LBJ. How many kids did you kill today?" In contrast, President Johnson helped hold the labor movement together. Even labor leaders who criticized the war heralded the Great Society and acknowledged that Johnson always lent labor his ear on important issues. Senator Eugene McCarthy's "victory" in New Hampshire, Robert F. Kennedy's entrance into the race, and then Johnson's stunning withdrawal changed the entire political scene.

McCarthy explicitly presented his candidacy as a viable alternative to polarization, "one last chance" for the system. As an advertisement in the *NY Times* entitled "Our Children Have Come Home" proclaimed, "Suddenly the kids have thrown themselves into politics, with all of their fabulous intelligence and energy. And it's a new election." Likewise, Robert F. Kennedy's campaign suggested that there was a viable alternative to the politics of "war and insanity," as represented by Johnson. Even if Robert F. Kennedy had a conservative past, his changing stance on Vietnam, seeming empathy for the poor, and charismatic and idealistic leadership could not be ignored.[28]

Before the New Hampshire primary, most well known new leftists argued that McCarthy had no chance and paid little heed to his campaign. But once Johnson withdrew it was no longer possible to dismiss electoral politics out of hand. This does not mean that the New Left rallied behind the McCarthy or Kennedy candidacies. On the contrary, new left leaders and organizations officially rejected both as symbols of liberal co-optation. For example, in the weeks preceding the Wisconsin primary, Paul Buhle asserted that McCarthy's campaign was a waste of time at best and a "positive detriment to the process of ideological clarification" at worst. SDS went ahead with its confrontational strategy of bringing the war home. Black Power activists laughed at the idea of working within the Democratic party, though they toyed with the prospect of supporting the Peace and Freedom ticket.[29]

Organized labor's response to Johnson's withdrawal was not much different. Most labor leaders had assumed that Johnson would run again and when he chose not to, they threw their support behind his anointed successor, Hubert H. Humphrey. Despite McCarthy's strong showing in New Hampshire and Kennedy's support in the polls, George Meany and most national union leaders viewed McCarthy and Kennedy as interlopers. Indeed, when the ADA endorsed McCarthy, several labor leaders resigned from it.[30]

But the declarations of New Left and organized labor leaders belied the fact that the ranks were attracted to these alternative candidacies. McCarthy's quixotic, antipolitical personality appealed to many new leftists and their sympathizers who had become alienated from traditional politics. McCarthy's supporters far outnumbered the doomsayers on college campuses. At SDS's Spring National Committee meeting, one contingent of SDS members presented a resolution on electoral politics that censured the National Office for issuing "encyclicals against electoral politics." The resolution emphasized that "the Electoral Process is not by its 'nature' bourgeois." SDS's leaders tabled the resolution but could not silence the avalanche of dissent that poured into national headquarters and local chapter offices. As one letter to the editor of *New Left Notes* declared, McCarthy's campaign represented "letting people decide," and that is what "I thought the American Revolution" and the New Left "was about."[31]

Similarly, Kennedy proved especially magnetic among Black Power's constituents. As one black militant informed Robert Coles, "Kennedy . . . is on our side. . . . We know it. He doesn't have to say a word." RFK also earned the private support or well wishes of several prominent new leftists, most notably Tom Hayden. He recalled that "the 'rational alternative' to the war and tumult, in the back of my mind, was Robert Kennedy. . . . My feelings were guarded. . . . And yet, in that year of turmoil . . . I thought that he alone . . . could understand the vertigo and pain that followed the hope of the early sixties."[32]

Furthermore, both candidates scored better in the primaries and polls than Hubert Humphrey among working-class Americans. In spite of George Meany's and COPE director Al Barkan's commands, both picked up some official trade union support. In the New Hampshire campaign, McCarthy took advantage of his Irish Catholic heritage to tap blue-collar support. He made regular appearances at factory gates, where reporters noted that workers favorably referred to him as "McCahty," although staffers wondered if they thought his first name was Joe. Robert Kennedy did even more strongly among Irish Catholic workers and other "Middle Americans." in the Indiana primary.[33]

Yet, Kennedy's assassination and McCarthy's subsequent collapse (coupled with the earlier assassination of Martin Luther King, Jr.) slammed shut the window of opportunity. What appeared to be a potential arena of collaboration rapidly turned into one of the primary arenas of confrontation. By the time of the convention, both the New Left and labor wanted little to do with one another.

While the New Left's radical stance grew out of its disillusionment with the political process on top of its dismay over the war and various domestic problems, labor's unwillingness to compromise nevertheless demands further explanation. For years liberals had sought to channel new left energy into politics. As prominent players within the Democratic party, labor officials could have endorsed McCarthy following Kennedy's assassination, rather than Humphrey, who had performed poorly in every presidential primary in which he had run. Instead, the AFL–CIO rallied behind the vice-president. They did so not because of McCarthy's record—he had gained COPE's endorsement in the past and had a much better senatorial rating than Lyndon Johnson—or because he could not win, since every Gallup and Harris poll showed McCarthy running better against Nixon than Humphrey. Rather, labor rejected McCarthy, and to a lesser extent Robert Kennedy, because they personified the spirit of dissent. Lewis Chester, Godfrey Hodgson, and Bruce Page explained in *An American Melodrama,* "Deep down they're afraid that if he wins the McCarthy supporters will replace them." Put another way, it was not ideology that kept the New Left and labor apart in 1968. Rather, labor leaders feared that McCarthy's nomination would unleash further revolt, which in turn would diminish their own power.[34]

In 1972, the question once again arose whether the electoral process would serve as an arena in which new leftists and labor could find common ground. Given the divisive conclusion of the Democratic campaign in 1968 and the rampage of workers on Wall Street in 1970, the chances for reconciliation seemed slim. But, a number of developments, from organizing efforts in the fields of California to local political campaigns, hinted that electoral politics could bring the New Left and labor together.

The chances for reconciliation were improved by the actions of Senator George McGovern, who between 1968 and 1972, in coalition with other reformers, shrewdly rewrote the Democratic party's rules. This made it easier for a reformer like McGovern to win the nomination. Henceforth, the support of the party bosses was not a prerequisite for winning the Democratic nomination. At the same time, McGovern established himself as an bona fide antiwar figure. In other words, McGovern and his campaign manager, Gary Hart, predicated McGovern's candidacy on the belief that it was possible to bridge the gap between the insurgents, who provided the base for the nomination, and the party regulars, especially organized labor, whose support they deemed crucial for success in November.[35]

Based on the writings and statements of organized labor, this strategy did not seem farfetched. In December 1971, for example, the AFL–CIO constitutional convention and George Meany claimed that labor's top priority was the defeat of Richard Nixon in 1972. Nonetheless, McGovern failed to win either the federation's or Meany's endorsement. Instead, both advocated a position of neutrality.[36]

Meany and other top AFL–CIO officials rationalized the federation's decision in every possible way. Meany declared that McGovern had *not* been a friend to labor. In addition, he accused McGovern of isolationism. Writing for the *AFL–CIO News,* Harvard political scientist John Roche seconded this charge, stating that McGovern's foreign policy represented a retreat to "Fortress America" of the 1930s. An article by Lane Kirkland, another top official with the AFL–CIO, justified the federation's stance in a different way. Kirkland claimed that the AFL–CIO was a political but "non-partisan" organization.[37]

Although technically correct this argument contradicted the AFL–CIO's history and recent statements by labor spokesmen. In fact, in every election since the creation of the AFL–CIO, 1956, 1960, 1964, and 1968, the labor federation had endorsed the Democratic ticket for president. COPE overwhelmingly endorsed Democratic candidates for Congress and state offices. Nearly every political analyst considered the labor federation to be an integral part of the Democratic party. Trade union members identified with the Democratic party and voted for Democratic candidates by a large margin. Indeed, a month before the 1972 convention, the *American Federationist* summarized the AFL–CIO's feelings toward the two parties, writing that the "GOP will be what it has always been," while the "Democrats are guaranteed a wide-open exercise in the democratic process." Only after McGovern won the nomination without its help did the AFL–CIO lay claim to nonpartisanship; only after the Democratic convention did the House of Labor abdicate its leadership role in the Democratic party and declare itself uninterested in defeating Richard Nixon.[38]

Moreover, Meany's and Roche's charges contrasted sharply with the record. COPE itself rated McGovern as having voted correctly 93 percent of the time in his fourteen years in Congress. The AFL–CIO had endorsed McGovern in each of his senatorial campaigns, and would do so again after 1972. COPE gave Nixon a dismal 13 percent rating. Not surprisingly, McGovern retorted that the labor federation's declaration of neutrality based upon the notion that there was no difference between Nixon and himself was absurd. McGovern's record as head of President Kennedy's Food for Peace program and support of the UN and Israel did not resemble the record of an isolationist of the 1930s. And his calls for reducing the defense budget did not add up to a dismantling of the American military. In addition, McGovern argued that America's continued presence in Vietnam left the U.S. isolated from its traditional European allies and damaged the nation's reputation worldwide.[39]

As in 1968, the AFL–CIO's espoused political convictions gave way to concerns over power. AFL–CIO leaders disliked the manner in which McGovern received the nomination more than the man. COPE director Al Barkan fumed at the "Harvard-Berkeley Camelots"— a group that included the New Left—and he declared that he had no intention of letting them take over the country. George Meany castigated the delegates at the convention as unrepresentative of America. In reference to the New York delegation, Meany stated: "What kind of delegation is this? . . . They've got six open fags and only three AFL–CIO people . . . !" Meany's contention that the 1972 convention shut out labor unionists was false. More trade unionists served as delegates in 1972 than had in 1968. However, the delegates were not the AFL–CIO power brokers, as they had been in the past. Consequently, AFL–CIO leaders chose to repudiate the insurgents over supporting their party. This is not to argue that an AFL–CIO endorsement would have translated into a McGovern victory, but the lack of an endorsement damaged McGovern's chances and the Democratic party. Ironically, the AFL–CIO deserved some blame for McGovern's nomination. As McGovern himself later observed: "By remaining aloof from the reform effort, labor not only forfeited its considerable influence but also helped maintain the division within the party that had opened in 1968."[40]

Labor movement opposition to McGovern, however, was hardly monolithic. Only a few unions endorsed Richard Nixon, most notably the Teamsters and the ILA, and the Teamsters' endorsement was tainted. In December 1971, President Nixon pardoned Jimmy Hoffa. Shortly afterward, Hoffa told panelist's on ABC's "Issues and Answers" that Nixon was the best candidate. Acting Teamster leader Frank Fitz-simmons agreed even though he had been an ardent opponent of the war throughout Nixon's first term. A number of large unions adopted a stance of neutrality, most prominently the Steelworkers and eleven Building Trades unions. But, an even larger number of unions (at least twenty-five) rejected Meany's counsel and endorsed McGovern.[41]

Many of the pro-McGovern unions had previously established themselves as dissenters within the labor movement by opposing the war. Yet, a few pro-war unions endorsed McGovern as well. CWA president Joseph Beirne, in particular, who had a long-standing record in support of Johnson's policies in Southeast Asia, urged McGovern to temper his disagreements with labor. In return Beirne pledged to work quietly for labor endorsements for the McGovern campaign. Both McGovern and Beirne upheld their ends of this agreement. In endorsing McGovern, several trade unions rebutted Meany's charges that McGovern was not a friend of labor. For example, *UAW Solidarity* ran a series of articles on McGovern's "pro-labor record" including his long-standing ties with the autoworkers, his strong COPE rating and his commitment to full employment. In its preelection issue, *UAW Solidarity* pleaded for a vote for "Peace, Jobs, and People." Leonard Woodcock explained, McGovern was a "son of the soil." His doctoral thesis alone, on the Ludlow massacre, showed that "anyone who took the time to read it would never believe the lie that George McGovern was not interested in or sympathetic to working men and women."[42]

On election day, polls showed that union households split their vote between Nixon and McGovern. Approximately 50 percent of union household members voted for McGovern, 48 percent for Nixon, up from 34 percent in 1968. Significantly, Nixon won the Wallace vote. McGovern's own bungling, especially the Eagleton fiasco, hurt him with workers, as it did with nearly every other group. Put another way, workers were just as torn by McGovern's candidacy as the House of Labor. Half proved willing to support an avowedly antiwar candidate, who had been nominated by a convention packed with insurgents, and whom the media commonly associated with the New Left. But the other half voted for an incumbent and politically shrewd conservative. (This breakdown of the vote does not account for the millions of Americans who chose not to vote, a sign of their alienation from both candidates and the electoral process itself.)[43]

Until shortly before McGovern received the nomination, most well known new leftists refrained from commenting on the election. In the summer of 1972, the thousands of students who joined McGovern's campaign broke this silence. Henceforth, new leftists of all persuasions came to recognize that McGovern's nomination was assured and spent much their time determining what to do. As the *Guardian* observed, "Does the position of a bourgeois candidate on a burning question before the masses—such as the Vietnam War—ever require left and progressive forces to rally behind a capitalist party? Or should the left support only Socialist and independent candidates, or even organize a boycott of elections?"[44]

The most "radical" new leftists never considered supporting McGovern. The Weathermen had gone underground, and PL disdained capitalist political parties. Avowedly socialist organizations, such as the SWP (YSA), ran their own candidates rather than endorse a Democrat.

A larger segment of the New Left objected to McGovern's candidacy but felt compelled to offer countless reasons for doing so. *Guardian* refused to endorse McGovern but simultaneously counseled against denouncing the "masses" who intended to vote for him. Dave Dellinger, Stanley Aronowitz, and Carl Davidson arrived at a similar position. They all admitted that McGovern and Nixon differed over the war. Still, they insisted that since both candidates accepted the premise of American imperialism neither deserved the New Left's support. "No fundamental changes in the nature of imperialism or of the state apparatus are in the offing as the result of the contest between Richard Nixon and George McGovern," read one *Guardian* editorial. Furthermore, to support McGovern would lend legitimacy to the Democratic party, an unabashedly imperialist and capitalist party. Participating in elections entails "joining in the process of reelecting the government when its task is to secure its disintegration," claimed Stanley Aronowitz. The Left would be better served by remaining independent of the electoral process and instead concentrating on "what it does best," namely orchestrating mass demonstrations against the war and educating the public about the nature of American imperialism. "Our job may not be to waste time attacking McGovern, who is clearly the best of the establishment politicians," wrote Dave Dellinger. "It may even be that our job is to push him as far as he can possibly go. But the way to do this . . . is to continue to build an enlightened, responsible people's movement."[45]

A number of well-known leftists and a large number of rank- and-file antiwar activists questioned this strategy. They saw it as betrayal of the antiwar cause in favor of purist politics. "Can you really talk about 'bourgeois parliamentary process and imperialism' while that little girl runs down the road with her clothes on fire from our napalm?" wrote Rhoda Good. "If Hitler lurks behind Nixon, as suggested . . . if McGovern wants to end the war and we want to end the war, he is the man to elect," exhorted Lucille Perlman. Activists did not support McGovern because he "personified the pure imperative of justice and the requirements of change," stated a *Ramparts* article, but because the Left could not afford to present the message that we care "too little" about Vietnam. I. F. Stone, who was one of the earliest critics of the war added, "I am all for keeping the heat on McGovern from the left . . . but not to the point of unrealistic tantrums. . . . the McGovern ticket, whatever its compromises, offers the country a real choice and a real change of direction for the first time in years."[46]

Many new leftists also criticized the fundamental reasoning of the anti-McGovernite segment of the New Left. Most importantly, the pro-McGovernites challenged the former to substantiate their claims of success. The anti-McGovernites certainly were not "building a durable left-wing alternative to electoral politics," retorted Paul Cowan. Nor did the anti-McGovernites display an ability to organize mass demonstrations anymore, argued the McGovern supporters. "What mass extra-legal parliamentary struggles are you referring to," asked one antiwar activist? The New MOBE had disintegrated; militant blacks had not staged a mass action in years; and only ecology and women's groups seemed capable of mobilizing large numbers of people.[47]

Finally, those who endorsed McGovern did so for the very same reasons that other new leftists advocated independence. Instead of seeing the election as a trap, as a mechanism for absorbing or dissipating dissent, the pro-McGovernites saw McGovern's campaign as a way to demonstrate the strength of the New Left and to induce others, especially workers, to move to the Left. David Kolodney argued that McGovern's success reflected the movement's success. "The candidate is only as radical as his constituency forces him to be." Another leftist wrote that McGovern was educating the American worker by "telling them to care about Vietnamese deaths. . . . True, he's not a socialist, but socialism is not a practical demand right now. Let's clear the way for socialism by supporting bourgeois capitalism as opposed to bourgeois fascism." In sum, Paul Cowan asserted, the anti-McGovernites displayed a "sickening cynicism." Their rationale was as disingenuous as that of George Meany. Both found faults with McGovern's record; both questioned his commitment to *their* cause. Neither offered a viable alternative; neither really wanted a Nixon victory. In contrast, the segment of the New Left that supported McGovern demonstrated a willingness to cooperate in the political world behind a viable candidate. As a result they helped to nominate a left-liberal politician for president, brought the issue of war into a presidential election, and fostered a spirit of cooperation with those segments of labor that rejected the reasoning of their own cynical leaders.[48]

In sum, the 1972 presidential election displayed the ambiguity of the relationship between the New Left and labor. Some new leftists and trade unionists rejected cooperating in politics, on any level, national or local. A second group of both movements entertained joining hands but balked when confronted with real electoral choices. Still another segment of the New Left forged effective political alliances with sympathetic trade unionists. Although such a coalition failed on the national level, it did succeed in electing candidates in certain locales and promised to influence an even greater number of elections in the coming years. Moreover, the events of 1972 demonstrated that neither the New Left nor labor were monoliths. While the leaders and ranks of both movements grappled with the question of whether to support McGovern, no single position won out. And those who championed principle, rather than compromise or political correctness, as opposed to common sense, hardly saw their cause flourish in the ensuing years.

Finally, the 1972 campaign marked the end of the New Left as a social movement. Beset by sectarian disputes, external pressures, physical and emotional exhaustion, and a less conducive setting, the New Left lost its momentum and dissipated into less substantial strands. Furthermore, shortly after the 1972 election, the economy took a dramatic turn, as the first of the oil crises of the 1970s introduced a period of stagnation. With this change, the entire context of American life and politics shifted. Throughout the 1960s, both the New Left and labor had assumed that the United States would remain the preeminent economic power. Neither really ever wondered what life would be like and what positions they should take in a less expansive or prosperous context. Those segments of both movements who had refused to endorse McGovern certainly felt that better times were ahead, that their causes were gaining momentum. Yet, a change in the economy actually hurt both the New Left and labor or at least played into the hands of conservatives who skillfully played on the middle-class fears of New Left and liberal positions. Put another way, the 1972 election marked the concluding chapter of the 1960s. Its major themes and concerns would not disappear from the American scene. But new ones would predominate and the subject of the New Left's relationship to labor became more academic than real in the process.

Conclusion

Contrary to the predominant view, the New Left and labor had a critical relationship throughout the 1960s. They interacted on both a personal and intellectual basis and shaped or influenced each other's histories. The social activist wing of the labor movement helped give birth to the New Left and through financial, emotional, and logistical aide nurtured its growth. To an extent, the early New Left rekindled the activist flame within the labor movement, pushing liberals to promote certain reforms they otherwise might not have supported (such as Joe Rauh making MFDP's case before the credential's committee of the Democratic party).[1]

The New Left appreciated labor's help and flirted with the idea of forging a realigned Democratic party, along the lines of the social democratic parties of Western Europe. As the New Left matured, however, its uncertainty over the value of coalition grew. Ties with the labor movement produced newfound opportunities, yet seemed to close off others. Moreover, with increased cooperation new leftists discovered—with a sense of betrayal—just how bound labor was to the established Democratic party and all of its conservative tendencies. Still, through the winter of 1964–65, disagreements did not override commonalities; cooperation, not confrontation, remained the predominant theme.

The escalation of the Vietnam War, emergence of Black Power, and the flowering of the counterculture altered the New Left's relationship to labor. These historically specific developments, more than anything else, drove a wedge between the two and accounted for the timing and nature of the rift. Nevertheless, even as these historical developments tore New Left and labor apart, the two found room to cooperate in local endeavors and in certain national campaigns, most notably behind the farm workers' drive for union recognition. In turn, these instances of collaboration laid the foundation for a reconciliation of differences between significant segments of both movements as the 1960s drew to a close.

Our study of the New Left's relationship to Labor reminds us that neither social movement should be viewed as a monolith. The New Left was not entirely cut off from the history of the Left in the United States. It shared ties and a concern for American workers, even if in a different degree and form than its predecessors. And it left a legacy of interaction with labor. By the same token, labor's commitment to the Democratic party, its anticommunism and support for the policy of containment, did *not* prevent it from aiding left-liberal groups, from SDS in the North to CORE and SNCC in the South (not to mention SCLC). Indeed, many have forgotten that labor was more concerned with the threat from the right than that from the Left in the early 1960s and that it sought allies to improve its image and prospects, and that of liberalism in general, on college campuses, in the South, and among unorganized workers. In addition, this study reveals that in the latter half of the 1960s and early 1970s, both the labor movement and the New left had internal factional differences and operated in contradictory manners. Student-labor peace initiatives took place alongside the rampage of construction workers on Wall Street. New leftists and trade unionists joined hands politically in some cases but rejected cooperation in other ones. Put another way, the image of the pro-war blue collar worker, epitomized by the fictional character Archie Bunker, and the concept of political backlash on the part of labor are in need of modification. If we continue to ignore these complexities and contradictions, so that we can present a "normative" picture of the New Left and labor, we will be doomed to misunderstanding the 1960s and the decades that have followed.

In other words, historians need to move beyond understanding the sixties in polemical and overly simplistic terms. It was not simply an era characterized by a move from the idealism of the Port Huron Statement to the madness of the Weathermen. It was not one in which the New Left and labor, or students and middle America, were solely confrontational. Nor was it a time when American youths came to hate their country and fellow countrymen. Some did but many others did not, as demonstrated by the willingness of large segments of the New Left to reconcile their differences with segments of labor in the late 1960s and early 1970s.

But, if this is valid, then how does one explain the conservative political shift of the 1970s and 1980s. Why was the liberal coalition unable to reconstitute itself? Why did a progressive coalition fail to form in its place?

A cardinal part of the established canon on the 1960s regards America's right-ward drift as one of the by-products of the polarization of the nation in the 1960s. According to this interpretation, the New Left pushed ethnic workers out of the Democratic party in 1968 and 1972. After the latter half of the 1960s, backlash against activism and the goals (or achievements) of the New Left became a pervasive theme. Not surprisingly, many of the same historians who emphasize the divisions between the New Left and labor ascribe to this "backlash" theory. In his updated study of the period, Irwin Unger portrays the late 1960s as a watershed in American history whereby liberalism declined and conservatism ascended. In particular, Unger argues that 1968 "was not just ferocious and tumultuous; it was also a year that changed America." Unger adds, "In that twelve month span the country pivoted. Old forces and currents lost their forward momentum and began to reverse; new ones appeared." In sum, Unger proclaims, "Nineteen sixty-eight was a turning point that marked the beginning of our own dubious age of privatism and social confusion. It was the year that the liberal consensus of the early sixties fell apart and was replaced by rancorous resistance to further social change." Likewise, William Chafe, in his highly respected text *The Unfinished Journey,* writes that 1968 marked a momentous moment in American history when " 'what might have been' now no longer seemed possible." Similarly, Irving Howe blames the excesses of the 1960s for the conservative developments of the decades that followed.[2]

Without suggesting that backlash against the New Left did not take place or that it has not had a significant impact on American life, these historians have overstated their case. A more balanced account of the 1960s, one which considers the impact of the entire era, produces a more nuanced understanding of the mood-swing of the 1970s and 1980s. If confrontation was not the only theme of the 1960s and early 1970s and if cooperation was a major theme of the early 1960s, then backlash alone can not explain the developments of the past two decades. Demographic and economic shifts over the past twenty years and the political skill of the Republican party have had as much, if not more, affect on recent politics as the legacy of the New Left. Moreover, the demise of liberalism, or the New Deal order, must be attributed at least as much to its successes, as to its excesses, or, put differently, to the legacy of cooperation as to the legacy of confrontation.

Ironically, new laws that were enacted in the first half of the decade created obstacles to sustaining the coalition that passed them in the first place. Liberal reforms, achieved to a large degree because of the pressure exerted by a radical flank (the New Left), forced the New Deal coalition to face its most fundamental contradiction: that it was a coalition of urban liberals and southern white supremacists. Most prominently, the Voting Rights Act of 1965 generated a substantial barrier to more reforms, overwhelming white southern resistance. Arguably the single most important piece of federal legislation of the decade, this law was a direct product of new left-labor collaboration. Since 1965, black involvement in politics, especially in the South, has increased at an astonishing rate. Twenty-five years after the act was passed, there were nearly twice as many black registered voters in the South and over twenty times as many elected black officials. As of 1992, for instance, an African American man is Congressman in Sunflower County, the one-time home of Fannie Lou Hamer.

Yet, the success of the civil rights coalition and black enfranchisement has resulted in the most significant political shift in the latter half of the twentieth century: white southern flight from the Democratic party. Especially in presidential elections, the once Democratically solid South has become the bastion of the Republican party. In 1980, 1984, and 1988, white southerners from the old confederate states voted over-whelmingly for Republican candidates. In 1964, 64 percent of white voters in the South identified with the Democratic party and Lyndon Johnson won almost 55 percent of their vote. Twenty years later, only 33 percent of whites in the South identified themselves as Democrats and Walter Mondale, the political heir to Hubert Humphrey, won just 30 percent of the southern white vote. Only in the election of 1976, when Jimmy Carter, a moderate Georgian, ran for President, did the Demo-crats come close to winning the white vote. Even then, Gerald Ford, a Republican from Michigan, out-polled Carter among white voters. Earl and Merle Black summarize the shift, "As a rule, presidential candidates of the Democratic party are no longer competitive among white south-ern voters. Not since Johnson's campaign has a majority of white south-erners voted Democratic, and only once since then—in Carter's 1976 candidacy—has a Democratic nominee won as much as 45 percent of the white vote."[3]

While backlash against the excesses of the New Left, the counterculture, black power, and "liberal" or anti-imperialistic foreign policy has con-tributed to this shift, it would be incorrect to give more weight to these factors than to the historical fact that the majority of whites in the South have refused to ally themselves with blacks. As soon as blacks moved into the Democratic party in significant numbers, whites moved out! This dilemma was compounded by the fact that in the same time span northern white workers, sometimes referred to as urban and suburban ethnics, were growing increasingly disillusioned with liberal programs, which they saw as operating against their best interests. The simultane-ous increase in welfare dependency and crime, which the Democratic party seemed incapable of addressing, angered the urban/suburban ethnics even more.

Does this mean that even if the New Left and labor could have maintained their cooperative relationship and constructed a progressive coalition akin to the one proposed by Bayard Rustin that the conservative political shift of the 1970s and 1980s could have been avoided? Or were Rustin, Howe, and others right in surmising that a New Left, bent on confrontation, would produce a backlash, which in turn, would create a force far more powerful than liberalism and one committed to maintaining the status quo, not gradual reform? Was the late 1960s a tragedy for progressivism broadly defined?

While there are no simple answers to these central questions, several general responses can be offered. First, the claim that the New Left wasted an opportunity ignores the historical forces that prevented such a coalition from forming in the first place. The Vietnam War, Black Power, and the counterculture tore apart liberals and the New Left because they were issues with which the New Deal coalition had to grapple if it was to go on to build a left-liberal coalition. Second, even if a consensus on these issues had been achieved, the coalition would have had to overcome other obstacles, most prominently that of race and southern white voting habits. History determined that the Democratic party carried with it certain baggage that mitigated against a sustained and successful left-liberal coalition, including the fact that it was an ideologically contradictory or inconsistent entity. John F. Kennedy went to his grave having failed to solve the riddle of winning passage of civil rights legislation without alienating the southern wing of his party. True, Lyndon Johnson won support for the Civil Rights Act of 1964 and other "race" reforms, but one of the results was the massive desertion of the South into the hands of George Wallace, the symbol of white supremacy, in 1968. The political ascendancy of blacks in the North, combined with the development of an urban underclass, presented one more barrier to coalition.[4]

This said, the 1960s represented a tragedy but not for the reasons suggested by Rustin. For progressives the tragedy lies in the fact that the opportunity to form a viable coalition diminished very rapidly after its greatest political triumphs in 1964 and early 1965. After the struggle of the early 1960s culminated with the Voting Rights Act of 1965 and the War on Poverty (as limited and as misconceived as it was), the next natural step would have been to unite the energies of the New Left and labor movement into a massive organizing drive of poor people, especially blacks. This was the task that Martin Luther King undertook in 1968. Such a drive or movement would have involved some type of redistribution of the wealth, the organizing of unorganized workers in the South, which in turn would have granted greater power to those historically without it. Economically the times were ripe for such an effort. Anticommunism had diminished in importance, as had overt racism—both historical barriers to such a drive. Labor had the muscle and political influence to consider such an effort and new leftists could have provided the necessary energy and idealism to have gotten such a movement off the ground.

Efforts were made along these lines, with the strike of sanitation workers in Memphis being one example. But following passage of the Voting Rights Act this was not the main thrust of the era. The New Left and labor, crucial segments of the left-liberal coalition, were generally busier attacking each other than joining forces. By the time that the Vietnam War ended and Black Power and the counterculture diminished in importance, conditions had changed dramatically. Increasing unemployment, global competition, massive budget deficits, middle-class tax revolts, deindustrialization, increased automation, and the depopulation of the Midwest and rise of the Sun Belt—all altered the parameters of change. Meanwhile, divisive cultural issues, from abortion to school prayer, and a resurgence of nationalism, arguably generated by backlash against the New Left, took the place of the war, black nationalism and the counterculture as issues that created rifts within the old New Deal coalition.

Tragically, neither the New Left nor labor saw such changes coming. Basking in the prosperity of the postwar years, both movements were optimistic about their ability to reform the world. By 1968, as evidenced by the extent to which both were willing to accept a Nixon victory, both saw each other as the main enemy and did not consider organized conservatives as much of a threat. The New Left ridiculously claimed that they would out-compete George Wallace and Spiro Agnew (or Ronald Reagan) for the votes or hearts of the New Right. Liberals expended more effort in fighting off George Wallace's entrée into the working class than did the New Left, but a large segment of labor rebuffed McCarthy and McGovern and other attempts to build alternative political coalitions in spite of its dislike for Richard Nixon. In other words, neither the New Left nor labor understood how small the window of opportunity was.

Does this mean that a progressive coalition, which would include veterans of the New Left (and its impulse) as well as segments of labor will never succeed? This is not the only conclusion one can draw from a study of the sixties. While the 1972 campaign marked the end of the New Left as a social movement, individual new leftists and new left ideas or goals have had an important afterlife. A number of new left leaders remained active politically, often carrying on the tradition of dissent. Tom Hayden, for example, nearly became a U.S. Senator in California in the mid–1970s and was elected to the state legislator in 1979. Julian Bond maintained his seat in the Georgia Assembly and Senate from 1965 to 1987. John Lewis won a seat in congress in 1986. Other new leftists won seats on town councils and still others were appointed to national and state posts. Impressive trade union support for Jesse Jackson in 1988 and David Dinkins in New York City in 1989, or the "rainbow coalition" that prevented Robert Bork's nomination to the Supreme Court, suggested that an important crosscurrent to that of backlash had begun to emerge as the eighties drew to a close.[5]

Even more important, on the local level, tens of veteran new leftists formed community or citizen action groups. These very same organizations often enjoyed the support or membership of trade union activists as well and younger men and women who were inspired to community activism by the struggles of the 1960s. While these community groups are outside the confines of traditional politics (defined as national, state, and local elections), they have had a significant affect on the public and private life of millions of Americans. In Harry Boyte's words, they have represented a "backyard revolution," in American life. Contrary to the predominant view, these grass roots organizations, many of which combine the strengths of the New Left and labor, show that most activists did not become part of the "Me decade." As participants in various "backyard revolutions," veteran activists have fought for a more democratic workplace, greater control over communities and a safer environment.[6]

Moreover, since the late 1960s, labor's political stances have evolved. While this evolution has not been dramatic, it is a shift nonetheless. The labor movement has spawned a distinct bloc of leaders and unions that routinely dissented against aggressive or expansionist foreign policy in the 1980s. Trade union leaders have allied themselves with left-leaning politicians and activist groups with increasing frequency, including calls for an end to American support for the Contras and sanctions against South Africa. William Winpisinger, head of the International Association of Machinists, for one, became a prominent critic of what the New Left called America's imperialist foreign policy. And Winpisinger's union was not part of the anti-Vietnam labor block in the late 1960s and early 1970s. Most of the unions that were part of this group, such as Local 1199, have retained their "anti-imperialist" bent.[7]

Without a doubt, a change in the historical context allowed labor to move to the left on certain issues—"just as external events called Middle America forth, just as surely did history dissolve it," Jonathan Rieder writes.[8] The Vietnam War initially had a dramatic affect on the New

Left's relationship to labor. Along with Black Power and the counterculture it drove a deep wedge between the two. As the war dragged on, however, it generated a massive peace movement, which included segments of the New Left and the labor movement. When the war came to an end, even more new leftists and trade unionists were able to find common ground. And the end of the Cold War removed one, if not the most important, reason for the disagreement in the first place.

The long-term impact of the Black Power and the counterculture is more difficult to gauge. Both disappeared as significant forces in the early 1970s. In common parlance, hippies were replaced by yuppies and militant black rhetoric gave way to pragmatic political pressure groups. Accordingly, neither should have remained a divisive force in the political arena. But as suggested earlier, backlash against programs associated with the militant civil rights movement, such as busing and affirmative action, and against "modernist" culture, the relative of the counterculture in much of the public's mind, abounds. Particularly in the South, the Republican party has rallied once solid Democrats behind conservative candidates by invoking traditional values—the flag, school prayer, and the family—and by tapping hundreds of years of racism upon the part of white workers, through subtle and not-so-subtle campaigning. And in the North, particularly in working-class urban and suburban districts, conservatives have made solid inroads among the backbone of the old New Deal coalition by shrewdly arguing that workers are the victims of reverse discrimination and special interest policies, which are the legacy of the sixties.[9]

But, to reiterate, we should not overstate the theme of backlash. It is more accurate to acknowledge the ambiguities of the latter part of the decade and its contradictory legacy. The political mood-swing of the 1970s and 1980s has not been as great as many commentators contend. Most notably, the Reagan years did not lead to the repeal of the New Deal nor many of the cornerstones of the Great Society, such as Medicare and the Voting Rights Act of 1965. Moreover, many of the reforms first raised by the New Left and later made into law by a broader coalition of forces and legal decisions still exist. To paraphrase one activist, to understand the changes wrought by the New Left one would have to have lived in the 1950s. Coat-hanger abortions, school prayer, atmospheric testing of atomic weapons, Jim Crow, wanton imperialism, mandatory ROTC, dress codes, dormitory curfews, the draft, bomb shelters, strident (domestic) anticommunism and, legal sexual and racial discrimination in the workplace and housing market were all part of American life before the sixties. Even though the New Left disappeared as a social movement, remnants of it, along with its labor allies have managed to resist the conservative crusade to return to the "good old" days. Especially when we consider the structural shifts that America has experienced since the late 1960s—a stagnating economy, the growth of the sunbelt and decline of the "rustbelt"—this accomplishment should not be underestimated. Perhaps Martin Luther King, Jr., who was busy trying to forge a coalition of antiwar advocates, trade unionists, poor people, and minorities was right when, on the on the eve of his assassination, he predicted, "We've got some difficult days ahead. But it doesn't matter with me now. Because I've been to the mountaintop. . . . And I've looked over. And I've seen the promised land. I may not get their with you. But I want you to know . . . that we, as a people, will get to the promised land."[10]

Appendix: Theory, Methodology, and Historiography

When I first began my research, over a decade ago, only a handful of scholarly works on the 1960s existed, especially as written by historians, except that which focused on the generation gap. Works on this subject abounded, from both the perspective of proponents and opponents of the developments of the sixties. When the youth rebellion rapidly dissipated and gave way to the parochialism of the me generation, which to an extent deflated the value of the generational school, interest among scholars in the 1960s waned. Following the publication of Irwin Unger's *The Movement* and William O'Neill's *Coming Apart,* little was written, except for personal reminiscences, such as James Forman's *The Making of A Black Revolutionary,* anthologies, and a couple of well-written books by professional journalists, most notably those by Kirkpatrick Sale and Milton Viorst.

But shortly after I completed my research, "historical" interest in the 1960s took off. Professional and semiprofessional historians delved into the "turbulent decade" with unusual verve. While their studies have added to our knowledge of the era, most share similar shortcomings and remain unfulfilling. Wini Breines and Maurice Isserman argue (and I tend agree with their argument) that the major works on the 1960s, such as Todd Gitlin's *The Sixties* and James Miller's, *Democracy Is in the Streets,* pay too much attention to male leaders, define the New Left too narrowly, and most important portray the developments of the 1960s as inevitable. In a review of Gitlin's and Miller's books, as well as one by Isserman himself, Jonathan Wiener adds that recent historians have overemphasized the early 1960s, and to an extent the end of the decade, at the expense of the middle years. Breines agrees with this complaint, calling for an examination of the 1960s on its own grounds, as embodied by the Economic Research and Action Projects and other prefigurative political movements. In addition, along with Wiener, she summons historians and sociologists to examine the middle 1960s, or what Wiener labels the "real 60s."[1]

To overcome the shortcomings of the recent works, Isserman and Breines suggest that historians develop local case studies. Undoubtedly local studies will improve our understanding of the 1960s. W. J. Rorabaugh's *Berkeley at War,*

Douglas McAdam's *Mississippi Summer,* and David Farber's *Chicago '68* have already added to our body of knowledge. Likewise, a closer examination of the middle sixties will add to our comprehension of the period. Nevertheless, I have chosen a different approach or method, a thematic one. Rather than examining the New Left in a particular locale, I have raised the question: "What was the relationship between the New Left and labor?" Ellis Hawley shed considerable light on the New Deal by examining its relationship to the subject of monopoly, and Samuel Hays shed light on the progressives by studying their relationship to conservation. In the same vein, by concentrating on an important historical theme, I have sought to shed light on the New Left, labor, and the 1960s—and more broadly on the history of liberalism in modern America by examining the relationship of the New Left to labor.

An additional shortcoming of most of the initial studies of the 1960s was their theoretical underpinning, or lack thereof. Simply stated, most who wrote on New Left subscribed to the "classical theory" school of social change. Liberal theorists, who were part of this school, contended that radicalism in the 1960s arose largely because of psychosociological reasons, not ideological or political ones. They claimed that America was pluralist, affluent, and nonideological and presumed that a natural state of equilibrium or consensus existed. Hence, only sociopsychological factors could explain the emergence of the New Left (or insurgencies in general).[2] Zbignew Brezinski, Lewis Feuer, Bruno Bettelheim, Alvin Toffler, and others depicted the tumult of the 1960s as a counterrevolution by youths. As society became increasingly rationalized it needed a larger and larger educated and technocratic class. Young students in the humanities and social sciences found themselves becoming increasingly obsolete. Hence, they rebelled "in a blind, mindless, and generally destructive way against rationalism, intellect, technology, organization, discipline, hierarchy, and all of the requisites of a post-industrial society." The New Left's turn to terrorism and anarchism was easy to predict according to this interpretative view. "Sensing their historical obsolescence, they lash[ed] out like the Luddites against the computers and managers that are consigning them into the 'dustbin of history.' "[3]

Theodore Roszak, Charles Reich, and many activists themselves rejected the claim that the New Left represented a counterrevolution. On the contrary, they argued, student radicals were in the vanguard. These scholars agreed with the New Left's critics that the world was changing rapidly, but they added that liberalism itself had reached a state of exhaustion and that young college students were the first group to recognize this. The young were not counter-revolutionaries; they were in the forefront of the dawning of the postindustrial age. Nonetheless, these same theorists concentrated on psychological and socio-logical determinants of change in substantiating their interpretation. Like the classical theorist, they posited that neither economics nor traditional ideologies explained the New Left.[4]

In an insightful review, Yale professor Kenneth Keniston disagreed with both of these interpretations. He did not see the youth rebellion as counterrevolution-ary and, though he sympathized with many student activists, he objected to

Reich's and Roszac's explanation of the New Left's behavior. Keniston aptly observed that classical theorists exaggerated the inevitability of the developments of the 1960s and underestimated the legitimacy of the New Left's causes as one of the sources for the emergence of the insurgency itself. Both theories were circular in their reasoning and lacked proper historical perspective to make the claims that they were making.[5] Yet, while Keniston sought to replace the classical theory with one of his own, ultimately he too lacked the requisite historical perspective for arriving at a much better sense of what was happening. For example, he could not predict the rapid decline of the New Left.

Subsequent works by historians, especially those written in the past ten years, have de-emphasized the importance of "youth," the generation gap and sociopsychological forces. Instead, they have focused on the events of the era in explaining the emergence of the New Left.[6] While these works improve upon those written by contemporaries, they have their own set of shortcomings. For instance, they do not compare the forces that gave rise to the New Left to those that gave rise to other prominent American social movements, such as the populists or abolitionists (as Howard Zinn did at the time). Perhaps they do not do this because they accept the New Left's claim that it was "new," both in a qualitative and chronological sense, that it was sui generis. In other words, they tend not to locate the New Left in history or ground their interpretations in any theory of social change.

Several sociologists and political scientists (and a handful of historians), all members of the "resource mobilization" school of social change, roughly defined, have begun to develop an alternative approach—one that deserves attention and praise. Through case studies of parts of the "movement," they have paved the way for a better understanding of the New Left, in particular, and social movements, in general. Overall, I agree with their theory of social change and feel that my work supports their's and vice versa.[7]

Unlike the classical school, the resource mobilization school sees insurgency as rational, not deviant, and emphasizes political, sociological and economic forces, rather than sociopsychological ones. It treats insurgency as a normal part of the political process and claims that favorable changes in the structure of political power along with resources provided by outside groups supply the basis for them to appear. In addition to nurturing insurgencies into existence, outside groups seek to control their ultimate behavior. Or as Mayer Zald and John McCarthy put it, "The resource mobilization approach emphasizes both societal support and constraint of social movement phenomena. It examines the variety of resources that must be mobilized.... The linkage of societal movements to other groups... and the tactics used by authorities to control or incorporate movements" is also the focus of resource mobilization theorists."[8]

As applied to the 1960s, changes in the structure of politics and the realignment of the Democratic party (for example, the election of John F. Kennedy and the increase in black political power) provided the opportunity for the New Left to emerge. At the same time, the liberal or social activist wing of the Democratic party, including labor, spurred the New Left's growth. It furnished the "free space"—to use Sara Evans' and Harry Boyte's designation, or the "pre-existing network of communication," to use Jo Freeman's words—to get the New Left off the ground.[9] "External support, however," as Craig Jenkins and others contend, "entails significant limits." Not only did the labor movement give birth to the New Left and nurture it into maturity, it also sought to control and/or restrict its development at the stage where it began to assert its independence.[10] Doug McAdam writes, "all social movements pose a threat to existing institutional arrangements in society . . . [because they] raise the specter of a restructuring of polity membership."[11] In the latter part of the 1960s, the specter of change was perceived by liberals as particularly threatening or unsettling because the New Left unleashed many new social movements, such as the women's, environmental, and gay movements and provided a model of effective action for even more movements.[12] As Jenkins and I note, however—and this is a modification of the resource mobilization model—fear of insurgency did not prevent all forms of collaboration. The coalition that formed around the United Farm Workers is a case in point.

To an extent, the resource mobilization school presents the latter stage, and hence the clash between the New Left and liberals, as inevitable. Certainly, structural forces made the confrontation likely. But I feel that the resource mobilization school has gone too far in this direction. They have overestimated the economic and sociological determinants at the expense of human agency or real decisions made by individuals with power. To reiterate my argument, historically specific developments better explain the divisions of the latter half of the 1960s than either generational or structural forces. For example, it is inaccurate to claim that the escalation of the Vietnam War, the emergence of Black Power, and the counterculture were inevitable. More specifically, they did not have to occur exactly when and how they did. If, for instance, LBJ had not escalated the Vietnam War in 1965, then divisions between the New Left and labor probably would not have been as deep as they were. As Irving Howe stated recently, "Suppose the United States had not become so deeply embroiled in the Vietnam War—how might this have affected the New Left? Probably toward a more gradual and harmonious development. Its growth would have been less rapid, but it might have found a path to a democratic radicalism suitable to the American temper."[13]

Another point of disagreement I have with the resource mobilization school, at least in terms of the plight of the New Left, is that it tends to overestimate the power of liberals. McAdam emphasizes the retrenchment of liberalism in the latter 1960s without noting that liberals too lost power. Liberals did not simply co-opt the New Left or control its growth by cutting off the resources that had allowed it to grow in the first place. Without a doubt, as Jenkins writes, as the insurgents "stepped up their demands," they challenged entrenched traditions and alienated "former allies."[14] But if a prominent conservative block had not existed, poised to muster countermovements, then the antagonisms that developed between the New Left and labor would have mattered less. It would have been easier for liberals and veteran activists to build on the "crosscurrents" and to have maintained a dominant political position.

Similarly, the resource mobilization school tends to underestimate the staying power of insurgencies and social movements. Ironically, McAdam, Jenkins, and Freeman each portray "their" specific group or movement—civil rights, farm, and women's movement—as having had a lasting impact upon and place in society. None of these movements died when the 1960s came to a close. Yet, McAdam, Jenkins, and Freeman imply that "their" movements were the exception, rather than the rule. Only Evans and Boyte arrive at the opposite conclusion, that the movements of the 1960s created the free space, or resources, for a large decentralized movement in the 1970s. While a revolution has not taken place, the New Left did not simply disappear; segments of it and individual activists have had substantial staying power.[15]

Moreover, such an understanding of the legacy of the New Left affords us the opportunity to better understand the early 1960s. Resource mobilization theorists claim that insurgencies develop out of resources provided by "allies." McAdam, Jenkins, and Freeman credit liberal foundations, church groups, independent leftists, and others with providing the resources out of which the New Left grew. Put another way, they provide the theoretical base for seeing labor as a crucial ingredient in the history of the 1960s, but do not move beyond their own assumption (or the traditional interpretation of the 1960s), that labor was part of the system (indeed part of the conservative wing), to see that labor played a major role in giving birth to the New Left. While labor was clearly less of a social movement in the 1960s than it had been in the 1930s, its social activism never completely died, as evidenced by its support for the New Left. Labor remained a home for many who dreamed of a renewal of social activism and/or of those who were not enamored by the main drift of America's domestic and foreign policies. In other words, the previous social movement provided the foundation for the next social movement.

Indeed, some recent analysts have suggested that a multiracial political coalition has begun to emerge or that the foundation for the birth of a modern populist movement exists. Kevin Phillips, for one, who adeptly predicted the success of the Republican party, argues that the social and economic conditions for the rebirth of a populist movement have been created by the excesses of conservatives.[16] Arthur Schlesinger insists that history travels in cycles and that the liberal cycle is destined to reemerge soon. Yet, neither Phillips and Schlesinger provide a good sense of the roots of the nascent populist movement. If the resource mobilization school and this study are correct, the remaining forces of the New Left and labor movement will provide the resources for a new social movement. They will provide the "pre-existing network of communication" or "free spaces" and some of the ideals for the emergence of the next movement dedicated to democracy and freedom for all. When that movement will appear or the precise shape it will take can not be predicted with any degree of accuracy. But its contours are already in the making.

Notes

Introduction

1. *NY Times,* 9 May 1970, pp. 1, 10.
2. *NY Times,* 12 May 1970, p. 1; 13 May 1970, p. 1.
3. *NY Times,* 21 May 1970, pp. 1, 22.
4. *NY Times,* 21 May 1970, pp. 1, 22.
5. *NY Times,* 27 May 1970, pp. 1, 18.
6. Unger, *The Movement,* p. 188.
7. Howe, ed. *Beyond the New Left,* p. 4.
8. Shostak, *Blue Collar Life,* p. 93.
9. For a more sophisticated view, see James Miller, *Democracy Is in the Streets* and Isserman, *If I Had a Hammer.* Both authors provide a sense of the connections between the Old Left and the New Left, though Miller does not follow through with this examination and Isserman focuses only on the early 1960s and a very narrow segment of the Left.
10. Leuchtenburg, *The Troubled Feast,* pp. 247–48.
11. Richard Rogin, "Joe Kelley Has Reached His Boiling Point," in *A History of Our Time,* ed. Chafe, p. 277.
12. Even recent depictions of the 1960s have not broken from this cannon. Irwin Unger's updated study of the period does not substantially vary from his original work. David Caute maintains that "the New Left remained a middle-class movement that made no headway within the trade unions, the backbone of the old communist, socialist and labor parties." Todd Gitlin laments the polarization of the latter part of the decade without taking into account or giving equal weight to earlier cooperation between the New Left and labor. And Burns's *Social Movements of the 1960s* examines the civil rights, student, antiwar, Black Power, and women's movement, without noting whatsoever any of their connections to the labor movement, including the Farm Workers' movement, which enjoyed the support of new leftists and trade unionists. Unger and Urwin, *Turning Point: 1968;* Caute, *The Year of the Barricade,* p. 34; Gitlin, *The Sixties;* Burns, *Social Movements of the 1960s.*
13. By the time this synthesis took place the New Left had come to redefine labor or at least reorient its position vis-à-vis the labor movement. Whereas in

the early 1960s, the New Left's relationship to labor involved primarily interactions with trade union leaders, by the early 1970s it tended to define labor as the working class and to interact with lower level trade union officials, particularly dissidents, rather than just top labor officials.

14. For a good review of the numerous contemporary studies of the 1960s, see Keniston, "Revolution or Counterrevolution?"; for a valuable bibliographic essay, see Hunter, O'Brien, and Naison, "Reading about the New Left"; more recent reviews include Isserman, "The Not-So-Dark and Bloody Ground," pp. 990–1010; Breines, "Whose New Left?" p. 545; and Wiener, "The New Left as History," pp. 173–88.

15. I understand that organized labor does not represent all workers and can misrepresent the views of its members. Accordingly, I have supplemented my discussion of labor drawn from labor presses and manuscript collections with public opinion surveys and qualitative studies of American workers. See Nelson Lichtenstein, "Labor-Liberalism in Crisis" (Paper delivered at the meeting of the Organization of American Historians, St. Louis, Missouri, 1989). In author's possession.

Chapter 1: We Shall Overcome

1. Martin Luther King, Jr., "I Have a Dream," in *Let Freedom Ring,* ed. Peter Levy, pp. 122–25.

2. Kahn, "The Power of the March," 315–20; Hedgemen, *The Trumpet Sounds,* pp. 167–69; "Marchers Master Plan," March on Washington, 1963, Vertical File, Schomburg Center, New York Public Library; Committee for Emancipation March for Jobs, "Call for March," in Richard Parrish Papers; A. Philip Randolph, letter to James Farmer, 26 Mar. 1963; "Minutes of the NAC CORE," 29 Mar. 1963; "March on Washington for Jobs and Freedom: 1st Plan of Operation"; all A:I, CORE Papers. Foner, *Organized Labor and the Black Worker,* pp. 346–50; "Unions Join Rights Assembly," *AFL–CIO News,* 31 Aug. 1963, p. 1. Saunders, ed., *The Day They Marched;* Josephine Schwartz, ed., "Songs for March on Washington," V:113, CORE Papers. A full collection of the speeches of the day can be found in March on Washington, 1963, Vertical (Clipping) File, Schomburg Center. A sense of the crowd's response to those speeches can be gained from *The Great March on Washington,* Motown, 1963.

3. "Shades of the Labor Movement of Old," *The Dispatcher,* 6 Sept. 1963, p. 2; Jay Garnet, "Muslim, Socialist, Nationalist, SNCC Views Heard in Chicago," *Militant,* 16 Sept. 1963; "SNCC Head Calls for New Protests," *Student Voice,* Oct. 1963; Bayard Rustin, Memo to the Chairmen of the March on Washington," 27 Sept. 1963, A:I, CORE Papers; Interview with Bob Zellner, 24 Nov. 1987, New York City. Nearly every discussion of the 1960s contains the obligatory description of the dispute over Lewis's speech. What they tend to overlook is that Lewis and SNCC agreed to alter the speech; it remained a militant speech; and SNCC and Lewis viewed the march favorably at the time.

4. "UPWA's Legislation and Civil Rights Conference," *Packinghouse Worker,*

Oct. 1963; "Transcript of Civil Rights and Legislative Conference," 23 Sept. 1963, Box 526, UPWA Papers.

5. "Transcript of Civil Rights and Legislative Conference."

6. "Leaflet: Conference on the Civil Rights Revolution," Box 400; "Call to Civil Rights and Legislation Conference," Box 466; "Transcript of Civil Rights and Legislative Conference." R. Helstein to J. Farmer, 4 Oct. 1963, Box 174, UPWA Papers; "UPWA's Legislation and Civil Rights Conference," *Packinghouse Worker,* Oct. 1963.

7. My view of Carliner's and Mahoney's roles is based on a survey of their correspondence found in SNCC Papers and Victor Reuther and Lewis Carliner Collection. Al Haber to Lew Carliner, 9 Oct. 1963; Lew Carliner to Sandra Hayden, 29 Aug. 1963; James Forman to Lew Carliner, 25 June 1963; Lew Carliner to William Mahoney, 19 July 1963; William Mahoney to Lew Carliner, 23 Oct. 1963; all in Box 17, Victor Reuther and Lewis Carliner Collection; William Mahoney to Tom Kahn, 29 Oct. 1963; Tom Kahn to Jack Conway, 10 Dec. 1963; Tom Kahn to Stanley Aronowitz, 10 Dec. 1963; all in Box 7, Student Activist Collection. See also "Notes On SNCC Conference," n.d., C:I:114, SNCC Papers; "Over 300 Attend SNCC Conference," *Student Voice,* 9 Dec. 1963. William Mahoney, "Report on Meeting with Union Leaders," 12 Dec. 1963, C:III, SNCC Papers.

8. "Notes on SNCC Conference"; William Mahoney, "Report on Meeting with Union Leaders"; Walter Tillow to Lew Carliner, 6 Dec. 1963, Box 17, Victor Reuther and Lew Carliner Collection.

9. While the links between labor and the New Left displayed at the March on Washington are readily apparent, only the most perceptive observers took note of these ties before this event. When the civil rights sit-ins swept across the South in early 1960, *New York Post* reporter William Shannon informed readers that "SIT-DOWNS" were taking place. In so doing, Shannon conjured up images of the "old left," namely the insurgency of industrial workers, while describing the emergence of the New Left in America. More significantly, a year earlier, in a study for the Young People's Socialist League, a relatively unknown Michael Harrington reported on the arrival of a New Left in America, evidenced by the increase in activism on college campuses, the outburst of black protest, and the revitalization of the labor movement. See William Shannon, "SITDOWNS," *NY Post,* Feb. and Mar. 1960; Michael Harrington, "The New Left: The Relevance of Democratic Socialism in Contemporary America," SLID Papers, Box 5.

10. On the League for Industrial Democracy, see the guide to the LID Collection, Tamiment Library, New York University and Unger, *The Movement,* pp. 51, 57; SLID Papers, Box 4, Student Activist Collection; James Miller, *Democracy Is in the Streets* and Isserman, *If I Had a Hammer.*

11. "SDS Constitution"; Interview with Michael Harrington by Kirkpatrick Sale, 6 Oct. 1969, in Oral History Collection, Tamiment Library, New York University; Interview with Stanley Aronowitz, by author, 25 June 1986, New York City.

12. Isserman, *If I Had a Hammer;* James Miller, *Democracy Is in the Streets,* pp. 73–75, 127–38; Harrington, *Fragments of the Century,* pp. 143–50.

13. I thank Ron Grele and Bret Eynon for helping me see these personal connections. "Minutes to NEC Meeting," 31 Aug.–2 Sept. 1962, Box 7, SLID Papers.

14. Irving Bluestone to Victor Reuther, 9 Sept. 1963, Victor Reuther and Lew Carliner Papers; Mildred Jeffrey to Walter P. Reuther, 25 June 1965; Mildred Jeffrey to Walter P. Reuther, 22 Dec. 1962; Mildred Jeffrey to Irving Bluestone, 13 Apr. 1965; all in Box 54, WPR Collection.

15. William Haber to Al Haber, 25 Apr. 1961; both in SLID Papers, Box 4; on William Haber, see *Who's Who in America,* 31:1181. Al Haber, "Students and Labor," SDS Papers; SDS, "Newsletter #2," Box 7, SLID Papers.

16. Haber even raised the possibility of SDS and the Industrial Union Department of the AFL–CIO forming a Student Labor Organizing Committee, whereby students and organized labor would cooperate around the goal of unionizing campus workers. Larry Rogin, educational director of the AFL–CIO, responded favorably, giving Haber the names of officials within AFSCME and the Building Service Unions who Rogin noted would prove "sympathetic."Al Haber to Larry Rogin, 10 Oct. 1960, Box 5, SLID Papers; Al Haber to Lew Carliner, 9 Oct. 1963, Box 17, V. Reuther and L. Carliner Papers.

17. Farmer, *Lay Bare the Heart,* ch. 15; Inge Powell Bell, *CORE and the Strategy of Nonviolence,* pp. 101, 181; A. Meier and E. Rudwick, *CORE,* pp. 6, 23, 82. See also CORE Papers, especially "Labor Unions," V:I.

18. Rorabaugh, *Berkeley at War,* pp. 23–24, 28–29, 44–45.

19. Glen, "On the Cutting Edge"; Horton, "The Highlander Folk School"; Interview with Bob Zellner, by author, 24 Nov. 1987, New York City.

20. Glen, "On the Cutting Edge"; Horton, "The Highlander Folk School"; Interview with Bob Zellner. In addition, Morris, *The Origins of the Civil Rights Movement,* details the foundations of the modern civil rights movement.

21. Reed, "The Southern Conference for Human Welfare."

22. Interview with Stokely Carmichael, Feb. 1991, York, Pa.; Clayborne Carson, "Stokely Carmichael," in *Biographical Dictionary of the American Left,* ed. Johnpoll and Klehr, pp. 66–67.

23. Russell Lasley and Charles Fischer to Sterling Stuckey, 7 Feb. 1961; Sterling Stuckey to Harold [*sic*] Lasley and Charles Fischer, 10 Feb. 1961; Russell Lasley to Whom It May Concern, 20 June 1961; "Tent City: Home of the Brave"; James Forman, "Memo," 8 Aug. 1961; all in Box 395, UPWA Papers; Interview with Charles Fischer, 27 Jan. 1987, UPWA Oral History Project, SHSW; Forman, *The Making of Black Revolutionaries,* pp. 130–37. The union raised funds for the Fayette League; in early 1961 Fischer and UPWA Vice President Russell Lasley traveled to Fayette County to express their support. Afterward, the Packinghouse Workers prepared a glossy pamphlet on the Fayette situation. Published by the Industrial Union Department (IUD) of the AFL–CIO, the pamphlet began with a ringing plea for aid written by Walter Reuther and then described the freedom struggle in Fayette County.

24. James Forman, telegram to Ralph Helstein, n.d., Box 174; James Forman,

telegram to Ralph Helstein, 10 Mar. 1962, Box 169; G. R. Hathaway, memo to R. Helstein, 5 July 1962; James Forman to R. Helstein, 4 Sept. 1962, both in Box 170; Jim Dombrowski to All Lenders, 1 Oct. 1965, Box 186; Myles Horton to R. Helstein, 10 Aug. 1962, Box 170 and Myles Horton to R. Helstein, 28 May 1964, Box 183; Bayard Rustin to Chairman UPWA, c/o R. Helstein, 27 Mar. 1963, Box 401, UPWA Papers. "Bull Scholarship Awarded," *Packinghouse Worker,* June 1963.

25. For financial information see folder marked "Union Solicitations, 1954–1965"; Tom Hayden to Walter P. Reuther, Mar. 1963, 2B, SDS Papers; Irving Bluestone to Tom Hayden, 9 July 1963; Walter P. Reuther to Tom Hayden, 31 July 1963; Irving Bluestone to Todd Gitlin, 16 Mar. 1964; all in Box 523, WPR Collection. Farmer quoted in James Farmer to Walter P. Reuther, 27 Feb. 1962, I:83, CORE Papers.

26. Nathaniel Minkoff to George Meany and William Schnitzler, 28 Apr. 1960; Aryeh Neier, memo to Victor Reuther, 11 Apr. 1960; Nathaniel Minkoff to George Meany, 19 July 1962; Nathaniel Minkoff to Walter P. Reuther, 27 Aug. 1963; all in Box 23, LID Collection. Also see "LID Contributions," Box 11, LID Collection.

27. "Union Solicitations," 2B, SDS Papers; Jack Conway to Dear Friend, 9 Nov. 1963, 2B, SDS Papers; Otha Brown to Todd Gitlin, 27 Dec. 1963; Todd Gitlin to Walter P. Reuther, 20 Dec. 1963; and Rennie Davis to Irving Bluestone, 25 Jan. 1964; Irving Bluestone to Rennie Davis, 11 Feb. 1964, in Boxes 195 and 523, respectively, WPR Collection; Todd Gitlin to Paul Booth, 28 Oct. 1963, Box 1, Paul Booth Papers; Lee Webb to Ralph Helstein, 16 Sept. 1963, Box 180, UPWA Papers.

28. Tom Hayden to Todd Gitlin, 2 Aug. 1963, Box 11, SDS Collection.

29. Irving Bluestone to Todd Gitlin, 16 Mar. 1964; Rennie Davis to Walter P. Reuther, 17 May 1964; Todd Gitlin to Walter P. Reuther, 14 May 1964; Irving Bluestone to Walter P. Reuther, 18 June 1963; Irving Bluestone to Larry Gettlinger, 5 Feb. 1965, Box 523, WPR Collection. Affiliates of SDS also solicited union funds and support. For example, the Liberal Study Group, a collection of SDS members within the National Student Association sought aid. So too did VOICE, the University of Michigan alternative student political party out of which SDS recruited several members. See Richard Rothstein to Ralph Helstein, 1 Aug. 1963; Bob Ross, to Ralph Helstein, 3 June 1962; and Nanci Hollander, to Ralph Helstein, 2 Mar. 1963, Box 170, 175, 176, respectively, UPWA Papers.

30. Meier and Rudwick, *CORE,* pp. 82, 149; Farmer, *Lay Bare the Heart,* chs. 15–17. "Labor Unions," V:I; "Financial Records, 21 Dec. 1954–9 Apr. 1965," V:141; Marvin Rich to Jacob Claiman, 20 Aug. 1963, V:141; Marvin Rich to AFSCME local 382, 24 Apr.1963, V:142; James Farmer to Walter P. Reuther, 3 Feb. 1965; James Farmer to Walter P. Reuther, 27 Feb. 1962, I:83; all in CORE Papers; Walter P. Reuther to James Farmer, 17 Jan. 1962, Box 488, WPR Collection; James Farmer to Arnold Zander, 4 Apr. 1961; President's Office, AFSCME Papers.

31. Zinn, *The New Abolitionists,* ch. 1. Carson, *In Struggle,* p. 71.

32. Even though SNCC did not keep a systematic record of its finances, a sense of them can be garnered from "Financial Records"; William Mahoney to Irving Bluestone, 19 Sept. 1963, A:I; John Lewis to Albert Fitzgerald, 8 July 1965, A:I; James Forman to Emil Mazey, 29 July 1962, A:IV; James Forman to Russell Lasley, 5 July 1962, A:IV; all in SNCC Papers; James Forman and Charles McDew to Walter P. Reuther, 29 Oct. 1962; Walter P. Reuther, memo to Emil Mazey, 18 Apr. 1963; both in Box 525, WPR Collection. Carl Megel to Presidents of locals, 16 May 1963, Box 6, American Federation of Teachers Collection. Martin Luther King, Jr., to Ralph Helstein, 7 Oct. 1962, Box 170; Martin Luther King, Jr., to Members of United Packing House Workers, 17 May 1961, Box 395; Earl Dickerson, NAACP Legal Defense Fund to Ralph Helstein, 18 Oct. 1963, Box 174, UPWA Papers.

33. Draper, *A Rope of Sand,* pp. 106–17.

34. In circulars and speeches Packinghouse officials from across the country rallied behind SNCC. In the spring of 1963 Herbert Walker, president of a midwestern local, invited SNCC activists Hollis Watkins and Jesse Harris to speak before District 3's UPWA convention on the situation in Mississippi. The convention urged locals to "adopt SNCC field representatives" and collected canned goods for immediate shipment to the South. Other SNCC representatives spoke before District 1 and District 7's convention in New York City and Atlanta, respectively, which likewise endorsed SNCC's struggle. Walker and UPWA vice-president Charles Hayes journeyed to Jackson and then Greenwood, where they met with Forman and other SNCC field representatives. At about the same time, UPWA locals began to work with SNCC's affiliate in Cambridge, Maryland. The union supported Gloria Richardson's voter registration drive, and she helped the union organize primarily black meat-packing and canning workers. "A Suggested Program of Support for the Student Non-Violent Coordinating Committee," Box 180, UPWA Papers; R. Helstein to Don Smith, 20 Feb. 1962, Box 396; Russell Lasley, "UPWA Fund for Democracy Drive," Box 398; Herman Walker to James Forman, 22 Apr. 1963, and UPWA Local 88, "Leaflet: To Support Student Non-Violent Coordinating Committee," 8 May 1963, both in Box 401. "Chicago Locals Send Help in Fight for Ballot Right," *Packinghouse Worker,* Mar. 1963; "District 3 Boost Per Capita Tax to Mount Big Organizational Drive" and "District 7 Convention," *Packinghouse Worker,* Apr. 1963; "District 1 Convention," and "About a Journey to Jackson," *Packinghouse Worker,* May 1963; "The View from the Eastern Shore," *Packinghouse Worker,* June 1963; "District 6 Cheers 20th Birthday," *Packinghouse Worker,* Apr. 1964; "How the Union Came to Town in Troubled Cambridge, Maryland," *Packinghouse Worker,* May 1964. Interview with Harry Alston, 27 Jan. 1986, UPWA Oral History Project. See also Herbert H. Haines, *Black Radicals and the Civil Rights Mainstream,* p. 84.

35. SDS, "Membership Bulletin," No. 3, Jan.-Feb. 1962; C. Clark Kissinger, "The BRUNS Strike: A Case Study in Student Participation in Labor," 2B, SDS Papers. A. Meier, *CORE,* pp. 109–11. Interview with Jeremy Brecher, Oral History of the New Left, Tamiment Library, New York University. "Reports on

Efforts to Organize an Active Unemployed Workers Committee on District #1 UPWA," 2B, SDS Papers.

36. Viorst, *Fire in the Streets,* p. 283; Einrich and Kaplan, "Yesterday's Discord," in *The Berkeley Student Revolt,* ed. Lipset and Wolin, pp. 10–36; "Report to Reader," *Guardian,* 4 July 1963, p. 2; "Bay Area Unions Hold Job Conference in S.F," *Guardian,* 26 Dec. 1963, p. 9.

37. "Wipe Out Job Bias, Labor Asks," *AFL–CIO News,* 4 Mar. 1961, p. 1; "Nation's No. 1 Problem: Denial of Civil Rights: Text of AFL–CIO Executive Council Resolution," *AFL–CIO News,* 23 Nov. 1963, p. 1. Editorial, "Don't Shush the Good Fight," *The Dispatcher,* 12 July 1963, p. 2; "Labor Must Join the Fight for Jobs and Freedom," *UE News,* 9 Sept. 1963. Michael Munk, "Southern Labor Leaders Play it Safe," *Guardian,* 19 Sept. 1963, p. 4; "The March," *Guardian,* 5 Sept. 1963, p. 2.

38. Meier, *CORE,* pp. 109–11. "UAW Locals Picket 5–10's," *UAW Solidarity* (Eastern Edition), Apr. 1960; Personal interview with Sam Meyers, 27 Aug. 1986, New York City; *Proceedings of the 18th UAW Constitutional Convention (1962),* pp. 280–82. The North Carolina State AFL–CIO is quoted in the *Packinghouse Worker,* Apr. 1960, p. 10; "Convention Tackles Key Issues," *Packinghouse Worker,* June 1960.

39. "Freedom Riders Describe Ordeal," *UAW Solidarity,* Aug. 1961; "Freedom Riders Detail Mob Violence in South," *AFL–CIO News,* 16 June 1962; "Shuttlesworth at UE Convention," *UE News,* 20 May 1963; "Abernathy Stirs Delegates with Message of Freedom," *UE News,* 23 Sept. 1963.

40. "Detroit Firemen Denounce Alabama 'Hose Tactics,'" *AFL–CIO News,* 18 May 1963, p. 2. "San Francisco Answers Birmingham: Inspiring March for Freedom," *The Dispatcher,* 31 May 1963. Walter P. Reuther, "The Cause of Freedom Is on Trial," *UAW Solidarity,* June 1963, p. 16; "One Nation, Under God, Indivisible, with Liberty and Justice for All," *UAW Solidarity,* July 1963, pp. 3–4. "Birmingham Seen as Proof of Need for Rights Law," *AFL–CIO News,* 18 May 1963, p. 1. The best surveys of public opinion on the civil rights movement are Hazel Erskine, "The Polls: Demonstrations and Race Riots," *Public Opinion Quarterly* (Winter 1967–68); Brink and Harris, *The Negro Revolution;* Schwartz, *Trends in White Attitudes toward Negroes;* Hamilton, *Class and Politics in the United States.*

41. Oates, *Let the Trumpet Sound,* pp. 215, 240, 253; David L. Lewis, *King,* pp. 200, 210–11; Widick, *Detroit,* p. 157; "Freedom Now," *UAW Solidarity,* June 1963; "125,000 Walk Quietly to Record Rights Plea," *Detroit Free Press,* 24 June 1963, pp. 1–3.

42. "Trade Union Leadership Council: Experiment in Community," *New University Thought,* vol. 3, no. 2 (1963): pp. 34–41; Widick, *Detroit,* pp. 154–61; Geschwender, *Class, Race and Worker Insurgency,* pp. 54–55. O'Brien, "The Development of the New Left," ch. 5; Lawrence Wittner, *Rebels against the War,* ch. 10 and epilogue; Memo to Leo Kramer files, 23 June 1959, Box 44, President's Office, AFSCME Collection. Todd Gitlin, *The Sixties,* pp. 85–94; Isserman, *If I Had A Hammer,* pp. 194–202.

43. "An Introduction to the Freedom School Project," n.d.; Peter Schnaufer to Elmer Wells, 10 Feb. 1964; Charles Coogen to AFT Civil Rights Committee, 30 June 1966, Box 5, President's Department, AFT Collection; "Introduction," Richard Parrish Papers. "Union Teachers Are Active in Mississippi: Civil Rights Schools," *American Teacher,* Summer 1964; "Adopt a Mississippi Freedom School," *American Teacher,* Summer 1964. There is also some information on the Prince Edwards County Freedom Schools in the Norma Becker Papers, SHSW.

44. Chafe, *Civilities and Civil Rights,* p. 67; David Danzig, "The Meaning of the Negro Strategy," *Commentary,* Feb. 1964, pp. 44–46; McElvaine, "Claude Ramsay, Organized Labor, and the Civil Rights Movement in Mississippi, 1959–1966," in *Southern Workers and Trade Unions, 1880–1975,* ed. Reed, Hough, and Gary Fink, pp. 109–42.

45. Michael Munk, "Southern Labor Leaders Play it Safe," *Guardian,* 19 Sept. 1963, p. 4; William Mahoney, "Report on Meeting with Union Leaders," 12 Dec. 1963, C:I, SNCC Papers; Personal Interview with Stanley Aronowitz, 25 June 1986, New York City. Erskine, "The Polls: Race Relations," 137–48; Schwartz, *Trends in White Attitudes toward Negroes;* William Brink and Harris, *The Negro Revolution;* Hamilton, *Class and Politics in the United States;* Gallup, *Gallup Poll Index.*

46. Jervis Anderson, *A. Philip Randolph,* ch. 20; Foner, *Organized Labor and the Black Worker,* chs. 21, 22; Ray Marshall, "The Negro and the AFL–CIO," in *Black Workers and Organized Labor,* ed. Meier, Bracey, and Rudwick, pp. 209–22. "Constitution of the NALC," Richard Parrish Papers.

47. Saul Miller, "AFL–CIO Performance Cited in Fighting Discrimination," *AFL–CIO News,* 21 Oct. 1961, p. 3. Herbert Hill, "NAACP Report: Racism within Organized Labor," A:I, CORE Papers. "NAACP Urged to Shun Split with Labor Allied," *AFL–CIO News,* 20 Oct. 1962; Herbert Hill, "Letter to the Editor," p. 155–59.

48. Meier and Rudwick, *CORE,* pp. 196–200 and 227–37; Michael Munk, "Negroes' Protests in the North Center on Lack of Jobs"; Henthoff, *The New Equality,* ch. 7.

49. Robinson, *George Meany and His Times,* ch 13; "End of Voting Curbs Backed by AFL–CIO: Rights Plan Advocated," *AFL–CIO News,* 24 Mar. 1962, p. 1; "Labor Urges Action to Halt Job Bias: Congress Pressed on FEPC Law," *AFL–CIO News,* 11 May 1963. "Bias Remedy Lies in Reform, Not Destruction," *AFL–CIO News,* 17 Nov. 1962, p. 12; "Randolph Urges Strengthening Historic Negro-Labor Alliance," *AFL–CIO News,* 23 Nov. 1963, p. 15; Randolph later told an interviewer that if he could do it over again, he would have tried to have avoided the debate with Meany, even though he insisted his charges had been valid, "The Reminiscences of A. Philip Randolph," Oral History, Columbia University, New York, 1973; (Press Release), "NALC Shifts from Strategy of Attack to Alliance with Labor," 11 Jan. 1966, Richard Parrish Papers; "Bias Charge Killed, ILGWU Vindicated," *AFL–CIO News,* 25 May 1963, p. 4; "Let Us Move Together, Meany Urges NAACP,"

AFL-CIO News, 13 July 1963, p. 8; "Labor for Civil Rights," *Justice,* 1 Aug. 1963.

50. Michael Munk, "Negroes' Protests in the North Center on Lack of Jobs"; Inge Powell Bell, *Core,* p. 181. The issue of the segmentation of the labor force and a partial bibliography and discussion of the subject can be found in, Gordon, et al., *Segmented Work.* For the ILGWU's ties to Chase Manhattan Bank, see "Interviews with SDS Staffers," in *The New Radicals,* ed. Jacobs and Landau, pp. 174–80.

51. SDS, "Port Huron Statement," SDS Papers; "Special Feature on U.S. Policy toward Cuba," *New University Thought,* vol. 1, no. 4 (1961); "Join Labor to Fight Reds," *AFL-CIO News,* 29 Apr. 1961, pp. 1–2; "Labor Pledges President Unstinting Support," *AFL-CIO News,* 12 Aug. 1961, p. 1; "U.S. Labor Pledges Support to Halt Soviet Aggression," *AFL-CIO News,* 27 Oct. 1967, p. 1; "AFL-CIO Backs U.S. On Cuba," *AFL-CIO News,* 17 Nov. 1962, p. 1. Ronald Radosh, "American Labor and the Root Commission to Russia," *Studies on the Left,* Winter 1962, pp. 34–47; "Editors Disagree on Cuba," *Liberation,* Jan. 1961, pp. 3–4; Sidney Lens, "Notes at Random," *Liberation,* June-July 1962, p. 12; Sumner Rosen, "Labor and the Politics of Peace," *Liberation,* Feb. 1962, p. 31; "Dancing to Kennedy's War Tune: Congress, Press and Labor Dutifully Mount Bandwagon," *Guardian,* 5 Nov. 1962, p. 5. Even when dead, JFK continued to be a point of contention between the New Left and labor. At SNCC's Jobs for Food Conference, IUD official Jack Conway and new leftists bickered over what Conway saw as the latter's lack of respect for the dead president and the new leftists countered that Conway refused to take on the Kennedy myth.

52. Sidney Lens, "Notes at Random," *Liberation,* Feb. 1962, p.12; Sumner Rosen, "Labor and the Politics of Peace," *Liberation,* Feb. 1962, pp. 31–35; Dave Dellinger, "Labor Action for Peace," *Liberation,* 1962, 27. Henthoff, *Peace Agitator;* Lens, *Unrepentant Radical.*

53. Sale, *SDS,* pp. 116–19; Conlin, *The Troubles;* Lader, *Power on the Left,* p. 172.

54. Charles McDew to Ralph Helstein, 21 Nov. 1963, A:I, SNCC Papers.

55. SDS, "Port Huron Statement," SDS Papers.

56. Richard Flacks quoted in "Port Huron: Agenda for a Generation [Symposium]," 147.

57. Cochran, ed., *American Labor in Midpassage* gives a sense of the mood of the labor movement and activists on the eve of the sixties. Emil Mazey quoted in *Proceedings of UAW's Constitutional Convention (1962),* pp. 282–83; Kevin Boyle, "The Dilemma of Liberalism: The UAW and Civil Rights, 1963–1968," paper presented at the 9th Annual North American Labor History Conference, 22 Oct. 1987, in author's possession.

58. Stanley Aronowitz recalls that the Amalgamated Clothing Workers benefited from their support of the civil rights movement, at least in so far as the Dan River Mills decided not to segregate the work force; Personal Interview with Stanley Aronowitz.

59. Irving Bluestone to Lew Carliner, 17 July 1962; Irving Bluestone, memo to Walter P. Reuther, 8 Jan. 1963, Box 523, WPR Collection.

60. Irving Bluestone, memo to Lew Carliner, 8 Jan, 1963, Box 523, WPR Collection; Nathaniel Minkoff to George Meany and Wm. Schnitzler, 28 Apr. 1960; Aryeh Neier, memo to Victor Reuther, 11 Apr. 1960; Tom Hayden to Walter P. Reuther, 29 Mar. 1963, Box 11, SDS Collection, Tamiment Library.

61. Unger, *The Movement,* ch. 3; Interview with Michael Harrington, by Sale.

62. Unger, *The Movement,* ch. 3. Interview with Michael Harrington, by Sale; Mildred Jeffrey to Walter P. Reuther, 12 Dec. 1962; and Mildred Jeffrey, letter to Walter P. Reuther, 22 Dec. 1963, Box 523, WPR Collection. On the lasting fondness of SDS members for Mildred Jeffrey, see Hayden, *Reunion: A Memoir,* chs. 4, 19. Nathaniel Minkoff to George Meany and Wm. Schnitzler, 28 Apr. 1960; Aryeh Neier, memo to Victor Reuther, 11 Apr, 1960, Box 11, SDS Collection.

Chapter 2: Coalition Politics or Nonviolent Revolution

1. The title of the chapter comes from an important article written by new left stalwart Staughton Lynd. See Staughton Lynd, "Coalition Politics or Nonviolent Revolution," *Liberation,* June-July 1965, pp. 18–25. For a fuller discussion of this article see chapter six.

2. McCord, *Mississippi;* Holt, *The Summer That Didn't End;* Carson, *In Struggle,* chs. 8, 9; Zinn, *SNCC,* ch. 5; Sellers, with Terrell, *The River of No Return,* chs. 8, 9; McAdam, *Freedom Summer,* p. 4.

3. Edward P. Morgan, "College Students Volunteering In Summer Civil Rights Fight," *AFL–CIO News,* 25 Apr. 1964, p. 7; Mike Quill, "As I Was Saying," *TWU Express,* July 1964, p. 20; "Journey of Land of Hate," *Oil and Chemical and Atomic Union News,* Oct. 1964, p. 11.

4. Editorial, *AFL–CIO News,* 27 June 1964, p. 6; *UE News,* 28 Dec. 1964, p. 8.

5. SNCC Papers, "Labor Organizations 1964–65," A:IX:22; "Mississippi Summer Project Pamphlet," CORE Papers, V:126; McCord, *Mississippi,* pp. 117–18; Myles Horton to Ralph Helstein, 7 July 1964; C. Conrad Brown to R. Helstein, 3 Oct. 1964; R. Helstein to M. Horton, 7 Oct. 1964, Box 183, UPWA Papers.

6. Julius Sukenik, cc Nora Becker, to Bob Moses, 1 Dec. 1963; COFO to Dear X, n.d; Louis Chafe to Norma Becker, 24 Mar. 1964; Louis Chafe to Norma Becker, 2 Mar. 1964; John O'Neal to Norma Becker, 6 Mar. 1964; Bob Moses to Ted Blecker, 10 Mar. 1964; Charles Coogen to Harry Van Arsdale, 8 Apr. 1964; Sandra Adickes to Dear Colleague, 15 Apr. 1964, Norma Becker Papers, SHSW.

7. "Press Release," 30 July 1964, Norma Becker Papers; *NY Daily Telegraph,* 4 Sept. 1964.

8. "Union Teachers Are Active in Mississippi Civil Rights Schools," *American Teacher,* Summer 1964, p. 13; "Press Release," n.d., Civil Rights, Box 5, American Federation of Teachers Collection; "Clipping File," Norma Becker Papers.

9. Joe Rauh, Jr., "Brief Submitted By the Mississippi Democratic Party,"

Mississippi Freedom Democratic Party Records, State Historical Society of Wisconsin (microfilm edition); Viorst, *Fire in the Streets,* pp. 249–56; Interview of Joe Rauh by Anne Romaine, n.d., SHSW; Dudley W. Buffa, *Union Power and American Democracy.* Among the people who Rauh introduced Robert Moses to was UAW official Mildred Jeffrey, a power within the Michigan Democratic party as well as the UAW. Also based on Rauh's contacts, Moses traveled to the UAW's convention in late March 1964. There, along with a contingent from SDS, he had a special meeting with Reuther. Considering Reuther's past support of civil rights efforts and his close ties with Rauh, Moses and his cohorts hoped to garner his support for MFDP. Partly due to the eclectic make-up of the group and of the ensuing discussion, Moses failed to gain such an endorsement. Nonetheless, Reuther did not tell Moses to discontinue his efforts. And Moses left not seeing his failure to attain an endorsement as a bad omen. See Holt, *The Summer That Didn't End,* pp. 149–67; McCord, *Mississippi;* and Interview of Joe Rauh by Anne Romaine.

10. James Miller, *Democracy Is in the Streets,* pp. 103–4; Kevin Boyle, "The Dilemma of Liberalism: The UAW and Civil Rights, 1963–1968" (Paper, in author's possession); Bayard Rustin, "The Meaning of the March on Washington," *Liberation,* Oct. 1963, pp. 11–13; Carson, *In Struggle,* pp. 103–6.

11. Leadership Conference on Civil Rights, memo to Cooperating Organizations, 13 Aug. 1964, A:I:53, CORE Papers; Casey Hayden, letter to Norman Hill, David Dennis, et al., 15 Aug. 1964, A:XVI:29, SNCC Papers; Carson, *In Struggle,* p. 123; Bob Moses to Ralph Helstein, 25 May 1964 and 11 June 1964; R. Helstein to B. Moses, 10 July 1964, Box 182, UPWA Papers.

12. Robert S. McElvaine, "Claude Ramsay, Organized Labor and the Civil Rights Movement in Mississippi, 1959–1966," in *Southern Workers and Their Unions,* ed. Reed, Hough, and Gary Fink, pp. 109–37.

13. "Freedom Ballot for Governor: Platform," MFDP Records; John Salter, *Jackson, Mississippi,* Forward, ch. 11; Interview with Bob Zellner; *Mine-Mill Union,* Mar. 1964, p. 2; Robert S. McElvaine, "Claude Ramsay."

14. Richard Rothstein, "ERAP: Evolution of the Organized," *Radical America,* Mar.-Apr. 1968; "Reports on Efforts to Organize an Active Unemployment Workers Committee," 2B:54, SDS Papers; Richard Flacks, "Organizing the Unemployed: The Chicago Project," in *The New Student Left,* p. 137–52; *Packinghouse Worker,* Sept. 1965, p. 12; *Packinghouse Worker,* June 1964, p. 14.

15. "Reports on Efforts to Organize an Active Unemployment Workers Committee," SDS Papers; Tom Hayden and Carl Wittman, "An Interracial Movement of the Poor," in *The New Student Left,* pp. 175–214; "Meeting of Executive Committee NC," 16 Jan. 1964, 2B:1, SDS Papers; Jim Williams, "On Community Unions," *Studies on the Left,* Summer 1964; Todd Gitlin, "The Radical Potential of the Poor," in Massimo Teodori, ed. *The New Left,* pp. 130–48.

16. Tom Hayden to Todd Gitlin, 2 Aug. 1963, SDS Collection, Box 11; "Fundraising: Individual Solicitations, 1964," and "Correspondence: UAW, 1963–1965," both in 2B:14, SDS Papers; "Union Solicitations, 1964–65," 2B:15;

Irving Bluestone to Walter Reuther, 6 Jan., 1964 and Irving Bluestone to Rennie Davis, 11 Feb., 1964, Folder 15, Box 523, WPR Collection. Ralph Helstein to Peter Dawdiowicz, 10 Apr. 1964, Box 182, UPWA Papers.

17. Ray Brown, "Our Crisis Economy," 2B:57, SDS Papers; "Conference on Community Movements and Economic Issues," 10 Apr. 1964, 2B:9, SDS Papers; Also see: "The Triple Revolution," *Liberation,* Apr. 1964, which was co-authored by a number of new leftists, independent leftists and labor intellectuals.

18. James O'Connor, "Toward A Theory of Community Unions," *Studies on the Left,* Spring 1964 and James O'Connor, "The Political Economy II," *Studies on the Left,* Summer 1964.

19. "SDS Economic Research and Action Projects: ERAP and the Labor Movement," SDS Collection, Box 11; "Prospects for a Newark Organizing Project," 2B:2, SDS Papers.

20. "The Intercollegiate Conference on Poverty in America," 24–26 Apr. 1964; Box 1, Paul Booth Papers.

21. Tom Hayden and Rennie Davis to Dear Friend, 4 June 1964, and Tom Hayden to Ben Seligman, 6 June 1964, both in Folder 16, Box 523, WPR Collection; Kirkpatrick Sale, *SDS,* ch. 7.

22. Andrew Kopkind, "Of, By, For the Poor," *New Republic,* 19 June 1965, p. 15; Patchen Dellinger, "On Location," *Liberation,* Sept. 1964, p. 31.

23. "Cleveland Community Project," 20–28 June; "Cleveland Report," 23 July 1964, both in 2B:2, SDS Papers; James Miller, *Democracy,* 197–203.

24. "Cleveland Report," 23 July 1964, SDS Papers.

25. "Cleveland: Continuation of Projects," n.d.; "CUFAW Speaks for Itself"; both in 2B:2, SDS Papers and "Cleveland Community People and Conference, 2B:92, SDS Papers.

26. Tom Hayden and Carl Wittman, "Summer Report: Newark Community Union," in *The New Radicals,* Paul Jacobs and Saul Landau, eds., pp. 166–70; Jesse Allen, "Newark: Community Union," in *The New Radicals,* pp. 171–74; Interview with Stanley Aronowitz; "Report: Newark Project," 30 June 1964, 2B:2, SDS Papers.

27. T. Hayden and C. Wittman, "Summer Report," and Jesse Allen, "Newark: Community Union," both in *The New Radicals;* Tom Hayden, *Reunion,* ch. 6.

28. Richie Parker, "Evaluation of the Trenton Project," and Richard Rothstein, "Baltimore JOIN," both in 2B:9, SDS Papers; "JOIN Community Union—Program for 1966," 2B:54, SDS Papers; Kirkpatrick Sale, *SDS,* ch. 9.

29. Hamish Sinclair, "Hazard, Ky.: Document of the Struggle," *Radical America,* Jan.-Feb. 1968; Peter Wiley, "Hazard: Socialism in Community Organizing, *Radical America,* Jan-Feb. 1968; Michael Harrington, *The Other America;* Harry Caudill, *The Night Comes to Cumberland;* Dick Greenberg, "Problems Relating to Unemployment in the Vicinity of Hazard, Ky.," and Mike Zweig, "Eastern Kentucky in Perspective," 2B:57, SDS Papers.

30. "Clippings File," Committee for Miners Papers (henceforth CFM Papers); "Hungary Ky. Miners Ready for All-Out War," *Guardian,* 17 Jan. 1963; Editorial,

"Berman Gibson is a Big Man," *Guardian,* 31 Jan. 1963; "Hazard, Guns at Mine Entrances," *Guardian,* 21 Feb. 1963.

31. Coal Adds to Woes of Ky. Miners," *Guardian,* 7 Feb. 1963; Editorial, "Berman Gibson is a Big Man," *Guardian;* "Gibson to Speak in N.Y.," *Guardian,* 10 Oct. 1963; "Miners Strike Raises Issues of Survival, Solidarity," *Liberation,* Mar. 1963. The Progressive Labor party sent food and supplies to Kentucky. Some PLers went to Hazard armed with weapons. Not wanting anything to do with their Maoist struggle the miners quickly sent PL packing.—PL was one of many small splinter groups from the Communist party. It espoused a traditional old left ideology, of working for a proletariat revolution. It would play an increasingly important role in the New Left. Progressive Labor Party, "Perspectives for the Left," in *The New Radicals,* pp. 181–90.

32. "Minutes," 7 Apr. 1963, CFM Papers.

33. "Summary of Tour by Arthur Gorson and Berman Gibson, May 14–28, 1964," "Report on Berman Gibson's Visit," Oct. 1963; "Washington Delegation Report," Box 12, CFM Papers.

34. "Clippings File," CFM Papers; Hamish Sinclair, "Hazard, Ky.: Committee for Miners," *Studies on the Left,* Summer 1965; Stanley Aronowitz, to Sidney Lens, 26 Mar. 1964 and Rob Burlage, "This is War?" 2B:57, SDS Papers.

35. "Clippings File," CFM Papers; "Appalachian Summer Project: Preliminary Proposal," 2B:59, SDS Papers.

36. Sally Susskind and Chuck Koehler, "Hazard Report," and "Report from Hazard," 17 July 1964, both in 2B:2, SDS Papers.

37. Steve Max, "Hazard," 10 Aug. 1964, 2B:59, SDS Papers; "CFM Reports," 7 Sept. 1964, 2B:135, SDS Papers.

38. Rennie Davis to Stanley Aronowitz and Art Gorson, 20 Nov. 1964; Richard Rothstein to Arthur Gorson, 9 Dec. 1964; Laurent Enchell to Lenore Belsky, 30 Apr. 1965; all in 2B:135, SDS Papers; Peter Wiley, "Hazard: Socialism in Community Organizing," *Radical America,* Jan.-Feb. 1968; Hamish Sinclair, "Hazard, Ky.: Document of the Struggle," *Radical America,* Jan.-Feb. 1968.

39. "Minutes," Jan. 1965; Berman Gibson to A. Gorson, 5 Feb. 1964; E. Tharp to H. Sinclair, 23 Feb. 1965; H. Sinclair to C. Braden, 6 Apr. 1965; Peter Wiley to A. Gorson, 13 Dec. 1964; S. Aronowitz to B. Gibson, 17 Feb. 1965; H. Sinclair to E. Tharp, 9 Apr. 1965; Sue Thrasher to H. Sinclair, 29 Apr. 1965; "Memo to Staff," 28 Apr. 1965, CFM Papers. A song that SDS member Jim Williams wrote entitled: "The Ballad for the Appalachian Committee for Full Employment," reflected SDS's sentiments toward the Hazard affair.

> He was poor, but he was honest
> Worked down in the Leatherwood Mine
> Now he walks the streets of Hazard in Kentucky
> Beggin' people for a dime . . .
> Berman Gibson is the leader
> Of our hearty little band

Well, he helped us get together
And together we will stand . . .
Well we once had us a union
It knew how to stand and fight
Now our union is a sell-out
Standing humble and contrite.
John L. Lewis is our leader
Now he is dead but won't lie down
Every time we have an election
His ghost comes haunting round.

40. "SDS: Voice of the National Office," 10 Aug. 1964, 2B:1, SDS Papers; "Notes for the NO Committee on ERAP," SDS Collection, Box 11.

41. "Cleveland Community Project Report," 20–28 June 1964; "Cleveland/ Continuation of Projects," SDS Papers, 2B:2; Tom Hayden and Carl Wittman, "Summer Report: Newark Community Union," [Draft], 2B:82, SDS Papers; "Report: Newark Community Project," 30 June 1964, SDS Papers, 2B:2.

42. "Apparatchick," *New Republic,* 24 July 1965, p. 7; Dick Flacks, "Some Problems, Issues, Proposals: 1965 National Convention Working Paper," SDS Collection, Box 11; Stanley Aronowitz, "Book Reviews," *Studies on the Left,* Winter 1964, pp. 58–73; Stanley Aronowitz, "Reply," *Studies on the Left,* pp. 70–71. Tom Hayden, *Reunion,* pp. 139–41.

43. The literature on the 1964 Democratic Convention is lengthy. Recent discussion include: David Garrow, *Bearing the Cross,* 346–51; Mary King, *Freedom Song,* 341–42; and Todd Gitlin, *The Sixties,* 152–62. Contemporary versions worth consulting are: James Forman, *The Making of a Black Revolutionary,* ch. 45; McCord, *Mississippi,* pp. 113–18; and Len Holt, *The Summer That Didn't End,* pp. 168–78. For Johnson's perspective, see Merle Miller, *Lyndon Johnson: An Oral Biography,* pp. 477–78.

44. Carson, *In Struggle,* ch. 9; Todd Gitlin, *The Sixties,* pp. 152–62; Henry Hampton, *Voices of Protest,* pp. 179–208.

45. Milton Viorst, *Fire in the Streets,* pp. 269–70.

46. Stokely Carmichael and Charles Hamilton, *Black Power,* p. 96; Staughton Lynd, "Coalition Politics or Nonviolent Revolution," *Liberation,* June-July 1965; Gitlin, *The Sixties,* pp. 171–77.

47. King, *Freedom Song,* p. 347; Dave Dennis to NAC CORE, 21 Sept. 1964, V:126, CORE Papers; Zinn, *SNCC,* ch. 12.

48. Staughton Lynd, "SNCC, The Beginning of Ideology," *The Activist,* Jan. 1965, pp. 11–12.

49. While the New Left infused the ERAPs and Mississippi Summer with great meaning, most trade unionists did not. They tended to view the MFDP as a favorable development. Similarly, they saw the ERAPs as an effective auxiliary to Johnson's War on Poverty. Moreover, in spite of SDS's unwillingness to explicitly exclude communists, which led to a break with LID, unions took no

unfavorable actions. Ironically, even Tom Kahn, who was the executive director of LID in 1965, wrote AFL–CIO Civil Rights director Donald Slaiman that he rejected the policy of disengaging from SDS because he did not see the differences between the student left and social democrats and progressive trade unionists to be "irreversible." Indeed, Ralph Helstein even supported SDS's foray into the magazine publishing business, providing financial and logistical aid for SDS's "New Era," which subsequently appeared as *New Left Notes.* See Tom Kahn to Donald Slaiman, 17 Aug. 1965; "Report of the Executive Secretary," Sept. 1964-Apr. 1965, Folder 18 and 23, respectively, Box 7, Student Activist Collection; Steve Max, "Field Secretary's Report on Student Activity," n.d., Student Activist Collection, Folder 27, Box 7; Ralph Helstein to Todd Gitlin, 6 Oct. 1964; T. Gitlin to R. Helstein, 3 Nov. 1964, 4 Dec. 1964, and 12 May 1964, Box 183, UPWA Papers.

50. "From the Editors: After the Election," *Studies on the Left,* Winter 1965, pp. 3–21; James Weinstein, Stanley Aronowitz, Lee Baxandall, Eugene Genovese and Helen Kramer, "Reply," *Studies on the Left,* Spring 1965, pp. 7–12; "Notes for the NO Committee on ERAP," SDS Collection, Box 11; Tom Hayden and Carl Wittman, "Summer Report: Newark Community Union," [Draft], 2B:82, SDS Papers.

51. On the continuation of JOIN see numerous clippings and documents, including financial ledgers, Boxes 5 and 6, Staughton Lynd Papers.

52. Aaron Henry, "Position Paper," 29 Aug. 1964; Council for United Civil Rights Leadership, "Report," 31 Dec. 1964; MFDP to Northern Supporters and Committees on Challenge, n.d.; "Statewide Meeting of MFDP," 16 May 1965; "Resolutions and Statements in Favor of MFDP Congressional Challenge," 12 June 1965, all in MFDP Records. LCCR to Dear Friend, 23 June 1965 and LCCR, "Statement on the Mississippi Challenge," 14 Sept. 1965, A:I:53, CORE Papers.

53. "Convention Bars Bias in the Party," *AFL–CIO News,* 29 Aug. 1964, p. 1, 11; "Speaker Sees Victory for Civil Rights as Basic to Future of America," *UE News,* 21 Sept. 1964, p. 8; "Convention Resolution, Civil Rights," *UE News,* 21 Sept. 1964, p. 5.

54. "Report on Mississippi with Fannie Lou Hamer," Norma Becker Papers; On the Chicago Area Friends of SNCC see A:IX:68–69 and A:IX:112, SNCC Papers, especially, Mississippi Report Dinner," 3 Oct. 1964 and Cynthia Washington to Muriel Tillinghast, 29 Aug. 1965.

55. For a general overview of Selma see: Garrow, *Protest at Selma* and Fager, *Selma, 1965.*

56. On the strength of the coalition, see Garrow, *Protest at Selma;* Philip Foner, *Organized Labor and the Black Worker,* p. 353; Oates, *Let the Trumpet Sound,* pp. 325–65.

57. "Sympathy Demonstrators in Oklahoma City," *Packinghouse Worker,* Apr. 1965, p. 6; "Selma! Anvil of Freedom," *UAW Solidarity,* Apr. 1965, p. 16; "Dist. One Members March in Rights Demonstrations," *UE News,* 22 Mar. 1965,

p. 1–3; "ILWU Vows to Hit Bigot Where It Hurts," *The Dispatcher,* 19 Mar. 1965, p. 1, 5; "Voting Law Spurred by Selma Brutality," *AFL–CIO News,* 13 Mar. 1965, p. 1; Garrow, *Protest at Selma,* pp. 73–77, 91–97 and 105–8.

On Sunday 7 March 1965, John Lewis and Hosea Williams led a contingent of six hundred marchers from Brown's chapel to the Pettus Bridge on the border of Selma. Their announced destination was Montgomery, Alabama, the state's capital. They never got across the bridge, as Alabama state troopers joined by Sheriff Jim Clark, launched a vicious assault on the nonviolent marchers. With nightsticks, tear gas, fists, and other assorted weapons, the troopers chased the marchers back into town, beating them at every opportunity. Over one hundred demonstrators suffered from serious injuries, including Lewis whose skull was fractured.

"Bloody Sunday," as the massacre on Pettus Bridge came to be known, outraged the nation. ABC-TV broke into *Judgment at Nuremberg,* the award-winning movie on the Nazi war-crime trials, to show film footage of the attacks. SNCC and King determined to stage a second march. Hence, on Tuesday 9 March, with King in the lead, marchers once again headed out toward the Pettus Bridge. Much to the surprise of most of the marchers, King turned the protest around rather than challenge state troopers and break a federal injunction against marching. Later that same evening, four Unitarian ministers were brutally assaulted in Selma by white ruffians; one of them, James Reeb, died from the attack. The night of Reeb's memorial service, President Johnson delivered one of the strongest speeches on civil rights in United States history, pledging to submit to Congress strong voting rights legislation. Two days later, Federal Judge Frank Johnson, no relation to the president, rescinded the injunction against the march. Hence, on 21 March thousands of marchers set out from Selma to Montgomery, this time protected by federal troops. Without incident, they arrived five days later in the city where Martin Luther King, Jr., had first emerged as a leader, during the Montgomery bus boycott, in 1955.

For a summary of polls on civil rights, see Hazel Erskine, "The Polls: Demonstrations and Race Riots," *Public Opinion Quarterly,* Winter, 1967–68; see also *Gallup Poll Reports,* which regularly asked the question, "Do you think the Johnson Administration is pushing integration too fast or not fast enough?" Respondents' desire for more legislation peaked in the spring of 1965, coinciding with Selma, and then fell dramatically following the Watts riot.

58. Public endorsements of the civil rights movement were some of the strongest ever issued. "We of the AFL–CIO are appalled by the police brutality in Selma, Alabama," Meany wrote in a telegram to President Johnson. ILWU president, Harry Bridges reacted even more adamantly, announcing: "It is time to quit talking. . . . It's time for a little action! We plan to let the sovereign state of Alabama know that we're going to put a boycott on it." The Steelworkers union called for an immediate "cessation of outrageous violations of people's rights and law of the land." Walter Reuther declared that: the "martyrdom" of James Reeb and Jimmy Lee Jackson, "must never be forgotten . . . for their tragic deaths must serve as constant reminders that the price people

must pay for freedom." "Sympathy Demonstrators in Oklahoma City," *Packinghouse Worker,* Apr. 1965, p. 6; "Selma! Anvil of Freedom," *UAW Solidarity,* Apr. 1965, p. 16; "Dist. One Members March in Rights Demonstrations," *UE News,* 22 Mar. 1965, p. 1–3; "ILWU Vows to Hit Bigot Where It Hurts," *The Dispatcher,* 19 Mar. 1965, p. 1, 5; "Voting Law Spurred by Selma Brutality," *AFL–CIO News,* 13 Mar. 1965, p. 1; Garrow, *Protest at Selma,* pp. 73–77, 91–97 and 105–8.

59. Erskine, "The Polls: Demonstrations and Race Riots." See also *Gallup Poll Reports* which regularly asked the question, "Do you think the Johnson Administration is pushing integration too fast or not fast enough?" Respondents' desire for more legislation peaked in the spring of 1965, coinciding with Selma, and then fell dramatically following the Watts riot.

60. "International and Local Unions of the AFL–CIO Joined in Protest," *AFL–CIO News,* 13 Mar. 1965, p. 3; "Selma March Rallies Nation to Negro Rights Struggle," *AFL–CIO News,* 20 Mar. 1965, p. 1; "Mission to Montgomery: ILGWU Mobile," *Justice,* 1 Apr. 1965, p. 1–2 and 5; "Multitudes Went to be Counted," *Oil, Chemical and Atomic Workers News,* Apr. 1965, p. 6. Among those to attend either the funeral or the march, or both, were: Charles Zimmerman, V.P., ILGWU; Robert Powell, V.P., Laborers; Thomas Donahue, Representative, Building Service Employees; David Sullivan, Pres. Building Service Employees; Walter Reuther, Pres. UAW; Mathew Guinen, Sect-Treas. TWU; Louis Simon, V.P. Clothing Workers; William Bowe, V.P. Sleeping Car Porters; Henry Van Arsdale, NYC Central Labor Council; Norman Hill, civil rights director of the IUD, AFL–CIO; Donald Slaiman, Dir. Civil Rights Dept. AFL–CIO; James Carey, Pres., IUE; Ralph Helstein, Pres. Packinghouse Workers; Max Greenberg, Pres. RWDSU; Russell Crowell, Pres. Laundry Workers; and Charles Coogen, Pres. AFT.

61. Garrow, *Protest at Selma,* pp. 88, 119, 123 and 131; "Labor Pledges Full Support to LBJ on Voting Rights," *AFL–CIO News,* 20 Mar. 1965, p. 1; Philip Foner, *Organized Labor and the Black Worker,* p. 353; "Across USA Labor Hails LBJ Stand on Voting," *Machinist,* 25 Mar. 1965, p. 4.

62. Editorial, "Selma Sheriffs Civilian Posse First Formed to Combat Labor," *AFL–CIO News,* 20 Mar. 1965, p. 1; "The Saddest Day in Selma, Ala.," *The Packinghouse Worker,* Apr. 1965, p. 4; "Selma . . . City Where Labor Unions Are Clubbed or Starved to Death," *Packinghouse Worker,* Apr. 1965, p. 6; James Hoffa, "Message from the General President: Brotherhood Should Be Our Guideline," *The International Teamster,* Apr. 1965, p. 3. One must wonder if Selma represented a missed opportunity to redirect the civil rights movement into a Southern-wide drive to organize workers, combining the energies of the New Left with the muscle of the labor movement. Several SNCC activists turned their attention to organizing workers at the local Coca Cola plant, but their effort was overshadowed by the political endeavors of their colleagues in Lowndes County and by events on the national scene, including the Vietnam War.

63. Jensen, *Strife on the Waterfront,* p. 319; "Multitude Went to be Counted," *Oil, Chemical and Atomic Workers News,* Apr. 1965, p. 6.

64. Carson, *In Struggle,* ch. 11; Braden, "The Southern Freedom Movement in Perspective," pp. 76–93; Bell, *CORE,* chs. 7, 10 and epilogue. "Alabama Bound: Selma and the Lowndes County Black Panther Party, 1964–1966," Panel with Silas Norman, Martha Norman, Robert Mants and Johnny Jackson, at "We Shall Be Moved: The Life and Times of SNCC, 1960–1966," Trinity College, Hartford, Connecticut, 14–16 Apr. 1988.

Chapter 3: Vietnam

1. Halberstam, *The Reckoning,* pp. 347–48; this same story has also been documented in Brett Eynon's oral history of Michigan SDS and antiwar activists and confirmed via a personal conversation with Irving Bluestone.

2. O'Brien, "The Development of the New Left in the United States, 1960–1965," chs. 12 and 13; *SDS,* ch. 11; On early differences on foreign policy, see Peter B. Levy, "The New Left and Labor," pp. 93–101.

3. "Full Support Pledged In Vietnam Retaliation," *AFL–CIO News,* 6 Mar. 1965, p. 4; "Meany Lauds LBJ's Vietnam Stand," *AFL–CIO News,* 1 May 1965, p. 1; Robert Randolph, "12,000 at U.C. Teach-in on Vietnam," *Guardian,* 29 May 1965; on the labor movement's reaction, see Foner, *American Labor and the Indochina War;* examples of labor's response can be found in: "New York Labor Voices Firm Support," *AFL–CIO News,* 30 Oct. 1965, p. 2; "Southeast Asia Policy Backed By Auto, Steel," *AFL–CIO News,* 30 Oct. 1965, p. 3; "President Johnson Hails Vietnam Help of Building Trades," *Building Tradesman,* 17 Dec. 1965, p. 1; "Unions Back President Lyndon Johnson on Vietnam Policy," *Pilot,* Dec. 1965; "SDS Call for March on Washington," *Liberation,* Mar. 1965, p. 46; Jack Smith, "The Demand is 'Peace'," *Guardian,* 24 Apr. 1965.

4. *NY Times,* 15 Dec. 1965.

5. AFL–CIO, *Proceedings of the AFL–CIO 6th Constitutional Convention: Vol. II: Daily Proceedings,* 9–15 Dec. 1965, Resolution No. 68; "Meany Blasts Critics of Johnson Policies," *AFL–CIO News,* 15 May 1965, p. 1. For opinions, see *Gallup Poll Index,* 1965.

6. Hal Benson, "Labor Project Organizers in Boston," *New Left Notes,* 2 Sept. 1966, p. 1; Nat Stillman, "SDS and Labor," *New Left Notes,* 2 Sept. 1966, p. 3; Kim Moody, Fred Epsteiner and Mike Flag, "Working Class: An SDS Convention Position Paper," *New Left Notes,* 9 Sept. 1966, pp. 6–7.

7. "Many U.S. Unions Stepping Up Peace Activities," *Guardian,* 9 Oct. 1965; Michael Munk, "U.S. Pressures Unions to Back War," *Guardian,* 30 Oct. 1965, p. 7; Editorial, *Dispatcher,* 19 Feb. 1965. See also Trade Unions for Peace, Vertical File. There is even some evidence that very early anti-war protests were instigated by union activists. For example, in Berkeley, mathematics Professor Stephen Smale, an activist within the local AFT was key in helping organize Vietnam Day. And later that fall, local longshoreman aided in the picketing of the Oakland Army terminal. See Fred Halstead, *Out Now!,* pp. 50–53, 88.

8. For information on SANE's March on Washington, see March on Washington, 27 Nov. 1965, Series I, Box 10, SANE Papers; Powers, *Vietnam,* pp. 89–94;

Patrick Gorman, "Letter to the Editor," *Guardian,* 30 Oct. 1965, p. 7; Carl Oglesby, "Speech at March on Washington," in *The New Radicals,* ed. Jacobs and Landau, pp. 257–66.

9. Sale, *SDS,* chs. 14–19; Zaroulis and Sullivan, *Who Spoke Up?,* pp. 106–7, 123–46; Mailer, *Armies of the Night;* Powers, *Vietnam,* ch. 11; *Mobilizer News,* 16 Oct. 1967; MOBE, "Newsletter," Vertical File; "Mass Protest Shakes Capital," *Guardian,* 28 Oct. 1967; Powers, *Vietnam,* pp. 54–79; Zaroulis and Sullivan, *Who Spoke Up?,* pp. 7–66 and 123–74; Halstead, *Out Now!.*

10. "Hate Peddlers Are Blasted As a Threat to America," *AFL–CIO News,* 16 Dec. 1967, p. 1; "Solid Support Voted U.S. On Viet Nam," *AFL–CIO News,* 16 Dec. 1967, p. 5; Roscoe Drummond, "The Right to Assent," *Justice,* 1 Dec. 1967, p. 12.

11. "Antiwar Sit-Ins Scored By Legion Commander," *AFL–CIO News,* 16 Dec. 1967, p. 5; Joseph Curran, "The War in Vietnam: Part of America's Historic Defense of Freedom," *Pilot,* Dec. 1967, pp. 1–3, 13; *The Carpenter,* Jan. 1966, p. 40.

12. Foner, *U.S. Labor and the Vietnam War,* pp. 7–8.

13. Radosh, *American Labor and United States Foreign Policy,* pp. 433–39; Sidney Lens, Editorial, *The Nation,* 19 Sept. 1966, p. 251.

14. "NMU Joins Thousands in Parade to Support Troops in Vietnam," *NMU Pilot,* June 1967, pp. 16–17; Murray Schumach, "70,000 Turn Out to Back U.S. Men in Vietnam War," *NY Times,* 14 Mar. 1967; James Wechsler, "Gleason's Glory," *NY Post,* 13 Dec. 1967, p. 7; AFL–CIO, *Proceedings of the AFL–CIO 7th Constitutional Convention: Vol. I: Daily Proceedings,* pp. 280, 363.

15. Oates, *Let the Trumpet Sound,* pp. 431–36; Lewis, *King,* pp. 356–61; Garrow, *Bearing the Cross,* ch. 10; *AFL–CIO News,* 15 Apr. 1967, p. 4; *Justice,* 1 Apr. 1967, p.12; *Justice,* 15 Apr. 1967, p. 2; *United Mine Workers Journal,* 15 May 1967, p. 9.

16. Martin Luther King Jr., "Declaration of Independence from the War in Vietnam," *Ramparts,* May 1967, p. 33; *Guardian,* 15 Apr. 1967, p. 13; "Peace Mobilization April 15 Centers on S.F. and N.Y.," *Guardian,* 25 Mar. 1967, p. 1.

17. On labor's support for LBJ's domestic policies, see Reuther, *The Brothers Reuther,* p. 448; Robinson, *George Meany and His Times,* pp. 240–41. Editorial, *Justice,* 15 May 1967, p. 12. Gillon, *Politics and Vision,* pp. 192–93.

18. Editorial, *Justice,* 15 May 1967, p. 12; on union growth during the war, see Leo Troy, "The Rise and Fall of American Trade Unions: The Labor Movement from FDR to RR," in *Unions in Transition,* ed. Lipset, pp. 75–85.

19. *AFL–CIO News,* 11 Dec. 1965, p. 10; Drew Middleton, "The Rights of Vietnam?" *American Federationist,* Mar. 1967, pp. 22–23; *UAW Solidarity,* Nov. 1965, pp. 14–15; *Seafarers Log,* 30 Apr. 1965, p. 24. Those unions which had been purged or managed to survive the 1950s within the AFL–CIO without renouncing their communist ties—the UE, ILWU, Local 1199 and District 65, were the exception.

20. Ronald Zieger, "George Meany, Labor Bureaucrat," in *Labor Leaders,* ed. Dubofsky and Van Tine.

21. David Sullivan, "A Report on Viet Nam," *American Federationist,* Oct. 1967, pp. 9–12.

22. Goulden, *Jerry Wurf,* ch. 6; Nelson Lichtenstein, "Labor-Liberalism in Crisis."

23. O'Neill, *Coming Apart,* ch. 8; Armbruster, *The Forgotten Americans,* 152–53; Richard Rogin, "Joe Kelley Has Reached His Boiling Point"; Richard Polenberg, *One Nation Divisible,* p. 223; Larrowe, *Harry Bridges,* pp. 376–80; Hoffer, *The Temper of Our Time;* Jim Hampton, "The Odds Say Hoffer Cannot Be an Uncommon Spokesman," *National Observer,* 11 Dec. 1967, p. 12. I also thank Lawrence N. Spitz, formerly of the USWA and Textile Workers for reminding me of the importance of the counterculture in shaping labor's views of the antiwar movement.

24. Sidney Lens, "Captive Unions," *Liberation,* Dec. 1965, pp. 5–6; Staughton Lynd, "Radical Politics and Nonviolent Revolution," *Liberation* Apr. 1966.

25. Marvin Garson, "When The Workers Start to Move," *Berkeley Barb,* 19–25 May 1967, p. 12; Paul Jacobs, "Three Tales of the CIA," *Ramparts,* Apr. 1967, pp. 25–28; Thomas Powers, *Vietnam,* ch. 10.

26. Carl Oglesby, "Liberalism and the Corporate State," in *The New Radicals,* ed. Jacobs and Landau, pp. 257–66; *The New Left,* ed. Teodori, p. 46. Radosh, "The Corporate Ideology: From Gompers to Hillman," *Studies on the Left,* Nov.-Dec. 1966; Ronald Radosh, *American Labor and the United States Foreign Policy,* chs. 10–14.

27. Radosh, "On Hanging Up the Red Flag," in *Political Passages,* ed. Bunzell.

28. Sidney Peck, "Notes on the Strategy and Tactics of the Movement Against the War," *New Politics,* Aug. 1968; Sidney Peck, "Working Paper # 1 On the Strategy and Tactics of the Movement Against the War," 10 Jan. 1968, Draft Copy, Cleveland Area Peace Action Coalition [henceforth CAPAC] Records; Halstead, *Out Now!,* p. 469; Lens, *Unrepentant Radical,* p. 341. Comments by Irving Bluestone, Labor History Conference, 23 Oct. 1987, Wayne State University.

29. Interview with Henry Foner, 18 June 1986, New York City, by author, was very useful in helping me reconstruct this period.

30. Foner, *American Labor and the Indochina War,* ch. 2; "Many Unionists Stepping Up Peace Activities," *Guardian,* 9 Oct. 1965; Trade Unions for Peace, Vertical File; Michael Munk, "U.S. Pressures Unions to Back War," *Guardian,* 30 Oct. 1965, p. 7; Editorial, "Don't Shoot—Negotiate!" *Dispatcher,* 19 Feb. 1965.

31. Foner, *American Labor and the Indochina War,* ch. 2; SANE Papers, "Trade Union Division," especially: Samuel Kalish to Moe Foner, 23 Nov. 1966 and Richard Liebes to Moe Foner, 23 Nov. 1966; *SANE World: Trade Union Division,* June 1966; *SANE World: Trade Union Division,* Dec. 1966; *SANE World: Trade Union Division,* Mar. 1967; Elaine Shinbrot, "Unionists Convene, Assail U.S. Vietnam Policy," *Guardian,* 31 Dec. 1966.

32. *SANE World: Trade Union Division,* Mar. 1967; "Leaflet: An Invitation to the Founding Conference of the Trade Union Division of L.A.," SANE Papers, "Trade Union Division."

33. On the origins of the LLAP, see "Call to a National Labor Leadership

Assembly for Peace," SANE Papers, "Trade Union Division"; Labor Leadership
Assembly for Peace, Vertical File; *Labor Voice For Peace,* Jan. 1968; "Unionists
Condemn War," *Guardian,* 25 Nov. 1967, p. 12; *Labor Voice For Peace,* Mar.
1968; "Executive Board—Labor Leadership Assembly for Peace," Box 3, Labor
Leadership Assembly for Peace Records.

34. Lifton, *Home From the War,* p. 237; Helmer, *Bringing the War Home,* pp.
51–52, 97–98, 216, 277; Kerry, *The New Soldier,* preface and appendix.

35. Peter B. Levy, "The Black Experience in Vietnam," *The Legacy,* ed.
Shafer.

36. Foner, *American Labor and the Indochina War,* pp. 55–56; AFL–CIO,
Proceedings of the AFL–CIO 7th Constitutional Convention: Vol. I, pp. 363.

37. Verba, "Public Opinion and the War in Vietnam," June 1967, pp. 317–33;
Erskine, "Current Polls: The Vietnam War," Fall 1968; *Gallup Poll Index,*
1965–1968. The graph actually underestimate dissent against the war. When 50
percent of the respondents stated that they disapproved of Lyndon Johnson's
policy an equal 50 percent did not approve of it. Rather, approximately ten to 20
percent of the respondents, on any given date, stated that they did not know or
had no opinion. Hence, for instance, when in December 1967 52 percent of the
national sampling stated that they disapproved of Johnson's policy, only 35
percent approved, not 48 percent as might be incorrectly extrapolated. It should
also be noted that it is difficulty to precisely track working class opinion of the
War because of the ways in which poll takers broke down their data. My graph
use the Gallup sub-grouping of manual workers. Others have used a combination of education, union membership and income. Unfortunately, none of the
latter pollsters surveyed union members on a regular basis. In addition, many of
those who disapproved of Johnson's handling of the war may have favored
escalation, not disengagement.

38. *Gallup Poll Index,* 1965–1968.

39. James Wright, "The Working Class, Authoritarianism, And the War in
Vietnam War," pp. 133–49; Katz, "Peace Liberals and Vietnam," pp. 21–39.

40. Foner, *American Labor and the Indochina War,* pp. 55–56; "Unionists
Condemn War," *Guardian,* 25 Nov. 1967, p. 12; "Radicals and Labor: Three
Letters to the Editor," *Guardian,* 2 Dec. 1967, p. 2; Stanley Aronowitz, "Left
May Have A Role in Unions," *Guardian,* 23 Dec. 1967; "Viewpoint," *Guardian,*
5 July 1972, pp. 8–9; Jeffrey Blankfurt, "The War Comes Home to Beallsville,
Ohio," *Ramparts,* July 1969, pp. 40–46; Doug Dowd, "Recession and the War,"
Liberation, Mar. 1970, p. 11; "War Creates Hard times for Workers," *Guardian,*
28 Feb. 1970, p. 9; Carl Davidson, "Workers Back Antiwar Campaign," *Guardian,*
6 Oct. 1971.

41. Foner, *U.S. Labor and the Vietnam War,* p. 72.

42. CAPAC Records, reel 1.

43. CAPAC Records, reel 1, especially, Jerry Gordon to All Labor Unions, 2
Apr. 1970; and, "Steering Committee for the National Conference," n.d. On the
origins of the New MOBE, see F. Halstead, *Out Now!,* p. 469.

44. Vietnam Moratorium Committee, "Leaflet: October 15, Viet Moratorium,"
in Vertical File on Vietnam Moratorium; "Millions Join October 15 Protests:

Moratorium," *Guardian,* 25 Oct. 1969, p. 4; "Vietnam Moratorium Observed Nationwide, Orderly," *NY Times,* 16 Oct. 1969, p. 1, 12, 19; Foner, *U.S. Labor and the Vietnam War,* pp. 88–90.

45. Zaroulis and Sullivan, *Who Spoke Up?,* pp. 277–95; "Parades for Peace and Patriotism," *Time,* 21 Nov. 1969, pp. 23–26; Kenneth Gross, "Give Peace A Chance," *The Nation,* 1 Dec. 1969, pp. 591–94; New MOBE, "Memo to Staff," 6 Nov. 1969, New MOBE Vertical File; "Up to 800,000 March in D.C., 250,000 In S.F.," *Guardian,* 22 Nov. 1969; Foner, *U.S. Labor and the Vietnam War,* p. 90.

46. Harlan Hahn, "Dove Sentiment Among Blue Collar Workers," *Dissent,* May-June 1970, p. 202; Sidney Lens, *Unrepentant Radical,* p. 363; Foner, *American Labor and the Indochina War,* pp. 74–81; "War Creates Hard Times for Workers," *Guardian,* 28 Feb. 1970, p. 9; On student support for labor, see Peter B. Levy, "The New Left and Labor," pp. 534–58; "We Take Our Stand," *UAW Solidarity,* Nov. 1969.

47. "Meany Backs President in Peace Efforts," *AFL–CIO News,* 11 Nov. 1969, p. 1; "Editorial: To Win the Peace," *AFL–CIO News,* 25 Nov. 1969, p. 4; "Support for Defense of Viet Nam Based on Firm Liberal Tenets," *AFL–CIO News,* 22 Nov. 1969, p. 4; John Roche, "Ivy Leaguer Rolls Back Cover on Radicals in Student Revolt," *AFL–CIO News,* 6 June 1970; John Roche, "Students Embrace Radicalism As Vehicle for Breaking System," *AFL–CIO News,* 22 Aug. 1970, p. 4.

48. Al Richmond, "Workers Against the War," *Ramparts,* Sept. 1970, pp. 28–32; "9 Hurt as Police Disperse Group in Midtown After Peace Rally," *NY Times,* 22 May 1970, p. 1; Jeremy Brecher, "Thoughts on the Next Crisis," *Liberation,* May 1970, p. 20; "Millions Protest Against the Cambodia Invasion," *Guardian,* 16 May 1970, pp. 6, 7; "N.Y. Workers, Students, Demand Peace," *Guardian,* 30 May 1970, p. 4; Walter Reuther, "Telegram," *UAW Solidarity,* June 1970.

49. "NCDWA Joins ALA & SCLC In march Against Racism and Repression," *The Distributive Worker,* May 1970, p. 8; "Washington Labor for Peace and Statements and Resolutions," Labor for Peace, Vertical File; CAPAC Records, especially: Cathy Perkins to Gus Scholle, 9 June 1970; and "National Emergency Conference: Scholle Calls for Coalition Between Labor-Students," [leaflet]. The typical view of the events of May 1970 also overlooks the working class background of many of the protestors. The fact that the most notable protest took place at Kent State University, a public university in the heart of industrial America, should at least suggest that the antiwar movement was not restricted to students of upper and middle class backgrounds.

50. Fred Cook, "Hard Hats, The Rampaging Patriots," *Nation,* 15 June 1970, pp. 712–19; Thomas Williams, "My Hard Hat Problems and Yours," *Esquire,* Oct. 1970, pp. 138–44.

51. Peter Roman, "Labor's War Discontents Widen," *Guardian,* 13 Mar. 1971; "Trade Unions Build Support for April 24," *Guardian,* 20 Mar. 1971; "800,000 Protest," *Guardian,* 5 May 1971.

52. Beirne quoted in, Foner, *U.S. Labor and the Vietnam War,* pp. 99–100.

53. See Gallup and Harris polls for this period and Foner, *U.S. Labor and the Vietnam War*.

54. Labor For Peace, Vertical File; Labor For Peace, District 65 Collection, folders 10–13; "Signers of the Open Letter, as of 9 Sept. 1971, CAPAC Records.

55. Hayden quoted in Zaroulis and Sullivan, *Who Spoke Up?*, p. 393; Staughton Lynd, "Guerilla History in Gary," *Liberation*, Oct. 1969, pp. 17–20; Staughton and Alice Lynd, eds., *Rank and File*, pp. 1–2; Jeremy Brecher, "Thoughts for the Next Crisis," *Liberation*, June 1970, pp. 18–22.

Chapter 4: Black Power

1. Flug, "Organized Labor and the Civil Rights Movement of the 1960s." pp. 322–46.

2. Flug, "Organized Labor and the Civil Rights Movement."

3. Jerry Menapace to Abe Feinglass, 26 July 1966; Abe Feinglass to Jerry Menapace, 28 July 1966, both in Philip S. Foner, et al., eds., *The Black Worker Since the AFL–CIO Merger, 1955–1980*, pp. 102–4.

4. Flug, "Organized Labor and the Civil Rights Movement" and Foner, et al, eds., *The Black Worker Since the AFL–CIO Merger, 1955–1980*, pp. 102–4.

5. Flug, "Organized Labor and the Civil Rights Movement."

6. Rustin, "From Protest to Politics."

7. "Detroit: A Quiet Appraisal," *UAW Solidarity*, Sept. 1967, p. 3, 9; Edward Morgan, "American Dream a Nightmare for Victims of Discrimination," *AFL–CIO News*, 6 June 1966, p. 7; "Probe of Riots Launched," *Labor*, 28 Aug. 1965, p. 6; John Lopez to William Oliver, n.d., WPR Collection; *AFL–CIO News*, 4 Mar. 1967, p. 9; "The Black Tragedy of Newark, Decay, Deterioration, Dismay," *Packinghouse Worker*, Oct. 1967, p. 4; "The Black Tragedy in Newark-Part II," *Packinghouse Worker*, p. 4, 9.

8. Editorial, *Oil, Chemical and Atomic Union News*, July 1967, p. 7; Editorial, *Butcher Workman;* Sept. 1967, p. 32; Editorial, *Dispatcher*, 16 Sept. 1966, p. 2; A study of the Newark local of the Teamster's newspaper revealed a similar attitude. Whereas before the riots the paper carried few stories on the civil rights movement or urban blight, afterwards, in spite of cries for law and order by local politicians, the IBT local called for jobs, housing and understanding. See Steven M. Darcy, "The Newark Riots and the New Jersey Teamsters," [unpublished paper] in author's possession.

9. Editorial, *Oil, Chemical and Atomic Union News*, Sept. 1967, p. 7; *Seafarers Log*, 17 Mar. 1967, p. 7; *Steel Labor*, Oct. 1967, p. 20.

10. Foner, *Organized Labor and the Black Worker*, pp. 363–74; *District Three Leader [IUE]*, May-June 1969, p. 8–9; *District Three Leader*, July 1968, p. 10; *District Three Leader*, Mar. 1968, p. 5; "Labor Set to Give Lead In Watts," *Packinghouse Worker*, Sept. 1965; Fine, *Violence in the Model City*, chs. 13 and 14.

11. *American Teacher*, May 1967, p. 8–9; *American Teacher*, Apr. 1968, p. 1, 7; *American Teacher*, Oct. 1967, p. 3. *American Teacher*, Apr. 1967, p. 4.

12. Fine, *Violence in the Model City,* ch. 16.

13. Jacobson, ed., *The Negro and the American Labor Movement,* pp. 16–17, 24–25; James Boggs, *Racism and the Class Struggle,* p. 91.

14. Garrow, *Bearing the Cross,* chs. 8, 9; Carson, *In Struggle,* chs. 10–14; Meier and Rudwick, *CORE,* chs. 10–12; Inge Bell, *CORE,* epilogue.

15. Carmichael and Hamilton, *Black Power,* pp. 53–55; Joyce Ladner, "White America's Response to Black Militancy," p. 212–13.

16. Floyd McKissick's views on labor can be found in John Lopez to William Oliver, n.d., WPR Collection. On Carmichael, see Viorst, *Fire in the Streets,* pp. 348–50.

17. James Haughton Papers, especially: *Fight Back,* vol. 1, no. 4 (June 1969); "Black Power-Myth Turned Around," n.d. and Marrion Sanders, "James Haughton Wants 100,000 More Jobs," *NY Times Magazine,* 14 Sept. 1969.

18. John Oliver Killens, "Black Labor and Black Liberation," *Black Scholar,* vol. 2, no 2 (Oct. 1970), pp. 33–39; Herbert Hill, "Black Protest and the Struggle for Union Democracy," *Issues in Industrial Society* vol. 1, no 1 (1969), pp. 19–29; Allen, *Black Awakening in Capitalist America,* p. 200.

19. Carmichael and Hamilton, *Black Power,* pp. 63–63 and 72–75.

20. Advocates of black power differed over the value of socialism, among themselves and over time. Carmichael once claimed that socialism was irrelevant to blacks, while the Black Panther party varied between describing race as more to equally important as class. See "To the R.N.A.," in *The Black Panthers Speak,* ed. Foner, p. 71; Eldridge Cleaver, "An Interview," in Teodori, *The New Left,* pp. 284–89; Huey Newton, "An Interview," *The Movement,* Aug. 1968; Carmichael, *Stokely Speaks,* p. ix; Lester, "The White Radical as a Revolutionary," in *Revolutionary Notes,* p. 46; *Packinghouse Worker,* Oct. and Nov. 1967.

21. Seale, *Seize the Time,* pp. 412–22; "On Violence," *The Black Panther,* 23 Mar. 1968, p. 19; Erskine, "The Polls: Demonstrations and Race Riots"; Brink and Harris, *Black and White,* ch. 6; Clayborne Carson, "Black Power Ten Years After," in *A History of Our Time,* ed. Chafe and Sitkoff; David Hilliard, "The Ideology of the Black Panther Party," in *The Black Panthers Speak,* ed. Foner, pp. 522–23; Nathan Wright, *Black Power and Urban Unrest,* ch. 1; Carmichael, "What We Want," *New York Review of Books;* Les Jarvis to Ceser Chavez, 10 June 1970, Box 59-B, United Farm Workers Collection; George Meany quoted in Jacobson, ed., *The Negro and the American Labor Movement,* pp. 15–16.

22. Jacobson, ed., *The Negro and the American Labor Movement,* pp. 15–16; "Cartoon: Hate-Peddlers at Work," *AFL–CIO News,* 22 Oct. 1966, p. 5; "Cartoon: The Game Nobody Wins," *AFL–CIO News,* 19 Aug. 1967, p. 4.

23. Gary Fink, ed., *AFL–CIO Executive Council Statements and Reports,* pp. 1920–22 and 2363–64.

24. Gary Fink, ed., *AFL–CIO Executive Council Statements and Reports,* p. 1212.

25. J.C. Rich, "Black Power Blows Up," *Hat Worker,* Oct. 1966, p. 5.

26. John Lopez to W. H. Oliver, "Assignment to Oakland," n.d. and William Oliver to Irving Bluestone, 18 July 1967, both in WPR, Box 488, Folder 3.

27. Floyd McKissick to Dear Friend, n.d.; William Oliver to Irving Bluestone, 18 July 1967, Folders 2 and 3, respectively, Box 488, WPR Collection.

28. Haines, "Black Radicalization and the Funding of Civil Rights, 1957–70." See also the financial records of CORE and SNCC: "Financial Records, Dec. 31 1954-April 9, 1965," V:1, CORE Papers; I:A:33 and VI:5, SNCC Papers.

29. "AFL–CIO Supports Joint Statement of Negro Leaders Condemning Riots, *AFL–CIO News,* 29 July 1967, p. 1, 12; Editorial, *Justice,* 15 Apr. 1967, p. 12; Editorial, *AFL–CIO News,* 23 July 1966, p. 4; "AFL–CIO Pres. George Meany Pledges Firm Support," *AFL–CIO News,* 22 Oct. 1966, p. 1, 10–11.

30. Bayard Rustin, "Civil Rights at Crossroads," *American Federationist,* Nov. 1966, pp. 15–20; AFL–CIO, *Proceedings of the AFL–CIO 8th Constitutional Convention, October 2–7, 1969,* pp. 104–12; *American Teacher,* Sept. 1966, p. 14.

31. "Sleeping Car Porters Pres. Sees Despair in Cry of Black Power," *AFL–CIO News,* 10 Sept. 1967; AFL–CIO, *Proceedings of the AFL–CIO 7th Constitutional Convention,* 7–12 Dec. 1967, pp. 337; A. Philip Randolph, "Keynote Address at Founding NALC Convention, May 18, 1960," James Haughton Papers.

32. Ray Marshall, "The Negro and the AFL–CIO"; Gus Tyler, "Contemporary Labor's Attitudes Toward the Negro," in Jacobson, ed. *The Negro and the Labor Movement,* 358–79; Coleman, "Labor Power and Social Equality," ch. 3.

33. By in large, commentators have paid little attention to the structural changes that faced labor in the mid and late 1960s and the impact they had on its views. Several works on the deindustrialization of America deal with the impact of economic change on labor in the 1970s and 1980s but a more careful analysis would lead scholars to realize that structural change threatened labor much earlier. In the early 1960s, the UAW called automation the number one problem, alongside with civil rights. The textile, garment, and electrical unions faced the problems associated with runaway shops before the oil crisis of the 1970s revealed the growing power of foreign nations to the public. Longshoremen confronted a revolution in their industry on the eve of the economic downturn of the 1970s. Coal, steel, rubber, and other basic industries had either already undergone or were about to undergo tremendous change. These industries were the wellspring of the social activist unions of the CIO. Most had not been organized until the late 1930s and early 1940s and did not win a secure position until after the mass strikes of 1946. Thus their period of strength, economically and politically, was in retrospect a short one. No sooner had they achieved a degree of power in society than they faced a foe at least as threatening as the company goons and spies of an earlier era, a loss of jobs and accordingly members. Cost of Living Agreements, or COLAs, eased the concerns of senior members but from the labor leaders' perspective remained irrelevant to the larger problem of structural economic change.

Boggs, *Racism and the Class Struggle,* p. 92; Jacobson, ed., *The Negro and the American Labor Movement,* Introduction; Grine, "America Against Herself: The Ideology of American Radicalism in the Nineteen Sixties"; Bloom, *Class, Race and the Civil Rights Movement.*

34. The best general works on the two affairs are Georgakas and Surkin, *Detroit: I Do Mind Dying;* Geschwender, *Class, Race and Worker Insurgency;* Ravitch, *The Great School Wars,* chs. 23–36; and Berube and Gittell, eds., *Confrontation at Ocean Hill-Brownsville.*

35. Geschwender, *Class, Race and Worker Insurgency,* ch. 6; Henle, "Some Reflections on Organized Labor and the New Militants," pp. 20–25; Michael Musuraca, "Labor Liberalism and Race: The UAW and the League of Revolutionary Black Workers," [unpublished paper in author's possession].

36. Geschwender, *Class, Race and Worker Insurgency,* p. 94–100; Eric Perkins, "The League of Revolutionary Black Workers and the Coming of the Revolution," *Radical America,* vol. 5, no. 2 (Mar.-Apr. 1971), pp. 50–62; "Finally Got the News."

37. [League Pamphlet] "Black Workers Protest UAW Racism: March on Cobo Hall," n.d., James Haughton Papers; J. Geschwender, *Class, Race and Worker Insurgency,* pp. 92–100.

38. Geschwender, *Class, Race and Worker Insurgency,* ch. 6;

39. Musuraca, "Labor Liberalism and Race"; *Eldon Revolutionary Ave. Union Movement,* vol. 2, no. 3, in James Haughton Papers.

40. Eric Perkins, "The League of Revolutionary Black Workers, *Radical America;*" Martha Glablerman, "Black Workers Organize Dodge Plant," *Guardian,* 23 Nov. 1968; "Detroit Union Radicals Act," *Guardian,* 8 Feb. 1969; "Special Supplement on Black Worker Insurgency," *Guardian,* 8 Mar. 1969; "The Dodge Rebellion," *Ramparts,* 30 Nov. 1969; Marrion Sanders, "James Haughton Wants 500,000 More Jobs," *NY Times Magazine,* 14 Sept. 1969; J. Jacobs, "Our Thing Is DRUM," *Leviathan,* 6 Mar. 1970, p. 2; "League of Revolutionary Black Workers," *Rat,* 25 Sept. 1970, p. 6; "From Repression to Revolution," *Radical America,* Mar. 1971, p. 81. In the same period, a caucus of the Black Panther party in the San Francisco Bay Area characterized Leonard Woodcock as a right-winger and defended using any means necessary to break from the chains of the union and company bosses. *Auto Worker Focus,* Aug. 1970, p. 3, in Philip Foner, et al, eds., *The Black Worker,* pp. 268–69.

41. Geschwender, *Class, Race and Worker Insurgency,* pp. 104–12; "UAW Rebuffs Black Extremists," *America,* 29 Mar. 1969, p. 346; Musuraca, "Labor Liberalism and Race."

42. Henle, "Some Reflections on Organized Labor and the New Militance"; Elliot quoted in, Thomas R. Brooks, "Black Upsurge in the Unions," *Dissent,* Apr. 1970, p. 131.

43. Carl Davidson, "Blacks Demand More Jobs," *Guardian,* 4 Oct. 1969; "Labor's Black Monday's Sunday Allies," *Ramparts,* Jan. 1970; Monroe Head and Dick Greeman, "Black Workers Close NJ Ford Plant," *Guardian,* 3 May 1969, p. 5; "Black Union Meets with Panthers," *Guardian,* 26 Apr. 1969, p. 5; Wilbur Haddock, "Black Workers Lead the Way," *Black Scholar,* vol. 5, no 3 (1973), pp. 43–48; "Black Brothers Have a Better Idea," *Movement,* Aug. 1969, pp. 8–9.

44. Charles Denby, "Black Caucuses in the Unions," *New Politics* vol. 3 (Summer 1968), pp. 10–17; McAfee, "Black Brothers Have a Better Idea."

45. Hampton and Fayer, *Voices of Freedom,* pp. 484–90.

46. Ravitch, *The Great School Wars,* p. 346; Berube and Gittell, *Confrontation at Ocean Hill-Brownsville,* Prologue and Prelude; Hampton, *Voices of Freedom,* pp. 491–92.

47. Ravitch, *The Great School Wars,* chs. 28–33.

48. Hampton, *Voice of Freedom,* 491–92; Ravitch, *The Great School Wars,* chs. 28–33.

49. Ravitch, *The Great School Wars,* chs. 28–33. Valuable material can also be found in Diane Ravitch Papers, in particular, see "Newsletter," n.d.; Rev. Herbert Oliver, "Press Release," 8 Sept. 1968; Rosalie Stutz, "The Community and the UFT," July 1967; and Ocean Hill-Brownsville School District Governing Board, "Statement," 31 May 1968; on the demonstrations and counter-demonstrations, see Hampton and Fayer, *Voices of Freedom,* pp. 485–510.

50. Berube and Gittell, *Confrontation at Ocean Hill-Brownsville.*

51. "Negro Union Leaders Support Teachers in New York School Strike," *AFL-CIO News,* 28 Sept. 1968, p. 6; Charles Coogen, "Race Separatism and the AFT," *American Teacher,* Jan. 1968, p. 2; Ravitch, *The Great School Wars,* pp. 369–70; "An Exchange of Views," in Berube and Gittell, *Confrontation at Ocean Hill-Brownsville,* pp. 139–55. Interview with Sam Meyer.

52. The most complete though extremely biased work on this subject is, Max Geltman, *The Confrontation,* quote from p. 4.

53. Hampton, *Voices of Freedom,* pp. 504–7.

54. Sol Stern, "Scab Teachers," *Ramparts,* 17 Nov. 1968, pp. 17–25; "Community Control of Our Schools: A Symposium," *Liberation,* Sept. 1968, pp. 26–39; Leah Fritz, "Schools for Anarchy," *Liberation,* Nov. 1968, pp. 5–6; "Birth of a Community by a Ocean Hill-Brownsville Resident," *Liberation,* Dec. 1968, pp. 16–27.

55. Ravitch, *The Great School Wars,* pp. 371–72.

56. *AFL-CIO News,* 21 Sept. 1968, p. 4; *AFL-CIO News,* 28 Sept. 1968, p. 6; Michael Harrington, "An Open Letter to Men of Good Will," in *Confrontation,* pp. 229–46; "The Freedom to Teach," [Advertisement placed in *NY Times,* 20 Sept. 1968] *American Teacher,* Oct. 1968, p. 5.

57. Sol Stern, "Scab Teachers," *Ramparts,* 17 Nov. 1968, pp. 17–25. Herbert Hill, "Reply," *Issues in Industrial Society* vol. 3 (1969), pp. 64–71.

58. Herbert Hill, "Reply."

59. "Negro Union Leaders Support Teachers in New York School Strike," *AFL-CIO News,* 28 Sept. 1968, p. 6.

60. Clarke Kissinger, "Who Supports George and Gene?" *Guardian,* 21 Sept. 1968; Stanley Aronowitz, "Opportunities for the New Left," *Guardian,* 26 Sept. 1968; Carl Davidson, "No Life of Riley," *Guardian,* 19 Oct. 1969.

Chapter 5: The Counterculture

1. For the original version of the song, see Guy and Candie Carawan, *Voices From the Mountains.* For other versions, see James Farmer, *Lay Bare the Heart,* ch. 3; Guy Carawan, *Freedom Is a Constant Struggle* and Glyn Thomas, "Songs of Protest," *RWDSU Record,* 10 and 24 Nov., p. 12; Dunaway, "Pete Seeger and the Modern American Topical Song Movements."

2. Hampton, *Guerilla Minstrels,* ch. 6.

3. Glyn Thomas, "Songs of Protest," *RWDSU Record,* 10 and 24 Nov., p. 12; Guy and Candie Carawan, *Freedom Is A Constant Struggle.*

4. On the emergence of the counterculture, see O'Neill, *Coming Apart,* ch. 8; Dickstein, *Gates of Eden;* Hodgson, *America in Our Time,* chs. 15–17; Braden, *The Age of Aquarius.* On Berkeley, see *Berkeley in the Sixties,* California Newsreal, 1990.

5. Eric Bentley, "The Red, White and the Black," *Liberation,* May 1970; Gitlin, *The Sixties,* p. 213.

6. While it would be incorrect to assert that the New Left and the counterculture were identical, both displayed a personal alienation from mainstream American culture.

7. Roszak, *The Making of the Counterculture.*

8. For the Port Huron and Cleaver quotes, see Marshall Berman, *The Politics of Authenticity,* pp. xvii-xvix; Mario Savio, "An End to History," in *The New Radicals,* ed. Jacobs and Landau, p. 230–34; Lasch, *The Agony of the American Left,* p. 182; Keniston, *Youth and Dissent;* Reich, *The Greening of America;* Roszak, *The Making of the Counterculture.*

9. Miles, *Ginsberg,* ch. 1.

10. Ibid., ch. 2.

11. Ginsberg quoted in Viorst, *Fire in the Streets,* p. 77; Miles, *Ginsberg.*

12. Marcuse, *Eros and Civilization;* Marcuse, *One Dimensional Man.*

13. Goodman, *Growing Up Absurd.*

14. Interview with Robinson Lillienthal, Newark, NJ, Dec. 1988, by author.

15. Peck, *Uncovering the Sixties,* pp. 22–32.

16. Ibid., pp. 22–32. An almost identical story is told by another Jewish working-class youth who went off to college and then became a spokesman for the counterculture, rock critic Richard Goldstein. See Richard Goldstein, "Son of the Return of the Repressed," *Village Voice,* 8 Mar. 1988, p. 23–28.

17. Rubin, *Do It,* pp. 12–13.

18. Gitlin, *The Whole World Is Watching,* Introduction and p. 113; *Life,* 10 Nov. 1967; Tom Kahn, "Youth Protest and the Democratic Process," *American Federationist,* 1 Apr. 1969, pp. 1–8; Richard Rogin, "Joe Kelley Has Reached His Boiling Point," in *A History of Our Time,* ed. Chafe, pp. 277–89; Polenberg, *One Nation Divisible,* pp. 224–25; Hoffer, *The Temper of Our Time;* Jim Hampton, "The Odds Say Hoffer Cannot Be an Uncommon Spokesman," p. 12; Arthur Shostak, *Blue Collar Life,* pp. 212–13. *NY Times,* 9 May 1970, p. 1.

19. Polenberg, *One Nation Divisible.*

20. Polls and surveys demonstrated the inchoate views of workers toward the

war and racial issues. As early as 1966, more workers disapproved of Johnson's conduct of the war than approved, although they did not express a clear view of what America should do instead. In the same years a large majority of white union members felt that blacks had it worse off than themselves but refused to call for more government action. On cultural issues Americans in general and workers in particular expressed themselves in a single voice. For example, a 1971 Roper study showed that Americans considered drug abuse to be a more serious problem than the Vietnam War, racial tension or the economy. See Armbruster, *The Forgotten Americans*, pp. 152–53.

21. William O'Neill, "The Counter-Culture," in *A History of Our Time*, ed. Chafe, p. 275.

22. Ibid., pp. 275–76; "What They Believe," *Fortune*, Jan. 1969, pp. 70–72; Jeremy Main, "Dissidence Among College Students Is Still Growing, And it Is Spreading Beyond the Campus," *Fortune*, June 1969, pp. 73–74; Yankelovich, *The Changing Values of Campus*, p. 7; Peter M. Swerdloff, "Hopes and Fears of Blue Collar Youth," *Fortune*, 9 Jan. 1969, pp. 148–52. Black workers throughout the latter half of the 1960s and early 1970s sympathized with the counterculture. As one black Akron, Ohio rubber worker told Peter Swerdloff: "Dropping out is cool, man—they are fighting the same power structure we are."

23. *Gallup Poll Index*, including "Miniskirts," June 1967 and "Morals," July 1968; Armbruster, *The Forgotten Americans*, pp. 152–53; Wattenberg, *The Real America*, ch. 20; John Sinclair quoted in Farber, *Chicago, '68*, p. 167.

24. Lawrence A. Mayer, "Young America: By the Number," *Fortune*, Jan. 1969.

25. Wolfe, *Radical Chic and Mau Mauing the Flak Catchers*.

26. Gabriel Fackre, "A Blue Collar White and the Far Right," *Christian Century*, 7 May 1969, pp. 645–48; Wattenberg, *The Real America*, p. 282.

27. Jerry Rubin quoted in Leuchtenburg, *The Troubled Feast*, p. 182; Hoffman, *Revolution For the Hell of It*, p. 57.

28. "Rebellion and Opportunity," *AFL–CIO News*, 8 June 1968, p. 4; "Editorial: The Other Youngsters," *AFL–CIO News*, 23 Aug. 1969, p. 4; Editorial, *International Teamster*, Oct. 1967, inside cover; Harry Bridges, "On the Beam," *Dispatcher*, 15 July 1969, p. 2.

29. Rubin, *Do It*, pp. 95–96; Abbie Hoffman cited in Hodgson, *America In Our Time*, pp. 308–9. Paul Krassner, one of the co-founders of the Yippies, wrote that he became a convert to countercultural revolution following the 1965 AFL–CIO convention when he became convinced of labor's middle class values, including its support of Vietnam. To that point in time, Krassner, an anarchist in sentiment, had served as a link between the old and New Left. See Paul Krassner, "The Birth of the Yippie Conspiracy," in *The Sixties Papers*, ed. Albert, p. 549.

30. Alden Whitman, "Max Eastman Is Sorry for Today's Rebels," *NY Times*, 9 Jan. 1969, p. 33.

31. Leamer, *The Paper Revolutionaries*; Rubin, *Do It*, pp. 95–96 and 116; Hoffman, "Revolution For the Hell of It"; in *The Sixties Papers*, pp. 53–64; Peck, *Uncovering the Sixties*, especially chs. 5, 6, 7. Gitlin, *The Whole World Is*

Watching discusses how individuals such as Hoffman and Rubin used the media to foster their ideas.

32. Simon Frith, "Rock and the Politics of Memory," in *The 60s Without Apology,* ed. Sayres, et al., pp. 67–68; Wiener, *Come Together,* p. 147; John Rockwell, *All American Music,* ch. 19; Jim Miller, ed., *The Rolling Stone Illustrated History of Rock and Roll.*

33. *Ramparts,* 15 June 1968, p. 37; Joanne Grant, ed., *Confrontation on Campus,* pp. 58–59.

34. Daniel Bell, "Columbia and the New Left," in *Confrontation,* p. 81.

35. Avorn, et al., *Up Against the Ivy Wall,* ch. 6; Barbara G. Myerhoff, "The Revolution as a Trip: Symbol and Paradox," in *The New Pilgrims,* ed. Altbach and Laufer, pp. 251–66.

36. Edward Morgan, "A Different View of Protesting Youth," *AFL–CIO News,* 14 Jan. 1967, p. 5.

37. On Joplin, see Friedman, *Buried Alive.*

38. Wattenberg, *The Real America,* chs. 19, 20; "50 Editors Look At Youth Problems," *AFL–CIO News,* 28 Sept. 1968, p. 5.

39. John Lopez to William Oliver, n.d., WPR Collection; Harris, *The Anguish of Change.*

40. Alan Brinkley, "Dreams of the Sixties," argues that the New Left and counterculture were rooted in a similar disaffection with American culture, but that ultimately the two trends clashed. The counterculture led to a quest for self-fulfillment, which ran against the New Left's call for political commitment. Unable to reconcile these two themes, the New Left collapsed.

41. M. A. Hutcheson, "Rebellion Road Is Not the Old Man's Road," *Carpenter,* July 1969, p. 40; Thomas Williams, "My Hard Hat Problems and Yours," *Esquire,* Oct. 1970, pp. 138–44; Discussion with Larry Spitz, Phoenix, Arizona, Mar. 1987.

42. Farber, *Chicago '68,* chs. 5, 6, 10. Farber argues that Chicago was not the focus of the protest, that the New Left sought a national confrontation and Chicago just happened to be the loci of it. To an extent Farber is correct. Yet, he underestimates the degree to which Chicago epitomized the establishment to new leftists.

43. Viorst, *Fire in the Streets,* ch. 12; Matusow, *The Unravelling of America,* p. 419; Zaroulis and Sullivan, *Who Spoke Up,* pp. 175–87; Farber, *Chicago '68,* p. 212.

44. Farber, *Chicago '68,* pp. 115–18; Matusow, *The Unravelling of America,* p. 419.

45. George Meany, "The AFL–CIO Program, 1968," *American Federationist,* Aug. 1968, p. 1; James Gannon, "Meany's All-Or-Nothing Political Bet," *Wall St. Journal,* 1 Oct. 1968, p. 18; "Unions Are Ready to Push in Chicago," *Business Week,* 17 Aug. 1968, p. 97.

46. David Farber, *Chicago '68,* pp. 158–61, 198–201 and 251–55; Todd Gitlin, *The Whole World Is Watching.* One of the reasons that so many attended the White Sox games that week was that Detroit Tiger Pitcher, Denny McLain was in the midst of his quest to become the first pitcher to win thirty games in a

single season since 1934. The fans' enthusiasm for McLain's quest reflected the cultural continuity of the 1960s that tended to be lost in the turmoil of the times. Ironically, McLain himself, was somewhat of a rebel or a nontraditionalist. He sported somewhat long hair and refused to behave—off the field—like the traditional clean-cut ballplayer.

47. Carl Davidson, "What Happened in Chicago?" *Guardian*, 7 Sept. 1968; Lester, *Revolutionary Notes*, pp. 153–56; Motherfuckers, "Respect for Lawlessness," *New Left Notes*, 16 Sept. 1968.

48. Noel Ignatin, "The Labor Scene at Convention Time," *New Left Notes*, 19 Aug. 1968; Viorst, *Fire in the Streets*, p. 453; David Stein, "Notes on a Police State," *Liberation*, Oct. 1968, p. 7; K. Sale, *SDS*, p. 501; Bill Ayers quoted in, Stern, *With the Weathermen*, p. 47; Carl Davidson, "From the New Left," *Guardian*, 5 Oct. 1968, p. 11; Farber, *Chicago '68*, p. 202.

49. Farber, *Chicago '68*, pp. 204–7; Matusow, *The Unravelling of America*, p. 423; Rosenberg, *Vietnam*, pp. 44–46 and 70–71; Polenberg, *One Nation Divisible*, pp. 220–31.

50. Levison, *The Working Class Majority*, p. 162.

51. Coles, *The Middle Americans*; "Editorial: The New Left," *AFL–CIO News*, 15 Mar. 1969; Rosenberg, *Vietnam*, chs. 2, 3; Jacob Epstein, "Blue Collars in Cicero," in *The World of the Blue Collar Worker*, ed. Howe, pp. 94–95.

52. Leamer, *The Paper Revolutionaries*, pp. 28–33, 115–17 and 163–65; Hodgson, *America In Our Time*, p. 345; Abe Peck, *Uncovering the Sixties*.

53. Leamer, *The Paper Revolutionaries*, p. 165.

54. Peck, *Uncovering the Sixties*, pp. 22–32, 310–11 and 320–21.

55. James Matles, "Young Worker Challenges The Unions Establishment," *UE News*, 2 Nov. 1968, pp. 5–6; "A Young Outlook," *United Rubber Worker*, July 1968, p. 5; Edward Morgan, "A Different View of Protesting Youth," *CWA News*, Feb. 1967; p. 4; Charles Michaelson, "Hair Back In Style," *RWDSU Record*, 24 Nov. 1968, p. 13.

56. Morgan, "A Different View of Protesting Youth"; Michaelson, "Hair Back in Style"; Matles, "Young Worker Challenges The Union Establishment."

57. Rubin, *Do It*, p. 92–92; "Students In Revolt," *Free Labour World*, June 1968, p. 3; For an example of a virulent attack on the New Left, see M.A. Hutcheson, "Rebellion Road," *Carpenter*, July 1969, p. 40.

58. Julian Beck, "Notes Toward a Statement on Anarchism and Theatre," in *The Sixties Papers*, ed. Albert, pp. 408–10; Gitlin, *The Sixties*, pp. 222–41, describes the Diggers as rooted in anarchist tradition. He implies they came from working class backgrounds.

59. Wiener, *Come Together*, ch. 7; Hampton, *Guerrilla Minstrels*, ch. 1; Fraser, ed., *1968*, pp. 116–17.

60. Gus Tyler, "Generation Gap or Gap Within a Generation?" in *The Seventies: Problems and Proposals*, ed. Harrington and Howe.

61. For information on People's Park, see Robert Sheer, "Dialectics of Confrontation," *Ramparts*, Aug. 1969, pp. 42–54; *Berkeley Barb*, from mid-April to mid-June 1969, especially articles by Stew Albert; Glick, "The People's Park."

62. Sheer, "Dialectics of Confrontation"; *Berkeley Barb,* 25 Apr.–1 May 1969; p. 1, 2–8 May 1969, p. 3; 2–8 May 1969, p. 4; Gitlin, *The Sixties,* pp. 353–62.

63. Robert Sheer, "Dialectics of Confrontation"; Todd Gitlin, *The Sixties,* pp. 353–62.

64. The Alameda Central Labor Council sought to mediate the dispute with Harry Bridges deploring the use of state troops. He wrote "Don't forget we had the same thing in 1934." Similiarly, the local Teachers' union endorsed the building and defense of the Park. See Sheer, "Dialectics of Confrontation"; "Proclamation," *Berkeley Barb,* 9–15 May 1969, p. 2; "Who Owns the Park?" *Berkeley Barb,* 9–15 May 1969, p. 2; "U.C. Clerks Hit Bricks," *Berkeley Barb,* 23–29 May 1969, p. 8; "The Battle of Berkeley," *Newsweek,* 2 June 1969, pp. 35–36; "Local 6 Tries to Help Resolve Berkeley Crisis," *Dispatcher,* 3 June 1969, p. 7; Glick, "The People's Park," pp. 217–20.

65. Lou Cannon, *President Reagan,* p. 534; *Berkely in the Sixties,* California Newsreel.

Chapter 6: Debating the Labor Question

1. On the French uprising, see Singer, *Prelude to Revolution;* "Interview with Herbert Marcuse," *Guardian,* 9 Nov. 1968; "France The Missing Vanguard," *Guardian,* 1 June 1968; Gordon Burnside, "Notes on the New Working Class," *New Left Notes,* 5 Aug. 1968, and Fraser, ed., *1968,* p. 201. A few new leftists expressed skepticism about the events, at least as they applied to the United States. See Staughton Lynd, "A Good Society," *Guardian,* 13 July 1968; Sidney Lens, "The Road to Power," *Liberation,* Nov. 1968.

2. "National Student Labor Project," *New Left Notes,* 24 June 1968; "Build the Campus Worker-Student Alliance," in *The University Crisis Reader, Vol. II,* ed. Wallerstein, pp. 296–300; "Ally With the Campus Worker," [*PL*] *New Left Notes,* 30 June 1968—following SDS's schism there were two *New Left Notes.* Unger, *The Movement,* ch. 6.

3. Mike Klonsky, "The State of SDS," *New Left Notes,* 24 June 1968; Sale, *SDS,* chs. 21–24; "Some Thoughts on Content and Style," *New Left Notes,* 8 July 1968; Les Coleman, "False Factionalism," *New Left Notes,* 18 Dec. 1968; Bernadine Dohrn, "No Class Today, Ruling Class Tomorrow!" *New Left Notes,* 8 Oct. 1968; Jim Pritchett, "Anti-Communism in the Movement," *New Left Notes,* 11 Dec. 1968; Jared Israel, "SLAP and the National Collective," *New Left Notes,* 18 Dec. 1968; "NC Supports Panthers," *New Left Notes,* 4 Apr. 1969; "One, Two, Three . . . Many SDS's," *Ramparts,* Sept. 1969.

4. Karen Ashley, Bill Ayers, Bernadine Dohrn, et al., "You Don't Need A Weatherman to Know Which Way the Wind Blows," in *The University Crisis Reader, Vol II,* ed. Wallerstein, pp. 260–93; "You Don't Need A Weatherman," *New Left Notes,* 18 June 1969.

5. Ashley, Ayers, Dohrn, et al., "You Don't Need A Weatherman to Know Which Way the Wind Blows"; Cathy Wilkerson quoted in Fraser, ed., *1968,* p. 312.

6. Unger, *The Movement,* ch. 6; Alan Adelson, *SDS,* ch. 13; Sale, *SDS,* chs. 21–24.

7. Adelson, *SDS,* ch. 13; Sale, *SDS,* chs. 21–24; Noel Ignatin, "Where Are We Heading?" *Guardian,* 6 July 1968; "RYM II," *New Left Notes,* 8 July 1969; Mike Klonsky, "Why I Quit," *New Left Notes,* 29 Aug. 1969; "Call for Action in Chicago," *New Left Notes,* 8 July 1969; "Bring the War Home," *New Left Notes,* 29 Aug. 1969; Mark Rudd, "Goodbye Mike," *New Left Notes,* 29 Aug. 1969.

8. Carl Davidson, "Adventurism," in *The University Crisis Reader, Vol II,* ed. Wallerstein, pp. 293; Greg Calvert, "A Left Wing Alternative," *Liberation,* May 1969; Julius Lester, "No-Longer-New Left," *Liberation,* Summer 1970; Paul Glussman, David Horowitz, Paul Booth and Todd Gitlin, "Symposium: One, Two, Three . . . Many SDS's,"*Ramparts,* Sept. 1969; Carl Oglesby, "Notes on a Decade Ready for the Dustbin," *Liberation,* Aug.-Sept. 1969; William Appleman Williams, "An American Socialist Community?" *Liberation,* June 1969; Charles Demby, *The Activist,* Feb. 1970.

9. Daniel Bell, "The End of Ideology in the West," in *The End of Ideology,* pp. 393–404.

10. Peter B. Levy, "The New Left and Labor," ch. 1; James Miller, *Democracy Is In the Streets,* ch. 6.

11. Henthoff, *Peace Agitator;* Lens, *Unrepentant Radical,* chs. 1–8.

12. C. Wright Mills, "A Who's What of Union Leadership," *Labor and Nation,* Dec. 1945, pp. 33–37; C. Wright Mills, "The People in the Unions," *Labor and Nation,* Jan.-Feb. 1947, pp. 28–31; C. Wright Mills, "What the People Think: Anti-Labor Legislation," *Labor and Nation,* Mar.-Apr. 1947, pp. 25–31; C. Wright Mills and Helen Schneider, "The Political Complexion of Union Leadership," *Labor and Nation,* July-Aug. 1947, pp. 10–12; "White Collar Unionism-Labor Democracy," *Labor and Nation,* May-June 1949, p. 17–20; C. Wright Mills, "All That and a Survey of the Left," *Labor and Nation,* Mar.-Apr. 1947, pp. 41–42; C. Wright Mills, "Grassroots Union With Ideas: The Auto Workers," *Commentary,* Mar. 1948, pp. 240–47; Mills, *The New Men of Power,* pp. 169 and 286.

13. Marcuse, "The Foundations of Historical Materialism," in *Studies in Critical Philosophy;* Clecak, *Radical Paradoxes,* pp. 175–78; Jay, *The Dialectical Imagination,* pp. 75–80.

14. Goodman, *Communitas.*

15. Mills, *The Marxists,* p. 128.

16. Williams, *Contours of American History,* p. 445; Goodman, *Growing Up Absurd,* p. 219; Marcuse, *Eros and Civilization,* pp. xiv and xxvi; and Marcuse, *One Dimensional Man,* pp. 21–34.

17. Peter B. Levy, "The New Left and Labor," ch. 1; James Miller, *Democracy Is In the Streets,* ch. 6; Mills, "The Big City: Private Troubles and Public Issues," in *Power, Politics and People,* p. 397; Mills, "Letter to the New Left," in *Power, Politics and People,* p. 256; Goodman, *Growing Up Absurd,* "Introduction"; Goodman, "Our Standard of Living," in *Drawing the Line,* pp. 255–63; Marcuse, *Eros and Civilization;* Harvey Swados, "The Myth of the Happy Worker," *The Nation,* 17 Aug. 1957.

18. On the Catholic Workers, see Piehl, *Breaking Bread*. For a sense of the writings of several independent socialists, see Cochran, ed., *American Labor at Midpassage;* the works of Paul Baran and Paul Sweezy, Philip Foner, Herbert Aptheker and others are also worth consulting.

19. Mills, "The New Left," in *Power, Politics and People,* p. 257; Oglesby, *The New Left Reader,* Introduction; for general discussions of New Left thought, see Guarsci, *The Theory and Practice of American Marxism;* and Clecak, *Radical Paradoxes.*

20. Tom Hayden, "The Politics of the Movement," *Dissent,* Jan.-Feb. 1965; Todd Gitlin, "The Radical Potential of the Poor," in *The New Left,* ed. Teodori, pp. 130–48; James O'Connor, "The Political Economy and Toward A Theory of Community Unions," *Studies on the Left,* Summer 1964.

21. Jim Williams, "On Community Unions," *Studies on the Left,* Summer 1964; "From the Editors: After the Election," *Studies on the Left,* Winter 1965, pp. 3–21; James Weinstein, Stanley Aronowitz, Lee Baxandall, Eugene Genovese and Helen Kramer, "Reply," *Studies on the Left,* Spring 1965, pp. 7–12.

22. "Against the Mainstream: Interview with James Matles of the UE," by Stanley Aronowitz, *Studies on the Left,* Winter 1965, pp. 43–54; Sidney Lens, "Radicalism: Is It Relevant," *Liberation,* May 1965.

23. Rustin, "From Protest to Politics"; Gus Tyler, "The New Challenge to Liberalism," *The American Federationist,* Nov. 1963, pp. 1–5.

24. Staughton Lynd, "Coalition Politics or Nonviolent Revolution," *Liberation,* June-July 1965.

25. Radosh, "On Hanging Up the Red Flag," pp. 217–18.

26. Dave McReynolds, "Transition: Personal and Political Notes," *Liberation,* Aug. 1965; Nat Henthoff, "Beyond the Generation Gap," *Liberation,* Aug. 1965; "Letter," *Liberation,* Oct. 1965; Irving Howe, "New Styles in Leftism," *Dissent,* Summer 1965.

27. The most incisive discussion of Black Power theory can be found in, Cruse, *The Crisis of the Negro Intellectual.* Lester, *Revolutionary Notes,* p. 16.

28. "Finally Got the News," Black Star Productions, 1970; Lester, *Revolutionary Notes,* p. 16.

29. Carmichael, "A Declaration of War," in *The New Left,* ed. Teodori, pp. 275–82; Carson, *In Struggle,* pp. 227, 237–38.

30. Carson, *In Struggle,* p. 270; William Melvin Kelley, "Black Power: A Discussion," *Partisan Review,* vol. 35, no. 2 (Spring 1968), pp. 216–17; Stokely Carmichael, "Comments," at "We Shall Not Be Moved" (SNCC Conference), 16 Apr. 1988.

31. Carmichael, "The Dialectics of Liberation," in *Stokely Speaks,* pp. ix, 77–97. Conlin, *The Troubles,* ch. 5; Julius Lester, "The White Radical as a Revolutionary," in *Revolutionary Notes,* p. 46; Cleaver, "The Black Man's Stake in Vietnam," in *Soul on Ice,* p. 125; Huey P. Newton, "An Interview," in *The New Left,* ed. Teodori, p. 289; Grine, "America Against Herself," p. 200; Rustin, "The Myth of the Black Revolt," in *The Black Revolution,* pp. 109–23.

32. John Conyers, "Politics and the Black Revolution," in *The Black Revolution*, pp. 223–34; Dymally, *The Black Politician.*

33. Mario Savio, "An End to History," in *The New Left*, ed. Teodori, p. 159; Wini Breines, *The Great Refusal*, p. 31.

34. Carl Davidson, "Toward a Student Syndicalist Movement of University Reform Revisited," in *The University Crisis Reader, Vol. II*, ed. Wallerstein, pp. 98–107; and Carl Davidson, "The Multiuniversity: Crucible of the New Working Class," in *The University Crisis Reader, Vol. I*, ed. Wallerstein, pp. 86–99.

35. Tom Hayden, "Two, Three, Many Columbias," in *The Politics and Anti-Politics of the Young*, ed. Brown.

36. Rudd, "Symbols of the Revolution," in *Up Against the Ivy Wall*, ed. Avorn, pp. 291–97.

37. James Turner, "The Black Students: A Changing Perspective," in *The Black Revolution*, pp. 161–73; Morrison and Morrison, *From Camelot to Kent State*, pp. 247–66; Avorn, et al., *Up Against the Ivy Wall*, p 48.

38. Keniston, *Youth and Dissent*, pp. 371–81.

39. SDS's response to student power can be traced in *New Left Notes*. For example, in January 1967, Nick Egleson, "Changes in Our Thinking," argued that a campus based movement was increasingly possible. By the Spring and Summer of 1967, however, the dominant argument called for moving away from just student orientation. See Robert Gotleib, George Tenney and Dave Gilbert, "Toward A Theory of Social Change in America," *New Left Notes*, 22 May 1967 and reports on the 1967 SDS convention, especially those on the draft and labor, *New Left Notes*, 26 June 1967; Carl Davidson, "The Multiuniversity: Crucible of the New Working Class"; and Carl Davidson, "The Praxis of Student Power: Strategy and Tactics," in *The University Crisis Reader, Vol. II*, ed. Wallerstein, p. 108.

40. John and Margaret Roundtree, "Youth as Class," *International Socialist Journal*, Feb. 1968.

41. Reich, *The Greening of America*, pp. 217–63; Theodore Roszak, "Youth and the Great Refusal," in *The Politics of Anti-Politics of the Young*, ed. Brown, p. 21.

42. Dave Gilbert, Bob Gotleib and Susan Southern, "Consumption: Domestic Capitalism," in *The New Left*, ed. Teodori, pp. 426–35; Conlin, *The Troubles*, pp. 79–80; on Gotleib, see Fraser, ed., *1968*, pp. 160.

43. Guarsci, *The Theory and Practice of American Marxism*, pp. 110–13; Gorz, *Strategy for Labor*, p. ix.

44. Greg Calvert, "In White America: Radical Consciousness and Social Change," in *The New Left*, ed. Teodori, pp. 412–17; Calvert and Neiman, *A Disrupted History.*

45. Greg Calvert, "In White America."

46. Carl Davidson, "The Multiuniversity: Crucible of the New Working Class," in *The University Crisis Reader, Vol. II*, pp. 96 and 99; Carl Davidson, "The New Radicals and the Multiuniversity," in *The New Left*, ed. Teodori, pp. 325; Fraser, ed., *1968*, p. 160.

47. Breines, *The Great Refusal*, ch. 6; Unger, *The Movement*, pp. 98–100; Sale, *SDS*, ch. 17.

48. Bernadine Dohrn, "Calvert's Conference," *New Left Notes*, 12 Dec. 1968; Greg Calvert, "A Left Wing Alternative," *Liberation*, May 1969; Carl Davidson, "Greg Calvert, Politics of Guilt," *Liberation*, June 1969; Greg Calvert, "Reply," *Liberation*, June 1969.

49. Ollman and Vernoff, *The Left Academy*, gives a sense of the strength of leftist thought in the wake of the organizational demise of the New Left.

50. Marcuse, *One Dimensional Man;* Marcuse, "Remarks at Guardian Dinner," in *The New Left Reader*, ed. Teodori, pp. 469–73; Marcuse, "An Essay on Liberation"; and "Freedom and the Historical Imperative," in *Studies in Critical Philosophy*.

51. For a brief autobiographical account of Aronowitz's career, see his *False Promises*, pp. 1–2. Stanley Aronowitz: "Left May Have Role in Unions," *Guardian*, 23 Dec. 1967, pp. 4–5; "Which Way for Labor," *Guardian*, 6 Jan. 1968, p. 5; "Public Workers Are Sold Out," *Guardian*, 17 Feb. 1968, p. 6; "Labor and Black Liberation: Partners?" *Guardian*, 25 May 1968, p. 7. Beginning 27 July 1968, though 28 September 1968, Aronowitz's column in the *Guardian*, "On the Line," explicitly examined the question: "What Role for the Working Class?" In these essays, Aronowitz clung to his hope for the revitalization of the labor movement, with the expectation that the rank and file could still act as an agent of change.

52. *Radical America's* editorial board initially consisted of Paul Buhle, Tom Cleaver, Henry Hostach Jr., Joseph Mewshaw and Don Slaughter, as managing editor. On *Radical America*, see James Green, ed. *Worker's Struggles Past and Present* and Buhle, *Marxism in the USA*, ch. 7.

53. Paul Buhle, ed. *Fifteen Years of Radical America*, vol. 16, No. 3; Paul Berman, "Spirit of '67," *Village Voice: Literary Supplement*, Sept. 1983, p. 16; James P. O'Brien, "The New Left," *Radical America*, vol. 2, no. 4–6; Buhle, *Marxism in* the USA, pp. 239–42.

54. Ollman and Vernoff, eds., *The Left Academy*, p. 1.

55. "No More Moanin' [Special Issue] *Southern Exposure*, vol. 1, nos. 3 and 4 and "Facing South," *Southern Exposure*, vol. 3, no. 4. Also Interview with Bob Hall, Columbia University Oral History Project.

56. Root and Branch, *Root and Branch: The Rise of the Workers Movements*, Introduction.

57. Fischer, ed., *The Revival of American Socialism*, p. vi-vii.

58. Martin Nicolaus, "The Crisis of Late Capitalism," in *The Revival of American Socialism*, pp. 3–21.

59. Irving Howe, "The Welfare State," in *The Revival of American Socialism*, pp. 63–80; Christopher Lasch, "From Culture to Politics," in *The Revival of American Socialism*, pp. 217–26.

60. John M. Cammet, "Socialism and Participatory Democracy," in *The Revival of American Socialism*, pp. 41–60.

61. John M. Cammet, "Socialism and Participatory Democracy," in *The Revival of American Socialism*, pp. 41–60.

62. Eugene Genovese, "Review of John Cammet's, 'Antonio Gramsci and the Origins of Italian Communism,'" in *Studies on the Left,* Mar.-Apr. 1967, pp. 83–107. "A Round Table: Labor, Historical Pessimism, and Hegemony," especially, John P. Diggins, "The Misuses of Gramsci," *Journal of American History,* vol. 75, no. 1 (June 1988), pp. 115–61.

63. At approximately the same time, several other journals, published by veteran socialists, began to include articles authored by new leftists, social democrats and trade unionists, including *New Politics.* For instance, in the fall and winter of 1972 and 1973, *New Politics* contained pieces by labor activists Paul Schrade and Don Stillman, as well as by Ronald Radosh, Julius Jacobson and David McReynolds. Concomitantly, Michael Harrington's commentary suggested that some sort of rapprochement with the New Left was developing. "Let me suggest . . . that the traditional protest of workers . . . and the unprecedented rebellion of the youth . . . may converge into transforming society." This statement was a far cry from the piercing critique that Harrington's colleague, Irving Howe, had leveled at the New Left in 1965. (Significantly, Harrington made it in the introduction to a book which he co-edited with Howe.) See *New Politics,* Fall 1972 and Winter 1973; Michael Harrington, "America Society: Burdens, Problems, Solutions," in *The Seventies,* ed. Howe and Harrington, pp. 36–37.

Chapter 7: Organizing the Unorganized

1. Good general works on the Farm Workers are Taylor, *Chavez and The Farm Workers;* Kushner, *Long Road to Delano;* Jacques Levy, *Chavez,* and Meister and Loftis, *A Long Time Coming.*

2. Meister and Loftis, *A Long Time Coming,* quoted on p. 134; and Jenkins, *The Politics of Insurgency,* p. 224. See also "Help Comes," *El Malcriado,* Oct. 1965.

3. See SNCC Papers, "Farm Workers," Series A:VIII; on Ganz, see Taylor, *Chavez and the Farm Workers,* pp. 141–50. See also Joe Schulman to CORE, 5 Nov. 1965; Terry Cannon to M. Farnham, 10 Apr. 1966; Cesar Chavez to Dear Friend, Dec. 1966 and Carolyn Miller to Jim Drake, 4 May 1966, all in the United Farm Workers Organizing Committee Collection (henceforth UFWOC), Box 2. The UFW was created out of the NWFA, Chavez's independent union, and the AFL–CIO's Agricultural Worker Organizing Committee (AWOC).

4. On Berkeley, see Social Protest Project, "Agricultural Labor Movement"; "The Pact Between Students and Farmworkers Reaffirmed," *El Malcriado,* 1 Mar. 1967; Caesar Chavez to Jean Himelock, 27 Oct. 1966, UFWOC Collection, Box 2.

5. "Student Committee for Agricultural Labor, 1965" "March to Madison, 1966," Box 3; and Dan Ortiz to Caesar Chavez, 13 May 1966, Box 2, UFWOC Collection; Nan Guerrero, "Migrant Unrest," *The New Student South,* vol. 4, no 1.

6. AFL–CIO, *Proceedings of the 7th Constitutional Convention, Vol. I;*
David Selvin, "The Rise of the Farm Workers Union," *American Federationist,*
May 1967, pp. 1–5; "Grape Strike Leaders Raise Cheers and Cash," *The Packinghouse Worker,* June 1966, p. 1; Meister and Loftis, *A Long Time Coming,* pp.
138–39; Jacques Levy, *Chavez,* pp. 201–5; Victor Reuther, *The Brothers Reuther,*
pp. 368–71; Jacques Levy, *Chavez,* pp. 201–5.

7. Dick Meister and Anne Loftis, *A Long Time Coming,* ch. 12; "Boycott," *El
Malcriado,* 22 Dec. 1965; "Boycott," *El Malcriado,* 26 Jan. 1966.

8. "AFL–CIO Fully Supports Consumer Boycott of DiGiorgio Corporation,"
AFL–CIO News, 14 May 1966, pp. 1–2; "National DiGiorgio Corp. Boycott
Asked in Delano Strike," *Mine-Mill Union,* June 1966, p. 6; "Boycott," *El
Malcriado,* 26 Jan. 1966, p. 1.

9. "SDS, SNCC *and* CORE Working on a 'Boston Grape Party,' " *New Left
Notes,* 25 Feb. 1966, p.2; Norman Potter, "Grape Strike Report Number 1," *New
Left Notes,* 18 Mar. 1966; "Busted, Fasting in U.C. Protest," *El Malcriado,* 15
Oct. 1968.

10. Sam Kushner, *Long Road to Delano,* p. 177.

11. "UFW Vertical File"; "Boycott Has Been 95% Effective," *El Malcriado,*
Aug. 1968; "A.P. Heir Expresses Support," *El Malcriado,* 15 Sept. 1968.

12. Sponsoring Committee of the Chicago Citizens Committee to Aid Delano
Farm Workers, Box 4, Lee Webb Papers, SHSW.

13. See assorted leaflets in "UFW Vertical File."

14. "Some Brutal Facts About Farm Labor," *RWDSU Record,* 2 Oct. 1966, p.
12. Here are some "brutal facts about farm labor," stated the *RWDSU Record.*
Farm workers earn wages well below federal minimum wages; they suffer from
long periods of unemployment and receive no protection from injury nor security for their old age. Moreover, "it is not unusual to have children working on
farms for wages."

15. Sister Mary Prudence, "The Nun's Tale," *Ramparts,* July 1966, p. 43;
Meister and Loftis, *A Long Time Coming,* ch. 5; Editorial, "Contemptible
Conduct by Certain Farmers," *OCAW News,* 2 Feb. 1965, p. 2.

16. Luis Valdez, "The Tale of La Raza," *Ramparts,* July 1966, p. 40; see also
John Lomax, "The Chicanos," *Many Pasts Vol. 2,* ed. Gutman and Kealey, pp.
443–65.

17. "Leaflet: Protest Govt. Buying Scab Grapes," Oct. 1968, Agricultural
Labor Support Committee, Social Protest Project; "Leaflet: UFW Day of Mobilization Against Pentagon Scabbing," n.d., UFW Vertical File.

18. Paul Jacobs, "Tales of the Delano Revolution," *Ramparts,* July 1966, p.
39; Paul Jacobs, *The State of the Unions.*

19. Paul Jacobs, "Tales of the Delano Revolution," *Ramparts,* July 1966,
p. 39; Paul Jacobs, *The State of the Unions;* Caesar Chavez, "Pereginacion,
Pentacia, Revolution," *New Left Notes,* 25 Mar. 1966, p. 1; Caesar Chavez,
"The Organizers Tale," *Ramparts,* July 1966, pp. 43–50; Taylor, *Chavez and
the Farm Workers,* p. 154; Kushner, *Long Road,* p. 178; "Telegram, from Dr.
Martin Luther King Jr. to Caesar Chavez," *El Malcriado,* 15 Apr. 1968.
This was one of King's last statements as he was assassinated shortly after

writing it. Chavez had a deep admiration for King and attended his funeral in April 1968.

20. Taylor, *Chavez and the Farm Workers,* ch. 12; Meister and Loftis, *A Long Time Coming,* ch. 10, 11.

21. Jacques Levy, *Caesar Chavez;* Taylor, *Chavez and the Farm Workers,* ch. 8; S. Kushner, *Long Road,* ch. 9; "NFWA and AFL-CIO Merge: A Movement Analysis," *New Left Notes,* 23 Sept. 1966.

22. Taylor, *Chavez and the Farm Workers,* p. 197.

23. "MFLU," Series A:XVII, SNCC Papers; Hammer, *To Praise Our Bridges,* p. 18; "Mississippi Freedom Labor Union, Origins," in *Black Protest,* ed. Grant, pp. 498-500; *NY Times,* 1 June 1965, p. 39; 4 June 1965, p. 17; 7 June 1965, p. 26; 6 June 1965, p. 1; *Student Voice,* 30 Apr. 1965; 6 June 1965.

24. "We Have No Government," in *Black Protest,* ed. Grant, pp. 500-505; "MFLU," SNCC Papers.

25. "MFLU," SNCC Papers; Liz Shirah, "Movement Turns to Economics," *Southern Patriot,* May 1965.

26. Claude Ramsay, "A Report on the Delta Farm Strike," 16 Aug. 1965; Don Slaiman to Anon., 15 Sept. 1965, Box 186, UPWA Papers; The Maryland Freedom Union sought to organize primarily poor black workers in Baltimore. Local CORE activists felt that the labor movement had failed but saw the need for economic power. Once they began to enjoy some success, however, they were opposed by local labor unionists and by national CORE officials. See Mike Flug, "Organized Labor and the Civil Rights Movement of the 1960s: The Case of the Maryland Freedom Union."

27. Leon Howell, *Freedom City* (Richmond: John Knox, 1969), pp. 30-37, 89; *NY Times,* 19 Aug. 1966, p. 20; 3 Dec. 1966, p. 42; 4 Dec. 1966, p. 5. Local supporters of the MFLU also included Mrs. Unita Blackwell, a member of the MFDP executive committee, who became Mayor of Mayersville, Mississippi.

28. "Farm Worker Strike: Revolt on the Rio Grande," *Southern Patriot,* June 1966; Doug Adair, "Texas Strike," *Liberation,* Aug. 1976; see also *El Malcriado* beginning in the late spring of 1966; AFL-CIO, *Proceedings of the Seventh Constitutional Convention, Vol. I,* pp. 438-41; "From TX: The Cry for Justice," *UAW Solidarity,* Mar. 1967; "In Texas A Time of Terror," *UAW Solidarity,* July 1967. On Brown, see David Danzig, "The Meaning of the Negro Strategy," *Commentary,* Feb. 1964, pp. 41-4; "Easter Caravan to Aid Farm Strikers in Texas," *AFL-CIO News,* 1 Apr. 1967; "Texas Rangers Break Strike," *Southern Patriot,* June 1967.

29. Nan Guerrero, "Migrant Unrest," *The New Student South,* Feb. 1967; Gene Guerrero, "Organizing Migrants," *The New Student South,* Oct. 1966.

30. "Millworkers United," *Southern Patriot,* June 1967; see also Chafe, *Civilities and Civil Rights,* pp. 173-76; Gene Guerrero, "Movement of Textile Workers," *New Student South,* Apr. 1967.

31. "Support Grows For Blue Ridge Strikers," *Southern Patriot,* Oct. 1967; Brenda Mull, "Blue Ridge Struggle Enters New Phase," *Southern Patriot,* Feb. 1968; Fred Lacy, "Blue Ridge Strike: The Untold Story," *MDS Newsletter,* Sept. 1968, pp. 2-3; "To Be Treated Like Human Beings," *MDS Newsletter,* Aug.

1966, pp. 1–5; "Blue Ridge Strike," *MDS Newsletter,* Oct. 1967; Anne Schunior, "Students and Workers Unite," *New Student South,* Apr. 1967.

32. Mike Smedberg, "The Duke Trustees and Labor," *New Student South,* Jan. 1969.

33. "Support Grows For Blue Ridge Strikers," *Southern Patriot,* Oct. 1967; Brenda Mull, "Blue Ridge Struggle Enters New Phase," *Southern Patriot,* Feb. 1968; Fred Lacey, "Blue Ridge Strike: The Untold Story," *MDS Newsletter,* Sept. 1968, pp. 2–3; "To Be Treated Like Human Beings," *MDS Newsletter,* Aug. 1966, pp. 1–5; "Blue Ridge Strike," *MDS Newsletter,* Oct. 1967.

34. Luke Carter, "Duke University Students Demand New Deal for Negro Workers," *Science,* 3 May 1968, pp. 513–17; Henry Boyte and Sara Evans, "Union Organizing at Duke," *New Left Notes,* 8 Apr. 1966, p. 2; "Students and Labor," *New Student South,* Apr. 1968. Outside the South, the SDS chapter at the University of Maine organized a support rally for striking textile workers at Owegan Woolen Mills. SDS in Boston helped the local Hospital Workers Union by raising money, mobilizing pickets and arranging for support from outside groups. Wisconsin student radicals lent their know-how and muscle to migrant Mexican-Americans who sought better wages and conditions from a local packing shed. And SDS at the University of Missouri demonstrated with non-academic employees of the Public Service Employees Union, who sought union recognition. Ken Kantro, "Maine Students Support Strike," *New Left Notes,* 11 Mar. 1966; "Boston Hospital Organizing," *New Left Notes,* 29 Apr. 1966; Hal Benson, "Labor Project in Boston," *New Left Notes,* 14 Oct. 1966; Jim Russell, "Migrant Strike," *New Left Notes,* 28 Oct. 1966; Gordon Burnside, "Missouri Report," *New Left Notes,* 18 Nov. 1966.

35. Unfortunately for historians SSOC's papers do not exist because a paranoid SSOC member, fearing government persecution, burnt them. Most of my discussion of SSOC, therefore, is based on interviews at the Oral History Collection of Columbia University, part of Ron Grele's and Bret Eynon's study of the 1960s. These include interviews of Sue Thrasher, Eugene Guerrero, Rob and Jackie Hall, Cathy Cade, Harlan and Barbara Joyce and Jeff Jones. I have also drawn on the reportage of the *Southern Patriot, The New Student South,* and the *MDS Newsletter* for the years 1966, 1967 and 1968 and a smattering of SSOC documents found in the collections of various individual activists.

36. Interviews with Sue Thrasher, Cathy Cade, Eugene Guerrero, Oral History Collection, Columbia University; "We Take Our Stand," 4 Apr. 1964; "Proposal of Organization"; Todd Gitlin to Sam Shirah, 4 Feb. 1964; "Southern Student Organizing Committee [Minutes of first and second meetings, prepared by Ronnie Parker]; all in Sam Shirah Papers. Several of SSOC's founders had participated in the Mississippi Summer white folks project.

37. Interview with Eugene Guerrero; "Millworkers Unite," *Southern Patriot,* June 1967; Gene Guerrero, "Movement of Textile Workers," *New Student South,* Apr. 1967.

38. Interview with Eugene Guerrero; "Millworkers Unite," *Southern Patriot,* June 1967.

39. Sacks, *Caring by the Hour,* ch. 2.

40. "Report on the SSOC Student and Labor Conference," 23–24 Apr. 1966, Lee Webb Papers; Robb Burlage, "On Political Strategy," *New Student South,* Mar. 1966. See also Steve Wise, "Working With Liberals," *New Student South,* (Nov. 1966).

41. *El Malcriado,* Sept. 1965; "Southern Labor Movement: Statement of Purpose," *MDS Newsletter,* 22 Aug. 1966.

42. *MDS Newsletter,* Oct. 1967.

43. Ibid., Interviews with Susan Thrasher, Bob and Jackie Hall, Eugene Guerrero, Jeff Jones, and Barbara and Harlan Joyce.

44. Interview with Bob Zellner, by author, 24 Nov. 1987, New York City; Robert Analavage, "Laurel Strike Is Broken," *Southern Patriot,* Jan. 1968.

45. Interview with Bob Zellner; Robert Analavage, "Workers Strike Back," *Southern Patriot,* Oct. 1968.

46. Interview with Bob Zellner; Robert Analavage, "Workers Strike Back," *Southern Patriot,* Oct. 1968; Jerry Lembcke and Tattam, *One Union In Wood,* ch. 7.

47. See numerous correspondences between Walter Tillow and Robert Lewis, Ben Smith and Jules Bernstein in the winter of 64–65; C.H. Mayer to Walter Tillow, 22 Dec. 1964; Walter Tillow to Carl Braden, 25 Dec. 1964; "List of Those Who Attended Labor Workshop"; all in Walter Tillow Papers.

48. Marjorie Merrill to Walter Tillow, 11 Feb. 1965; Judy Walborne, "The SNCC Labor Conference at Highlander"; Hershel Kaminsky to Walter Tillow, 10 Feb. 1965, Harold Gibbons to Walter Tillow, 29 Jan, 29, 1965; all in Walter Tillow Papers.

49. The best work on the strike is Joan Turner Beifuss, *At the River I Stand.* See also Green, "Labor in the South"; J. E. Stanfield, "Memphis: More than a Garbage Strike," *Current,* May 1968; "Memphis Garbage Worker Strike," *Southern Patriot,* Mar. 1968.

50. Beifuss, *At the River I Stand,* pp. 27–31.

51. Ibid., chs. 2–4.

52. Ibid., ch. 4.

53. Earl Green, "Labor in the South," ch. 5; see also Foner, *Organized Labor and the Black Worker, 1619—1973,* ch. 24; Goulden, *Jerry Wurf,* ch. 5.

54. Lewis, *King,* pp. 378–97; Oates, *Let the Trumpet Sound,* ch. 7; Norman Pearlstine, "A Powerful Negro Coalition," *Wall Street Journal,* 8 Mar. 1968.

55. Beifuss, *At the River I Stand,* ch. 10.

56. Ibid., chs. 11, 12; quoted pp. 277–79.

57. Lewis, *King,* pp. 378–97; Oates, *Let the Trumpet Sound,* ch. 7; Earl Green, "Labor In the South," ch. 6; P. Foner, *Organized Labor,* pp. 383–85.

58. "Summary of Violence," *Guardian,* 14 Apr. 1968, p. 2; Robert Allen, "King: His Death and Dilemma," *Guardian,* 13 Apr. 1968; "The Execution of Dr. King," *Ramparts,* May 1968; Eldridge Cleaver, "Requiem for Nonviolence," *Ramparts,* May 1968; Lester, "The Death of Martin Luther King, Jr." and "The Funeral of Martin Luther King, Jr.," in *Revolutionary Notes,* pp. 82–90.

59. Beifuss, *At the River I Stand,* chs. 14, 15; quote from pp. 340–51.

60. Ibid., pp. 340–51.

61. Ibid., ch. 16.

62. "Labor, Rights Coalition Presses Hospital Strike," *AFL-CIO News,* 12 Apr. 1969; "Negro Leaders Swell Support of Striking Hospital Workers," *AFL–CIO News,* 26 Apr. 1969; "Meany Pledges Labor Aid In Charleston," *AFL–CIO News,* 3 May 1969; Foner, *Women and the American Labor Movement,* ch. 22; Steven Hoffius, "Charleston Hospital Workers' Strike, 1969," in *Working Lives,* ed. Mark Miller, pp. 244–58; Jack Bass, "Strike at Charleston," *New South,* Summer, 1969, pp. 35–44; Foner, *Organized Labor and the Black Worker,* pp. 386–96; Jim Grant, "The Organized Unorganized," *Southern Exposure,* vol. 4, no. 1–2, pp. 132–35.

63. Sacks, *Caring By the Hour,* pp. 52–53.

64. Jack Conway and Woodrow L. Ginsburg, "The Extension of Collective Bargaining to New Fields," 29 Dec. 1966; "Resolution: AFL–CIO IUD Community Center," Tom Kahn to Robert Curvin, 31 Dec. 1965; "Conference on Working Poor and Union Centers," 31 Mar. 1966; "JOIN the IUD Community Union," [leaflet]; "The Lawndale Union to End the Slums"; all in Box 32, George Chiakulas Collection; Brooks, *Walls Came Tumbling Down,* p. 276–77. In addition to being influenced by SDS's ERAPs, the I.U.D. projects displayed the influence of independent activists Saul Alinsky. See Horwitt, *They Call Me Rebel.*

65. A good history of labor in the 1960s has yet to be written. Most works on the labor movement in the postwar era focus on two themes: 1) labor's stagnancy under the leadership of George Meany (largely the result of the purge of the communists and the marriage of the House of Labor to the Democratic party). This led to Meany's unquestioning support for the Cold War, including Vietnam and the labor movement's poor record on integration, especially in the craft unions. 2) The failure of labor to launch a successful organizing drive, especially amongst women or in the South. Perhaps when a history of labor of the 1960s is written, it will paint a more complex picture of labor's political views, based in part on my discussions here, and will note that the labor movement actually grew during the 1960s from 18.1 million to 20.7 million members. (In terms of the percent of the total work force it had a slight decline, from 23.6 percent to 22.6 percent of the total work force.) Much of this growth came among public employees and from white collar workers, two of the most likely recipients of New Left support. Though labor union membership in the South did not take off, it did increase in absolute size. Obviously, compared to the period 1935–45, labor's performance in the 1960s can be seen as dismal. But in comparison to the history of labor from 1945 to 1985, the 1960s look much better.

Chapter 8: Solidarity on the Labor Front

1. Morry Wright, "Oil Strike Given Help By Students," *Guardian,* 15 Feb. 1969, p. 4; Rich Hyland, "Workers Join Students," *Guardian,* 15 Feb. 1969, p. 4; "S.F. State Students, Workers Ally," *Guardian,* 15 Mar. 1969, p. 8; "Bay Area Oil Striker Killed," *Guardian,* 15 Mar. 1969, p. 8; "Workers Call Standard Oil

Boycott," *Guardian,* 8 Mar. 1969, p. 9; Morry Wright, "Oil Strike in Bay Area," *Guardian,* 15 Mar. 1969, p. 3; "Viewpoint: Victory in Oil," *Guardian,* 15 Mar. 1969, p. 12; Jeff Jones, "Reciprocal Support," *New Left Notes,* 21 Feb. 1969; "Boycott Standard Oil," *New Left Notes,* 17 Apr. 1969, p. 2; "Standard Oil: Interview of G.T. Jacobs," *New Left Notes,* 24 Apr. 1969.

2. "Meany Warns G.E. Struggle All-Out Challenge to Labor," *AFL–CIO News,* 18 Nov. 1969; "Labor Rallies Full Support of G.E.," *AFL–CIO News,* 1 Nov. 1969; "$50 Million All-Union Fund Urged to Aid G.E. Srikers," *UAW Solidarity,* Dec. 1969, p. 2. " Minutes of Movement to Support the GE Strikers," 3 Jan. 1970, Box 1, Paul Booth Papers.

3. Peter Brimlow, "A Look Back At Boulwarism," *Forbes,* 29 May 1989, pp. 246–47.

4. Stanley Aronowitz, "Opportunity for Left Seen in G.E. Strike," *Guardian,* 6 Dec. 1969, p. 18; "Viewpoint: G.E. Strike," *Guardian,* 6 Dec. 1969, p. 10; Carl Davidson, "Workers-Scabs Clash in G.E. Strike," *Guardian,* 8 Nov. 1969, p. 5; Fred Kushner, "Marrch-Support G.E. Strikers," *New Left Notes,* 13 Nov. 1969; "7500 Support G.E. Workers," *New Left Notes,* 10 Dec. 1969; "Workers Attack 'National Interest'," *Progressive Labor,* Feb. 1970, pp. 3–6.

5. The best source on the student-worker alliance in the Boston area is the underground newspaper, *The Old Mole.* See Jon Schwartz, "on Strike Against G.E." *Old Mole,* 7–21 Nov. 1969, p. 7; "Strike Against G.E. Has Many Sides," *Old Mole,* 21 Nov.–4 Dec. 1969, pp. 8–9; "Come to Tea With G.E. at B.C.: RSVP, Yessiree!" *Old Mole,* 21 Nov.–4 Dec. 1969, pp. 8–9; "Unholy Cross," *Old Mole,* 17 Dec.–8 Jan. 1970, p. 8; "G.E. Disrupter at MIT," *Old Mole,* 9–27 Jan. 1970, p. 8; "MIT Occupation," *Old Mole,* 23 Jan.–5 Feb. 1970, p. 3.

6. "G.E. at B.U." *Old Mole,* 7–21 Nov. 1969, p. 9; "B.U.(st)," *Old Mole,* 5–16 Dec. 1969, p. 3; "Boston Students," *UE News,* 15 Dec. 1969.

7. "5 Jailed for B.U. Sit-in," *Old Mole,* 17 Dec.–8 Jan. 1970, p. 2; "BU Strike," *Old Mole,* 6–19 Mar. 1970, p. 6.

8. Susy Orchard, "Women's Work at G.E.," *Old Mole,* 9–27 Jan. 1970, p. 8; "Bread and Roses Learn From G.E. Women," *Old Mole,* 6–19 Feb. 1970, p. 14.

9. Matles and Higgins, *Them and Us,* ch. 17; Hal Benson to Lee Webb, n.d.; Steve Max to Lee Webb, n.d.; Walter [Tillow] to Lee Webb, 17 May 1966; Lee Webb to Hal Benson, n.d.; all in Box 4, Lee Webb Papers. "Students and District 1 Members Talk," *UE News,* 23 Mar. 1971; "Boston Students," *UE News,* 15 Dec. 1969.

10. "G.E. Bargaining Unit Disavows SDS Acts," *AFL–CIO News,* 22 Nov. 1969, p. 3; "G.E. Strikers Strengthened By Wide Boycott Support," *AFL–CIO News,* 20 Dec. 1969, p. 1.

11. "Parallel to G.E. Struggle Seen In Student Unrest," *AFL–CIO News,* 20 Dec. 1969, p. 3; "G.E. Strike Activity Spurs Youth to Do Their Thing," *AFL–CIO News,* 17 Jan. 1970, p. 3.

12. "N.C. Resolves: Support G.E. Strike," *New Left Notes,* Jan. 1970, p. 4; "G.E. And SDS," *New Left Notes,* 5 Feb. 1970, p. 1; "G.E. Strike Ends: Victory for the Workers or the Bosses," *New Left Notes,* 16 Mar. 1970,

p. 15; Walter Linder, "Sellout Is Still The Word," *Progressive Labor,* June 1970, pp. 11–15.

13. "Movement to Support the G.E. Strikers," *Liberation,* Feb. 1970, pp. 5–12; "G.E. Strike: A Settlement," *Old Mole,* 20 Feb.–5 Mar. 1970; Jon Schwartz and Bill Callahan, "The Emergence of a Workers Left," *Old Mole,* 20 Feb.–5 Mar. 1970, p. 8; "G. E. Strike Appears Over," *Guardian,* 2 Feb. 1970, p. 7; Stanley Aronowitz, "Analysis of G.E. Strike Settlement," *Guardian,* 14 Feb. 1970; "Students and District 1 Members Talk," *UE News,* 23 Mar. 1971.

14. Stanley Aronowitz and Jeremy Brecher, "Notes on the Postal Strike," *Root and Branch,* June 1970, pp. 1–5; Kevin Bradley and Tom Condit, "The Postal Strike," *International Socialist,* Apr. 1970; Karl Fisher, "The Mail Strike," *Fifth Estate,* 15 Apr. 1970, p. 1; "Mail Impaled," *Helix,* 26 Mar. 1970, p. 3; "Great Strikers of Our Time," *Helix,* 9 Apr. 1970; "Govt. Workers Revolt," *Long Beach Free Press,* 2 Apr. 1970, p. 1.

15. Jack Weinberg, "Reasons Why the Postal Workers Strike," *L.A. Free Press,* 27 Mar. 1970, p. 9; "The Postal Strike," *Old Mole,* 3 Apr. 1970, p. 3; Kevin Bradley and Tom Condit, "The Postal Strike," *International Socialist,* Apr. 1970.

16. "Reflections on the Postal Strike," *Distant Drummer,* 2 Apr. 1970, p. 5; Jack Weinberg, "Reasons Why the Postal Workers Strike," *L.A. Free Press,* 27 Mar. 1970, p. 9; Kevin Bradley and Tom Condit, "The Postal Strike," *International Socialist,* Apr. 1970.

17. "Reflections on the Postal Strike," *Distant Drummer,* 2 Apr. 1970, p. 5; "Great Strike of Our Time," *Helix,* 9 Apr. 1970.

18. "Strike Stamped," *Berkeley Tribe,* 3 Apr. 1970, p. 4; Jeremy Brecher and Stanley Aronowitz, "Notes on the Postal Strike," *Root and Branch,* June 1970. pp. 1–5; Kevin Bradley and Tom Condit, "The Postal Strike," *International Socialist,* Apr. 1970.

19. Wayne Price, "Racism in Auto," *Workers Power,* 11 Sept. 1970, p. 5; James Coleman, "GM on the Attack," *Workers Power,* 9 Oct. 1970; p. 5; "GM Strike: Wallposter," *Fifth Estate,* Nov. 1970; "Shut Down GM: In 1937 We Did It," *Rising Up Angry,* Fall 1970, p. 9; "Mark of Accidents," *Berkeley Tribe,* 12 Dec. 1970.

20. "Shut Down GM," *Rising Up Angry,* Fall 1970; "The Strike and the UAW," *Fifth Estate,* Nov. 1970; "Back to Work at GM," *Berkeley Tribe,* 12 Dec. 1970.

21. "On the Line With the UAW," *L.A. Free Press,* 18 Sept. 1970, p. 13; Karl Fischer and James Coleman, "Auto Strike: 1970," *Workers Power,* 11 Sept. 1970, pp. 3–4; Karl Fisher, "Auto: Organize to Win," *Workers Power,* 25 Sept. 1970, p. 4; James Coleman, "GM on the Attack," *Workers Power,* 9 Oct. 1970, p. 5.

22. Carl Wagner to Paul Booth, 16 Nov. 1970; "Detroit Meeting of ALA Worker-Student Strike Support Area Coordinators," 24 Oct. 1970; "Support the Auto Workers Strike Against GM"; all in Box 4, Paul Booth Papers.

23. "Support Auto Workers," *New Left Notes,* 28 Sept. 1970; "Boycott GM," *New Left Notes,* 24 Oct. 1970, p. 5; "March on GM: SDS Rallies 2600," *New Left Notes,* 22 Nov. 1970; "Over 1000 People Demonstrate in Solidarity with GM,"

Guardian, 21 Nov. 1970, p. 2; "Support the Auto Workers' Strike Against GM," Paul Booth Papers.

24. See biography of Paul Booth, Paul Booth Papers. The Labor Workshop consisted of veteran new leftists and reform-minded trade unionists, such as Steve Zelluck of the AFT, Peter Brandon, Stanley Aronowitz and Ken McEldowney (a former SDS member himself). It met on an irregular basis, beginning with a conference in Morgantown, West Virginia, in October 1969, with the expressed goal of fostering rank and file militancy. As McEldowney's put it: the Labor Workshop sought "to parallel the various functions of the union and demonstrate that we in fact represent the rank and file." This strategy resembled that of several other New Left adventures throughout the 1960s, most notably that of MFDP and of various freedom schools and universities. Ken [McEldowney] to Paul Booth, 22 July 1969; "Report on Morgantown Conference," Oct. 1969; "Report on Washington Meeting," Jan. 1970; all in Box 4, Paul Booth Papers.

25. Steve Max to Paul Booth and Lee Webb, n.d., Box 4, Lee Webb Papers.

26. Gannon, *Biographical Dictionary of the Left,* pp. 429–31; John Cory, "Spokesman for the New Left," *NY Times Magazine,* 23 Jan. 1966, pp. 12–18; *NY Times,* 28 Dec. 1965, p. 10.

27. John Cory, "Spokesman for the Left"; Interview with Staughton Lynd, St. Louis, Missouri, Apr. 1989, by author.

28. Staughton Lynd, "Guerilla History in Gary," *Liberation,* Oct. 1969, pp. 17–20; Staughton and Alice Lynd, eds., *Rank and File,* pp. 1–2.

29. Staughton Lynd, "Ernest Mandel's America," in S. Lynd and Alperovitz, *Strategy and Program;* Interview with Staughton Lynd.

30. Joel Stein, "Review of *American Working Class in Transition,* by Kim Moody," *Root and Branch,* June 1970, p. 28; Kim Moody and Sy Landy, "The Unions Under Monopoly Capitalism," *Workers Power,* May 1970, p. 9; In addition to Booth, Lynd and Moody, many other New Left veterans turned their attention, some permanently to labor. Jack Weinberg, for instance, went to work in a Detroit auto plant in 1968 and subsequently married a union organizer. See Morrison, *From Kent State to Camelot,* pp. 231–32.

31. James Green, *The World of the Worker,* p. 220; Ted Farrow, "Vega Speedup," *Workers Power,* Mar. 1972, p. 1.

32. Kit Lyons, "Lordstown's Revolt Against Speedup," *Workers Power,* 4 Feb. 1972, p. 1; James Green, *World of the Worker,* p. 220.

33. John Hillinson, "Lordstown," *Liberation,* Apr. 1972, p. 24; Gil Green, *What's Happening to Labor,* pp. 195–97. As they had with the GE, Postal Workers and GM strikes, new leftists heralded the action of the rank and file against greedy mine operators and "bought off" union leaders. Bill Gerchow, "Reign of Terror in the UMW," *Workers Power,* Feb. 1970, p . 7; Jack Weinberg, "Mountain Men to Review Traditions," *L.A. Free Press,* Feb. 1972, p. 12.

34. Gil Green, *What's Happening to Labor,* p. 201; James Green, *World of the Worker,* p. 214 and 244; Staughton Lynd, "Conversations With Steel Mill Rebels," *Ramparts,* Dec. 1972.

35. Samuel R. Friedman, *Teamster Rank and File;* "Teamster Insurgency,"

Guardian, 3 June 1970; "Striking Phone Workers," *Guardian,* 26 June 1972; "LA Teamsters Wildcat Aided by Students," *Liberation,* 13 June 1970; George Sullivan, "Steelhaulers," *Liberation,* May 1971; George Sullivan, "One Workingman's Revolution," *Liberation,* May 1971. On the AFT challenge, see Alan Newman to Whom It May Concern, 20 June 1974, Folder 16, Box 5, Teaching Assistant's Association Papers [henceforth TAA Papers]. Indeed, if the New Left press was a perfect reflection of its attitudes, which it is not, than one might conclude that the New Left had become an appendage of labor, as stories on the rise of the rank and file were rivaled only by those on the women's and gay liberation movements and the Black Panthers. In sharp contrast to the focus of the underground press of the mid–1960s, the papers now highlighted the actions and concerns of the working class. New papers appeared, including *The Bay Area Worker, Workers Voice* (Dayton), *Strike Back* (New York City), *Movin on Up* (Cincinnati), *We the People* (Madison), *On the Line* (St. Louis), *Workers Power* (Detroit) and *Rising Up* (Philadelphia). *The Dayton Worker Voice* issue of August 1972 exemplified the coverage of these publications, with articles on working conditions in local factories, local strikes, a recent black workers conference, unemployment, the Vietnam Vets Against the War (presumably a working class organization) and the costs of the Vietnam War. In addition, periodicals of smaller old left groups, such as *People's World, Militant* and *International Socialist,* which had always covered labor issues, increased their readership, especially among student activists, and covered an even broader array of worker issues than the underground press. Furthermore, the most widely read New Left journals, *Liberation, Ramparts* and *Guardian* increased their coverage of the same. For example, *Guardians'* September 1970 issue contained the following stories: "Farmworkers Extend Strike Action"; "Rail, Auto Workers Near Strike"; "GOP Woos Working Class Votes"; "Teachers for Peace in Vietnam"; "Auto Workers Halt Largest Corporation"; and "New Films Distort Workers."

36. On Madison in general, see "The War At Home" and Buhle, *History and the New Left*.

37. Peter Wiley, "A History," [Draft] n.d., Folder 1, Box 1; Henry W. Haslich Jr., "The University of Wisconsin Teaching Assistants Association," n.d., Folder 21, Box 6; both in TAA Papers.

38. Peter Wiley, "A History"; Henry Haslich, "The Univ. of Wisc. Teaching Assistant Association," and "The Madison Teaching Assistants' Association: From Pressure Group to Industrial Union," n.d.; all in Folder 21, Box 6, TAA Papers.

39. Ibid.

40. Ibid.

41. Ibid.

42. Ibid.; "Is The TAA A Bread-And-Butter Union?" *TAA Newsletter,* Oct 6, 1969, Folder 11, Box 1, TAA Papers.

43. Moreover, the TAA also aided organizing drives among other teaching assistants around the country. It played an especially helpful role in getting one started at the University of Minnesota. *TAA Newsletter,* 17 Nov. 1969; *TAA*

Newsletter, 30 Oct. 1970; see also the minutes of meeting in 1969 and 1970, Folder 4, Box 1, TAA Papers.

44. "Minutes," 3 Feb. 1969; "Minutes," 4 Dec. 1969; "Minutes," 10 Mar. 1969; "Minutes," 5 Apr. 1970; "Minutes," 23 Sept. 1970; all in Folder 4, Box 1, TAA Papers.

45. *TAA Newsletter,* 12 Nov. 1973; TAA, "History" [pamphlet] in author's possession.

46. "Resolution," 3 Dec. 1974, Folder 5, Box 1, TAA Papers; see also Folder 1, Box 7, TAA Papers. On Muehlenkamp, see Leon Fink and Brian Greenberg, *Upheaval in the Quiet Zone.*

47. *UAW Solidarity,* Dec. 1970, p. 6; "UAW Students Launch Joint Project," *UAW Solidarity,* Mar.-Apr. 1971; John D. Compton, "Victory at GE: How It Was Done," *American Federationist,* July 1970, pp. 1–8; Tom Kahn, "American Youth: Which Way Now," *American Federationist,* Sept. 1970, pp. 1–5; Editorial, "Students Now Our Allies," *El Malcriado,* 15 June 1970, p. 2; "Worker-Student Coalition Seen," *El Malcriado,* 15 June 1970, p. 6.

48. James Higgins, "Unions and Campus: Talking Together," *The Nation,* 6 Sept. 1971, pp. 171–74; Penn Kemble, "Rediscovering American Labor," *Commentary,* Apr. 1971, pp. 45–52; Benjamin Masse, "Intellectuals Start Wooing Trade Unions," *America,* 9 Jan. 1971, p. 33; Victor Reuther quoted in, Deborah Shapley, "Labor-Campus Link," *Science,* 30 Oct. 1970, pp. 516–18; Anon., "Academic-Labor Alliance Formally Established," *Science,* 6 Nov. 1970, p. 614.

49. Patti Lee Parmalee, "Bay Area Meeting On Working Class," *Guardian,* 21 Feb. 1970.

50. Boyte and Evans, *The Backyard Revolution.*

51. Hartmann, *From Margin to Mainstream;* Harrison, *On Account of Sex,* chs. 5–7.

52. Harrison, *On Account of Sex,* 176–82; Hartman, *From Margin to Mainstream.*

53. Hartman, *From Margin to Mainstream,* 62–76; Harrison, *On Account of Sex,* ch. 10; Foner, *Women and the American Labor Movement,* ch. 24; Freeman, *The Politics of Women's Liberation,* pp. 55–56.

54. Freeman, *The Politics of the Women's Movement,* pp. 57–63; Hartman, *From Margin to Mainstream,* pp. 62–72.

55. Ruth Milkman, "Women Workers, Feminism and the Labor Movement," in *Women, Work and Protest,* ed. Milkman, p. 307.

56. Foner, *Women and the American Labor Movement,* p 516.

57. Freeman, *The Politics of Women's Liberation,* p. 166.

58. Annamarie Troger, "The Coalition of Labor Union Women: Strategic Hope, Tactical Despair," *Radical America,* Fall 1975.

59. Patricia Cayo Sexton, "Workers (Female) Arise!" *Dissent,* Summer 1974, pp. 380–96.

60. Ruth Milkman, "Women Workers, Feminism and the Labor Movement," in *Women Work, and Protest,* ed. Milkman, p. 315.

61. Cathy Tuley, "Clerical Workers Unite," in *Modern American Women,* ed. Ware, pp. 378–83.

62. Baxandall, Gordon, and Reverby, eds., *America's Working Women,* p xvi.

63. *The American Annual,* 1969, 1970, and 1971.

Chapter 9: Testing the Political Waters

1. Greenstone, *Labor in American Politics;* White, *The Making of the President, 1960;* James Miller, *Democracy Is In the Streets;* Gitlin, *The Sixties.*

2. Carson, *In Struggle,* chs. 3–4, 9.

3. Zinn, *SNCC,* ch. 12; Viorst, *Fire in the Streets,* pp. 269–70; Carmichael and Hamilton, *Black Power,* p. 96.

4. Carmichael quoted in Lawson, *In Pursuit of Power,* pp. 57, 61.

5. Bond quoted in Lawson, *In Pursuit of Power,* p. 91 and Nathan Wright, *What Black Politicians Are Saying,* pp. 136–37; Marble, *Race, Reform and Rebellion,* p. 167; Dymally, ed., *The Black Politician,* pp. 11–13, 61–63; Carl Braden, "How Poor People Built Political Power," *The Southern Patriot,* Feb. 1971, pp. 1–8; Evers, *Evers;* E. C. Foster, "A Time of Challenges: Afro-Mississippi Political Developments Since 1965," *Journal of Negro History,* Spring, 1983.

6. Lawson, *In Pursuit of Power,* p. 97.

7. Aaron Henry to Dear Friend, 9 Aug. 1968, Box 4, Aaron Henry Papers; *Congressional Quarterly Weekly Report,* 23 Aug. 1968, pp. 2242–54; *Congressional Quarterly Weekly Report,* 30 Aug. 1968, pp. 2283–2308; *NY Times,* 21 Aug. 1968, p. 1. The credential committee ruled in favor of challengers in two other cases, both of which involve racial discrimination. Georgia's delegation was split in half, with Lester Maddox's and Julian Bond's slate receiving equal voting rights. The Alabama regulars were forced to take a loyalty oath, to support the party nominee, not George Wallace, and a handful of insurgents from the National Democratic party took the seats of those delegates who proved unwilling to do so. Notably, Joe Rauh assisted the Georgia and Alabama challengers.

8. Lawson, *In Pursuit of Power; Congressional Quarterly Weekly Report,* 23 Aug. 1968, pp. 2242; *Congressional Quarterly Weekly Report,* 30 Aug. 1968, pp. 2283–2308.

9. Metcalf, *Up from Within;* Christopher, *Black Americans in Congress;* see also the special issue of *The Black Scholar,* Oct. 1975, which examines "Black Politics," including: John Conyers Jr., "Toward Black Political Empowerment: Can the System Be Transformed?" pp. 2- 7; Daniel Powell, "PAC to COPE: Thirty-Two Years of Southern Labor in Politics," in *Essays in Southern Labor History,* ed. by Fink and Merle Reed, pp. 244–57; Evers, *Evers,* Rustin, "Coalition: the Only Route to Victory," *Memo From COPE,* 27 Apr. 1970; Bayard Rustin, "Labor and Minorities: Power at the Polls," *Memo From COPE,* 15 Mar. 1971; Hampton and Fayer, *Voices of Protest,* pp. 621–46.

10. William Strickland, "Whatever Happened to the Politics of Black Liberation?" *Black Scholar,* Oct. 1975, pp. 20–26; Amiri Baraka, "Needed: A Revolutionary Strategy," *Black Scholar,* Oct. 1975, pp. 42–43; Julius Hobson, "Black

Power: Right or Left?" in *The Black Politician*, ed., Dymally, pp. 132–35; Marble, *Race, Reform and Rebellion*, pp. 137–38 and 150.

11. Marble, *Race, Reform and Rebellion*, pp. 137–38; Poinsett, *Black Power Gary Style*, pp. 77–88, 96; Brisbane, *Black Activism*, ch. 11.

12. "Hatcher Inaugurated at Gary: Asks Labor Help in Remaking Steel City," *Steel Labor*, Feb. 1968, p. 2; Richard Hatcher, "Address," *Steel Labor*, Sept. 1968, p. 3.

13. Richard Hatcher, "Address," *Steel Labor*, Sept. 1968, p. 3.

14. Harman Henkin, "Three Days on Mifflin Street," *The Nation*, 26 May 1969, pp. 653–54; Paul Bluestein, "Madison's Golden Coalition," *The Nation*, 25 June 1973, pp. 817–20; Dan Schwartz, "Madison Elects Radical Mayor," *Ramparts*, July 1973, pp. 12–14; John Patrick Hunter, "And in Madison," *New Republic*, 30 Mar. 1968, pp. 18–19.

15. Phil Huslanger, "Madison's Radical Mayor," *The Progressive*, June 1975, p. 31; Paul Bluestein, "Madison's Golden Coalition," *The Nation*, 25 June 1973, pp. 817–20; Dan Schwartz, "Madison Elects Radical Mayor," *Ramparts*, July 1973, pp. 12–14.

16. Dan Schwartz, "Madison Elects Radical Mayor," *Ramparts*, July 1973, pp. 12–14; Philip Altbach and Dennis Carlson, "Militants in Politics," *Society*, July-Aug. 1976, pp. 54- 57.

17. Edward Glynn, "Enter Ron Dellums: Radical," *America*, 5 Dec. 1970, pp. 483–87; Christopher, *Black Americans in Congress* , pp. 272–77; George Metcalf, *Up from Within*.

18. Earl Caldwell, "Black Insurgent Who Won Berkeley Race is an Outspoken Radical," *NY Times*, 14 June 1970, p. 46.

19. Bush, *The New Black Vote*, pp. 315–36.

20. R.W. Apple Jr., "Negro Candidate Succeeds Too Well," *NY Times*, 24 Sept. 1970, p. 32.

21. *Memo From Cope*, 26 Oct. 1970, p. 3; "Legislative Contests Hold Balance of Power," *Dispatcher*, 23 Oct. 1970, p. 2.

22. Jack Slater, "Ron Dellums and the Politics of Niggers," *Ebony*, May 1972, pp. 88–95.

23. Shirley Chisholm, "Ghetto Power: The Value of Positive Political Action," in *The Black Politician*, ed. Dymally, pp. 40–43, 57–60; Chisholm, *Unbound and Unbossed*, describes her rise to Congress; John Knifer, "Farmer and a Woman in Lively Bedford-Stuyvesant Race," *NY Times*, 26 Oct. 1968, p. 21.

24. Chisholm, *Unbound and Unbossed;* New York State AFL-CIO, *COPE Newsletter*, Oct. 1968.

25. Chisholm, *Unbound and Unbossed*, pp. 163–69; Schlesinger, *The New Reformers*, p. 27.

26. Foner, *Women and the American Labor Movement*, pp. 110–111 and 115.

27. Foner, *Woman and the American Labor Movement*, p. 115.

28. Chester, *An American Melodrama*, p. 97 and McCarthy, *The Year of the People*, pp. 68–84; Chafe, *The Unfinished Journey*, pp. 348–56.

29. Johnny Appleseed, "Eugene and Lyndon," *New Left Notes*, 25 Mar. 1968,

p. 1; Greg Calvert, "Elections and the Elect," *New Left Notes,* 25 Mar. 1968, p.
1; Paul Buhle, "On Electoral Politics," *The Call,* Mar. 1968.

30. Gillon, *The Politics and Vision,* pp. 192–93.

31. James Weschler, "What Makes McCarthy Run," *The Progressive,* Jan.
1968, p.p. 23–26; "Tabled Resolutions: Electoral Politics," *New Left Notes,* 8
Apr. 1968; John Lamb, "The Real McDove," *New Left Notes,* 15 Apr. 1968, p. 2;
Anon., "Working for McCarthy," *New Left Notes,* 22 Apr. 1968.

32. Chafe, *The Unfinished Journey,* pp. 360–73; Chester, *An American Melodrama,* pp. 62–97; Hayden, *Reunion,* pp. 263–69 and 285–90. Hayden very closely
watched the Kennedy campaign, even talking with top RFK aide Richard Goodwin.

33. Evidence of working class support for both RFK and McCarthy can be
found in various poll data. See *Gallup Poll Index,* May 1968, pp. 9–13. These
surveys showed that among manual workers, in April 1968, 34 percent of the
respondents favored RFK, 27 percent McCarthy, 23 percent Humphrey and 16
percent had no opinion. Among people who had incomes below $4,999, the
candidates were favored in the same order.

34. Chester, *An American Melodrama,* pp. 144–45 and 548; Parmet, *The
Democrats,* ch. 12.

35. Schlesinger, *The New Reformers;* Schlesinger established the journal *The
New Democrat* in part to monitor the Commissions efforts and to push or stimulate
"fresh thinking in the Democratic Party"; White, *The Making of the Presidency,*
ch. 2; McGovern, *Grassroots,* ch. 7; Ken Bode, "Democratic Party Reform,"
New Republic, 10 July 1972, pp. 19–23; Hart, *Right From the Start,* p. 77.

36. George Meany, "No Return to Isolationism," *American Federationist,*
Oct. 1972, pp. 13–14; "The 9th Convention," *American Federationist,* Dec.
1971; this article stated that "The AFL–CIO's ninth convention gave a ringing
vote of 'no confidence' to President Nixon's handling of the economy. In the
process, it made the defeat of Nixon in 1972 its primary objective and found a
new unity in labor in pursuit of this goal." McGovern, *Grassroots,* chs. 7, 10; "A
Policy of No Endorsement," *AFL–CIO News,* 22 July 1972, p. 1; "Meany Spells
Out Reasons For Policy on 1972 Election," *AFL–CIO News,* 12 Aug. 1972, p. 5;
John Roche, "McGovern's Come Home Line Smacks of 1930s Isolationism,"
AFL–CIO News, 19 Oct. 1972.

37. George Meany, "No Return to Isolationism," *American Federationist,*
Oct. 1972, pp. 13–14; McGovern, *Grassroots,* chs. 7, 10; "A Policy of No
Endorsement," *AFL–CIO News,* 22 July 1972, p. 1; "Meany Spells Out Reasons
For Policy on 1972 Election," *AFL–CIO News,* 12 Aug. 1972, p. 5; John Roche,
"McGovern's Come Home Line Smacks of 1930s Isolationism," *AFL–CIO News*
19 Oct. 1972; Lane Kirkland, "We Are Non-partisan, We Are Non-Political,"
American Federationist, Sept. 1972, pp. 11–12.

38. Lane Kirkland, "We Are Non-Partisan, We Are Not Non-Political," *American
Federationist,* Sept. 1972, pp. 11–12; Rex Hardesty, "Focus on the Conventions,"
American Federationist, June 1972, pp. 1–5.

39. McGovern, *Grassroots,* chs. 7, 10.

40. Ibid., p. 192; White, *The Making of the Presidency, 1972,* p. 38, 178;
Wittiker, *How to Lose Everything in Politics Except Massachusetts.*

41. For a listing of union endorsements of McGovern and Nixon, see *AFL–CIO News* in the weeks after the convention; McGovern estimated that twenty-five unions endorsed him, although his campaign manager Gary Hart claimed that he received endorsements from forty-five unions, see McGovern, *Grassroots,* ch. 10; Hart, *Right From the Start,* p. 309. Among those to endorse him were the UAW, AFSCME, UE, District 65, Meatcutters, Lithographers, Transport Workers Union, Newspaper Guild, ACWA, CWA, AIW, Textile Workers, Furniture Workers, ILGWU, IUE, RWDSU, Woodworkers, Molders, Brewery Workers and IAM.

42. Frank Wallach, "Washington Report: What's McGovern Really Like?" *UAW Solidarity* Sept. 1972, p. 2; "Woodcock Almost Was McGovern's Running Mate," *UAW Solidarity,* Sept. 1972, p. 8; "McGovern's Pro-Labor Record," *UAW Solidarity,* Oct. 1972, p. 1; "For Peace, Jobs, People: Vote McGovern-Shriver," *UAW Solidarity,* Nov. 1972, p. 1; "Son of the Soil," *UAW Solidarity,* Nov. 1972, p. 5.

43. White, *The Making of the Presidency, 1972,* ch. 13; Hart, *Right From the Start,* part 4; Carroll, *It Seemed Like Nothing Happened,* ch. 5.

44. "Should the Left Back McGovern," *Guardian,* 23 Aug. 1972.

45. "Should the Left Back McGovern," *Guardian,* 23 Aug. 1972; Carl Davidson, "What Makes McGovern Run?" *Guardian,* 21 June 1972, p. 1, 3; Carl Davidson, "Behind the Democrats' New Face," *Guardian,* 9 Aug. 1972, pp. 1, 7; "Viewpoint," *Guardian,* 21 June 1972, p. 6, 7; Dave Dellinger, "Conversations With the Vietnamese in Paris," *Liberation,* Sept. 1972, pp. 11–18; Stanley Aronowitz, "The 1972 Election: Opportunity or Trap?" *Liberation,* Sept. 1972.

46. See Letters to the Editor in the *Guardian* for the weeks of 30 Aug., 6 Sept., and 13 Sept. 1972; Barbara Demming, "Letter," *Liberation,* Sept. 1972; David Kolodney, "McGovern and the Left: Time For a Stand," *Ramparts,* Sept. 1972, p. 6; I.F. Stone is quoted in letter to the editor by Lucille Perlman, *Guardian,* 13 Sept. 1972.

47. David Kolodney, "McGovern and the Left," *Ramparts,* Sept. 1972, p. 6; L.T. Pethou, "Letter," *Guardian,* 6 Sept. 1972. A number of leftist organizations ran candidates, none of whom received a significant number of votes. Socialist Worker nominee(s) Linda James and Evelyn Reed received 62,290 votes; Communist Gus Hall got 25,222; 78,801 Americans voted for Dr. Benjamin Spock. In contrast, Nixon received upward of 47 million votes, McGovern over 29 million. And American party candidate William Schmitz gained over one million votes.

48. David Kolodney, "McGovern and the Left," *Ramparts,* Sept. 1972, p. 6; L.T. Pethou, "Letter," *Guardian,* 6 Sept. 1972; Paul Cowan, "Comment," *Liberation,* Sept. 1972.

Conclusion

1. Haines, *Black Radicals and the Civil Rights Movement,* argues that radicals legitimized liberal demands, prompting them to extend their call for more reforms. As part of the radical flank, the New Left can be seen as having

legitimized and furthered liberalism (which included labor) in the first half of the 1960s.

2. Unger, *The Turning Point,* p. 3; Howe, *A Margin of Hope;* Chafe, *The Unfinished Journey,* p. 380.

3. Black and Black, *Politics and Society in the South,* pp. 269–70; Jaynes and Williams, Jr., eds., *A Common Destiny,* pp. 230–44. In the 1992 election Bill Clinton, a moderate Democrat from Arkansas cut into the Republican hold on the South, winning a large percentage of the black vote and a large percentage of the white vote than his predecessors, Mondale and Dukakis. He also won labor's support. Whether he can hold together this coalition remains to be seen.

4. The literature on opportunities missed by the Left is extensive. The most thoughtful pieces note that by not taking certain steps future progressives essentially sealed their fate or at least added to the obstacles that would have to be overcome in the future. See Nelson Lichtenstein, "From Corporatism to Collective Bargaining: Organized Labor and the Eclipse of Social Democracy in the Postwar Era," in *The Rise and the Fall of the New Deal Order,* ed. Fraser and Gerstle, pp. 122–52. For an even more extreme presentation of this view, see Davis, *Prisoners of the American Dream.*

5. No good work on the subject of former new leftists in politics exists. Contrary to a common perception, that the New Left "sold out," moved onto Wall Street or onto Madison Avenue, most systematic studies of the 1960s show that many sixties "radicals" remained politically active in the 1970s and 1980s. See McAdam, *Freedom Summer;* Fraser, et al, *1968: A Student Generation in Revolt,* especially pp. 366–70, 393–400 and Flacks and Whalen, *Beyond the Barricades.*

6. Boyte, *The Backyard Revolution;* see also Evans and Boyte, *Free Spaces* and Breines, *Community and Organization in the New Left, 1962–1968,* especially Preface to Second Edition.

7. Winpisinger, *Reclaiming Our Future.*

8. Jonathan Rieder, "The Rise of the Silent Majority," in *The Rise and Fall of the New Deal Order,* ed. Fraser and Gerstle, p. 265.

9. Jonathan Rieder, "The Rise of the Silent Majority"; Thomas Byrne Edsall, with Mary D. Edsall, "Race," *Atlantic Monthly,* May 1991, pp. 53–86.

10. Martin Luther King, Jr. "I See the Promised Land," 3 Apr. 1968, in *A Testament of Hope,* ed. Washington, p. 286.

Appendix

1. For a good review of the numerous contemporary studies of the 1960s, see Keniston, "Revolution or Counterrevolution?"; a valuable bibliographic essay is Allen Hunter, James P. O'Brien and Mark Naison, "Reading About the New Left," *Radical America,* 1972; more recent reviews include Maurice Isserman, "The Not-So-Dark and Bloody Ground: New Works on the 1960s," *American Historical Review,* Oct. 1989, pp. 990–1010; Wini Breines, "Whose New Left?" *Journal of American History* 75 (Sept. 1988), p. 545; and Jon Wiener, "The New Left as History," *Radical History Review* vol. 42 (1988), pp. 173–88.

2. This perspective shaped studies of the past as well as the contemporary scene. Most notably, Richard Hofstadter's *Age of Reform* applied the concept of "status anxiety" to explain the rise of the populists and the progressives. Other historians argued that the American Revolution and writing of the constitution could be accounted for without reference to economic or ideological factors, a view that contrasted sharply with that put forth by "progressive" historians.

3. Keniston, "Revolution or Counterrevolution?" p. 531–32. Keniston, himself, rejected these interpretations.

4. Keniston, "Revolution or Counterrevolution?" pp. 531–32.

5. Ibid., pp. 537–38.

6. Hayden, *Reunion,* shows how Hayden, who was a bit alienated from mass America, was radicalized by his contact with the civil rights movement. Gitlin, *The Sixties,* emphasizes the cultural context out of which his radicalism grew, while at the same time showing how the Vietnam War and counterculture allowed the New Left to explode. James Miller, *Democracy Is In the Streets* and Isserman, *If I Had a Hammer,* delve into some of the more subtle origins of the New Left, including its ties to the Old Left.

7. I have taken some liberty in using the term resource mobilization theorists. Consensus does not exist on the definition or utilization of the theory which I describe. Nonetheless, especially when compared to the "classical" theory, I think it is fair to identifying a separate resource mobilization school. See Zald and McCarthy, eds., *The Dynamics of Social Movements;* Freeman, *The Politics of Women's Liberation;* Jenkins, *The Politics of Insurgency;* McAdam, *Political Process and the Development of Black Insurgency, 1930–1970;* and to a degree, Evans and Boyte, *Free Spaces;* and Morris, *The Origins of the Civil Rights Movement.*

8. Zald and McCarthy, eds., *The Dynamics of Social Movements;* pp. 11–12.

9. Evans and Boyte, *Free Spaces,* pp. 201; Freeman, *The Politics of Women's Liberation:,* pp. 66–67.

10. Jenkins, *The Politics of Insurgency,* p. 2.

11. McAdam, *Political Process and the Development of Black Insurgency, 1930–1970,* p. 26.

12. Jenkins, *The Politics of Insurgency,* pp. 220–21.

13. Howe, *A Margin of Hope,* p. 294–95.

14. McAdam, *Political Process;* Jenkins, *The Politics of Insurgency,* pp. 221–22.

15. Evans and Boyte, *Free Spaces;* Boyte, *Backyard Revolutions.*

16. Phillips, *The Politics of Rich and Poor.*

Bibliography

Manuscripts

AFSCME Collection. President's Office, Arnold Zander. Archives of Labor and Urban Affairs [henceforth ALUA]. Wayne State University. Detroit, Michigan.

American Federation of Teachers Collection. ALUA.

Stanley Aronowitz Papers. State Historical Society of Wisconsin [henceforth SHSW]. Madison, Wisconsin.

Norma Becker Papers. SHSW.

Paul Booth Papers. SHSW.

Robb Burlage Papers. SHSW.

George Chiakulas Collection. ALUA.

Cleveland Area Peace Action Council (CAPAC) Papers. SHSW. Microfilm edition.

Committee for Miners Papers. SHSW.

Congress of Racial Equality Papers, 1944–68. Martin Luther King, Jr. Center for Nonviolent Social Change. Atlanta, Georgia. Microfilm edition.

James Haugton Papers. Schomberg Center for Research in Black Culture. New York, New York.

Labor Leadership Assembly for Peace, Papers. SHSW.

Labor for Peace. District 65 Collection. Tamiment Institute, New York University. New York, New York.

League of Industrial Democracy Collection. Tamiment Institute.

Staughton Lynd Papers. SHSW.

March on Washington, 1963. Clipping File. Schomberg Center.

Mississippi Freedom Democratic party, Records. SHSW. Microfilm edition.

National Mobilization Committee to End the War Papers. Swarthmore Peace Collection. Swarthmore College, Swarthmore, Pennsylvania.

Richard Parish Papers, 1950–75. Schomberg Center.

Diane Ravitch Papers [Research Material for *The Great School Wars*]. Teachers College, Columbia University, New York, New York.

Walter P. Reuther Papers. UAW President's Office. ALUA.

Victor Reuther and Lewis Carline Collection. UAW International Department. ALUA.

SANE Papers. Swarthmore Peace Collection.

Sam Shirah Papers. SHSW.
Social Protest Project. Bancroft Library. University of Califorinia, Berkeley.
Student Activist Collection. ALUA.
Students for a Democratic Society Collection. Tamiment Institute.
Students for a Democratic Society Papers, 1958–70. SHSW. Microfilm edition.
Student Nonviolent Coordinating Committee Papers, 1959- 1972. Martin Luther
    King, Jr. Center for Nonviolent Social Change. Atlanta, Ga. Microfilm edition.
Student Peace Union Records, 1958–64. SHSW.
Teaching Assistants Association, American Federation of Teachers, Local 3220,
    Records, 1966–76. SHSW.
Walter Tillow Papers. SHSW.
George Tselos Papers, 1961–71. SHSW.
Underground Newspaper Collection, 1963–75. Microfilm.
United Farm Workers. Verticle File. Tamiment Institute.
United Farm Workers Collection. ALUA.
United Packinghouse, Food and Allied (AFL–CIO) Papers, (UPWA) 1937–68.
    SHSW.
Vietnam Vertical File. [File includes folders on: Fifth Avenue Vietnam Peace
    Parade Committee; Labor Leadership for Peace; Labor-Student Coalition for
    Peace; National Coordinating Committee to End the War in Viet Nam; New
    MOBE; Student Mobilization Committee to End the War in Vietnam; Trade
    Unions for Peace.] Tamiment Institute.
Lee Webb Papers. SHSW.

Newspapers and Journals

NEW LEFT PERIODICALS (YEARS EXAMINED)

The Activist, 1961–70
Berkeley Barb, 1965–72
Berkeley Tribe, 1968–70
The Fifth Estate, 1968–72
Guardian, 1950–72
Helix, 1968–72
International Socialist, 1968–72
Kaleidoscope, 1968–71
Liberation, 1956–72
Mobilizer News (Spring Mobilization), 1967
Movement: Bay Area Friends of SNCC, 1964–65
New Left Notes (SDS), 1966–72
New Politics, 1968–72
New Student South, 1966–69
New University Thought, 1960–71
Old Mole (Boston), 1968–70
Radical America, 1967–74
Ramparts, 1962–75
Rising Up Angry, 1968–72

Root and Branch, 1969–70
Southern Patriot (SCEF), 1960–70
Studies on the Left, 1959–67
Workers Power, 1968–72

LABOR PERIODICALS

Advance (ACTWU), 1962–68
AFL–CIO News, 1958–74
American Federationist (AFL–CIO), 1960–74
American Teacher (AFT), 1962–70
The Carpenter, 1960–72
CWA News, 1963–72
The Dispatcher (ILWU), 1960–72
District Three Leader (IUE), 1965–70
El Malcriado (UFWOC), 1965–72
The International Teamster, 1962–72
Justice (ILGWU), 1960–69
Oil, Chemical and Atomic Union News, 1962–68
Mine-Mill Union, 1960–68
Pilot (NMU), 1962–69
The Packinghouse Worker, 1960–69
RWDSU Record, 1962–69
Steel Labor, 1960–72
UAW Solidarity, 1959–74
UE News, 1960–72
United Mine Workers Journal, 1962–69

Books, Articles, and Dissertations

Aaron, Daniel. *Writers on the Left.* New York: Avon, 1961.
Abzug, Bella. *Bella! Mrs. Abzug Goes to Washington.* New York: Saturday Review Press, 1972.
"Academic-Labor Alliance Formally Established." *Science* (6 Nov. 1970), 614.
Adelson, Alan. *SDS.* New York: Scribner, 1972.
———. "Unlikely Alliance: Student Radicals Seek Workers Cooperation in Fighting the System." *Wall St. Journal,* July 16, 1969, p. 1.
AFL–CIO. *Proceedings of the AFL–CIO 6th Constitutional Convention, Vol. 2: Daily Proceedings.* Washington, D.C. 1965.
AFL–CIO. *Proceedings of the AFL–CIO 7th Constitutional Convention, Vol. 1: Daily Proceedings.* Washington, D.C., 1967.
AFL–CIO. *Proceedings of the AFL–CIO 8th Constitutional Convetion, Vol 1: Daily Proceedings.* Washington, D.C., 1969.
Albert, Stew, and Judith Clair Albert, eds. *The Sixties Papers.* New York: Praeger, 1984.
Allen, Robert. *Black Awakening in Capitalist America.* Garden City: Doubleday, 1969.

Altbach, Philip, and Dennis Carlson. "Militants in Politics." *Society,* July-Aug. 1976, pp. 54–57.

Altbach, Philip G., and Robert S. Laufer, eds. *The New Pilgrims: Youth Protest in Transition.* New York: David McKay, 1972.

Anderson, Alan B., and George W. Pickering. *Confronting the Color Line: The Broken Promise of the Civil Rights Movement.* Athens: Georgia University Press, 1986.

Anderson, Jervis. *A. Philip Randolph: A Biographical Portrait.* New York: Harcourt Brace, 1972.

Anderson, Perry. *Considerations on Western Marxism.* London: New Left Books, 1979.

Anson, Robert Sam. *McGovern: A Biography.* New York: Holt, Rinehart and Winston, 1972.

Aptheker, Herbert. *The World of C. Wright Mills.* New York: Marzani and Munsell, 1960.

Armbruster, Frank E. *The Forgotten Americans: A Survey of Values, Beliefs and Concerns of the Majority.* New Rochelle, N.Y.: Arlington House, 1972.

Armbruster, Trevor. *Act of Vengeance: The Yablonski Murders and Their Solution.* New York: Saturday Review Press, 1975.

Aronowitz, Stanley, *False Promises: The Shaping of American Working Class Consciousness.* New York: McGraw Hill, 1973.

Avorn, Jerry et. al. *Up against the Ivy Wall.* New York: Atheneum, 1969.

Bacciocco, Edward J. *The New Left in America: Reform to Revolution, 1956 to 1970.* Palo Alto: Stanford University Press, 1974.

Baraka, Imamu Amir. "Needed: A Revolutionary Strategy." *Black Scholar* (special issue on "Black Politics"), Oct. 1975, pp. 42–43.

Baran, Paul. *The Longer View: Essays toward a Critique of Political Economy.* New York: Monthly Review Press, 1963.

Baran, Paul, and Paul Sweezy, *Monopoly Capital: An Essay on the American Economic and Social Order.* New York: Monthly Review Press, 1966.

Baritz, Loren, ed. *The American Left: Radical Political Thought in the Twentieth Century.* New York: Basic Books, 1971.

Bass, Jack. "Strike at Charleston." *New South,* Summer 1969, pp. 35–44.

Baxandall, Rosalyn, Linda Gordon, and Susan Reverby, eds. *America's Working Women.* New York: Random House, 1970.

Beifuss, Joan Turner. *At the River I Stand: Memphis, the 1968 Strike, and Martin Luther King.* Brooklyn, N.Y.: 1989.

Bell, Daniel. *Confrontation: The Student Rebellion and the Universities.* New York: Basic Books, 1968.

———. *The End of Ideology: On the Exhaustion of Political Ideas in the Fifties.* Rev. ed. New York: Collier Books, 1961.

———. *The Radical Right: The New American Right.* Garden City, N.Y.: Doubleday, 1963.

Bell, Inge Powell. *CORE and the Strategy of Nonviolence.* New York: Random House, 1968.

Berman, Marshall. *The Politics of Authenticity: Radical Individualism and the Emergence of Modern Society.* New York: Atheneum, 1970.

Berman, Paul. "Spirit of '67." *Village Voice Literary Supplement,* Sept. 1983, p. 10.

Berube, Maurice, and Marilyn Gittell. *Confrontation at Ocean Hill-Brownsville: The New York School Strikes of 1968.* New York: Praeger, 1969.

Black, Earl, and Merle Black. *Politics and Society in the South.* Cambridge: Harvard University Press, 1987.

The Black Revolution: An Ebony Special Issue. Chicago: Johnson, 1970.

Bloom, Jack M. *Class, Race, and the Civil Rights Movement.* Blomington: Indiana University Press, 1987.

Blustein, Paul. "Madison's Golden Coalition." *The Nation,* 25 June 1973, pp. 817–20.

Bode, Ken. "Democratic Party Reform." *New Republic,* 10 July 1972, pp. 19–33.

Boggs, James. *Racism and the Class Struggle.* New York: Monthly Review Press, 1970.

Bond, Julian. *A Time to Speak, a Time to Act: The Movement in Politics.* New York: Simon and Schuster, 1972.

Bonnell, Victoria E., and Chester W. Hartman. "Cambridge Votes on the Vietnam War." *Dissent,* Mar.-Apr. 1968, pp. 103–6.

Boyte, Harry C. *The Backyard Revolution: Understanding the New Citizen Movement.* Philadelphia: Temple University Press, 1980.

Braden, Anne. "The Southern Freedom Movement in Perspective." *Monthly Review* (special issue) 17:3 (1965), pp. 1–93.

Braden, William. *The Age of Aquarius: Technology and the Cultural Revolution.* Chicago: Quadrangle, 1970.

Brauer, Carl. *John F. Kennedy and the Second Reconstruction.* New York: Columbia University Press, 1977.

Breines, Wini. *The Great Refusal: Community and Organization in the New Left.* New York: Praeger, 1982.

Breines, Wini. "Whose New Left?" *Journal of American History* 75 (Sept. 1988), p. 545.

Brink, William, and Lou Harris, *Black and White: A Study of U.S. Racial Attitudes Today.* New York: Simon and Schuster, 1967.

——. *The Negro Revolution in America.* New York: Simon and Schuster, 1964.

Brinkly, Alen. "Dreams of the Sixties." *New York Review of Books.* 34:10 (1987).

Brody, David. *Workers in Industrial America: Essays on the 20th Century Struggle.* New York: Oxford University Press, 1980.

Brooks, John. *The Great Leap.* New York: Harper and Row, 1960.

Brooks, Thomas. *Walls Come Tumbling Down: A History of the Civil Rights Movement.* Englewood Cliffs, N.J.: Prentice-Hall, 1974.

Brown, Michael, ed. *The Politics and Anti-Politics of the Young.* Beverly Hills, Calif.: Glencoe Press, 1969.

Buhle, Paul. *History and the New Left: Madison Wisconsin, 1950-1970.* Philadelphia: Temple University Press, 1990.

———. *Marxism in the USA: From 1870 to the Present Day.* London: Verso, 1978.

Buffa, Dudley W. *Union Power and American Democracy: The UAW and the Democratic Party, 1935–72.* Ann Arbor: University of Michigan Press, 1984.

Bunzell, John H. *Political Passages: Journeys of Change through Two Decades.* New York: Free Press, 1988.

Burns, Stewart. *Social Movements of the 1960s.* Boston: Twayne, 1990.

Bush, Ron, ed., *The New Black Vote.*

Calvert, Greg, and Carol Neiman. *A Disrupted History: The New Left and the New Capitalism.* New York: Random House, 1971.

Cantor, Milton. *The Divided Left: American Radicalism, 1900–1975.* New York: Hill and Wang, 1978.

Carawan, Guy. *Freedom Is a Constant Struggle and Songs of the Freedom Movement.* New York: Oak, 1968.

Carawan, Guy, and Candie Carawan. *Voices from the Mountains.* New York: Knopf, 1975.

Carmichael, Stokely, and Charles Hamilton. *Black Power: The Politics of Liberation in America.* New York: Vintage Books, 1967.

———. *Stokely Speaks.* New York: Random House, 1971.

———. "What We Want." *New York Review of Books,* 26 Sept. 1966.

Carroll, Peter. *It Seemed Like Nothing Happened.* New York: Holt, Rinehart and Winston, 1982.

Carson, Clayborne. *In Struggle: SNCC and the Black Awakening of the 1960s.* Cambridge: Harvard University Press, 1981.

Caudill, Harry. *The Night Comes to Cumberland.* Boston: Little Brown, 1963.

Caute, David. *The Year of the Barricades: A Journey through 1968.* New York: Harper and Row, 1988.

Chafe, William H. *Civilities and Civil Rights: Greensborough, North Carolina, and the Black Struggle for Freedom.* New York: Oxford University Press, 1980.

———. *The Unfinished Journey.* New York: Oxford University Press, 1986.

Chafe, William H., and Harvard Sitkoff, eds. *A History of Our Time: Readings on Postwar America.* New York: Oxford University Press, 1983.

Chester, Lewis, Godfrey Hodgson, and Bruce Page. *An American Melodrama: The Presidential Campaign of 1968.* New York: Viking, 1968.

Chisholm, Shirley. *Unbound and Unbossed.* Boston: Houghton Mifflin, 1970.

Christopher, Maurine. *Black Americans in Congress.* Rev. ed. New York: Thomas Crowell, 1975.

Cleaver, Eldridge. *Soul on Ice.* New York: McGraw-Hill, 1968.

Clecak, Peter. *Radical Paradoxex: Dilemmas of the American Left, 1945–1970.* New York: Harper Torchbooks, 1973.

Cochran, Bert, ed. *American Labor in Midpassage.* New York: Monthly Review Press, 1959.

———. *Labor and Communism: The Conflict That Shaped American Unions.* Princeton: Princeton University Press, 1977.

Coleman, Vernon T. "Labor Power and Social Equality," Ph.D. diss., University of California at Los Angeles, 1984.

Coles, Robert. *The Middle Americans.* Boston: Little Brown, 1971.

Collier, Peter, and David Horowitz. *Second Thoughts: Former Radicals Look Back at the Sixties.* Lanham: Madison Books, 1989.

Conlin, Joseph. *The Troubles: A Jaundiced Glance Back at the Movement of the 1960s.* New York: Franklin Watts, 1982.

Crawford, Alan. *Thunder on the Right: The "New Right" and the Politics of Resentment.* New York: Pantheon, 1980.

Cruse, Harold. *The Crisis of the Negro Intellectual: A Historical Analysis of the Failure of Black Leadership.* New York: Quill, 1984.

Danzig, David. "The Meaning of the Negro Strategy." *Commentary,* Feb. 1964, pp. 41–46.

Davis, Mike. *Prisoners of the American Dream: Politics and Economics in the History of the U.S. Working Class.* London: Verso, 1986.

DeBenedetti, Charles. "On the Significance of Citizen Peace Activism: America, 1961–1975." *Peace and Change* 9:2/3 (Summer 1983), pp. 6–20.

Dellinger, Dave. *More Power Than We Know: The People's Movement toward Democracy.* Garden City, N.Y.: Doubleday, 1975.

Denisoff, R. Serge, ed. *The Sociology of Dissent.* New York: Harcourt Brace Jovanovich, 1974.

Dickstein, Morris. *Gates of Eden: American Culture in the Sixties.* New York: Basic Books, 1977.

Diggins, John P. *The American Left in the Twentieth Century.* New York: Harcourt Brace Jovanovich, 1973.

———. *Up from Communism: Conservative Odysseys in American Intellectual History.* New York· Harper and Row, 1975.

Draper, Alan. *A Rope of Sand: The AFL–CIO Committee on Political Education, 1955–1967.* Westport, Conn.: Praeger, 1989.

Draper, Hal. *The Rediscovery of Black Nationalism.* New York: Viking, 1969.

Draper, Theodore. *The Roots of American Communism.* New York: Viking, 1957.

DuBofsky, Melvyn, and Warren Van Tine, eds. *Labor Leaders in America.* Urbana: University of Illinois Press, 1987.

Dunway, David Kin. "Pete Seeger and the Modern American Topical Sons Movement." Ph.D. diss., University of California, Berkeley, 1981.

Dye, Thomas R. *The Politics of Equality.* Indianapolis: Bobbs-Merrill, 1971.

Dymally, Mervyn M. *The Black Politician: His Struggle for Power.* Belmont, Calif.: Duxbury Press, 1971.

Edsall, Thomas Byrne, with Mary D. Edsall. "Race." *Atlantic Monthly,* May 1991, pp. 53–86.

Erskine, Hazel. "The Polls: Demonstrations and Race Riots." *Public Opinion Quarterly* 31:4 (1967–68), pp. 678–83.

———. "The Polls: Is War a Mistake?" *Political Science Quarterly* 34:1 (1970), pp. 135–50.

———. "The Polls: Race Relations." *Public Opinion Quarterly* 26:1 (1962), pp. 137–48.

Evans, Sara. *Personal Politics: The Roots of Women's Liberation in the Civil Rights Movement and the New Left.* New York: Viking, 1979.

Evans, Sara, and Harry Boyte. *Free Spaces: The Sources of Democratic Change in America.* New York: Harper and Row, 1986.

Evers, Charles. *Evers.* New York: World Publishing, 1971.

Fager, Charles E. *Selma, 1965.* New York: Charles Scribner, 1974.

Farber, David. *Chicago '68.* Chicago: University of Chicago Press, 1988.

Farmer, James. *Lay Bare the Heart.* New York: Arbor House, 1985.

Ferber, Michael, and Staughton Lynd. *The Resistance.* Boston: Beacon Press, 1971.

Fine, Sidney. *Violence in the Model City: The Cavanaugh Administration, Race Relations, and the Detroit Riot of 1967.* Ann Arbor: University of Michigan Press, 1989.

Fink, Gary, ed. *AFL–CIO Executive Council Statements, 1956–1977.* Westport, Conn.: Greenwood Press, 1977.

Fink, Gary, and Merle Reed, eds., *Essays on Southern Labor History.* Westport, Conn.: Greenwood Press, 1977.

Fink, Gary, Leslie Hough, and Merle Reed, eds. *Southern Workers and Their Unions, 1880–1975: Selected Papers.* Westport, Conn.: Greenwood Press, 1981.

Fink, Leon, and Brian Greenberg. *Upheaval in the Quiet Zone: A History of Hospital Workers' Union, Local 1199.* Urbana: University of Illinois Press, 1989.

Fischer, George ed. *The Revival of American Socialism: Selected Papers of the Socialist Scholars Conference.* New York: Oxford University Press, 1971.

Flacks, Richard, Jim Hawley, Michael Harrington, and Barbara Haber. "Port Huron: Agenda for a Generation [Symposium]." *Socialist Review* 17:3/4 (May-Aug. 1987), pp. 105–64.

Flug, Michael. "Organized Labor and the Civil Rights Movement of the 1960s: The Case of the Maryland Freedom Union." *Labor History* 31:3 (Summer 1990), 322–46.

Foner, Philip S. *American Labor and the Indochina War: The Growth of Union Opposition.* New York: International Publishers, 1971.

———. *The Black Panthers Speak.* Philadelphia: Lippincott, 1970.

———. *Organized Labor and the Black Worker, 1619–1973.* New York: International Publishers, 1974.

———. *U.S. Labor and the Vietnam War.* New York: International, 1989.

———. *Women and the American Labor Movement.* New York: Free Press, 1980.

Foner, Philip S., Ronald L. Lewis, and Robert Cvornyek, eds. *The Black Worker since the AFL–CIO Merger, 1955–1980.* Philadelphia: Temple University Press, 1984.

Forman, James. *The Making of Black Revolutionaries: A Personal Account.* New York: Macmillan, 1972.

Foster, E. C. "A Time of Challenges: Afro-Mississippi Political Development since 1965." *Journal of Negro History,* Spring 1983, pp. 185–200.

Franklin, Bruce, ed. *From the Movement toward Revolution.* New York: Van Nostrand Reinhold, 1971.

Franklin, John Hope, and August Meier, eds. *Black Leaders of the Twentieth Century.* Urbana: University of Illinois Press, 1982.

Fraser, Ronald, ed. *1968—A Student Generation in Revolt: An International Oral History.* New York: Pantheon, 1988.

Fraser, Steve, and Gary Gerstle, ed. *The Rise and the Fall of the New Deal Order, 1930–1980.* Princeton: Princeton University Press, 1989.

Freeman, Jo. *The Politics of Women's Liberation: A Case Study of an Emerging Social Movement and Its Relation to the Policy Process.* New York: David McKay, 1975.

Friedman, Myra. *Burried Alive: The Biography of Janis Joplin.* New York: Bantam, 1974.

Friedman, Samuel R. *Teamster Rank and File: Power, Bureaucracy, and Rebellion at Work and in a Union.* New York: Columbia University Press, 1982.

Gallup Opinion Index. N.J.: American Institute of Public Opinion, 1962–72.

Gannon, Francis X. *Biographical Dictionary of the Left.* Boston: Western Islands, 1969.

Garrow, David J. *Bearing the Cross: Martin Luther King, Jr., and the Southern Christion Leadership Conference.* New York: William Morrow, 1986.

———. *Protest at Selma: Martin Luther King, Jr., and the Voting Rights Act of 1965.* New Haven: Yale University Press, 1978.

Geltman, Max. *The Confrontation: Black Power, Anti-Semitism, and the Myth of Integration.* Englewood Cliffs, N.J.: Prentice-Hall, 1970.

Georgakas, Dan, and Marvin Surkin. *Detroit: I Do Mind Dying.* New York: St. Martin's Press, 1975.

Geschwender, James A. *Class, Race, and Worker Insurgency: The League of Revolutionary Black Workers.* Cambridge: Cambridge University Press, 1977.

Gillon, Steven M. *Politics and Vision: The ADA and American Liberalism, 1947–1985.* New York: Oxford University Press, 1987.

Gitlin, Todd. *The Sixties: Years of Hope and Days of Rage.* New York: Bantam, 1987.

———. *The Whole World Is Watching: Mass Media in the Making of the New Left.* Berkeley: University of California Press, 1980.

Glen, John Mathew. *Highlander: No Ordinary School.* Lexington: University Press of Kentucky, 1989.

Glen, John Mathew. "On the Cutting Edge: A History of Highlander Folk School," Ph.D. diss., Vanderbilt, 1985;

Glick, Stanley Irwin. "The People's Park." Ph.D. diss., State University of New York at Stony Brook, 1986.

Goldman, Eric. *The Tragedy of Lyndon Johnson.* New York: Alfred Knopf, 1968.

Goodman, Paul. *Drawing the Line: The Political Essays of Paul Goodman.* Ed. Taylor Stoehr. New York: Free Life Editions, 1977.

———. *Growing Up Absurd: Problems of Youth in the Organized Society.* New York: Vintage Books, 1956.

———. *New Reformation: Notes of a Neolithic Conservative.* New York: Random House, 1970.

———. *People or Personnel: Decentralizing and the Mixed System.* New York: Random House, 1905.

———. *Like a Conquered Province: The Moral Ambiguity of America.* New York: Vintage, 1968.

———. *The Society I Live In Is Mine.* New York: Horizon Press, 1962.

———. *Utopian Essays and Practical Proposals.* New York: Random House, 1962.

Goodman, Paul, and Percival Goodman. *Communitas: Means of Livelihood and Ways of Life.* Rev. ed. New York: Vintage Books, 1960.

Gordon, David et. al. *Segmeted Work, Divided Workers* (Cambridge: Cambridge University Press, 1982.

Gorz, Andre. *Strategy for Labor: A Radical Proposal.* Trans. Martin A. Nicolaus and Victoria Ortiz. Boston: Beacon Press, 1967.

Goulden, Joseph C. *Jerry Wurf: Labor's Last Angry Man.* New York: Atheneum, 1982.

———. *Meany.* New York: Atheneum, 1972.

Grant, Joanne, ed., *Confrontation on Campus: the Columbia Pattern for the New Protest.* New York: Signet, 1969.

———, ed., *Black Protest.* New York: Fawcett, 1968.

Green, Earl Jr. "Labor in the South: A Case Study of Memphis: The 1968 Sanitation Strike and Its Effect on an Urban Community." Ph.D. diss., New York University, 1980.

Green, Gil. *What's Happening to Labor.* New York: International Publishers, 1976.

Green, James. *The World of the Worker: Labor in Twentieth-Century America.* New York: Hill and Wang, 1980.

———, ed. *Workers Struggles Past and Present: A Radical America Reader.* Philadelphia: Temple University Press, 1983.

Greenstone, J. David. *Labor in American Politics.* Chicago: University of Chicago Press, 1977.

Grine, Omar. "America against Herself: The Ideology of American Radicalism in the Nineteen Sixties." Ph.D. diss., Columbia University, 1971.

Gross, Kenneth. "Give Peace a Chance." *The Nation,* 1 Dec. 1969, pp. 591–94.

Gutman, Herbert, and Gregory S. Kealey, eds., *Many Pasts: Reading in American Social History, Vol. 2.* Englewood Cliffs, N.J.: Prentice-Hall, 1973.

Guarsci, Richard. *The Theory and Practice of American Marxism, 1957–1970.* Lanham, Md.: University Press, 1980.

Haines, Herbert H. "Black Radicalization and the Funding of the Civil Rights, 1957–1970." *Social Problems* 32:1 (Oct. 1964), 31–43.

———. *Black Radicals and the Civil Rights Mainstream, 1954–1970.* Knoxville: University of Tennessee Press, 1988.

Halberstam, David. *The Reckoning.* New York: William Morrow, 1986.

Haley, Alex. *The Autobiography of Malcolm X.* New York: Grove Press, 1964.

Hall, Burton, ed. *Autocracy and Insurgency in Organized Labor.* New York: Dutton, 1972.

Halstead, Fred. *Out Now! A Participant's Account of the American Movement against the Vietnam War.* New York: Monad Press, 1978.

Hamilton, Richard F. *Class and Politics in the United States.* New York: Wiley, 1972.

———. "Liberal Inteligentsia and White Backlash." *Dissent,* Winter 1972, pp. 225–32.

Hammer, Fannie Lou. *To Praise Our Bridges: An Autobiography.* Jackson: KIPCO, 1967.

Hampton, Henry, and Steve Fayer. *Voices of Freedom: An Oral History of the Civil Rights Movement from the 1950s through the 1980s.* New York: Bantam, 1990.

Hampton, Jim. "The Odds Say Hoffer Cannot Be an Uncommon Spokesman." *National Observer,* 11 Dec. 1967, p. 12.

Hampton, Wade. *Guerilla Minstrels: John Lennon, Joe Hill, Woodie Guthrie and Bob Dylan.* Knoxville: University of Tennessee Press, 1980.

Hardman, J. B. S., and Maurice F. Neufield, eds. *The House of Labor: Internal Operations of American Unions.* New York: Prentice-Hall, 1951.

Harrington, Michael. *Fragments of the Century.* New York: E. P. Dutton, 1973.

Harrington. Michael, and Irving Howe, eds., *The Seventies: Problems and Proposals.* New York: Harper and Row, 1972.

———. *The Long Distance Runner: An Autobiography.* New York: Henry Holt, 1988.

———. *The Other America: Poverty in the United States.* New York: Macmillan, 1962.

Harris, Louis. *The Anguish of Change.* New York: Norton, 1973.

Harrison, Cynthia. *On Account of Sex: The Politics of Women's Issues, 1945–1968.* Berkeley: University of California Press, 1988.

Hart, Gary. *Right from the Start.* New York: Quadrangle, 1973.

Hartmann, Susan M. *From Margin to Mainstream: American Women and Politics since 1960.* Philadelphia: Temple University Press, 1989.

Hayden, Tom. "The Politics of the Movement." *Dissent,* Jan.-Feb. 1966, pp. 75–87.

———. *Rebellion in Newark: Official Violence and Ghetto Response.* New York: Random House, 1967.

———. *Reunion: A Memoir.* New York: Random House, 1988.

Hedgemen, Anna Arnold. *The Trumpet Sounds: A Memoir of Negro Leadership.* New York: Holt, Rinehart and Winston, 1964.

Helmer, John. *Bring the War Home.* New York: Free Press, 1974.

Henkin, Harman. "Three Days on Mifflin Street." *The Nation,* 26 May 1969, pp. 653–54.

Henle, Peter. "Some Reflections on Organized Labor and the New Militiants." *Monthly Labor Review,* July 1969, pp. 20–25.

Henthoff, Nat. *The New Equality.* 2d ed. New York: Viking, 1965.

———. *Peace Agitator: The Story of A. J. Muste.* New York: Macmillan, 1963.

Herring, George C. *America's Longest War: The United States and Vietnam, 1950–1975.* New York: John Wiley and Sons, 1979.

Higgins, John. "Union and Campus: Talking Together." *Nation,* 6 Sept. 1971, pp. 171–74.

Hill, Herbert. "Letter to the Editor," *Labor History* 32:7 (Winter 1991), 155–59.

Hodgson, Godfrey. *America in Our Time.* New York: Vintage, 1976.

Hoffer, Eric. *The Temper of Our Time.* New York: Harper and Row, 1960.

Hoffman, Abbie. *Revolution for the Hell of It.* New York: Dial Press, 1968.

Holt, Len. *The Summer That Didn't End.* New York: William Morrow, 1965.

Horowitz, Irving Louis. *C. Wright Mill: An American Utopian.* New York: Free Press, 1983.

Horwitt, Sanford P. *Let Them Call Me Rebel: Saul Alinsky—His Life and Legend.* New York: Alfred Knopf, 1989.

Horton, Aimee I. "The Highlander Folk School: A History of the Development of Its Major Programs Related to Social Movements in the South, 1932–1961." Ph.D. diss., University of Chicago, 1961.

Howe, Irving, ed. *Beyond the New Left.* New York: McCall Publishing, 1970.

———. *A Margin of Hope: An Intellectual Biography.* New York: Harcourt Brace Jovanovich, 1982.

———. "New Styles in Leftism." *Dissent,* Summer 1965, pp. 295–323.

———. *The World of the Blue-Collar Worker.* New York: Quadrangle, 1972.

Howe, Irving, and Lewis Coser. *The American Communist Party: A Critical History, 1919–1957.* Boston: Beacon Press, 1957.

Howe, Irving, and Michael Harrington, eds. *The Seventies: Problems and Proposals.* New York: Harper and Row, 1972.

Howell, Leon. *Freedom City.* Richmond: John Knox, 1969.

Huberman, Leo, and Paul M. Sweezy. *Cuba: Anatomy of a Revolution.* 2d ed. New York: Monthly Review Press, 1961.

Isserman, Maurice. *If I Had a Hammer: The Death of the Old Left and the Birth of the New Left.* New York: Basic Books, 1987. Rpt., Urbana: University of Illinois Press, 1993.

———. "The Not-So-Dark and Bloody Ground: New Works on the 1960s." *American Historical Review* 94:4 (Oct. 1969), pp. 990–1110.

Jacobs, Harold, ed. *Weatherman.* Berkeley, Calif.: Ramparts Press, 1971.

Jacobs, Paul. *The State of the Unions.* New York: Atheneum, 1963.

Jacobs, Paul, and Saul Landau. *The New Radicals: A Report with Documents.* New York: Random House, 1966.

Jacobson, Julius, ed. *The Negro and the American Labor Movement.* Garden City, N.Y.: Anchor, 1968.

Jaynes, Gerald D., and Robin M. Williams. *A Common Destiny: Blacks and American Society.* Washington, D.C.: National Academy Press, 1989.

Jenkins, J. Craig. *The Politics of Insurgency: The Farm Workers Movement in the 1960s.* New York: Columbia University Press, 1985.

Jensen, Vernon. *Strike on the Waterfront.* Ithaca, N.Y.: Cornell University Press, 1974.

Johnpoll, Bernard K., and Harvery Klehr, eds. *Biographical Dictionary of the American Left.* Westport, Conn.: Greenwood Press, 1986.

Junkerman, John. "Lordstown: Yesterday's Rebels Are Running Scared." *The Progressive,* Aug. 1983, pp. 18–21.

Kahn, Tom. "The Power of the March." *Dissent* 10:4 (1963), pp. 315–20.

Kampleman, Max M. *The Communist Party vs. the CIO: A Study in Power Politics.* New York: Praeger, 1957.

Katz, Milton S. "Peace Liberals and Vietnam: SANE and the Politics of Responsible Protest," *Peace and Change* 9:2/3 (Summer 1983), pp. 21–39.

Keeran, Roger. *The Communist Party and the Auto Workers Unions.* Bloomington: Indiana University Press, 1980.

Kemble, Penn. "Rediscovering American Labor." *Commentary,* Apr. 1971, pp. 45–52.

Kempton, Murray. "Marching on Washington." In *Freedom Now: The Civil Rights Struggle in America.* Ed. Alan F. Westin. New York: Basic Books, 1964, pp. 271–89.

Keniston, Kenneth. "Revolution or Counterrevolution?" In *Twentieth Century America: Recent Interpretations.* 2d ed. Ed. Barton Bernstein and Allen J. Matusow. San Diego: Harcourt Brace Jovanovich, 1972.

———. *Youth and Dissent: The Rise of a New Opposition.* New York: Harcourt Brace Jovanovich, 1971.

Kerry, John. *The New Soldier.* New York: Collier, 1971.

King, Mary. *Freedom Song.* New York: Random House, 1987.

Kolko, Gabriel. *Wealth and Power in America.* New York: Praeger, 1962.

Kushner, Sam. *Long Road to Delano.* New York: International Press, 1975.

Lader, Lawrence. *Power on the Left: American Radical Movements since 1946.* New York: Norton, 1979.

Ladner, Joyce. "White America's Response to Black Militancy." In *Black America.* Ed. John F. Szwerd. New York: Basic Books, 1970, pp. 212–13.

Larrowe, Charles P. *Harry Bridges: The Rise and Fall of Radical Labor in the United States.* New York: Lawrence Hill, 1972.

Lasch, Christopher. *The Agony of the American Left.* New York: Alfred Knopf, 1969.

———. *The New Radicalism in America, 1889–1963: The Intellectual as a Social Type.* New York: Vintage, 1963.

Laslett, John. *Labor and the Left: A Study of Socialist and Radical Influences in the American Labor Movement, 1881- 1924.* New York: Basic Books, 1970.

Laslett, John M., and Seymour Martin Lipset. *Failure of a Dream? Essays in the History of American Socialism.* Garden City, N.Y.: Anchor Books, 1974.

Lawson, Steven. *In Pursuit of Power: Southern Blacks and Electoral Politics, 1965–1982.* New York: Columbia University Press, 1985.

Leamer, Lawrence. *The Paper Revolutionaries: The Rise of the Underground Press.* New York: Simon and Schuster, 1972.

Lembcke, Jerry, and William M. Tattam. *One Union in Wood.* New York: International Press, 1984.

Lens, Sidney. *The Crisis of American Labor.* New York: A. S. Barnes, 1961.

———. *Unrepentent Radical: An American Activist's Account of Five Turbulent Decades.* Boston: Beacon Press, 1980.

Lester, Julius. *Look Out Whitey! Black Power Gon' Get Your Mama.* New York: Grove Press, 1969.

———. *Revolutionary Notes.* New York: Grove Press, 1969.

Leuchtenburg, William. *A Troubled Feast: American Society since 1945.* Rev. ed. Boston: Little Brown, 1979.

Levenstein, Harvey A. *Communism, Anticommunism, and the CIO.* Westport, Conn.: Greenwood Press, 1981.

Levison, Andrew. *The Working-Class Majority.* New York: Penguin, 1974.

Levy, Jacques E. *Cesar Chavez: Autobiography of La Causa.* New York: Norton, 1975.

Levy, Peter B. "The New Left and Labor: A Misunderstood Relationship." Ph.D. diss., Columbia University, 1986.

Levy, Peter B., ed. *Let Freedom Ring.* (New York: Praeger, 1992).

Lewis, David L. *King: A Biography.* 2d ed. Urbana: University of Illinois Press, 1978.

Lifton, Robert J. *Home from the War: Vietnam Veterans, Neither Victims nor Executioners.* New York: Simon and Schuster, 1973.

Lipsett, Seymour Martin, ed. *Unions in Transition.* San Francisco: ICS, 1986.

Lipset, Seymour Martin, and Sheldon Wolin, eds. *The Berkeley Student Revolt: Fact and Interpretations.* Garden City, N.Y.: Anchor Books, 1965.

Lynd, Alice, and Staughton Lynd. *Rank and File: Personal Histories by Working Class Organizers.* Boston: Beacon Press, 1973.

Lynd, Staughton. "Coalition Politics or Nonviolent Revolution." *Liberation* 10:4 (1965), 18–25

Lynd, Staughton. "The New Radicals and Participatory Democracy." *Dissent,* Summer 1965.

Lynd, Staughton, and Gar Alperovitz. *Strategy and Program: Two Essays toward a New American Socialism.* Boston: Beacon Press, 1973.

Lyttle, Clifford M. "The History of the Civil Rights Billof 1964." *Journal of Negro History* 51:4 (1966), p. 287.

McAdam, Doug. *Freedom Summer.* New York: Oxford University Press, 1988.

———. *Political Process and the Development of Black Insurgency, 1930–1970.* Chicago: University of Chicago Press, 1982.

McAuliffe, Mary Sperling. *Crisis on the Left: Cold War Politics and American Liberals, 1947–1954.* Amherst: University of Massachusetts Press, 1978.

McCarthy, Eugene. *The Year of the People.* Garden City, N.Y.: Doubleday, 1969.

"McCarthy for President." *The Progressive,* Mar. 1968, pp. 3–5.

McCord, William. *Mississippi: The Long, Hot Summer.* New York: Norton, 1965.

McGovern, George. *Grassroots.* New York: Random House, 1977.

Magdoff, Harry. *The Age of Imperialism and the Economics of U.S. Foreign Policy.* New York: Monthly Review Press, 1969.

Mailer, Norman. *Armies of the Night.* New York, Signet, 1968.

Marable, Manning. *Race Reform and Rebellion and the Second Reconstruction in America, 1945–1982.* Jackson: University of Mississippi Press, 1984.

Marcuse, Herbert. *Eros and Civilization: A Philosophical Inquiry into Freud.* Boston: Beacon Press, 1955.

————. *Negations: Essays in Critical Theory.* Trans. Jeremy J. Shapiro. Boston: Beacon Press, 1968.

————. *One-Dimensional Man: Studies in the Ideology of Advanced Industrial Society.* Boston: Beacon Press, 1964.

————. *Studies in Critical Philosophy.* Trans. Joris De Bres. London: New Left Books, 1972.

Marshall, Ray. "The Development of Organized Labor." *Monthly Labor Review,* Mar. 1961, pp. 65–73.

————. "The Negro and the AFL–CIO." In *Black Workers and Organized Labor.* Eds. August Meier, John Bracey, Jr., and Elliot Rudwick. Belmont: Wadsworth Publishing, 1971, pp. 199–227.

Massé, Benjamin L. "Intellectuals Start Wooing Trade Unions." *America,* 9 Jan. 1971, p. 33.

Matles, James J., and James Higgins. *Them and Us: Struggles of a Rank-and-File Union.* Englewood Cliffs, N.J.: Prentice-Hall, 1974.

Matusow, Allen. *The Unravelling of America.* New York: Harper and Row, 1984.

Meier, August, and Elliot Rudwick. *CORE: A Study in the Civil Rights Movement, 1942–1968.* New York: Oxford University Press, 1973.

Meier, August, and Francis Broderick, eds. *Negro Protest Thought in the Twentieth Century.* Indianapolis: Bobbs-Merrill, 1965.

Meister, Dick, and Anne Loftis. *A Long Time Coming: The Struggle to Unionize America's Farm Workers.* New York: Macmillan, 1977.

Metcalf, George. *Up from Within: Today's New Black Leaders.* New York: McGraw-Hill, 1971.

Michner, James. *Kent State: What Happened and Why.* New York: Random House, 1971.

Miles, Barry. *Ginsberg: A Biography.* New York: Simon and Schuster, 1989.

Milkman, Ruth, ed. *Women, Work, and Protest: A Century of U.S. Women's Labor History.* Boston: Routledge and Keegan Paul, 1985.

Miller, Herman P. *Rich Man, Poor Man.* Rev. ed. New York: Thomas Crowell, 1971.

Miller, James. *Democracy Is in the Streets: From Port Huron to the Siege of Chicago.* New York: Free Press, 1984.

Miller, Jim, ed., *The Rolling Stone Illustrated History of Rock and Roll.* Rev. and updated. New York: Rolling Stone, 1980.

Miller, Mark, ed. *Working Lives: The Southern Exposure History of Labor in the South.* New York: Pantheon, 1980.

Miller, Merle. *Lyndon Johnson: An Oral Biography.* New York: Ballantine, 1980.

Mills, C. Wright. *The Causes of World War Three.* New York: Simon and Schuster, 1958.

———. *Listen Yankee: The Revolution in Cuba.* New York: Ballantine, 1960.

———. *The Marxists.* New York: Delta Books, 1963.

———, with Helen Schneider. *The New Men of Power: America's Labor Leaders.* New York: Harcourt Brace, 1948.

———. *Power, Politics, and People: The Collected Essays of C. Wright Mills.* Ed. Irving Louis Horowitz. New York: Oxford University Press, 1967.

———. *The Power Elite.* New York: Oxford University Press, 1956.

Moody, Kim. *An Injury to All: The Decline of American Unionism.* London: Verso, 1988.

Morris, Aldon. *The Origins of the Civil Rights Movement.* New York: Free Press, 1984.

Morrison, Joan, and Robert K. Morrison. *From Camelot to Kent State: The Sixties in the Words of Those Who Lived It.* New York: Times Books, 1987.

Newfield, Jack. "Can the Children of Camus Cure the Newark Plague." *Village Voice,* 5 Aug. 1965, pp. 1, 10.

Oates, Stephen B. *Let the Trumpet Sound: The Life of Martin Luther King, Jr.* New York: New American Library, 1982.

O'Brien, James P. "The Development of a New Left in the United States, 1960–1965." Ph.D. diss., University of Wisconsin, 1971.

Oglesby, Carl, ed. *The New Left Reader.* New York: Grove Press, 1969.

Ollman, Bertoll, and Edward Vernoff, eds. *The Left Academy: Marxist Scholarship on American Campuses.* New York: McGraw-Hill, 1982.

O'Neill, William. *A Better World: The Great Schism—Stalinism and the American Intellectual.* New York: Simon and Schuster, 1982.

———. *Coming Apart: An Informal History of America in the 1960s.* Chicago: Quadrangle, 1971.

Parmet, Herbert S. *The Democrats: The Years after FDR.* New York: Oxford University Press, 1976.

Peck, Abe. *Uncovering the Sixties: The Life and Times of the Underground Press.* New York: Pantheon, 1985.

Pells, Richard H. *Radical Visions and American Dreams: Culture and Social Thought in the Depression Years.* New York: Harper and Row, 1973.

Phillips, Kevin. *The Politics of Rich and Poor.* New York: Random House, 1980.

Piehl, Mel. *Breaking Bread: The Catholic Worker and the Origins of Catholic Radicalism in America.* Philadelphia: Temple University Press, 1982.

Pohlhaus, Francis. "Watch on the Potomac." *Crisis* 71:4 (1964), p. 365.

Poinsett, Alex. *Black Power, Gary Style: The Making of Mayor Richard Gordon Hatcher.* Chicago: Johnson, 1970.

Polenberg, Richard. *America Divisible: Race, Class, and Ethnicity in Postwar America.* New York: Penguin, 1980.

Powers, Thomas. *Vietnam: The War at Home.* Boston: G. K. Hall, 1984.

Press, Howard. *C. Wright Mills.* Boston: Twayne, 1978.

Progressive Labor Party. *Revolutionary Today: U.S.A.—A Look at the Progressive Labor Movement and the Progressive Labor Party.* New York: Exposition Press, 1970.

"The Power of Political Protest." *The Progressive,* May 1968, pp. 3–4.

"Probe of Riots Launched." *Labor,* 28 Aug. 1965, p. 6.

Purcell, Theodore V., and George Cavanaugh. *Blacks in the Industrial World.* New York: Free Press, 1972.

Radosh, Ronald. *American Labor and United States Foreign Policy.* New York: Random House, 1969.

Ransford, H. Edward. "Blue Collar Anger: Reacting to Student and Black Protest." *American Sociological Review* 3:3 (1972), pp. 333–46.

Ravitch, Diance. *The Great School Wars: New York City, 1805–1973: A History of the Public Schools as Battlefield of Social Change.* New York: Basic Books, 1974.

Reed, Linda. "The Southern Conference for Human Welfare and the Southern Christian Education Fund, 1938–1968." Ph.D. diss., Indiana University, 1986.

Reich, Charles A. *The Greening of America.* New York: Random House, 1970.

Report of the National Advisory Commission on Civil Disobedience. New York: Bantam, 1968.

Reuther, Victor. *The Brothers Reuther and the Story of the UAW: A Memoir.* Boston: Houghton Mifflin, 1976.

Robinson, Archie. *George Meany and His Times: A Biography.* New York: Simon and Schuster, 1981.

Rorabaugh, W. J. *Berkeley at War: The 1960s.* New York: Oxford University Press, 1989.

Rosenberg, Milton J., Sidney Verba, and Philip Converse. *Vietnam: The Silent Majority.* New York: Harper and Row, 1970.

Roszak, Theodore. *The Making of the Counterculture.* Garden City, N.Y.: Doubleday, 1969.

Rovere, Richard H. *Senator Joe McCarthy.* New York: Harper and Row, 1959.

Rubin, Jerry. *Do It! Scenarios of the Revolution.* New York: Simon and Schuster, 1970.

Rustin, Bayard. *Down the Line.* Chicago: Quadrangle, 1970.

———. "From Protest to Politics: The Future of the Civil Rights Movement." *Commentary,* Feb. 1965, pp. 25–31.

Sacks, Karen Brodkin. *Caring by the Hour: Women, Work, and Organizing at Duke Medical Center.* Urbana: University of Illinois Press, 1988.

Sale, Kirkpatrick. *SDS.* New York: Random House, 1973.

Salter, John. *Jackson Mississippi.* Hicksville, N.Y.: Exposition Press, 1979.

Saunders, Doris E., ed. *The Day They Marched.* Chicago: Johnson Publishing, 1963.

Sayres, Sonya et al. *The 60s without Apology.* Minneapolis: University of Minnesota Press, 1984.

Schlesinger, Arthur, Jr., *The Vital Center.* Boston: Houghton Mifflin, 1949.

Schlesinger, Stephen. *The New Reformers.* Boston: Houghton Mifflin, 1973.

Schwartz, Milton A. *Trends in White Attitudes toward Negroes.* Report No. 19. Chicago: University of Chicago, 1967.

Scimecca, Joseph A. *The Sociological Theory of C. Wright Mills.* Port Washington, N.Y.: Kennikat Press, 1977.

Seale, Bobby. *Seize the Time: The Story of the Black Panther Party and Huey P. Newton.* New York: Vintage, 1968.

Sellers, Cleveland, with Robert Terrell. *The River of No Return: The Autobiography of a Black Militant and the Life and Death of SNCC.* New York: William Morrow, 1973.

Serwer, Arnold. "Gene McCarthy's Winning of Wisconsin." *The Progressive,* 1 Apr. 1968, pp. 24–27.

Sexton, Brendon, and Patricia Cayo Sexton. *Blue Collar and Hard Hats.* New York: Random House, 1971.

Sexton, Particia Cayo. "Workers (Female) Arise." *Dissent* 18:4 (1971), pp. 365–74.

Shafer, Michael, ed., *The Legacy: The Vietnam War in the American Imagination.* Boston: Beacon Press, 1990.

Shapley, Deborah. "Labor-Campus Link: Union Heads, Academic Leaders Discuss Alliance." *Science,* 30 Oct. 1970, pp. 516–18.

Shostak, Arthur B. *Blue-Collar Life.* New York: Random House, 1969.

Singer, Daniel. *Prelude to Revolution: France in May 1968.* New York: Hill and Wang, 1970.

Sitkoff, Harvard. *The Struggle for Black Equality, 1954–1980.* New York: Hill and Wang, 1981.

Stanfield, J. E. "Memphis: More Than a Garbage Strike." *Current,* May 1968.

Starobin, Joseph. *American Communism in Crisis, 1943- 1957.* Cambridge: Harvard University Press, 1972.

Stern, Susan. *With the Weathermen.* New York: Doubleday, 1975.

Stolz, Mathew F., ed. *Politics of the New Left.* Beverly Hills, Calif.: Glencoe Press, 1971.

Strickland, William. "Whatever Happened to the Politics of Black Liberation?" *Black Scholar* (special issue on "Black Politics") Oct. 1975, pp. 20–26.

Sundquist, James L. *Politics and Policy: The Eisenhower, Kennedy, and Johnson Years.* Washington, D.C.: Brookings Institute, 1968.

Sutherland, Elizabeth. *Letters from Mississippi.* New York: McGraw-Hill, 1965.

Swados, Harvey. *A Radical at Large: American Essays.* London: Hart-Davis, 1968.

Sweezy, Paul M. *The Theory of Capitalist Development: Principles of Marxian Political Economy.* New York: Monthly Review Press, 1942.

Taylor, Ronald B. *Chavez and the Farm Workers.* Boston: Beacon Press, 1975.

Teodori, Massimo, ed. *The New Left: A Documentary History.* Indianapolis: Bobbs-Merrill, 1969.

Terkel, Studs. "A Steelworker Speaks." *Dissent,* Winter 1972, pp. 9–21.

Thelwell, Michael. *Duties, Pleasures, and Conflicts: Essays in Struggle.* Amherst: University of Massachusetts Press, 1987.

Unger, Irwin. *The Movement: A History of the American New Left, 1959–1972.* New York: Dodd Mead, 1974.

Unger, Irwin, and Debi Urwin. *Turning Point: 1968.* New York: Charles Scribner's, 1988.

Verba, Sidney et al. "Public Opinion and the War in Vietnam." *American Political Science Review* 61:2 (1967), pp. 317–33.

Vickers, George R. *The Formation of the New Left: The Early Years.* Lexington, Mass.: D. C. Heath, 1975.

Viorst, Milton. *Fire in the Streets: America in the 1960s.* New York: Simon and Schuster, 1979.

Wallerstein, Immanuel, and Paul Starr, eds. *The University Crisis Reader: The Liberal University under Attack.* Vol. 1. New York: Random House, 1971.

———. *The University Crisis Reader: Confrontation and Counter Attack.* Vol. 2. New York: Random House, 1971.

Ware, Susan, ed., *Modern American Women: A Documentary History.* Chicago: Dorsey, 1989.

Washington, James Melvin, ed., *A Testament of Hope: The Essential Writings of Martin Luther King, Jr.* San Francisco: Harper and Row, 1986.

Waters, Pat. "Workers, White and Black, in Mississippi." *Dissent,* Winter 1972, pp. 70–77.

Wattenberg, Ben J., *The Real America.* Garden City: Doubleday, 1974.

Wattenburg, Ben J., ed. *The Statistical History of the United States: From Colonial Times to the Present.* New York: Basic Books, 1976.

Weschler, James. "Gleason's Glory." *New York Post,* 13 Dec. 19—, p. 7.

———. *Revolt on the Campus.* New York: Covici and Friede, 1935.

Whalen, Charles, and Barbara Whalen. *The Longest Battle: A Legislative History of the 1964 Civil Rights Act.* New York: New American Library, 1985.

Whalen, Jack, and Richard Flacks. *Beyond the Barricades: The Sixties Generation Grows Up.* Philadelphia: Temple University Press, 1990.

White, Theodore. *The Making of the Presidency.* New York: Atheneum, 1973.

Widick, B. J. *Detroit: City of Race and Class Violence.* Chicago: Quadrangle, 1972.

Wiener, Jonathan. *Come Together: John Lennon in His Times.* New York: Random House, 1984. Rpt., Urbana: University of Illinois Press, 1991.

———. "The New Left as History." *Radical History Review* 42 (1988), pp. 173–87.

Wilkins, Roy. *Standing Fast: The Autobiography of Roy Wilkins.* New York: Vintage, 1982.

Williams, William Appleman. *Americans in a Changing World: A History of the United States in the Twentieth Century.* New York: Harper and Row, 1978.
———. *Contours of American History.* Chicago: Quadrangle, 1961.
———. *The Tragedy of American Diplomacy.* Rev. ed. New York: Delta, 1962.
Winpisinger, William W. *Reclaiming Our Future: An Agenda for America.* Boulder, Colo.: Westview Press, 1989.
Wittiker, Kristi. *How to Lose Everything in Politics Except Massachusetts.* New York: Mason and Lipscomb, 1974.
Wittner, Lawrence S. *Rebels against War: The American Peace Movement, 1941–60.* New York: Columbia University Press, 1969.
Wolfe, Tom. *Radical Chic and Mau Mauing the Flak Catchers.* New York: Bantom Books, 1970.
Wortman, Max S., Jr., ed. *Critical Issues in Labor and Text and Readings.* New York: Macmillan, 1969.
Wright, James D. "The Working Class, Authoritarianism, and the Vietnam War." *Social Problems* 20:2 (Fall 1972), pp. 133–49.
Wright, Nathan Jr. *Black Power and Urban Unrest.* New York: Hawthorne, 1967.
Wright, Nathan, Jr. *What Black Politicians Are Saying.* New York: Hawthorne, 1972.
Yankelovich, Daniel. *The Changing Values on Campus and Political and Personal Attitudes of Today's College Students.* New York: Washington Square, 1972.
Young, Alfred, ed. *Dissent: Explorations in the History of American Radicalism.* DeKalb: Northern Illinois University Press, 1968.
Zald, Mayer N., and John D. McCarthy, eds. *The Dynamics of Social Movements: Resource Mobilization, Social Control, and Tactics.* Cambridge: Winthrop, 1979.
Zaroulis, Nancy, and Gerald Sullivan. *Who Spoke Up? American Protest against the War in Vietnam, 1963–1975.* Garden City, N.Y.: Doubleday, 1984.
Zeiger, Robert H. *American Workers, American Unions, 1920–1985.* Baltimore: Johns Hopkins University Press, 1986.
Zinn, Howard. *Postwar America, 1945–1971.* Indianapolis: Bobbs-Merrill, 1973.
———. *SNCC: The New Abolitionists.* Boston: Beacon Press, 1964.

Index

Abel, I. W., 67
Abernathy, Ralph, 68, 145
Abolitionists, 199
Abortion, 164, 175, 192, 194
Abzug, Bella, 131, 176
Activist, The, 6
Adair, Doug, 135
Adickes, Sandra, 27–28
Afro-American, 65
Agnew, Spiro, 60, 173, 192
Albany, Georgia, 84
Albert, Stew, 105
Allen, Jesse, 33
Allen, Robert, 70
Alliance for Labor Action, 59, 122, 154
All in the Family, 91
Altbach, Philip, 173
Amalgamated Clothing Workers, 162
American Congress for Cultural
   Freedom, 50, 125
Americans for Democratic Action
   (ADA), 28–29, 41, 173, 177
American Federation of Labor-Congress
   of Industrial Organization (AFL-CIO):
   funding of New Left, 14–15; and civil
   rights movement, 17–22; and southern
   unions, 19; and foreign policy, 21,
   52–53; and Mississippi Summer, 27;
   and Mississippi Freedom Democratic
   party, 41; and Selma, Alabama, 42; 1964
   convention, 47–48; and Vietnam War,
   47–53; and civil rights movement, 64;
   and Black Power, 71–72, 75; 1919 convention, 74; and League of Revolutionary Black Workers, 77–78; and Ocean
Hill-Brownsville, 81; and 1968 Democratic party convention, 101; and farm
   workers, 128–34; and Mississippi Freedom Labor Union, 134–35; and sanitation workers strike, 142; and community
   unions, 145–46; and GE strike, 148–51;
   and TAA, 160; and women's movement, 162; and election of 1968, 177;
   and George McGovern, 179–82; and
   Republican party, 180. *See also* Committee on Political Education (COPE);
   names of individual trade unions
American Federation of State, County,
   and Municipal Employees (AFSCME):
   mentioned, 12, 145; and Vietnam War,
   49, 60; and sanitation workers strike,
   141–46; and TAA, 159; and black
   mayors, 170
American Federation of Teachers: 12, 19,
   27–28, 42, 48, 68, 74, 155, 159–60; and
   Ocean Hill-Brownsville, 78–83
American Institute for Free Labor
   Development, 50, 160
American Jewish Congress, 7
Amalgamated Meatcutter's Union, 32, 49,
   64–65, 155
American Workers' party, 111
Analavage, Robert, 134
Anti-Semitism, 80
Anticommunism, 6, 11, 21–22, 24, 41, 49,
   77, 99, 133, 188, 192, 194
Antiwar movement, 1–2, 47, 49–51, 53,
   158–59
Applachia, 31, 34

Appalachian Committee for Full
  Employment, 35, 37
Aptheker, Bettina, 12
Apthecker, Herbert, 12, 50, 113
Arnold, Thurmond, 52
Aronowitz, Stanley, 5, 10, 35, 33, 58, 122,
  124, 127, 148, 182–83
Ashland, Massachusetts, 148
Atlanta, Georgia, 169
Atlantic City. *See* Democratic party

Backlash, 3, 66, 174, 188–89, 191–92
Baez, Joan, 84, 96, 171
Baker, Ella, 41
Bakery Drivers Union, 90
Baldwin, James, 9–10
Baraka, Amiri (Leroi Jones), 171
Barber's Union, 104
Barkan, Al, 178, 180
Barnett, Ross, 84
Barry, Marion, 13, 170
Bay of Pigs, 21
Beatles, The, 85
Beats, The, 88–89
Beck, Julian, 105
Becker, Norma, 27–29
Beifuss, Joan Turner, 144
Beirne, Joseph, 62, 181–82
Belafonte, Harry, 144
Bell, Daniel, 54, 97, 111, 118
Berkeley Barb, 103
Berkeley, California, 5, 105–6, 117,
  173–74. *See also* University of Califor-
  nia at Berkeley
Berkeley at War, 197
Berknap, Michael, 1
Berman, Paul, 123
Bettelheim, Bruno, 198
Bevel, James, 146
Birmingham, Alabama, 18
Black, Earl, 190
Black intellectuals, 70
Black nationalism, 68–69, 110, 153
Black Organizing Project, 142
Black Panther party, 70–72, 88, 110, 154,
  173–74
Black Panther party, of Lowndes County,
  Alabama, 169
Black Power: mentioned, 4, 63–83,

115–17, 121, 135; and electoral politics,
  171–75, 190–91
Black Power, 70
Black students, 159
Black studies, 118
Bluestone, Barry, 11, 46
Bluestone, Irving, 11, 24, 30, 46
Boggs, James, 68–69
Bond, Julian, 169, 171, 192
Boorstin, Daniel, 111
Booth, Heather, 162
Booth, Paul, 146, 154–55
Boozer, George, 104
Bork, Robert, 193
Boston College, 148
Boston Grape party, 130
Boston University, 148–51
Boudin, Kathy, 32
Boulware, Lemuel, 148
Boulwarism, 148
Boyle, Kevin, 28
Boyle, Tony, 157
Boyte, Harry, 138, 193, 200–201
Bracero program, 132
Braden, Anne, 13, 138–41
Braden, Carl, 13, 138–41
Brando, Marlon, 171
Brandon, Peter, 138
Bread and Roses, 149
Brecher, Jeremy, 16, 62
Breines, Wini, 197
Brennan, Peter, 2, 131
Breslin, Jimmy, 131
Brezinski, Zbignew, 118, 198
Bridges, Harry, 94–95
Bronx Science High School, 90
Brooke, Edward, 51
Brooklyn, New York, 174–75
Brooks, Owen, 135
Brookwood Labor College, 111
Brotherhood of Sleeping Car Porters,
  7
Brown, Sam, 59
Brown v. *Board of Education,* 19
Brown, Hank, 19, 135
Brown, H. Rap, 68, 143, 177
Brown, James, 116
Brown, Ray, 30
Buhle, Paul, 123, 177

Building Trades, 20, 62, 69–70, 75, 174, 181
Bunker, Archie, 91, 188
Burlage, Robb, 35–36, 138–39

Cade, Cathy, 138
Calvert, Greg, 120–21, 127
Cambodia, invasion of, 60, 93, 159
Cambridge Nonviolent Action Committee, 7
Cambridge, Massachuesetts, 151
Cammet, John, 125
Campbell, Leslie, 80
Campus workers, 136
Carawan, Guy, 85
Carey, James, 12
Carliner, Lew, 9–10
Carlson, Dennis, 173
Carmicael, Stokely: mentioned, 13–14, 42, 67, 69–72, 143, 171; and MFDP, 41; and King assassination, 144; and Black Power, 169
Carpenter's Union, 99
Carter, Hodding, 170
Case Western Reserve, 55
Cash, W. J., 137
Castro, Fidel, 116
Catholic worker movement, 113
Catholics, 168
Caudill, Harry, 34–35
Cavanagh, Jerome, 19
Central Intelligence Agency (CIA), 50, 160
Chafe, William, 189
Chaney, James, 27–28, 32
Chapel Hill, North Carolina, 145
Chapin, Ralph, 105
Charleston, South Carolina, 145
Charlotte, North Carolina, 145
Chavez, Cesar, 128–34, 145
Chester, Lewis, 179
Chester, Pennsylvania, 30
Chiakulas, Charles J., 146
Chicago Area Industrial Union Department, 146–47
Chicago Citizens Committee to Aid the farm workers, 131
Chicago organizing school, 154, 156

Chicago protest (1968), 55, 99. *See also* Democratic party
Chicago *Seed,* 90
Chicago '68, 198
Chicanos, 132–33
Chisholm, Shirley, 174, 176
Chomsky, Noam, 161
Church-Labor Conference, 29
Ciampi, P. J., 142, 145
Cicero, Illinois, 102
Cimino, Frank, 32
Citizen action groups, 193
Citizens United for Adequate Welfare, 32–33
Civil Rights Act of 1964, 26–27, 162, 191
Civil rights movement. *See* Student Nonviolent Coordinating Committee; National Association for the Advancement of Colored People; Congress of Racial Equality; Black Power; Black Panther party; Martin Luther King, Jr.; Stokely Camichael
Clark, Jim (Sheriff), 43
Clay, William, 170
Cleage, Albert, 68
Cleaver, Eldridge, 88, 144
Cleveland Area Peace Action Coalition, 59, 61–62
Coalition for Peace, 61
Coalition of Labor Union Women, 163–64
Cohelan, Jeffrey, 173
Cold war liberals, 52–53
Cold war, 50, 194
Coles, Robert, 178
Collins, Judy, 35
Columbia University, 49, 78, 88, 96–97, 118, 121
Commentary, 111
Comming Apart, 197
Committee for the Miners, 35, 37
Committee on Political Education (COPE), AFL-CIO, 15, 28, 170, 174, 178
Committee on the Move for Equality (COME), 142
Communication Workers of America, 62, 181
Communist party, 13, 49, 71
Community control, 79–82, 174
Community organizing, 154–55

Community unions, 14, 30–31, 145–46

Congress of Racial Equality: mentioned, 4, 7, 69, 73; ties to labor, 12, 15; and building trades, 20; and Hazard, Kentucky, 35; and Vietnam War, 51; and farm workers, 129–30; and Mississippi Freedom Labor Union, 134–35

Connor, "Bull," 133

Construction worker rampage, 1–3, 60–61, 63, 165, 179, 188

Construction unions. *See* Building trades

Contours of American History, 112

Conway, Jack, 10, 30–31

Coogen, Charles, 27, 131

Corporate liberalism, 54, 109, 118

Counterculture: mentioned, 4, 63, 84–107, 158; public opinion of, 92

Country Joe and the Fish, 96

Cowan, Paul, 183–84

Cowley, John, 125

Crosby, Stills, Nash & Young, 96

Cuban missle crisis, 21

Cuban revolution, 21

Curran, Joseph, 47, 49,

Curvin, Robert, 67

Dahl, Robert, 111

Daily Worker, 11, 103

Daley, Richard, 41, 99–100, 160

Danville, Virginia, 10, 138

Davidson, Carl, 101, 117–18, 120, 182

Davidson, Ray, 43–44

Davis, Caroline, 162

Davis, Leon, 55, 59

Davis, Ossie, 144

Davis, Rennie, 14, 31, 100, 146

Days of Rage, 101–2

Deindustrialization, 192

Delacour, Michael, 105–6

Delano, California, 129–30

DeLeon, Daniel, 123

Dellinger, Dave, 22, 102, 182–83

Dellums, Ronald, 173–74, 176

Delta ministry, 135

Demby, Charles, 110

Democracy Is in the Streets, 197

Democratic party: realignment of, 11, 23, 28–29, 41; national convention (1964),

18, 38–39, 168, 176; national convention (1968), 49, 99–100; mentioned, 90, 100, 190–91, 199; reform of, 179–80; national convention (1972), 180–81

Dennis, Dave, 41

Dennis, Eugene, 13

Dennis, Gene, Jr., 13

Detroit Federation of Teachers, 28

Detroit (Michigan) riot, 67–68, 76

Diggers, The, 105

Dinkins, David, 193

Dissent, 113

District 65 (RWDSU), 7, 16, 41, 104. *See also* Retail Workers

Dixiecrats, 11, 29

Dodge Revolutionary Union Movement (DRUM), 76–78

Dohrn, Bernadine, 121

Dombrowski, Jim, 138

Donaldson, Ivanhoe, 124

Douglass, Frederick, 82

Dow Chemical, 158

Dreiser, Theodore, 112

Drugs, 92–93, 95, 97

Duke University, 137–38

Dylan, Bob, 84–86

Eachus, Ron, 161

Eagleton, Thomas, 182

Eastman, Max, 88, 95

Economic Research and Action Projects (ERAPs), 4, 12, 14–15, 30- 34, 37–38, 46, 146, 197

Economy, 35, 52, 62, 93–94, 189

Eiban, Hank, 32

Eisenhower, Kay, 165

El Malcriado, 128

Eldon Axle and Gear Revolutionary Union Movement (ELRUM), 76

Elections: of 1964, 41, 47, 66, 190; of 1960, 167–68; of 1968, 176–79, 190; of 1972, 179–85; of 1976, 190

Electoral politics, 167–85

Environmental movement, 132, 183, 200

Epstein, Joseph, 102

Epsy, Mike, 135

Equal Pay Act of 1963, 162

Equal Rights Amendment, 162–63, 175

Eros and Civilization, 89

Evans, Sara, 137–38, 200–201
Evers, Charles, 169–70
Evers, Medgar, 169

Fackre, George, 94
Fair housing laws, 67
Farber, David, 99–100, 198
Farm workers, 161, 187, 136. *See also*
  United Farm Workers of America
Farmer, James, 9, 12, 20, 29, 84, 174–75
Farrow, Ted, 157
Fayettee, Tennessee, 13
Feel Like I'm Fixin to Die Rag, 96
Fein, Otto, 32
Feinglass, Abe, 64–65, 161
Feldman, Sandra, 78–79
Feminism, 149, 175. *See also* Women's
  movement
Fenster, Leo, 59
Feuer, Lewis, 118, 198
Fields, Bobby, 72
Fine, Sidney, 68
Finley, Murray, 131
Firefighters, 18
Fischer, Charles, 13
Fischer, Sylvia, 13
Fitzimmons, Frank, 181
Flacks, Richard, 11, 23, 131
Flag, Mike, 48
Folk music, 85
Foner, Henry, 55
Foner, Philip, 113
Food and Tobacco Workers, 85
Ford Revolutionary Union Movement
  (FRUM), 76
Foreign policy, 47. *See also* Cold War
Foreman, Clark, 13
Forman, James, 10, 13, 15–16, 19, 42, 197
Fraser, Douglas, 59
Free Speech movement (Berkeley), 12,
  26, 54, 87, 117
Free Student Union, 12
Freedom Marches, 18
Freedom Rides, 15, 17, 78, 84
Freedom Schools, 68
Freedom Village, 135
Freeman, Jo, 164, 200–201
Freemont, California, 154
Fuerst, John, 154

Galbraith, John Kenneth, 111
Gallagher, J. D., 140
Gallup polls, 19, 48
Gannon, James, 100–101
Ganz, Marshall, 129
Garson, Barbara, 12
Garson, Marvin, 54
Garvey, Marcus, 74
Gary, Indiana, 155, 171
General Electric strike, 147–51, 161, 166
General Motors strike, 153–56, 166
Generation gap, 39, 98, 119, 197, 199
Genovese, Eugene, 125–26
Germano, Joseph, 171
Gibbons, Harold, 12, 55–56, 59, 141, 161
Gibson, Berman, 34
Gibson, Ken, 171
Gilbert, David, 119
Gilbert, Ronnie, 35
Ginsberg, Allen, 88–89
Gitlin, Todd, 14–15, 197
Give Peace a Chance, 105, 110
Gleason, Thomas, 2, 50–51
Glenn, Grady, 59
Goldberg, Arthur, 48
Goldfinger, Nat, 31
Goldwater, Barry, 29, 39, 47, 66
Good, Rhoda, 183
Goodman, Andrew, 27–28
Goodman, Paul, Goodman, 32, 89, 112
Gordon, Jerry, 59
Gorman, Patrick, 49, 56, 59
Gorson, Arthur, 35–36
Gorz, Andre, 119–20
Gotbaum, Victor, 49, 61
Gotleib, Bob, 119
Gramsci, Antonia, 125–26
Grape boycott, 130–32
Grapes of Wrath, 128
Grass Roots Organizing Workers
  (GROW), 139–40
Great Depression, 94
Great Society, 26, 52, 194
Great Speckled Bird, 139
Green Beret, 99
Green, James, 157
Greensboro, North Carolina, 136
Greenwich Village, 35, 95
Greenwood, Mississippi, 169

Greer, Frank, 161
Gregory, Dick, 9, 100
Grossman, Jerome, 59
Guardian, 34, 70, 122, 147, 182
Guerrero, Gene, 138–39
Guerrero, Nan, 136
Guthrie, Arlo, 154
Guthrie, Woody, 74, 85
Gutman, Herbert, 123

Haber, Allan, 12
Haber, William, 12
Halstead, Fred, 59
Hamer, Fannie Lou, 39, 42, 134, 170, 190
Hamilton, Charles, 70
Hamlet, Ed, 138
Hamlin, Mike, 77
Hampton, Wade, 84
Hamtramck, Michigan, 76
Harlem (New York), 78
Harrington, Michael, 24, 34, 54, 81, 114–15, 126
Hart, Gary, 179
Hartz, Louis, 111
Harvard University, 148, 161
Harvest of Shame, 128
Hat Worker, 72
Hatcher, Richard, 171–72
Hattiesburg, Mississippi, 28
Haughton, James, 69–70
Haw River, North Carolina, 136
Hawk, David, 59
Hawley, Ellis, 198
Hayden, Casey, 138
Hayden, Tom, 24, 30–31, 41, 50, 62, 100, 118, 124, 178, 192
Hays, Samuel, 198
Hazard, Kentucky, 10, 34–37, 141
Helix, 152
Helmer, John, 57
Helstein, Ralph, 13, 15–17, 22–23, 30, 131
Hendrix, Jimi, 98
Henry, Aaron, 67, 169–70
Heyns, Roger, 106
Higgins, George, 8
Highlander Center, 141
Highlander Folk School, 12–13, 85
Higson, Mike, 140

Hill, Herbert, 20, 81–82
Hill, Norman, 7, 138
Hillinson, John, 157
Hippies, 53, 90–91, 94, 103, 151
Historiography of 1960s, 2–3, 41, 197
History, African American, 68, 81–82
Hitler, Adolph, 183
Hodgson, Godfrey, 179
Hoffa, Jimmy, 181
Hoffer, Eric, 53, 91
Hoffman, Abbie, 55, 90, 94–96, 100, 121, 124
Hofstadter, Richard, 111
Hollander, Nanci, 146
Holmes, Robert, 60
Holy Cross, 148–49, 151
Homosexuality, 88, 98
Honeymooners, The, 103
Hooks, Benjamin, 142
Horton, Myles, 12, 138–39, 141
Horton, Zilphia, 85
Hospital workers, 145–46. *See also* Local 1199
Howard University, 13
Howe, Irving, 3, 54, 115, 118, 124, 189, 200
Humphrey, Hubert, 38–39, 177–78

Ifship, David, 161
Imperialism, 70, 77, 115, 118, 148, 182, 194
In White America, 120
Independent leftists, 111–15, 121–27
Industrial Workers of the World, 118, 123
Integration (of schools), 68, 78–79
Intercollegiate Conference on Poverty, 31
International Ladies Garmant Workers Union (ILGWU), 14, 17–22, 20, 49, 51, 155
International Longshoremen Association (ILA), 2, 43, 50, 181
International Longshoremen and Ware-housemens Union (ILWU): mentioned, 8, 15, 94; and civil rights movement, 18; and Vietnam War, 48; and farm workers, 130; and GE strike, 148; and politics, 174
International Machinists Association, 30, 193

International Socialists, 58, 152–53, 155
International Socialist Journal, 119, 152
International Union of Electrical Workers (IUE), 31, 67–68, 148, 150
Invaders, The, 142, 144
Ishie, Herbert, 140
Isolationism, 180
Israel, 180
Isserman, Maurice, 197
Itlong, Larry, 129–30, 133
Iushewitz, Morris, 131

Jackson State, 61
Jackson, Jesse, 143, 192
Jackson, Jimmy Lee, 44
Jackson, Maynard, 170
Jackson, Mississippi, 19, 169
Jacobs, G. T., 147
Jacobs, Paul, 132
Jacobson, Julius, 68
Jeffrey, Mildred, 11, 24–25
Jeffrey, Sharon, 11, 32, 146
Jenkins, Craig, 200–201
Jobs or Income Now (JOIN), 16, 41, 47
Joe, 91
John Birch Society, 82, 133
Johnson, Lyndon, and the Great Society, 26; and Mississippi Summer, 27; and MFDP, 38–39; mentioned, 144, 191, 200
Jones, T. O., 141–42, 145
Joplin, Janis, 97–98
Jordan, Barbara, 170
Jordan, Vernon, 73
Judaism, 90

Kahn, Tom, 7, 91, 115, 161
Karenga, Ron, 72
Katz, Martin, 171
Kelley, Joe, 91
Kelley, William Melvin, 116
Kempton, Murray, 115
Keniston, Kenneth, 198–99
Kennedy, John F.: mentioned, 17, 18, 66, 162, 167–68, 191; assassination of, 26; and civil rights, 168
Kennedy, Robert, 144, 176–78
Kent State, 2
Kerner Commission, 67, 81

Kerr, Clark, 117
Key, V. O., 70
King, Corretta Scott, 145
King, Ed, 29
King, Martin Luther, Jr.: and March on Washington, 7–8; mentioned, 18, 44, 46, 66, 108–9, 191, 195; and MFDP, 39; and Vietnam War, 51; and antiwar movement, 56; and farm workers, 133; and sanitation workers strike, 143–46; and Chicago, 146; assassination of, 178
Kirkland, Lane, 180
Kirshner, William, 133
Kissinger, C. Clark, 16
Klonsky, Mike, 109, 121
Knowland, William, 174
Koehler, Chuck, 36, 141
Kolodny, David, 184
Kopkind, Andrew, 32
Kosik, Jim, 154
Krupa, John, 171
Ku Klux Klan, 140
Kunkin, Arthur, 103, 153

Labor: intellectuals, 5, 110, 112; history, 5; definition of, 6; opinion of civil rights movement, 18, 20–21; in Hazard, Kentucky, 35; in Selma, Alabama, 42–44; press, 103–4, 160–61; organizing, 128–46; education, 162. *See also* AFL-CIO; *names of individual unions and labor leaders*
Labor Action for Peace, 22, 62
Labor and Nation, 111
Labor for Equal Rights Now, 175
Labor Leadership Assembly for Peace, 56–58
"Labor question," The, 108–28
Labor Workshop, 154–56
Lafayette, Bernard, 13, 131
Lasch, Christopher, 124–25
Laurel, Mississippi, 140
Lavine, John, 42
Lawson, James, 142
Lawson, Stephen, 169–70
Leadership Conference for Civil Rights (LCCR), 29, 33, 41
League of Industrial Democracy (LID), 7, 10–11, 24, 91

League of Revolutionary Black Workers, 76–78
Leamer, Lawrence, 95, 103
Leary, Timothy, 97
Lemisch, Jesse, 123, 131
LeMoyne College, 145
Lennon, John, 105
Lens, Sidney, 22, 50, 53–54, 59, 111, 122
Lesbianism, 164. *See also* Homosexuality
Lester, Julius, 101, 115
Leuchtenburg, William, 3
Levi Strauss, 137–38
Levison, Andrew, 102
Lewis, John, 8, 13–14, 29, 29
Lewis, John L., 36, 157
Liberal intellectuals, 111–12
Liberal party, 175
Liberalism, 24, 26, 66, 75, 107, 173, 185–88, 191, 198
Liberation, 6, 58, 111, 114, 155
Liberation News Service, 103
Lichtenstein, Nelson, 53
Lillienthal, Robinson, 89
Lindsay, John, 1, 131
Lipset, Seymour Martin, 118
Living Theater, 105
Livingston, David, 55, 59
Local 1199, 16, 41, 55, 145, 160, 193
Loeb, Henry, 142, 145
Loftis, Anne, 128
London, Jack, 11
Lopez, John, 72–73, 98
Lordstown, 156–57
Los Angeles *Free Press,* 103, 153
Lovestone, Jay, 50, 52
Lucy in the Sky with Diamonds, 105
Lynch, Lincoln, 65
Lynd, Alice, 63
Lynd, Staughton, 5, 41, 50, 54, 63, 114, 155–57
Lynn, Massachusetts, 149
Lyrical left, 95

Madar, Olga, 164
Madison, Wisconsin, 5, 158–62, 172. *See also* University of Wisconsin
Mahoney, William, 9–10
Mahwah, New Jersey, 78

Main, Jeffrey, 92
Making of a Black Revolutionary, The, 197
Malcolm X, 8, 21, 79, 82
Mallet, Serge, 119, 120
Mantle, Mickey, 116
Maplewood, New Jersey, 33
Marable, Manning, 171
March Against Racism and Repression, 61
March on Washington (1963), 7–8, 18, 22, 41, 49, 78
March on Washington movement, 68, 74
March, Ronald, 77
Marcuse, Herbert, 54, 89, 112, 122
Martin, Tommy, 136
Marx, Groucho, 95
Marx, Karl, 89, 95, 112
Marxism, 70–71, 95, 116, 120–26
Maryland Freedom Union, 64–65
Mason, Lucy Randolph, 13
Mass media, 95, 100
Masses, The, 95, 103
Massie, Mae, 67
Mattles, James, 150
Max, Steve, 11, 154–55, 162
May uprising (France), 108–9
Mayer, Arnold, 15
Mays, Willie, 116
Mazey, Emil, 22–23, 31, 48–49, 56, 77
McAdam, Douglas, 27, 198, 200–201
McCarthy, Eugene, 144, 170, 176–79
McCarthyism, 24
McCoy, Rhody, 79
McDew, Charles, 22
McGovern, George, 167, 170, 179–85
McKissick, Floyd, 51, 65, 68, 73
McReynolds, David, 115
Meany, George: and Birmingham demonstrations, 18; and March on Washington, 19; dispute with A. Philip Randolph, 20–21; and antiwar movement, 48; and anticommunism, 50, 52–53; and trade unionists for peace, 55–57; and Black Power, 71; and counterculture, 86; and 1968 Democratic party convention, 100; and farm workers, 133, 135; and TAA, 160; and John F. Kennedy, 168; and Shirley

Meany, George (*Continued*)
Chisholm, 174; and Eugene McCarthy, 177–78; and Richard Nixon, 179; and Democratic convention (1972), 180–81
Medicare, 194
Meese, Edwin, 106
Meier, August, 51, 115
Meister, Dick, 128
Melman, Seymour, 161
Memphis, Tennessee. *See* Sanitation workers strike
Menapace, Jerry, 64–66
Meredith, James, 135, 169
Meyer, Sam, 55, 59
Meyer, Herbert H., 149
Michigan Democratic party, 29
Michigan State University, 154
Middle America, 3, 85–86, 92
Midwest Academy, 162
Mikulski, Barbara, 176
Militant Labor Forum, 35
Militant, The, 103
Milkman, Ruth, 163
Miller, Dottie, 138–39
Miller, James, 197
Mills, C. Wright, 54, 111–12
Mine Workers for Democracy, 157
Minh, Ho Chi, 48, 116
Miniskirt, 93
Mississippi Freedom Democratic party, 28–29, 38, 63, 81, 140, 168–70, 187
Mississippi Freedom Labor Union (MFLU), 134–35
Mississippi Freedom Schools, 27–28, 155
Mississippi State AFL-CIO, 170
Mississippi Summer (1964), 4, 19, 26–30, 41–42, 78, 129, 134
Mississippi Summer, 198
Mississippi Teachers Association, 170
Mitchell, Parren, 170
Monsonis, Jim, 16
Monthly Review, 113
Moody, Kim, 16, 48, 156
Moratorium, 59
Morgan, Edward P., 27, 67, 104
Moses, Robert, 17, 28, 31, 42
Movement, The, 197
Muehlenkamp, Bob, 160
Municipal Employees Union, 170

Munk, Michael, 22
Muste, A. J., 30, 111

National Association for the Advancement of Colored People (NAACP), mentioned, 7, 15–16, 73, 141–42, 170; and report "Racism within Organized Labor," 20–21; and Mississippi Summer, 27
Nader, Ralph, 157
Nashville, Tennessee, 138
National Alliance of Postal and Federal Employees, 65
National Conference for a New Politics (NCUP), 154, 176
National Council of Churches, 7
National Mobilization Committee to End the War in Vietnam (MOBE), 49, 51, 55, 59
National Maritime Union, 47
National Organization of Women, 163, 176
National Review, 70
National Student Association, 50, 150–51
National Urban League, 73
Nazi Germany, 89
Negro American Labor Council, 7, 20–21, 55, 69, 74,
Network of Economic Rights, 175
New Deal coalition, 189, 191
New Detroit movement, 68
New Directions in Labor, 154
New Left: origins 4, 10–11; definition of, 5–6; family ties to labor, 11–12; views on foreign policy, 21–22; and George Meany, 22; and Democratic party, 39; and Lyndon Johnson, 39; Left and liberalism, 40–41; historiography, 188. *See also* Students for a Democratic Society; Student Nonviolent Coordinating Committee; Congress of Racial Equality; and names of individual new leftists, such as Tom Hayden.
New Left Notes, 118, 178
New MOBE, 59, 148, 192
New Right, 24, 82–83, 107, 185, 188–89, 192, 194
New working class, 119–22, 160, 165

New York City: Building Trades Council,
  2; Central Labor Council, 27–28, 131;
  mentioned, 78–82
New York intellectuals, 79
New York State AFL-CIO, 175
New York State Commission on Human
  Rights, 20
New York University, 90
Newark, New Jersey, 33, 37–38, 67–68,
  78, 171
Newark Committee for Full Employment,
  33
Newark State, 154
Newfield, Jack, 115
Newport Jazz Festival, 85
Newspaper Workers, 16
Newton, Huey, 173
Nicaragua, 193
Nicolaus, Martin, 124
Nine to Five, 164
Nixon, Richard, mentioned, 2, 58, 60, 133,
  157, 161, 183, 192; and postal workers
  strike, 151–52
Nkrumah, Kwame, 116
Nonviolence, 129, 133
Nonviolent Action Group, 9, 13
Noplis, Babe, 36
North Carolina State AFL-CIO, 17
North Carolina University, 136
North Vietnam, 50
Northeastern University, 148
Nuclear Test Ban Treaty, 19
Nuclear weapons, 194

O'Connor, James, 31
O'Neill, William, 92, 197
Oakland, California, 173–74
Ocean Hill-Brownsville, 76, 78–82; 160
Ochs, Phil, 35
Oglesby, Carl, 49; 113
Oil and Chemical Workers of America,
  43–44, 147
Oil crisis, 185
Okie from Muskogee, 99
Old Left 3, 5–6, 34, 125, 156. See also
  Communist party
Old Mole, 151–52
Oliver, William, 72
Oliver, C. Herbert, 80

Ollman, Bertell, 123
Operating Engineers, 30
Ortiz, Daniel, 129

Pace College, 1
Page, Bruce, 179
Palace Hotel (San Francisco), 16
Parrish, Richard, 19
Participatory democracy, 36, 81, 125,
  156
Peace movement, 18
Peace and Freedom party, 177
Peck, Abe, 89–90
Peck, Sidney, 55, 58–59, 161
Pentagon demonstration, 49, 55
People's Park, 105–6, 173
Perdew, John, 141
Perkins, Eric, 77
Perlman, Selig, 70
Perlman, Lucile, 183
Personal politics, 87, 163
Peterson, Estelle, 162
Phillips, Kevin, 201
Plaquemine, Lousiana, 9
Poinsett, Alex, 171
Polish Americans, 77
Pollack, Sam, 32
Poor People's Campaign, 33, 68, 114–15,
  143, 191
Populists, 199, 201
Pornography, 98
Port Huron Statement, 45, 87, 188
Postal workers strike, 151–53
Postindustrialism, 119, 198. See also
  Deindustrializaiton
Potofsky, Joseph, 161
Potter, Paul, 32
Powell, Daniel, 170
Presidential Commission on the Status of
  Women, 162
Presley, Elvis, 97, 116
Prince Edwards County, Virginia, 19
Princeton University, 120
Progressive Labor party (PL): mentioned,
  96, 108–9, 121–22, 139; and GE strike,
  148–51
Pro-war (Vietnam) movement, 1–2, 47
Public employee unionism, 143–44
Public opinion: on race, 42–43; of

Public opinion (*Continued*)
Chicago (1968) demonstration, 101; of
Eugene McCarthy, 179
Pulpworkers, 140

Quakers, 89
Quill, Michael, 27

Raby, Al, 131
Race riots, 66–68. *See also names of individual race riots, such as Detroit riots*
Racial discrimination, 194
Radical America, 5, 77, 121–24, 157–58, 164
Radical feminists, 163–64. *See also* Women's movement
Radosh, Ronald, 21, 50, 54, 114
Rags, 103
Ramparts, 6, 51, 58, 80, 173, 183
Ramsay, Claude, 19, 135, 140, 169
Randolph, A. Philip: and March on Washington, 7–8; mentioned, 12, 17, 68–71, 117; and dispute with George Meany, 20–21; and MFDP, 39; and Black Power, 73–74; and Ocean Hill-Brownsville, 81–82
Rank and File, 155
Rauh, Joe, 28, 41, 187
Ravitch, Diane, 79
Reagan, Ronald, 106–7, 133, 192
Rector, James, 106
Red Diaper Babies, 11–12
Reeb, James, 42–44
Reed College, 16, 89
Reese, Arthur, 28, 84, 105
Reich, Charles, 119, 198–99
Reider, Jonathan, 193
Republican party, 168, 201,
Resistance, The, 48
Resource mobilization theory, 199–200
Retail Clerks, 12, 130, 141. *See also* District 65
Reuther, Roy, 46
Reuther, Victor, 50, 161
Reuther, Walter: and March on Washington, 8; mentioned, 12, 17, 35, 41, 46–47; and SDS, 14; and Birmingham protests; and MFDP, 39; and antiwar movement, 48; and anticommunism, 50; and Viet-

nam War, 60–61; and riots, 68; and CORE, 73; and farm workers, 130, 133; and sanitation workers strike, 144–45; and John F. Kennedy, 168
Revolutionary Youth movement, 109, 139
Rice, Shirley, 145
Rich, J. C., 72
Rich, Marin, 12, 15
Richardson, George, 67
Richmond, California, 147,
Richmond, Virginia, 175
Rising Up Angry, 153
Robinson, Cleveland, 7, 61, 161
Roche, John, 60, 179
Rockefeller, David, 2
Rock 'n Roll, 85, 95, 105
Rodriguez, John, 161
Rogin, Richard, "Joe Kelley Has Reached His Boiling Point," 3
Rolling Stones, The, 97
Romaine, Howard, 138
Romano, Peter, 2
Romney, George, 31
Roosevelt, Eleanor, 17
Roosevelt, Franklin D., 168
Root and Branch, 124
Rorabaugh, W. J., 197
Rosenblum, Frank, 56, 59
Ross, Bob, 11, 146
Ross, William, 51
Rossman, Michael, 12
Roszak, Theodore, 87, 119, 198–99
ROTC, 194
Rothstein, Richard, 36, 146
Roundtree, Margaret, 119
Rubin, Jerry, 55, 90, 94–96, 100, 121
Rucker, Betty, 58
Rudd, Mark, 78, 118
Rustin, Bayard: mentioned, 7, 9, 66, 68, 70, 114, 116–17, 191; and MFDP, 39; *From Protest to Politics,* 66, 114; and Black Power, 73–74; and sanitation workers strike, 143–46; debate with Staughton Lynd, 155
Rutger's University, 151
Ryan, William, 35

Sachs, Karen, 145
Sadlowski, Ed, 158

Sale, Kirkpatrick, 197
Salter, John, 29
Samuels, H. D., 161
San Francisco Mine Troupe, 105
San Francisco State, 147, 173
SANE, mentioned, 48–49; trade union
    division, 55–56
Sanitation workers strike (Memphis),
    141–46, 192
Savio, Mario, 87, 117
Schiller, Ed, 16
Schlesinger, Arthur Jr., 111, 201
School prayer, 192, 194
Schrade, Paul, 59, 154
Schunior, Anne, 136
Schwerner, Michael, 27–28, 32
Scottsboro boys, 89
Seafarers, 11, 130
Seale, Bobby, 71, 100, 173
Sears Roebuck & Co., 12
Seeger, Pete, 85, 139
Segal, Ben, 31
Segregation, 194
Sellers, Cleveland, 29
Selma, Alabama, 42–44, 63
Service Employees International Union,
    164
Sexton, Brendan, 30
Sexton, Patricia Cayo, 164
Sexual discrimination, 162, 176, 194
Sexual revolution, 97–98
Shanker, Albert: mentioned, 27, 78–82;
    and sanitation workers strike, 144; and
    TAA, 160
Sheer, Robert, 173
Sherr, Max, 103
Shirah, Liz, 134, 140
Shirah, Sam, 137–38, 140
Shiskin, Boris, 17
Shostak, Arthur, 3
Sinclair, Hamish, 35
Sinclair, John, 92
Sinclair, Upton, 11
Sit-ins, 17
Sixties, The, 197
Slaiman, Donald, 150
Sloan, Cliff, 2
Smith, Howard, 162
Smith, Maxine, 142

Social activist unions, 6, 23, 53–54, 74–74
Social democrats, 66, 68, 114–15, 126, 187
Social movements, theory of, 199–201
Socialism, 124–26, 156, 184
Socialist Scholars Conferences, 5, 121–25
Socialist party, 113–14, 123, 155
Socialist Worker party, 153, 155, 182
Soglin, Paul, 172, 176
Solidarity Foreover, 105, 110
South Africa, 153, 193
Southern Christian Leadership Confer-
    ence (SCLC), 7, 27, 67, 73, 143, 146
Southern Conference Education Fund
    (SCEF), 13, 134, 139–40
Southern Conference for Human Wel-
    fare (SCHW), 13
Southern Exposure, 123–24, 139
Southern Labor Action Movement
    (SLAM), 139
Southern Patriot, 134
Southern Student Organizing Committee
    (SSOC), 123, 136–39
Southern, Susan, 119
Southern Tenants Farmers' Union, 123
Southwestern College, 145
Space program, 26
Sparticist league, 112
Spellman College, 155
Spitz, Lawrence, 53
Spock, Benjamin, 144
Spragens, John, Jr., 135
Standard Oil of California, 147
Starr, William, 97
Steinbeck, John, 128
Steinem, Gloria, 131
Stern, Sol, 80
Stillman, Nat, 154
Stone, I. F., 183
Strike city, 135
Student League for Industrial
    Democracy. See Students for a
    Democratic Society
Student Mobilization Committee, 58
Student Nonviolent Coordinating Com-
    mittee (SNCC): mentioned, 4; and
    UPWA, 9–10, 13–14; "Jobs and Food
    Conference," 9–10; ties to labor, 12–13;
    and Hazard, Kentucky, 35; and fed-
    eral government, 40; Friends of SNCC,

SNCC (*Continued*)
    42; and Vietnam War, 59; and Black
    Power, 69; and farm workers, 129–32;
    and Mississippi Freedom Labor Union,
    134–35; and southern labor movement,
    140–41; community unions, 146; and
    women's movement, 163; and Kennedy
    Administration, 168; and Black Pan-
    ther party, 169
Student Peace Union, 18
Student power, 117–18, 120
Students and Labor, 12
Students for a Democratic Society
    (SDS): mentioned, 2, 4; and March on
    Washington, 7; origins of, 10–11; and
    UAW, 14–15; and strike support, 16;
    and foreign policy, 22; "Port Huron
    Statement," 23–24; and AFL-CIO, 23;
    and LID, 41; and Committee for the
    Miners, 35–36; and Vietnam War,
    47–49, 58–59; and League of Revolu-
    tionary Black Workers, 77; and 1969
    con vention, 108–11; and farm workers,
    129–32; and community unions, 145;
    and oil workers strike, 147; and GE
    strike, 148–51; and UE, 150; and GM
    strike, 154; and Eugene McCarthy, 177;
    and election of 1968, 177–78;
Studies on the Left, 6, 21, 114, 122, 125,
    155, 158
Susskind, Sally, 36
Sutherland, Elizabeth, 129
Swarthmore College (SDS chapter), 30,
    35
Sweezy, John, 164
Sweezy, Paul, 124

Taft-Hartley Act, 6
Taxes, 61, 192
Teaching Assistants Association (TAA),
    158–62
Teamsters, 35, 55, 60, 133, 181
Teamsters for Democracy, 158, 160
Tennessee AFL-CIO, 142
Tet Offensive, 55, 57
Texas AFL-CIO, 19, 135
Texas, farm workers movement, 135
Textile workers, 136–39
Tharp, Everette, 37

Third World Liberation Front, 121
Thomas, Norman, 9, 54, 115
Thrasher, Sue, 138
Tillow, Walter, 10, 140–41, 150
Toffler, Alvin, 118, 198
Trade Union Leadership Council, 19
Trade unionists for peace, 48, 55, 59–60,
    188
Transit Workers Union, 27
Trenton, New Jersey (ERAPs), 33
Tripp, Luke, 77
Tuley, Cathy, 165
Tyler, Gus, 52, 105, 126

Underground newspapers, 103–4
Unemployment, 66
Unger, Irwin, 3, 189, 197
United Automobile Workers (UAW): and
    March on Washington, 7, and Crusade
    Against Poverty, 10; ties to New Left,
    11–12; and funding of SDS, 14–15; and
    MFDP, 28; and ERAPs, 30; and
    Vietnam War, 49; and civil rights
    movement, 65; and urban riots, 67–68;
    and Black Power, 72–73; and Local 3,
    77; and League of Revolutionary Black
    Workers, 76–78; mentioned 111, 123;
    and GM strike, 153–56; and Lordstown
    strike, 157; and Women's Department
    of, 162 63, 175; and women's move-
    ment, 163–64, 175; and George
    McGovern, 181–82;
United Black Brothers, 78
United Civil Rights Leadership, 41
United Electrical Workers (UE), 15, 41,
    48, 104, 147–51,
United Farm Workers of America
    (UFWA), 5, 128–34; 174, 200
United Federation of Teachers. *See*
    American Federation of Teachers
United Mine Workers, 34–37, 51, 157
United Packinghouse Workers of America
    (UPWA): and March on Washington,
    8; "Civil Rights and Legislation
    Conference," 8- 9; and SNCC, 9–10,
    13–16; and sit-ins, 17; and ERAPs, 30,
    33; and Selma protests; and urban riots,
    67; and Black Power, 73; and farm
    workers, 129–30; and SDS, 154

United Rubber Workers, 104
United Steel Workers of America,
    171–72, 181
University of California at Berkeley, 26,
    106, 117, 129, 173
University of California, Los Angeles, 154
University of California at Santa Barbara,
    106
University of Florida, 129
University of Illinois, 154
University of Michigan, 2, 154
University of Nebraska, 129
University of Southern California, 97
University of Wisconsin (Madison) 16,
    129, 158–62,

Van Arsdale, Harry, 27, 131
Veblen, Thorsten, 125
Verba, Sidney, 102
Vernoff, Edward, 123
Viet Cong, 49, 60, 116
Vietnam Day Committee, 48
Vietnam War: mentioned, 1–4, 46–63;
    and public opinion of, 48, 57, 60–61;
    relationship to counterculture, 86, 92;
    and politics, 169, 173, 180
Vietnam veterans, 156
Vietnam Veterans Versus the War, 56–57,
    62
Viorst, Milton, 41, 197
Voter Education project, 15, 168
Voter registration, 33
Voting Rights Act of 1965, 26, 42–44, 66,
    134, 190–92, 194

Wagner Act, 70, 134
Wald, George, 161
Wallace, George, 42, 84, 95, 182, 191–92
War on poverty, 4, 26, 35, 37, 173, 191
Washington, Booker T., 82
Washington, D.C., 170
Waskow, Art, 30
Watson, John, 77
Watts (Los Angeles) riots, 67
Wayne State, 77, 154
We Shall Overcome, 85, 105, 110
Weathermen, The, 109–11, 122, 165, 167,
    182, 188
Weavers, The, 35

Webb, Lee, 131, 154
Weinberg, Jack, 151
Weinberg, Nat, 161
Weschler, James, 51
Which Side Are You On?, 84, 86,
    105
White Citizens' Council, 19
White, John, 65
White folks project, 141
White supremacy, 191
Whiteville, North Carolina, 138
Who, The, 96
Wiener, Jonathan, 197
Wiley, George, 129
Wilkerson, Cathy, 109
Wilkins, Roy, 20, 39, 51, 143
Williams, Claude, 124
Williams, Hosea, 143
Williams, Jim, 138, 154
Williams, Joyce, 124
Williams, Thomas, 99
Williams, William Appleman, 54, 112
Winpisinger, William, 193
Wisconsin AFL-CIO, 160
Wittman, Carl, 30, 38
Wolfgang, Myra, 59
Women workers, 156
Women's Bureau, 162
Women's movement: and labor
    movement, 149–50; mentioned,
    162–65, 183, 200; and poltics, 175–76
Woodcock, Leonard, 46, 61, 161, 181
Woodcock, Leslie, 46
Woodstock, 96
Woodworkers, 140
Work conditions, 77
Worker Student Alliance (WSA), 108–9,
    147
Workers Power, 157
Working-class youths, 109
World War I, 46
Wurf, Jerry, 12, 142–44
Wyatt, Addie, 164

Yablonski, Jock, 157
Yankelovich, Daniel, 92
Yellow Submarine, 85
Young, Alfred, 123
Young Americans for Freedom, 24

Young, Andrew, 170
Young Democratic Club, 169–70
Young Socialist Alliance, 12, 58
Young, Whitney, 73

Youth movement, 119, 197

Zald, Mayer, 199
Zellner, Bob, 13–14, 138–40

PETER B. LEVY is an assistant professor of history at York College of Pennsylvania. His publications include *Let Freedom Ring: A Documentary History of the Modern Civil Rights Movement* and *100 Key Documents in American Democracy.* He has had articles published in *Labor History, Industrial and Labor Relations Review, Peace and Change,* and *Maryland Historical Magazine.* He received his Ph.D. from Columbia University in 1986, where he studied with Eric Foner.

Books in the Series
The Working Class in American History

Worker City, Company Town: Iron and Cotton-Worker
Protest in Troy and Cohoes, New York, 1855–84
Daniel J. Walkowitz

Life, Work, and Rebellion in the Coal Fields:
The Southern West Virginia Miners, 1880–1922
David Alan Corbin

Women and American Socialism, 1870–1920
Mari Jo Buhle

Lives of Their Own: Blacks, Italians, and Poles
in Pittsburgh, 1900–1960
John Bodnar, Roger Simon, and Michael P. Weber

Working-Class America: Essays on Labor, Community,
and American Society
Edited by Michael H. Frisch and Daniel J. Walkowitz

Eugene V. Debs: Citizen and Socialist
Nick Salvatore

American Labor and Immigration History, 1877–1920s:
Recent European Research
Edited by Dirk Hoerder

Workingmen's Democracy: The Knights of Labor and
American Politics
Leon Fink

The Electrical Workers: A History of Labor
at General Electric and Westinghouse, 1923–60
Ronald W. Schatz

The Mechanics of Baltimore: Workers and Politics
in the Age of Revolution, 1763–1812
Charles G. Steffen

The Practice of Solidarity: American Hat Finishers
in the Nineteenth Century
David Bensman

The Labor History Reader
Edited by Daniel J. Leab

Solidarity and Fragmentation: Working People and
Class Consciousness in Detroit, 1875–1900
Richard Oestreicher

Counter Cultures:
Saleswomen, Managers, and Customers
in American Department Stores, 1890–1940
Susan Porter Benson

The New England Working Class and
the New Labor History
Edited by Herbert G. Gutman and Donald H. Bell

Labor Leaders in America
Edited by Melvyn Dubofsky and Warren Van Tine

Barons of Labor: The San Francisco Building Trades
and Union Power in the Progressive Era
Michael Kazin

Gender at Work: The Dynamics of Job Segregation
by Sex during World War II
Ruth Milkman

Once a Cigar Maker: Men, Women, and Work Culture
in American Cigar Factories, 1900–1919
Patricia A. Cooper

A Generation of Boomers: The Pattern of Railroad
Labor Conflict in Nineteenth-Century America
Shelton Stromquist

Work and Community in the Jungle:
Chicago's Packinghouse Workers, 1894–1922
James R. Barrett

Workers, Managers, and Welfare Capitalism:
The Shoeworkers and Tanners of Endicott Johnson,
1890–1950
Gerald Zahavi

Men, Women, and Work: Class, Gender, and Protest
in the New England Shoe Industry, 1780–1910
Mary Blewett

Workers on the Waterfront: Seamen, Longshoremen,
and Unionism in the 1930s
Bruce Nelson

German Workers in Chicago: A Documentary History
of Working-Class Culture from 1850 to World War I
Edited by Hartmut Keil and John B. Jentz

On the Line: Essays in the History of Auto Work
Edited by Nelson Lichtenstein and Stephen Meyer III

Upheaval in the Quiet Zone:
A History of Hospital Workers' Union, Local 1199
Leon Fink and Brian Greenberg

Labor's Flaming Youth: Telephone Operators
and Worker Militancy, 1878–1923
Stephen H. Norwood

Another Civil War: Labor, Capital, and the State
in the Anthracite Regions of Pennsylvania, 1840–68
Grace Palladino

Coal, Class, and Color:
Blacks in Southern West Virginia, 1915–32
Joe William Trotter, Jr.

For Democracy, Workers, and God:
Labor Song-Poems and Labor Protest, 1865–95
Clark D. Halker

Dishing It Out: Waitresses and Their Unions
in the Twentieth Century
Dorothy Sue Cobble

The Spirit of 1848: German Immigrants, Labor Conflict,
and the Coming of the Civil War
Bruce Levine

Working Women of Collar City: Gender, Class, and
Community in Troy, New York, 1864–86
Carole Turbin

Southern Labor and Black Civil Rights:
Organizing Memphis Workers
Michael K. Honey

Radicals of the Worst Sort: Laboring Women
in Lawrence, Massachusetts, 1860–1912
Ardis Cameron

Producers, Proletarians, and Politicians: Workers and
Party Politics in Evansville and New Albany, Indiana,
1850–87
Lawrence M. Lipin

The New Left and Labor in the 1960s
Peter B. Levy